First Corinthians

INTERPRETATION
A Bible Commentary for Teaching and Preaching

INTERPRETATION

A BIBLE COMMENTARY FOR TEACHING AND PREACHING

James Luther Mays, *Editor*
Patrick D. Miller Jr., *Old Testament Editor*
Paul J. Achtemeier, *New Testament Editor*

RICHARD B. HAYS

First Corinthians

INTERPRETATION

A Bible Commentary
for Teaching and Preaching

WESTMINSTER
JOHN KNOX PRESS
LOUISVILLE • KENTUCKY

© 2011 Westminster John Knox Press

2011 paperback edition
Originally published in hardback in the United States
by Westminster John Knox Press in 1997.
Louisville, Kentucky

11 12 13 14 15 16 17 18 19 20—10 9 8 7 6 5 4 3 2 1

Scripture quotations from the New Revised Standard Version of the Bible
are copyright © 1989 by the Division of Christian Education of the National
Council of the Churches of Christ in the U.S.A. and are used by permission.
Italic emphasis has been added in some quotations.

The excerpt on p. 117 was previously published in Richard B. Hays, *The Moral
Vision of the New Testament: Community, Cross, New Creation* (San Francisco: HarperSanFrancisco, 1996), pp. 50-51.

**Library of Congress Cataloging-in-Publication Data is on file at the
Library of Congress, Washington, D.C.**

ISBN: 978-0-664-23440-9 (paper edition)

SERIES PREFACE

This series of commentaries offers an interpretation of the books of the Bible. It is designed to meet the need of students, teachers, ministers, and priests for a contemporary expository commentary. These volumes will not replace the historical critical commentary or homiletical aids to preaching. The purpose of this series is rather to provide a third kind of resource, a commentary which presents the integrated result of historical and theological work with the biblical text.

An interpretation in the full sense of the term involves a text, an interpreter, and someone for whom the interpretation is made. Here, the text is what stands written in the Bible in its full identity as literature from the time of "the prophets and apostles," the literature which is read to inform, inspire, and guide the life of faith. The interpreters are scholars who seek to create an interpretation which is both faithful to the text and useful to the church. The series is written for those who teach, preach, and study the Bible in the community of faith.

The comment generally takes the form of expository essays. It is planned and written in the light of the needs and questions which arise in the use of the Bible as Holy Scripture. The insights and results of contemporary scholarly research are used for the sake of the exposition. The commentators write as exegetes and theologians. The task which they undertake is both to deal with what the texts say and to discern their meaning for faith and life. The exposition is the unified work of one interpreter.

The text on which the comment is based is the Revised Standard Version of the Bible and, since its appearance, the New Revised Standard Version. The general availability of these translations makes the printing of a text in the commentary unnecessary. The commentators have also had other current versions in view as they worked and refer to their readings where it is helpful. The text is divided into sections appropriate to the particular book; comment deals with passages as a whole, rather than proceeding word by word, or verse by verse.

Writers have planned their volumes in light of the requirements set by the exposition of the book assigned to them. Biblical books differ in character, content, and arrangement. They also differ in the way they have been and are used in the liturgy, thought, and devotion of the church. The distinctiveness and use of particular books have been taken into account in decisions about the approach, emphasis, and use of space in the commentaries. The goal has been to allow writers to develop the format which provides for the best presentation of their interpretation.

The result, writers and editors hope, is a commentary which both explains and applies, an interpretation which deals with both the meaning and the significance of biblical texts. Each commentary reflects, of course, the writer's own approach and perception of the church and world. It could and should not be otherwise. Every interpretation of any kind is individual in that sense; it is one reading of the text. But all who work at the interpretation of Scripture in the church need the help and stimulation of a colleague's reading and understanding of the text. If these volumes serve and encourage interpretation in that way, their preparation and publication will realize their purpose.

The Editors

For Judy

And if I have prophetic powers, and understand all mysteries
and all knowledge . . . but do not have love, I am nothing.

(1 Corinthians 13:2)

ACKNOWLEDGMENTS

It is a pleasure to acknowledge several persons and institutions without whose aid this commentary would not have been written.

I began writing the commentary during a stay in Cambridge, England, in the summer of 1995. I am grateful to the Warden of Tyndale House, Dr. Bruce W. Winter, for his gracious hospitality and for a number of illuminating conversations about ancient Corinth and about Paul's relation to the popular rhetoricians of his day.

A substantial portion of the manuscript was completed during a sabbatical leave in Jerusalem at the Tantur Ecumenical Institute for Theological Studies during the spring semester of 1996. Dr. Thomas F. Stransky, C.S.P., the Rector of Tantur, and all the Tantur staff provided indispensable support during my time there. I would like to record my special thanks to Betty and Martin Bailey and to Genevieve Daleh for their generous assistance. My thanks also to the École Biblique for according me the privilege of using their research library. Thanks are due as well to Dean Dennis Campbell and to Duke University for making this leave time possible.

Andy Wakefield, my research assistant at Duke, prepared an extensive bibliography on 1 Corinthians for me at the beginning of the project. I have learned much from many scholars who have written on this letter, though the format of the present commentary does not permit full acknowledgment of my intellectual debts. Particular mention must be made, however, of the excellent commentaries by C. K. Barrett, Gordon Fee, and Wolfgang Schrage. These three commentators have exemplified not only careful attention to exegetical detail but also profound theological concern for the text's subject matter.

My special gratitude goes out to students in my seminars on 1 Corinthians at Yale Divinity School and Duke Divinity School during the years 1982–95. Their questions, ideas, and insights into Paul's letter have stimulated my thinking in more ways than I can record here.

Finally, thanks are due above all to the one to whom this commentary is dedicated, my wife, Judy, who has embodied the meaning of Paul's dictum: "Love bears all things."

Richard B. Hays

CONTENTS

RESPONSES TO CONTESTED ISSUES IN CORINTH
1 CORINTHIANS 7:1—15:58

Introduction

Reading Someone Else's Mail:
The Challenge of Interpretation

When we read Paul's First Letter to the Corinthians, we are literally reading somebody else's mail. This letter was originally addressed to a fledgling mission church, a small band of people in the ancient Mediterranean city of Corinth. No doubt the Corinthian Christians of Paul's day would have preferred that this correspondence not be broadcast to the ages, for it portrays them in an unflattering light and divulges a number of things that they might well, with the wisdom of hindsight, wish to have kept private. Fortunately for us, however, the letter was preserved, widely circulated, and ultimately canonized as a part of the New Testament. Thus, we are given a privileged glimpse of one particular tension-filled moment in the life of the first generation of the Christian movement. The letter, though not written to us, allows us to overhear a fascinating argument in progress.

What are *we* to do with the information gained by eavesdropping on this conversation between the agitated apostle and his refractory followers? How does it speak to us? Paul, after all, was not aiming to write timeless truth or even a general theological treatise; rather, he was giving direct pastoral instruction for one community that faced a specific set of problems in the middle of the first century. For example, was it permissible to eat meat sold in the market if the meat came from an animal sacrificed to a pagan god? What does it mean to take Paul's advice on such a topic, addressed to ancient people in a very different world almost two thousand years ago, and to declare it to be Scripture? What hermeneutical maneuvers permit us to read these particular pastoral instructions as God's word to us? We are so accustomed to thinking of 1 Corinthians as part of "our" Bible that we seldom see the full complexity of this interpretive problem.

To discern *how* the word comes to us through this ancient letter, we must be alert to discovering imaginative *analogies* between the world of the letter and the world we inhabit. While recognizing that 1 Corinthians is not written to us, we learn to read it as though it were. We project ourselves imaginatively into the faraway life of the Corinthian congregation and thereby learn to see our own lives in strange

1

and challenging new ways. The act of preaching (or teaching) such a text in the church requires us to create a metaphorical overlap between then and now and to listen expectantly for God's truth. Since it is *God's* truth for which we listen, however, our work of interpretation must never be confused with mere imaginative cleverness on our part; we can read someone else's mail as God's word to us only because God has chosen—oddly, we might think—to convey ongoing guidance to his people through the finite medium of this specific text. So the church confesses, and so we preach. Interpretation, then, always involves a dialectical process of distancing ourselves from the text enough to see its foreignness and then allowing the text to draw near again and claim us.

If this is the task of interpretation, there can be no fixed formulas to follow. To be sure, the church's tradition of interpretation offers rich guidance about how to understand the text. This commentary is informed by that tradition in many ways, both explicit and implicit, although the format of the series does not allow for thorough acknowledgment of all the ways in which the work of predecessors has shaped the exposition in these pages. Still, different interpreters in different historical settings will produce diverse readings; Paul's letter will shed light from different angles, depending on where we stand. This commentary, then, will seek to offer one reading, offering some suggestions about how the word of God comes to the church today through 1 Corinthians. The specific suggestions offered here for teachers and preachers are intended as stimuli to the reader's imagination, put forward in the hope that they will encourage others to carry forward the task of proclaiming the word freshly: "For you can all prophesy one by one, so that all may learn and all be encouraged" (1 Cor. 14:31).

The Setting of the Letter

In order to listen intelligently to Paul's conversation with the Corinthians, we must first know a few things about the letter's setting and occasion. We cannot, of course, know as much as we would like; numerous details of the background are unknown to us, and therefore the text contains many allusions that remain opaque to posterity. In reading 1 Corinthians we see, at best, through a glass darkly. Nonetheless, we can sketch in some information that provides a helpful context for our reading of the letter.

The city of Corinth

2

Corinth was a prosperous commercial crossroads in classical antiquity. Its location on the Isthmus of Corinth, overlooking the two ports of Cenchreae and Lechaeum, allowed it to command a major east-west trade route between the Aegean and Ionian seas. The sea voyage around the southern coast of the Peloponnesian peninsula was considered difficult and dangerous; consequently, merchants shipping goods between Asia and Italy preferred to send their cargo via Corinth. Small ships could actually be carted across the isthmus; shipments from larger vessels were unloaded, transferred on land to the other side, and reloaded at the other port. The economic benefits of such activity for the city of Corinth were described by the ancient geographer Strabo, writing in 7 B.C.E.:

> Corinth is called "wealthy" because of its commerce, since it is situated on the Isthmus and is master of two harbors, of which the one leads straight to Asia, and the other to Italy; and it makes easy the exchange of merchandise from both countries that are so far distant from each other. . . . [I]t was a welcome alternative, for the merchants both from Italy and from Asia, to land their cargoes here. And also the duties on what by land was exported from the Peloponnesus and what was imported to it fell to those who held the keys. And to later times this remained ever so.
>
> (*Geography* 8.6.20)

Additionally, Corinth hosted the Isthmian games, an athletic festival second only to the Olympic games in importance. This event, held once every two years, attracted large crowds and generated additional revenue for the city. The importance of the Isthmian games for Corinth may be gauged by the fact that the most prestigious political office in the city was that of the *agōnothētēs*, the sponsor of the games.

Corinth's prosperous commercial life, however, was interrupted in 146 B.C.E. when the Roman army captured the city, destroyed its buildings, and either executed or enslaved its inhabitants. The site stood virtually abandoned until, on the initiative of Julius Caesar, the city was refounded as a Roman colony in 44 B.C.E., less than a hundred years before Paul's arrival on the scene. Many of the colonists were former slaves, Roman freedmen who would have discovered in the newly refounded city opportunities for economic and social advancement not available to them elsewhere. For example, Roman Corinth was unusual in permitting freedmen (i.e., former slaves) to be elected as *duoviri*, the chief magistrates of the city. In our reading of Paul's letter, it will be useful to remember that he was writing to a church in a city only a few generations removed from its founding by colonists seeking upward social mobility. (In this respect there is a significant analogy between Paul's Corinthian readers and the American readers of this commentary.) We should also bear in mind that the laws, political structures, and cultural customs of Corinth were significantly determined by its orientation toward Rome, even though it was a Greek city.

3

The older, pre-Roman Corinth had apparently acquired—at least among the Athenians—a reputation as a center of sexual promiscuity: The comic playwright Aristophanes, for example, coined the verb *korinthiazesthai*, meaning "to fornicate." In older commentaries, one sometimes finds exaggerated accounts of the flagrant licentiousness of Corinth. More recently, however, scholars have shown that such accounts represent misinterpretation of the sources. Sacred prostitution was not ordinarily part of Greek religious practice, and Strabo's story of a thousand temple prostitutes in the temple of Aphrodite on Acrocorinth—which in any case referred to the ancient city before its destruction, not the city of Paul's time—has been discredited by historical and archaeological investigations. C. K. Barrett puts the topic of Corinthian sexual *mores* in its proper perspective: "In Paul's day, Corinth was probably little better and little worse than any other sea port and commercial center of the age" (Barrett, 3).

The accounts of Strabo and of the second-century C.E. writer Pausanias indicate that the city supported numerous sites of pagan worship and was adorned by magnificent statues of gods and goddesses in public places, including a large statue of Athena in the middle of the *agora* (marketplace). There was nothing unusual about this. Every significant city in the Greco-Roman world displayed similar temples and statuary. Athens, for instance, is described in Acts 17:16 as being "full of idols." The Corinthian Christians would have been confronted on a daily basis by these imposing symbolic reminders of the religiopolitical world out of which they had been called. When Paul wrote of "many gods and many lords" in the world (1 Cor. 8:5), his words brought vivid images to mind for his readers. Consequently, Paul was faced with a major task of reshaping the thinking of his Corinthian converts into the symbolic world of Judaism and the emergent Christian movement, in which one God alone was to be worshiped.

From Acts 18:1–17 we know that there was also a Jewish community in Corinth, as confirmed by a passing comment by Paul's contemporary Philo of Alexandria (*Legatio ad Gaium* 281). An inscription referring to the "Synagogue of the Hebrews" has been found in the excavation of the site, but we have no information about the size of the Jewish community, and it appears from the content of Paul's letters to Corinth that most members of Paul's fledgling Christian community were of Gentile, rather than Jewish, ancestry. This meant that Paul was faced with a massive task of *resocialization*, seeking to reshape the moral imaginations of these Gentile converts into patterns of life consonant with the ways of the God of Israel.

Other information about the social and historical background will

4

be brought forward at pertinent places in the commentary. For further discussion of the ancient sources and the archaeological investigation of Corinth, see the collections of material compiled by Jerome Murphy-O'Connor in *St. Paul's Corinth* and by Ben Witherington, III, in *Conflict and Community in Corinth.*

The occasion of the letter

Paul had founded the Christian community in Corinth through his preaching and teaching (Acts 18:1–11); consequently, he describes himself as having planted the community (1 Cor. 3:6), or having laid its foundation (3:10), or even as having "fathered" it (4:15). According to Luke's account, Paul spent eighteen months in Corinth (Acts 18:11), sufficient time to develop significant relationships there and to provide extensive instruction. In accordance with his mission of organizing new communities, once the church was up and running, he moved on. It is likely that Paul left Corinth during the year 51 C.E. and that the letter known to us as 1 Corinthians was written some time later, probably during the interval 53–55 C.E. The letter itself indicates that it was written from Ephesus during the spring of the year, prior to Pentecost (1 Cor. 16:8). (The chronology of Paul's missionary activity is a complicated problem, and the precise date of the letter need not concern us here; for discussion of these matters, see the standard New Testament introductions and commentaries on 1 Corinthians.) Paul had been away long enough for new problems and serious misunderstandings to arise within the Corinthian community. From the letter itself we learn that he had written to them at least once previously (5:9); this correspondence, unfortunately, is lost to us, unless a fragment of it is preserved in 2 Cor. 6:14—7:1.

Two convergent factors precipitated Paul's writing of 1 Corinthians. First, he had received a report from "Chloe's people"—presumably members of the household headed by a woman named Chloe—that there was serious dissension within the community (1 Cor. 1:11; 11:18). Their report presumably also included alarming information about other problems within the Corinthian church: sexual immorality (5:1–8; 6:12–20), legal disputes (6:1–11), abuses of the Lord's Supper (11:17–34), and controversies about the resurrection of the dead (15:1–58). Second, the Corinthians themselves had written to Paul (7:1a) asking for his advice about several things. Their letter had certainly posed questions about sex within marriage (7:1b–40) and eating meat that had been offered to idols (8:1—11:1); probably it had also raised the issues of spiritual gifts in the community's worship (12:1—14:40) and Paul's collection for Jerusalem (16:1–4). Whether this letter also addressed the theological issue of the resurrection is more difficult to say. In any case, the convergence of the secondary report with the Corinthians' own letter provoked Paul to compose an extended epistle taking up all these issues and reframing them in light of his gospel proclamation.

The character of his response suggests that he sees the members of the Corinthian church as standing—contrary to their own self-perception—at a moment of crisis and testing (10:11–13). Will they heed Paul's words and recover a disciplined unity in the faith? Or will their community disintegrate before the forces of pride, rivalry, and spiritualized self-indulgence? Paul tellingly remarks, "I do not want to see you just in passing" (16:7); a longer visit will be required to sort out all the problems of which he has been apprised. The letter, then, is a stopgap measure until Paul himself can get there to deal with the issues in greater depth (11:34b).

The Corinthian church and its "theology"

Because our only source of information about the Corinthian church is Paul's correspondence, the pertinent information will emerge in the course of the commentary. Thus, a lengthy description is not necessary here. Still, a few summary remarks may be useful.

The Corinthian church, founded by Paul, had been in existence for only about five years at the time of the writing of this letter. The community had a few Jewish members, including Crispus (1:14), described in Acts 18:8 as a leader of the Corinthian synagogue. If the Sosthenes named in the salutation of Paul's letter (1:1) is the same person mentioned in Acts 18:17, then at least two prominent Jewish leaders in Corinth had joined the Christian movement. Most of the members of the community, however, were Gentile converts. Some of these, like the Titius Justus mentioned in Acts 18:7, may have been attracted to Judaism before Paul came to Corinth to preach (i.e., they had been "Godfearers," Gentile adherents of the synagogue who had not taken the step of becoming full Jewish proselytes by undergoing circumcision). We do not know the number of Christians in Corinth, but archaeological investigations have provided the basis for some informed guesswork. Because Christians met in private homes and had no public buildings, the size of their gatherings was limited by the size of the villas of the most affluent members of the community. According to the calculations of Jerome Murphy-O'Connor, such houses could have accommodated no more than thirty to fifty people for the common meal. It is, therefore, likely that there were several separate house church gatherings, meeting in the homes of leaders such as Stephanas

(16:15–18). Over time, such house church communities might have developed different practices and even acknowledged different leaders, thus exacerbating the problem of factions within the community. If each of the factions mentioned in 1:12 represents a different house church (a possible but uncertain assumption), there might have been as many as 150 to 200 Christians in the city at the time of Paul's writing. It is impossible, however, to be certain about this; there could have been more or fewer. My own guess is that these figures are on the high side.

One thing that we do know, however many Christians there may have been in Corinth, is that they represented a spectrum of differing social and economic classes, ranging from prosperous household heads to slaves. This socioeconomic diversity—highly unusual for any voluntary association either in the ancient world or today—created some tensions and difficulties within the church. This is most evident in the case of the problems surrounding the Lord's Supper, where the "haves" were disregarding and shaming the "have-nots." Other issues that Paul addresses in his letter may also have had socioeconomic dimensions, as the commentary will explain.

The phenomenon of status diversity in the Corinthian church may come as a surprise to those who are used to thinking of early Christianity as a movement of the underclass. This impression has been encouraged by a certain reading of Paul's statement in Corinthians 1:26: "Consider your own call, brothers and sisters: not many of you were . . . powerful, not many were of noble birth." Clearly the church was not *primarily* a movement of the privileged classes, but the very way that Paul qualifies his formulation ("not many") should suggest to us that some of the Corinthian believers were in fact wealthy and wellborn. This supposition is confirmed by other evidence, including the interesting fact that Erastus, a city official of Corinth who became part of Paul's mission team (see Rom. 16:23; Acts 19:22; 2 Tim. 4:20), was a man wealthy enough to fund and dedicate a costly public pavement for the city. An inscription found in the city reads, "Erastus, for his aedileship, constructed [this pavement] at his own expense." Wayne Meeks, in his careful study *The First Urban Christians*, has concluded that many of the early Christians were characterized by "status inconsistency": that is, they may have been economically prosperous but not of high status in their culture for other reasons. The somewhat unstable and anomalous social status of some key members of the Corinthian church may have contributed to the volatility of the community's quarrels.

What role did theology play in these disputes? Critics have speculated ceaselessly about the "theology" of the Corinthians and its

7

sources. Wolfgang Schrage has catalogued at least thirteen different theories about the character of "the Corinthian theology" (Schrage, 38–63). All such theories are hypotheses constructed through "mirror-reading," extrapolating the thought of the Corinthians based on Paul's response to them. One of the most elaborate constructions of this kind is Antoinette Wire's attempt (*The Corinthian Women Prophets*) to piece together the theology of a group of female prophets at Corinth whose activity was, hypothetically, the primary provocation for Paul's writing of the letter. Such reconstructive work can be pursued only with great caution. The few fragments of information that we have do not necessarily add up to a theology, and, given the splintered character of the community, it is methodologically uncertain which people at Corinth might have held the various views that Paul opposes. For example, were the people who said that "it is a good thing for a man not to touch a woman" (7:1b) the same people who denied the resurrection of the dead (15:12; see the commentary on these passages)? Or do these views belong to different groups within the community? We can formulate guesses about such matters, but they remain nothing more than guesses.

Furthermore, it is not always clear that the problems addressed by Paul have their basis in explicitly *theological* ideas. It is *Paul* who frames the issues in theological terms; indeed, this is an important part of his pastoral strategy, as we shall see. For example, it is doubtful that the Corinthians thought of themselves as promulgating a "realized eschatology"; it is Paul who uses his eschatological theology to critique various things that the Corinthians were doing. In many cases, the practices of the Corinthians were motivated by social and cultural factors—such as popular philosophy and rhetoric—that were not consciously theological at all. The brilliance of Paul's letter lies in his ability to diagnose the situation in theological terms and to raise the inchoate theological issues into the light of conscious reflection in light of the gospel.

Consequently, this commentary will not presuppose any elaborate reconstruction of the Corinthians' theology. As we work through the letter, we will build up some cumulative impressions of what Paul's original readers might have thought, but these impressions will remain sketchy and hypothetical; they will not be used to construct a systematic picture that will in turn govern our reading of the text. What we can analyze with some confidence is *Paul's* theology as he articulates it in this letter; that is the primary focal point of our interest.

The unity and structure of the letter

8

Before turning to Paul's theology we must comment on one more matter that has a bearing on our reading: the question of the literary unity and structure of the letter. When we read this text are we really reading a single letter, or has it been artificially constructed by an editor who has pieced together excerpts from more than one letter of Paul? The canonical 2 Corinthians, for example, is almost certainly a composite product of the latter sort. In the case of 1 Corinthians, however, there are good reasons to think that the text printed in our New Testament represents substantially what Paul wrote to the Corinthians on a single occasion. Margaret Mitchell's important study of the rhetorical composition of the letter (*Paul and the Rhetoric of Reconciliation*) has argued persuasively that the letter should be read as an extended appeal for unity. When the text is read this way, virtually all the pieces fit together in the service of a unified argument. Because our concern in this commentary is with matters of theological substance rather than with the formal rhetorical structure of the letter, we will not set forth Mitchell's structural analysis in detail, but the working assumption of my exposition is that the letter should be read as a unified whole.

That judgment still leaves open, of course, the precise determination of the Greek text of 1 Corinthians. The letter is preserved in numerous ancient manuscripts, and these manuscripts do not agree in all details. Thus, critical judgments about the text are necessary. In general, this commentary will presuppose the Greek text printed in the 27th edition of the Nestle-Aland *Novum Testamentum Graece*. At one or two points, however, we will have to consider the possibility that the scribes who transmitted the text in the centuries following Paul may have introduced alterations or additions. The most important of these is the notorious instruction for women to be silent in church (1 Cor. 14:34–35). I will argue that these verses were not originally part of the letter that Paul wrote; the reader is referred to that section of the commentary for the evidence for this position.

Apart from such technical problems, the letter is to be read as a unity. When we read it that way, attending particularly to Paul's fundamental theological concerns, what themes stand out in Paul's exposition?

Major Theological Themes in the Letter

1. *Christology.* Because Paul's letter to the Corinthians deals primarily with their behavioral problems rather than with doctrine per se, the central place of christology in Paul's thought can sometimes be overlooked in studies of the letter. Yet from beginning to end Paul interprets every issue in light of "the testimony of Christ" (1:6). Paul's gospel is fundamentally the story of Jesus crucified and raised from the

dead (2:2; 11:23–26; 15:3–5), and he insists that the identity of the community must be shaped with reference to this story. God has redefined "wisdom" through Christ's death and resurrection (1:30), and the meaning of love is exemplified in him (8:11; 11:1). The christology of the letter does not emphasize Jesus' death as a means of atonement for sin; rather, Paul highlights Jesus' role as the initiator of a new apocalyptic age, the precursor of a new humanity set free from death (15:20–28). The exact relation between Jesus Christ and God the Father is not spelled out in 1 Corinthians; some passages express Christ's subordination to God (3:23; 11:3; 15:28), while others link them together in the closest possible relation (8:6; 12:4–6). In any case, it is impossible to understand this letter without attending carefully to Paul's insistence that Jesus Christ has defined the new cosmic situation in which we live and move—and that his self-sacrificial death defines the pattern for the life of the community.

2. *Apocalyptic eschatology.* Paul repeatedly seeks to impress upon the Corinthians that they are living in a time of eschatological urgency, in which "the ends of the ages have met" (10:11). The cross has brought the old age to an end, and the power of the Spirit in the community is a sign of God's new order. Yet the community still lives between the times, awaiting "the day of our Lord Jesus Christ" (1:8) and proclaiming his death "until he comes" (11:26). As the commentary will demonstrate, virtually every page of Paul's letter seeks to reframe the Corinthians' vision of existence within this "already/not yet" eschatological dialectic.

3. *Embodied existence.* Against the Corinthians' tendency to deprecate the physical body, Paul repeatedly insists on the meaningfulness of the body and its actions. Our bodies are created by God, sanctified in the present through union with Christ (6:12–20), and destined for ultimate redemption through resurrection (15:35–58). This has implications for many issues, including sexual morality, marriage, the sharing of economic resources, and the nature of our future hope.

4. *The primacy of love.* Reacting to the Corinthians' overemphasis on knowledge and wisdom, Paul affirms that love must rule over all other values and virtues (8:1–13; 12:31b–13:13; 16:14). This claim of the primacy of love—which is, of course, grounded in the story of Jesus—sets Paul's teaching apart from the other philosophical and religious options that exercised such powerful fascination for the Corinthians.

10

5. *The transformation of power and status through the cross.* As we shall see throughout the letter, Paul repeatedly argues that the gospel overturns the world's notions of power and social standing.

Those who acclaim a crucified Christ as Lord find that God has chosen what is "low and despised" in the world to "reduce to nothing things that are, so that no one might boast in the presence of God" (1:28–29). This has earth-shaking implications for the social structure of the community of Christ's people. As the body of Christ, they are linked together—rich and poor, slave and free—in a network of mutual love and concern. Old status distinctions no longer count "in the Lord," and all power relations must be reinterpreted in light of the cross. The Corinthians had some difficulty grasping this vision (e.g., 11:17–22, 27–34), but Paul insists that it is a necessary entailment of the gospel.

Major Focal Points in This Commentary

Beyond the themes that Paul himself stresses, the commentary will draw attention to several second-order observations that emerge from our analysis of the letter. These observations highlight important aspects of Paul's response to the Corinthians situation, and the reader may find it useful to have some of the recurrent ones enumerated briefly in the beginning.

1. *Paul's pastoral task: community formation.* Paul is not concerned just with individual edification of believers or with doctrinal teaching in the abstract; rather, his pastoral task is the organization and nurturing of a community. His constant goal is to call the Corinthians to understand their corporate existence as the church. One implication of this is that theology and ethics are bound together inseparably in Paul's thought: To think theologically is to reflect about the shaping of the community's life together. A second implication of this observation pertains to our task of interpreting the letter: To read 1 Corinthians rightly, we must hear ourselves addressed *as the church.* If we fail to keep this perspective in mind—if we suppose that we can understand the letter as isolated scholars or "spiritual" persons—we are likely to misread the letter at every turn.

2. *Conversion of the imagination.* In order to form a Christian community identity within a pluralistic pagan world, Paul repeatedly calls his readers to a "conversion of the imagination." He invites them to see the world in dramatically new ways, in light of values shaped by the Christian story. Many of the problems at Corinth were caused by the Corinthians' understandable tendency to think and act in ways that were entirely normal within the cultural world of the Greco-Roman city, such as taking one another to court or accepting invitations to meals held in the temples of the gods. Paul, however, calls on them to change in fundamental ways and to shape a different kind of community, rethinking their inherited sociocultural norms and practices, as

11

well as their ingrained conceptions of value, honor, and leadership. Social historians refer to this process of change as "resocialization." Paul
elsewhere refers to it as transformation through the renewing of the
community's mind (Rom. 12:2). This process of transformation is complex, because not everything in the Corinthians' previous life needed
to be changed; for example, Paul insists that marriage to non-Christian
spouses should be honored and maintained if possible (1 Cor. 7:12–
16). Thus, a detailed process of discernment is required. One important aspect of this discernment and imaginative conversion is for the
Gentile Corinthians to learn to envision themselves as the heirs of Israel's story (e.g., 10:1–22).

3. *The social location of theological thinking.* The internal divisions
within the Corinthian church were in part attributable to socioeconomic factors. Recent scholarship has suggested that the Corinthians'
differing views on "knowledge" and spiritual gifts may have been related to class and status differences within the church. Certainly the
problems surrounding the Lord's Supper had a socioeconomic aspect.
Some who had enough food to eat were humiliating "those who have
nothing" (11:22). Throughout the commentary, we shall try to observe
the ways in which the Corinthian disputes may be symptomatic of social differences and, just as importantly, the ways in which Paul's interpretation of the gospel seeks to overcome such differences.

4. *Paul as hermeneutic theologian.* Paul characteristically reasons
theologically by reflecting imaginatively on scriptural texts and traditions. Even in 1 Corinthians, where scriptural interpretation is not the
major focus of the argument as it is in Galatians and Romans, Paul repeatedly appeals to Israel's Scripture as a basis for his counsel to the
community. In order to follow his arguments, we must attend carefully
to his innovative interpretations of the Old Testament texts and to the
rhetorical effects created by his use of them. The commentary will give
particular attention to this matter, which should be of special interest
to teachers and preachers who must themselves consider how to develop their own message for the community on the basis of Scripture.
At the same time, we should recognize also that Paul's hermeneutical
reflection sometimes begins not from the Old Testament but from
early Christian confessional and liturgical traditions (e.g., 11:23–25;
15:3–5). Here too we can learn much by observing his manner of bringing these traditions to bear upon the practical issues that face the community.

5. *Paul as model for ministry.* Paul explicitly offers himself as a
model to be imitated (4:16–17; 11:1). Throughout the commentary, we
will explore what it would mean to take him as a model for ministry

12

and pastoral theology. By way of preview, we can say that the model is both compelling and daunting. Paul attempts to address all particular pastoral problems in light of fundamental theological considerations; somehow he finds that the message of Jesus Christ crucified and risen speaks to every concern of the Corinthian community. Paul is not afraid of confrontation: It seems that his gospel may *generate* problems, not solve them, for the word of the cross poses a challenge to the comfortable assumptions of Paul's readers. Furthermore, in his relationship with his congregation, Paul will not tolerate slackness and mediocrity; he calls them again and again to excellence—the excellence of love as defined by the gospel—and accountability. Finally, as a pastoral theologian, he thinks with imaginative freedom but with simultaneous fidelity to the foundational kerygmatic tradition, and he urges his readers to do the same. This is a hard act to follow, but those called to ministry in Christ's church have no choice but to try.

OUTLINE OF THE LETTER

13

INTERPRETATION

Opening the Letter: A Community Called by God

1 CORINTHIANS 1:1–9

1:1–3
Salutation

When we open the Corinthians' mail, we find ourselves confronted immediately by some remarkable claims about God's designs for the community of people to whom Paul writes. The opening sentence of the letter declares not only that Paul is a special agent of Jesus Christ but also that the Corinthians are a community specially summoned by God for service: "the church of God that is in Corinth . . . sanctified in Christ Jesus, called to be saints" (1 Cor. 1:2). This does not mean that the Corinthians have some special vocation that sets them apart from other Christians; rather, they—along with all other Christians—are set apart from a confused and perishing world, marked by God as God's people. Paul regards all the members of all his churches as "the saints," the elect of God. Thus, he and his readers are caught up in a cosmic drama, and they must play a distinctive role in God's action to rescue the world.

Paul himself is "called to be an apostle of Christ Jesus by the will of God" (v. 1). We know from Paul's other letters that he understands his calling to be specially focused on the mission of preaching the gospel to the Gentiles (Gal. 1:16); here he highlights the motif of God's *call*, which both authorizes and motivates his mission. It is God, not Paul, who ultimately initiates and drives the proclamation of the gospel.

"Sosthenes the brother," mentioned as co-sender of the letter (1 Cor. 1:1), is probably the same person described by Luke in Acts 18:17 as a leader of the synagogue in Corinth. According to that account, he was roughed up by a crowd of Corinthian Jews who were frustrated by the decision of the Roman proconsul Gallio to ignore their complaints against Paul. Why they picked on Sosthenes is not clear in the Acts narrative; perhaps if he had not already become a Christian convert he was at least perceived as sympathetic to Paul. By the time of the writing of this letter—two to four years later—Sosthenes was apparently with Paul in Ephesus, sharing in Paul's missionary work. If he was a notable Corinthian convert who had suffered for the gospel, he might have been a person of some influence among the Corinthian Christians. Thus, though he is not mentioned again in the text, his appearance in the salutation perhaps lends some additional weight to the appeals that Paul will make throughout the letter. This is the first indication of a fact we will note repeatedly: Paul employs considerable political tact in addressing the touchy situation in the Corinthian church.

Just as Paul is called by God, so too are the Christians at Corinth. They are called to be *hagioi*, "saints." This term does not apply—as in later Christian usage—only to a few especially holy individuals; rather, all the members of the community are gathered up into this calling. To be "sanctified" means to be set apart for the service of God, like Israel's priests or the vessels used in the Temple. Long before, in the Old Testament, the call to be a sanctified people had been addressed to the people of Israel as a whole: "The LORD spoke to Moses, saying: 'Speak to all the congregation of the people of Israel and say to them: You shall be holy [*hagioi*], for I the LORD your God am holy [*hagios*]' " (Lev. 19:1–2 LXX). Thus, when Paul applies this language to the Corinthians, he is echoing God's call to Israel. This is the first of many times in the letter that Paul implicitly addresses and describes the Corinthian Christians—a predominantly Gentile group—as members of the covenant people of God, Israel. Whatever their background, they have now been caught up into the story of God's gracious elective purpose. They are to serve as a covenant people, representing God's kingdom within a world that does not know God. "Now therefore, if you obey my voice and keep my covenant, you shall be my treasured possession out of all the peoples. Indeed, the whole earth is mine but you shall be for me a priestly kingdom and a holy [*hagion*] nation" (Exod. 19:5–6a LXX).

As this passage from Exodus suggests, to be God's covenant people entails certain obligations of obedience: If the church is to represent God rightly in the world, certain norms and standards must be kept. Thus, when Paul addresses the Corinthians as "sanctified in Christ Jesus," he introduces a tension that will play itself out throughout the letter, for the Corinthians' actual conduct seems to be terribly out of synch with their vocation to be God's covenant people. At this point, however, the tension remains unexpressed; the emphasis in the letter's salutation remains on *God's* initiative in calling and sanctifying this community.

Paul goes on to make another point: The Corinthians are not unique or isolated in their calling. They are "sanctified in Christ Jesus . . . *together with all those who in every place call on the name of our Lord Jesus Christ*" (1 Cor. 1:2). Even in the opening address of the letter, Paul places the church at Corinth and its particular concerns

16

within a much wider story, encouraging them to see themselves as part of a network of communities of faith stretching around the Mediterranean world. The importance of this broader framework will emerge as the letter proceeds. We will see that Paul chides the Corinthian Christians for their prideful presumption that their spiritual freedom liberates them from accountability to others: "[D]id the word of God originate with you? Or are you the only ones it has reached?" (14:36). The answer is, of course, that the word of God has reached many and that the Corinthians must see themselves as part of a much larger movement, subject to the same Lord whose authority governs the church as a whole. They are not spiritual free agents. The church of God that is in Corinth is just one branch of a larger operation.

Thus, the letter salutation establishes the identity of the apostle and his addressees. Everything that follows is founded upon these identity ascriptions: God is the one who *calls*, and the church, not just at Corinth but everywhere, is the community of people who respond by *calling* on the name of Jesus Christ. Upon this community at Corinth Paul pronounces a blessing: "Grace to you and peace from God our Father and the Lord Jesus Christ" (1:3). Those who participate in the covenant community are the recipients of God's freely given mercy, and they therefore stand within the sphere of God's peace, a peace that should extend to their relationships with one another.

1:4–9
Thanksgiving

Paul characteristically opens his letter with a word of thanksgiving for the community to which he writes. This thanksgiving section artfully foreshadows many of the issues that Paul will address in the letter as a whole. Three theological themes stand out in the thanksgiving section of 1 Corinthians: (1) *the grace of God*, who is the giver of all the gifts enjoyed by the Corinthian church; (2) *the eschatological framework* of Christian existence; and (3) *God's call to community* in and with Jesus Christ. Let us consider each of these themes in turn.

Paul focuses his thanksgiving initially on the grace (*charis*) of God, stressing that this gift has been given to the Corinthian community in (or perhaps *by*) Christ Jesus. This grace is said to be manifest particularly in that the Corinthian church has been "enriched . . . in speech

17

and knowledge of every kind" (v. 5). This account of the situation would no doubt seem apt and pleasing to those members of the Corinthian church who prided themselves on precisely these aspects of their spiritual experience: the possession of privileged knowledge and the ability to speak with spirit-endowed eloquence, including speaking in tongues. After reading the letter as a whole, however, we cannot miss the ironic undertone here. It is precisely these gifts of speech and knowledge that have become the instruments of division in the community. Paul never denies that such knowledge and speech are authentic gifts of God; indeed, he gives thanks for them rather than deploring them. At the same time, however, he stresses that they are *gifts of God*; that is, they are not expressions of the Corinthians' own autonomous spiritual capacity or brilliance. When Paul later writes, "What do you have that you did not receive? And if you received it, why do you boast as if it were not a gift?" (4:7), we see that he has already laid the theological groundwork in the thanksgiving section for a stinging critique of the Corinthians' spiritual pride. If the Corinthians can consider themselves already rich (4:8), it is only because they have been *made* rich by God (1:5). Thus, boasting is excluded. When Paul observes that the Corinthians are "not lacking in any spiritual gift" (v. 7), he pointedly used the word *charisma*: "manifestation of grace." The Corinthians themselves may have spoken of these speech-gifts as "spiritual" (*pneumatika*) (cf. 12:1), but the word "spiritual" does not actually appear in Paul's Greek here in verse 7. Whatever endowments of speech and knowledge the Corinthians have, they have them only by God's *grace* as gifts which serve to confirm "the testimony of Christ," not to aggrandize the members of the church.

Second, Paul sets his thanksgiving for the Corinthians' "giftedness" within the framework of a not-yet-fulfilled hope: "[Y]ou are not lacking in any spiritual gift *as you wait for the revealing of our Lord Jesus Christ*" (1:7). No matter how richly blessed the community may be in the present, Paul insists that they have not yet received that for which the church ultimately longs: the revelation (*apokalypsis*) of Jesus Christ, his final coming again to triumph over the powers of evil and death (cf. 15:20–28). Thus, the church's present existence is a time of waiting, a time in which they must be sustained and strengthened by Christ in anticipation of the end. Furthermore, as Paul suggests in 1:8, the day of Christ's *parousia* will also be a day of *judgment*. Thus, the community must rely upon Christ's own work in their midst to prepare them for that day, so that they might be "blameless" at the final reckoning. The Corinthians, if they were listening carefully, may have heard all this talk of waiting and preparation for judgment as a sobering

18

corrective to their enthusiastic spiritual experience in the present. That, of course, is precisely Paul's aim. Throughout the letter, he recalls the Corinthians' attention again and again to the future-directed character of the gospel and highlights the motif of the church's ultimate accountability to God's judgment. At the same time, Paul's tone here in the thanksgiving section is not one of warning or exhortation; rather, he gratefully affirms that the community can stand confidently as they wait, for "God is faithful" (v. 9a). It is God, the giver of the gifts, who has called the community and who undergirds their hope.

The third motif sounded in the thanksgiving is more subtly expressed than the other two, but it is no less important: God has called the Corinthians "into the fellowship (*koinōnia*) of his Son, Jesus Christ our Lord" (v. 9b). The formulation is ambiguous: the word *koinōnia* can refer both to the spiritual relationship to Jesus Christ and to the community of people who are called together into that relationship. In fact, in Paul's understanding, these two realities are inseparable. To be "in Christ" *is* to be in the fellowship of the church. The community's calling is not just to perform a mission or to obey certain norms; rather, the community is finally called into a relationship of intimate mutuality with one another in Christ. This is one of the most distinctive aspects of the early Christian movement. To participate in the church was to find oneself summoned to close and even sacrificial relationships with others, including those of other social classes, those with whom one might ordinarily have nothing at all in common. What the members of the church had in common was simply their shared calling to participate in the new family created by God's grace; that is why Paul addresses the members of his churches as "brothers and sisters." It is not surprising that such a new self-understanding might have been difficult for newly formed Christian communities, such as the one at Corinth, to grasp and internalize. Thus, when Paul concludes his thanksgiving by reminding the Corinthians that they have been called into Christ's *koinōnia*, he is sounding a theme whose manifold variations he will continue to play from beginning to end in this letter.

REFLECTIONS FOR TEACHERS AND PREACHERS

By the end of the first nine verses, Paul has sketched a sweeping picture of the Corinthian church's calling: They have been called by God to participate in a movement, along with others all around the known world, to extend the destiny of Israel by living as a covenant people set apart for the service of God. God has lavished upon them spiritual gifts that enable their mission of bearing witness to the grace of Jesus Christ, and God supports and strengthens the community

19

during the present age, while they await God's final judgment of the world. During the time of waiting, God prepares and sanctifies the community and brings them together into close fellowship with Christ and with one another. In short, Paul portrays the Corinthians as important players in a grand story scripted by God.

Teachers and preachers in the church would do well to learn from Paul's way of framing the church's identity. We are apt to think of the church's life and mission on a small, even trivial, scale. We tend to locate the identity of our communities within some denominational program, or within local politics, or within recent history. But Paul urges us instead to understand the church in a cosmic frame of reference that points toward the final triumph of God's righteousness, the setting right of all things in Jesus Christ. When we understand ourselves as actors within that epic drama, we undergo a crucial shift of perspective. On the one hand, the stakes are raised. Our actions belong to a larger pattern of significance than that of our own lives, and the church's obedience to God's will matters urgently, because it is part of God's strategy for the eschatological renewal of the world. On the other hand, at the same time, we can gain a better sense of proportion about our own striving and failures, for God is faithful, and it is God who is at work in calling us and preparing us for his gracious ends. Thus, by reading the opening passage of the Corinthians' mail, we can learn to see ourselves within the story of God's grace in such a way that despair and pride and petty conflict should fall away.

We might also learn from Paul's opening paragraph something about the practice of giving thanks. Even though the Corinthian church is riddled with problems, Paul offers a word of thanksgiving to God for the very community that he is setting out to correct. Despite all present difficulties, he sees this church as the work of God in the world, and he discerns in their midst gifts for which God is to be thanked. As Dietrich Bonhoeffer wrote in *Life Together*:

> If we do not give thanks daily for the Christian fellowship in which we have been placed, even where there is no great experience, no discoverable riches, but much weakness, small faith, and difficulty; if on the contrary, we only keep complaining to God that everything is so paltry and petty, so far from what we expected, then we hinder God from letting our fellowship grow according to the measure and riches which are there for us all in Jesus Christ.
>
> This applies in a special way to the complaints often heard from pastors and zealous members about their congregations. A pastor should not complain about his congregation, certainly never to other people, but also not to God. A congregation has not been entrusted to him in order that he should become its accuser before God and

men. . . . What may appear weak and trifling to us may be great and glorious to God. . . . The more thankfully we daily receive what is given to us, the more surely and steadily will fellowship increase and grow from day to day as God pleases.

(Bonhoeffer, 29–30)

Paul models the thankful stance that Bonhoeffer prescribes. He is able to give thanks to God for the problematical Corinthian church because he recognizes that Christian community is, as Bonhoeffer aptly observes, "not an ideal which we must realize; it is rather a reality created by God in Christ in which we may participate" (30).

A Call for Unity in the Community
1 CORINTHIANS 1:10—4:21

1:10–17
Factions in the Community

The fundamental theme of the letter is sounded in 1:10: "Now I appeal to you, brothers and sisters, by the name of our Lord Jesus Christ, that all of you be in agreement and that there be no divisions among you, but that you be united in the same mind and the same purpose." Everything that follows, especially in 1 Corinthians 1:11—4:21, must be understood as an elaboration of this appeal. Paul, writing to a community torn by divisions (*schismata*), calls for unity. The word in 1:10 translated by the NRSV as "united" may carry the connotation of restoration to a prior condition, the putting in order of something that has fallen into disarray. (The same verb is used in Mark 1:19/Matt. 4:21 to describe the "mending" of fishing nets; NEB felicitously translates this word in 1 Cor. 1:10 as "firmly joined.") Paul had left the Corinthian community in a relatively harmonious condition; now he has learned, to his dismay, that quarrels are splitting the church.

The source of this information is "Chloe's people." Their precise identities are unknown, but presumably they were slaves or retainers of a household headed by a woman named Chloe. We do not know

21

whether Chloe lived in Corinth or in Ephesus, where Paul wrote the letter, but we can presume that her emissaries had traveled between the two cities on business and had brought Paul news of disturbing developments in the Corinthian church.

The divisions at Corinth should not necessarily be understood to be clearly organized parties. The evidence of the letter as a whole suggests rather that there are inchoate dissensions and arguments brewing. In this volatile situation, according to the report of Chloe's people, the Corinthian Christians are rallying around the names of various preachers and leaders: "[E]ach of you says, 'I belong to Paul,' or 'I belong to Apollos,' or 'I belong to Cephas,' or 'I belong to Christ' " (v. 12). That Paul himself had been unaware of the existence of a "Paul party"—indeed, that he thoroughly disapproves of such an idea—shows that these slogans have probably arisen spontaneously within the Corinthian church, without any direct encouragement from the leaders whose names were being bandied about. Despite many scholarly speculations, it is not possible to assign a distinct ideological program to each of these factions. Indeed, Paul's remarks here suggest that the emergent factions may be created more by personal allegiance to particular leaders than by clearly defined theological differences.

Apollos, according to Acts 18:24–28, was a learned Jew from Alexandria who was deeply grounded in Scripture and who "taught accurately the things concerning Jesus" with great passion and eloquence. He had already been operating as a Christian preacher at Ephesus before coming into contact with representatives of the Pauline mission. According to the story in Acts, Paul's coworkers Priscilla and Aquila took Apollos in hand and gave him further instruction, particularly concerning baptism. The Pauline congregation at Ephesus then sent him with their blessing to Corinth, where "he greatly helped those who through grace had become believers" (Acts 18:27; see 18:27—19:1). The emphasis placed by Luke on Apollos's eloquence and his effective ministry in Achaia may provide some important clues for understanding Paul's argument in 1 Corinthians 1:17—2:5, in which he disparages the sort of wisdom that is displayed in rhetorical skill: Even though Paul had founded the community, some Corinthians may have found Apollos the more impressive figure and sought to lead the community in different directions under the banner of his name.

"Cephas" is the Aramaic name of Peter (1 Cor. 15:5; Gal. 2:8–9). It is unclear whether he had actually visited Corinth or whether he was merely a widely recognized leader in the early church whose reputation and personal influence had spread to Corinth.

Most puzzling is Paul's disapproving reference to those who say "I

22

belong to Christ." Is that not what every Christian should say? In context, it would seem that some of the Corinthians must have been claiming Christ as their leader in an exclusivistic way ("We are the ones who *really* belong to Christ, but we're not so sure about you"). Such a claim might be coupled with a boastful pretension to have direct spiritual access to Christ apart from any humanly mediated tradition. Indeed, it is not hard to see how some of the Corinthians might have developed just such a position on the basis of Paul's own preaching (cf. Gal. 1:11–12). Paul sees, however, that when "I belong to Christ" becomes the rallying cry of one contentious faction within the church, Christ is de facto reduced to the status of one more leader hustling for adherents within the community's local politics.

Paul regards this situation as scandalous. Consequently, he poses a series of biting rhetorical questions (v. 13). The first of these questions ("Has Christ been divided?") would be more precisely translated, "Has Christ been divided up and parceled out?" The community's dissension has created an absurd situation, Paul suggests, in which Christ is treated as a commodity or a possession to be haggled over. Thus, the one body of Christ (an image that will appear explicitly later in the letter) has been fragmented into interest groups. Even more telling are the next two questions, which make the point that no merely human preacher can ever be the basis for the church's faith and unity. The form in which these questions are posed in the Greek indicates that they are rhetorical questions that demand a negative answer: "Paul wasn't crucified for you, was he? Or you weren't baptized in the name of Paul, were you?" The community's life before God depends entirely on Jesus' death on a cross (cf. 11:26; 15:1–3), and the Lord into whose dominion the community has been transferred in baptism is Jesus Christ alone. The church is saved and sustained only in the name of Jesus. When this truth is kept clearly in focus, petty rivalries and preferences for different preachers are seen in their true light: They are simply ridiculous.

Perhaps some of the difficulty was caused by misunderstandings among the Corinthians about the meaning of baptism. This would explain why Paul declares himself glad that he did not baptize many people at Corinth (vv. 14–16). Baptism does not create some special bond of allegiance to the baptizer. Indeed, the act of baptism as such is of such slight importance to Paul that he claims not even to remember how many people he did baptize at Corinth, except for a few prominent community leaders such as Crispus, Gaius, and Stephanas. The "afterthought" of verse 16 functions rhetorically to emphasize the relative triviality of the issue of who baptized whom: "Well, all right, so I did baptize the household of Stephanas, but beyond that I don't even know

23

whether I baptized anyone else!" Paul's fundamental mission is to preach the gospel, not to baptize (v. 17a). In other words, in Paul's apostolic work the ministry of the Word is all-important, whereas the ministry of "sacrament" has only secondary significance; the community should not be divided by different sacramental practices, because its fundamental ground of unity lies in the proclaimed gospel. Perhaps the Corinthians really were splitting up into divergent house-church communities that placed undue emphasis on who had performed their baptisms; on the other hand, perhaps all this is merely an elaborate rhetorical flourish on Paul's part, a *reductio ad absurdum* of the Corinthians' tendency to magnify the messengers and miss the message.

It is noteworthy that the three persons named here by Paul were all wealthy or prominent, or both, in the community. Gaius is described in Romans 16:23 as "host" to Paul, and to "the whole church" in Corinth; this would mean he had a large enough house to accommodate gatherings of the community. Crispus was a "ruler of the synagogue" (*archisynagōgos*) converted by Paul's missionary preaching (Acts 18:8), and Stephanas, head of the first household of converts in Achaia, is singled out by Paul as a leader whom the other members of the community should recognize and serve (1 Cor. 16:16–17). Apparently Paul, after baptizing a few such converts, entrusted the subsequent performance of baptisms to these prominent persons. Two significant observations follow from these facts. First, Paul has no conception of baptism as a sacrament that must be administered only by specially ordained persons, nor does he have any proprietary interest in regulating its administration. Second, the church at Corinth preserved and reproduced—apparently with Paul's implicit blessing—many of the status distinctions and household authority structures that were already present in the Corinthian social setting before Paul's arrival. As we shall see later in the letter, this recapitulation of socioeconomic status distinctions within the church had begun to produce problems that Paul needed to confront (11:17–34; on this whole problem, see especially Gerd Theissen, *The Social Setting of Pauline Christianity*.)

In contrast to the ministry of baptizing, Paul insists that his commission from Christ is "to proclaim the gospel," and that this proclamation is to be carried out "not with eloquent wisdom" (literally, "not in the wisdom of a word"). The antithesis posited here sets unadorned gospel-preaching over against a "wisdom" presented with rhetorical skill and flair; indeed, Paul is convinced that such slick presentations would have the effect of making the cross of Christ "empty" (1:17b). This contrast between rhetoric and gospel becomes the theme to which Paul next turns his attention (1:18—2:5).

24

REFLECTIONS FOR TEACHERS AND PREACHERS

It requires no great leap of imagination to hear the thematic introduction of this letter to the Corinthians (1:10–17) as addressed also to us. Sadly, the church in these days finds itself no less riddled by conflict than was the Corinthian congregation. We are "by schisms rent asunder, by heresies distressed" ("The Church's One Foundation").

Those who teach and preach on this passage will have no difficulty in persuading their congregations to discern the parallels between the Corinthian divisions and the church's present disunity. The more challenging task will be to enable today's readers and hearers to embrace the foundation for unity that Paul identifies: the cross of Jesus Christ and baptism into his name. Note well that Paul does *not* appeal to the Corinthians to stop bickering in the name of expediency or humanitarian tolerance. Instead, he points to Jesus Christ as the one ground of unity. The Letter to the Ephesians offers an authentic exposition of Paul's theology at this point: Christians are called "to maintain the unity of the Spirit in the bond of peace" because their identity is defined by "one Lord, one faith, one baptism" (Eph. 4:3–5). Any attempt by the community to define itself in other terms—whether in the names of leaders or doctrines or good causes—will promote schism in the church and make our actions into a ridiculous parody of the faith we confess.

There can be no doubt that our denominational divisions perpetuate the sort of fragmentation of Christ that Paul deplored. Each one of us says, "I belong to Luther," or "I belong to Calvin," or "I belong to Wesley," or "I belong to the Church of Christ." The division of the Christian communions is a scandal, and we should hear in Paul's letter to Corinth a reproach to ourselves for perpetuating this tragic state of affairs.

Likewise, wherever there are cults of personality in the church, Paul's indictment hits home. When the charisma and ambition of the preacher begin to loom larger than the gospel of the cross, something is dreadfully wrong. When the faithful start to align and define themselves in terms of one particular leader, a red flag should go up. This can happen on a large scale, as with TV preachers, or on a small scale, as when "groupies" gather around the pastor in a local congregation. Paul has forewarned us about the potential of such movements to divide the church.

It is at the level of the local congregation that Paul's warnings are finally most pertinent. It is easy to deplore the brokenness of the church universal, but it is a hard thing to attend carefully to the ways in which factions and quarrels damage the daily life of our own congregations. This is the hard thing to which Paul's letter calls us. Wherever we see tears in the fabric of our congregational life, we need to

25

recall 1 Corinthians 1:10–17 and draw the appropriate conclusions: We are called to work and pray diligently for the healing of our divisions.

Keeping this passage in focus as the keynote of 1 Corinthians will help us see that Paul's basic concern throughout the letter is the wholeness and integrity of the community. Paul does not write this letter to address the atomistic problems of isolated individuals at Corinth. Rather, he calls on the community as a whole to take responsibility for relinquishing rivalry and overcoming divisions. In our time, divisions in the local church may arise more often over "issues" (such as homosexuality, abortion, or the naming of God in prayer) than over the personal appeal of particular leaders. Either way, Paul's calling to the church is clear: unity in Christ. Only when that unity is kept in sight will we be able to work in good faith to be "united [restored] in the same mind and the same purpose."

1:18—2:5
The Foolishness of the Cross
Excludes Boasting

Following his initial appeal for unity in the church, Paul now moves on a different argumentative tack. He launches into an extended meditation on the meaning of the cross, seeking to show that prideful confidence in human wisdom is antithetical to the deepest logic of the gospel. The fundamental theme of this section of the letter is the opposition between human wisdom (*sophia*) and the "word of the cross" (1:18). The cross is interpreted here as an apocalyptic event, God's shocking intervention to save and transform the world.

The twin pillars upon which Paul's exposition is constructed are the Old Testament quotations in 1:19 and 1:31. Both of these are taken from passages that depict God as one who acts to judge and save his people in ways that defy human expectation. Paul thus links the gospel of the cross to the older story of judgment and grace told in Israel's Scripture.

In this part of the letter, Paul makes no explicit reference to the problems at Corinth; the theme of divisions in the church does not reappear until 3:1–4. Nonetheless, he is artfully laying the theological groundwork for his critique of the Corinthians' divisiveness. As we read through this section, we begin to see Paul's diagnosis of the root causes of the Corinthian conflict. They are caught up in rivalries because they glory in the superficially impressive human wisdom of this age. They

are boasting about their own possession of wisdom and rhetorical eloquence—or at least they are infatuated with leaders who manifest
these skills. God, however, has revealed in Christ another kind of wisdom that radically subverts the wisdom of this world: God has chosen
to save the world through the cross, through the shameful and powerless death of the crucified Messiah. If that shocking event is the revelation of the deepest truth about the character of God, then our whole
way of seeing the world is turned upside down. Everything has to be
reevaluated in light of the cross.

Our familiarity with "the cross" as a theme of Christian preaching
may tend to obscure the astonishing imaginative power of this passage.
Paul has taken the central event at the heart of the Christian story—
the death of Jesus—and used it as the lens through which all human
experience must be projected and thereby seen afresh. The cross becomes the starting point for an epistemological revolution. Thus, Paul
provides the categories necessary for a fresh critical evaluation of divisions in the church and, more fundamentally, of our understanding of
wisdom, power, and wealth. For anyone who grasps the paradoxical
logic of this text, the world can never look the same again.

God's Foolishness and Human Wisdom (1:18–25)

The unit begins with a forceful statement of the central paradox,
backed by the first Scripture quotation. The word (*logos*) of the cross,
which looks like nonsense to a lost and perishing world, is the power of
God for salvation to those who believe (cf. Rom. 1:16). Though this
state of affairs may seem surprising, it accords with the prophetic word
of Isaiah declaring that God will destroy the wisdom of the wise (1 Cor.
1:19, quoting Isa. 29:14).

Throughout this passage we must bear in mind that the term "wisdom" in the Corinthian setting can refer both to the possession of exalted knowledge and to the ability to express that knowledge in a
powerful and rhetorically polished way. Much of the controversy
at Corinth may have been stirred up by the tendency for the new
Christians to regard Paul and other Christian preachers as rhetors
competing for public attention and approval alongside other popular
philosophers. Paul's forceful rebuttal is designed to reframe the categories of the debate and to put the gospel in a category apart from other
varieties of "wisdom" on offer in the popular marketplace of ideas. The
gospel is not an esoteric body of religious knowledge, not a slickly
packaged philosophy, not a scheme for living a better life; instead, it is

27

an announcement about God's apocalyptic intervention in the world, for the sake of the world.

The apocalyptic perspective is signaled by the way in which Paul describes the encounter between world and gospel in verse 18: as the word of God breaks into the world, it divides all humanity in two. The present participles that describe the two contrasting groups of hearers (those who *are perishing* and those who *are being saved*) indicate, significantly, that Paul sees the judging and saving activity of God as underway in the present moment; he describes the church not as those who *have been* saved, but as those who *are being* saved. The distinction is important, because he will continue to insist throughout the letter on the not-yet-completed character of salvation in Christ. Part of the trouble with those who claim wisdom is that they suppose themselves already to have arrived, already to be in possession of the full truth. For Paul, however, the power of God is presently afoot in the world through the gospel, bringing both destruction and deliverance (cf. Rom. 1:16–18). The books are not closed yet; the eschatological verdict has not yet been rendered. Thus, as the power of God is at work in the world through the proclamation of the gospel, members of the church find themselves on a trajectory toward salvation, but they cannot unqualifiedly claim salvation as a present possession.

For now, however, Paul is making another point. This apocalyptic sundering of humankind creates a sharp epistemological division as well: The whole world is now perceived differently by those who are being saved. In the present, the Christian community's fixation on a crucified Lord appears the height of absurdity to those who are on the way to destruction. It is not wisdom but *mōria*, "foolishness." (The Greek root is preserved in the English word "moron.") The Corinthians who celebrate their own wisdom, therefore, are celebrating something other than the gospel, showing in fact that they will still see the world from the perspective of the old unredeemed age. Those who are being saved, however, recognize the cross for what it is, the power of God, and this changes the way they understand everything else as well.

Paul sees this paradoxical situation prefigured in Scripture. He quotes a prophecy of Isaiah:

"I will destroy the wisdom of the wise,
and the discernment of the discerning I will thwart."
(1:19, quoting Isa. 29:14)

28   Isaiah's verb "I will destroy" (*apolō*) is echoed by Paul's reference in 1:18 to "those who are perishing" (*apollymenois*, literally "those who are being destroyed"). Pointedly, the thing that God will particularly

annihilate, according to Isaiah, is *sophia*, "the wisdom of the wise"—
precisely the thing that the Corinthians now prize.

We will understand the full force of Paul's meaning only if we note
the wider context from which the Old Testament quotation comes. In
Isaiah, the passage is a judgment oracle against Judah, whose political
and religious leaders are trusting in their own wise and "realistic" plans
to protect the kingdom by making a military alliance with Egypt, rather
than listening to the word of the prophet and trusting in God. In order
to grasp the pertinence of the text to the Corinthian situation, we must
recall the full oracle, including especially the verse before the one that
Paul quotes.

> The Lord said:
> Because these people draw near *with their mouths*
> and honor me *with their lips,*
> while their hearts are far from me,
> and their worship of me is a human commandment learned by rote;
> so I will again do
> amazing things with this people,
> shocking and amazing.
> *The wisdom of their wise shall perish,*
> and the discernment of the discerning shall be hidden.
> (Isa. 29:13–14; emphasis added)

Isaiah's point is that God-talk is cheap and that God's action will shut
the mouths of the wise talkers. Did Paul recall this full context when
choosing an opening sermon text to chastise the Corinthians who were
puffed up about their ability to speak in tongues and to speak about the
things of God with eloquent rhetorical flourish? We may be reasonably
sure that he did. The Corinthians, with their prized speech-gifts, make
a show of possessing wisdom and honoring God with their lips, but
their fractious behavior shows that in fact their hearts are far from God.
Thus, like Judah in Isaiah's oracle, they stand under the sentence of divine judgment which will nullify their professed wisdom and unmask
their professed piety as a sham.

This is the first of a string of Scriptural quotations that undergird
Paul's argument in this section (1 Cor. 1:19, 31; 2:9, 16; cf. also
3:19–20). As we shall see, each quotation—with the possible exception
of the obscure case of 2:9—triggers chains of association with the original
Old Testament context from which it is drawn. This is characteristic of
Paul's use of Scripture, and it offers rich poetic and theological possibilities for the preacher who follows these chains of association.

Having stated his paradoxical thesis about the word of the cross and
supported it by a suggestive scriptural citation, Paul cranks the tension

29

of the passage even higher by developing a series of contrasts between the wisdom of the world and the foolishness of the *kērygma* (vv. 20–25). The rhetorical questions of verse 20 pose a direct challenge to the world's talkers: the wise philosopher (*sophos*), the scribe (*grammateus*: the expert in Jewish Law), and the "debater of this age" (the popular rhetorician). All belong to "this age" (note again Paul's use of apocalyptic categories) and all are therefore swept away—or simply made to appear ridiculous—by God's strange way of manifesting grace.

In the ancient Greco-Roman world, rhetorical eloquence was highly prized. Powerful orators received the same sort of acclaim and public adulation that is today lavished on movie stars and sports heroes. But Paul now regards all this acclaim as utterly negated by God. Where are they now? he asks rhetorically (cf. Isa. 19:12). The question presupposes that their talk has already been swept away by God's shocking and amazing act of reversal: the cross.

Philosophers, Torah scholars, and, most significantly, popular orators—all the esteemed pundits of Paul's day—fail to understand what is really going on in the world. Their vaunted wisdom has failed to grasp the truth about God. Paul suggests that this failure is itself a mysterious part of God's own purpose. It is "in the wisdom of God" that the world has failed to know God through wisdom (v. 21). Why? Because God's ways are, as Isaiah declared, shocking and amazing, contrary to what our fallen minds would consider common sense. In contrast to "this age," God has exploded common sense by an eschatological revelation of the truth "through the foolishness (*mōria*) of our proclamation (*kērygma*)." The word *mōria* points to the utter craziness of the gospel message by commonsense standards. How can the ignominious death of Jesus on a cross be the event of salvation for the world? One would have to be a fool to believe *that*. Yet that is precisely what the gospel declares.

Paul's language throughout this section revels in the paradoxical twists of God's grace. This is not, however, just a Pauline rhetorical tour de force. The fundamental theological point is that if the cross itself is God's saving event, all human standards of evaluation are overturned. This outlandish message confounds Jews and Greeks alike, who quite understandably seek evidence of a more credible sort, either empirical demonstrations of power ("signs") or rationally persuasive argumentation ("wisdom"). But the apostle offers neither. Instead, "we proclaim Christ crucified" (v. 23).

The scandal of this message is difficult for Christians of a later era to imagine. To proclaim a *crucified* Messiah is to talk nonsense. Crucifixion was a gruesome punishment administered by the Romans to "make an example" out of rebels or disturbers of the *Pax Romana*. As

30

a particularly horrible form of public torture and execution, it was designed to demonstrate that no one should defy the powers that be. Yet Paul's gospel declares that the crucifixion of Jesus is somehow the event through which God has triumphed over those powers. Rather than proving the sovereignty of Roman political order, it shatters the world's systems of authority. Rather than confirming what the wisest heads already know, it shatters the world's systems of knowledge.

All of this is understandably baffling to Paul's hearers in the ancient Mediterranean world. Jews, who have suffered long under the burden of foreign oppression, quite reasonably look for manifestations of God's *power: signs* like those done by Moses at the time of the exodus, perhaps portending at last God's powerful deliverance of his people again from bondage. The Messiah should be a man of power, manifesting supernatural proofs of God's favor. Greeks, with their proverbial love of learning, quite reasonably look for *wisdom:* reasonable accounts of the order of things presented in a logically compelling and aesthetically pleasing manner. The Christ should be a wise teacher of philosophical truths. But no! God has blown away all apparently reasonable criteria: the Christ is a crucified criminal.

Those at Corinth who have been converted to the Christian faith through Paul's preaching certainly ought to know that, because his whole message was "Christ crucified" (cf. 2:2). This proclamation of the crucified one is a stumbling block (*skandalon*) to Jews and craziness to Greeks, but for those who are part of God's elect people—made up now of Jews and Greeks together, those who are "the called ones" (1:24; cf. 1:2, 9) at Corinth and elsewhere—this mind-warping paradox is God's power and God's wisdom.

Paul's relentless focus on the cross is suggested in verse 25 in a way that is difficult to appreciate in English translation. The words translated by NRSV as "foolishness" and "weakness" are not abstract nouns but substantive adjectives, so that a very literal translation would read, "For the foolish thing of God is wiser than humans, and the weak thing of God is stronger than humans." This foolish and weak thing is the event of the cross itself. The cross is the key to understanding reality in God's new eschatological age. Consequently, to enter the symbolic world of the gospel is to undergo a conversion of the imagination, to see all values transformed by the foolish and weak death of Jesus on the cross.

God's Calling Excludes Human Boasting (1:26–31)

To illustrate his point, Paul turns the spotlight on the Corinthians themselves. Even though a few members of the community may have enjoyed relative affluence, this church is on the whole not a gathering of the elite. "Not many" of them were highly educated or wealthy or powerful. Nonetheless, as Paul has insisted, they have been called by God as God's own covenant people (1:2). Paul reminds them of this *calling* (v. 26; cf. v. 24). God has not called Caesar or persons of senatorial rank to represent the gospel in the world; instead, he has called this motley assembly which embraces freedmen, tradespeople, and slaves—along with a few people of higher standing (hence "not many," rather than "none"). The mixed socioeconomic status of the church was one of the most striking features of the early Christian movement. Then, as now, voluntary societies tended to be socially homogeneous. The fact that the early Christian assembly brought together people of diverse rank and background who acknowledged one another as "brothers and sisters" (v. 26) was one of its distinctive characteristics. (As we shall see, precisely this socioeconomic diversity may also have been one of the causes of trouble in the Corinthian church.)

God's mysterious election of this unlikely group of people symbolizes the pattern of eschatological reversal, deeply imbedded in Israel's prophetic tradition, which also characterizes the message and ministry of Jesus. "God chose what is foolish in the world to shame the wise; God chose what is weak in the world to shame the strong; God chose what is low and despised in the world, things that are not, to reduce to nothing things that are" (vv. 27–28). This account of God's action corresponds closely to the story in Hannah's prayer (1 Sam. 2:1–10) and Mary's song of praise (Luke 1:46–55). God "raises up the poor from the dust," and he has "brought down the powerful from their thrones and lifted up the lowly." Or, in terms of Jesus' own vision, the tax collectors and prostitutes are entering the kingdom of God ahead of those who appear to be respectable and religious (Matt. 21:31).

Paul's understanding of the cross leads him to a similar understanding. If God "justifies the ungodly" (Rom. 4:5), then one would expect that the church will be a mixed lot. And, indeed, that was empirically the case at Corinth. In Paul's view, the relatively low status of most of the Corinthian Christians is a sign of what God did in the cross and therefore is doing in the world: overturning expectations. God is creating his new community out of unimpressive material precisely to exemplify the power of his own unmerited grace. The social composition of the church is an outward and visible sign of God's paradoxical election.

32   What is the purpose of the sign? Paul's answer is clear and emphatic: "so that no one might boast in the presence of God" (1 Cor. 1:29). It is axiomatic in the Old Testament that no human flesh (the

word that Paul actually uses in v. 29) can stand before the awesome holiness of God or contribute anything that God needs. All self-assertion
must melt away before the flame of God's presence. Accordingly, God
has elected to shame the wise and powerful of the world by creating an
eschatological community made up of people whom the world scorns;
this is an illustration of God's apocalyptic action of abolishing "the
things that are" and bringing a new creation into being *ex nihilo* ("out
of nothing," v. 28). That point is underscored in verse 30: God is the
source of the very existence of the Corinthian community; they have
been brought into being by God in Christ Jesus.

Here Paul makes a crucial move: Christ Jesus "became for us
wisdom (*sophia*) from God, and righteousness and sanctification and
redemption." He is in effect saying to the Corinthians, "You want wisdom? All right, here is the wisdom that God has provided us: Christ
Jesus. And remember, that means Christ Jesus *crucified!*" This reiterates what Paul has already said in verses 23–24. The identification of
Christ with wisdom cannot be separated from the very specific event
of the cross, which ironically deconstructs all human wisdom.

At this point, much theological discussion in our time has gone seriously astray, as some have championed a form of "wisdom christology" that celebrates Jesus as a teacher of wise aphorisms and an
affirmer of human potential, entirely separated from the passion narratives and the cross. Nothing could be more antithetical to what Paul
means when he equates Christ with wisdom in this passage. His whole
point is that it is the *crucified Christ* who is the wisdom of God. Furthermore, he hastens to add a string of explanatory appositives: he
became wisdom for us—and also righteousness, sanctification, and redemption. All three of these words reconnect the significance of Jesus
with the story of God's redemption of Israel to be a holy people in
covenant with him. There is no such thing as wisdom apart from
covenant relationship with God (righteousness) that leads to holy living (sanctification) made possible by God's act of delivering us from
slavery (redemption) through the cross. Those who are in Christ participate in this covenantal reality. That is what Paul is saying to the
Corinthians who revel in their possession of the divine *sophia.* To embrace wisdom christology as an alternative to a christology focused on
the cross is to recapitulate the Corinthian mistake.

The clincher of the argument is provided, then, by Paul's second
Scripture quotation, which articulates the message toward which the
whole argument has been driving: "Let the one who boasts, boast in the
Lord" (v. 31). This text emphatically precludes any possibility of glory-
ing in human wisdom. It is God who is the source of salvation, God who

33

deserves all the glory. There is no room for human self-assertion. "The Lord" in this text, in accordance with characteristic Pauline usage, probably refers to Christ, as the writer of the hymn "In the Cross of Christ I Glory" understood, and as the close parallel in Galatians 6:14 confirms.

Where does this culminating Scripture quotation come from? The usual view is that it is adapted from Jeremiah 9:24, which is part of a proclamation of judgment against Israel, "because they have forsaken my law that I set before them, and have not obeyed my voice, or walked in accordance with it, but have stubbornly followed their own hearts and have gone after the Baals, as their ancestors taught them" (Jer. 9:13–14). The immediate context of the Jeremiah citation resonates not just with 1 Corinthians 1:31 but with the whole foregoing passage:

> Thus says the Lord: Do not let the wise man [*ho sophos*] boast in his wisdom [*sophia*], do not let the strong man boast in his strength, do not let the wealthy man boast in his wealth; but let the one who boasts boast in this, to understand and know that I am the Lord; I act with mercy and justice and righteousness upon the earth, for in these things is my will, says the Lord.
>
> Jer. 9:22–23 LXX=Jer. 9:23–24 MT

When this whole passage is called up in memory, its appropriateness to Paul's argument is evident: it looks as though Jeremiah has provided not only the clincher quote against boasting but also the pattern for Paul's threefold rhetorical dismissal of the wise, the powerful, and the well-born in 1 Corinthians 1:26–28. Even the reference to Christ as becoming "righteousness" in verse 30 might be heard as an echo of the last part of Jeremiah 9:24.

There is, however, another equally possible source for the quotation. The Septuagint version of Hannah's prayer has a long conclusion that is lacking in the Hebrew text of 1 Samuel 2:10:

> Do not let the wise man (*ho phronimos*) boast in his understanding [*phronēsei*),
> And do not let the powerful man boast in his power,
> And do not let the wealthy man boast in his wealth,
> But let the the one who boasts boast in this,
> To understand and know the Lord
> And to do justice and righteousness in the midst of the earth.
>
> (1 Kgdms. 2:10 LXX)

The wording is nearly identical to Jeremiah 9:24, but the context is different: whereas Jeremiah 9 pronounces judgment, Hannah's song celebrates God's gracious blessing and, most significantly, highlights the theme of reversal of status, a theme that has dominated Paul's whole discussion of wisdom and folly, strength and weakness, in 1 Corinthians

1:18–31. The passage in 1 Kingdoms 2:10 LXX, however, lacks the key link-words *sophos* and *sophia*, which are present in Jeremiah. Does Paul's brief citation in 1:31 allude distinctly to one or the other of these passages? It is difficult to say; possibly we should hear echoes of both. It is clear, however, that Paul's disparagement of wisdom, power, and privilege draws upon Old Testament sources. The God with whom the Corinthians must learn to deal is the God of Jeremiah and Hannah, a God who acts surprisingly for the salvation of his people, demands just actions from them in response, and leaves no scope for human pride.

Preaching the Cross (2:1–5)

Paul points also to his own missionary preaching—which of course the Corinthians had experienced directly in the recent past—to illustrate the argument that he is pursuing. He reminds them that he did not preach with dazzling rhetoric or intricate wisdom. Instead, he proclaimed "the testimony of God" (this reading is to be preferred to "the mystery of God") in simple and blunt terms: "I decided to know nothing among you except Jesus Christ, and him crucified." The hyperbolic formulation underscores Paul's point emphatically: the Corinthians' own faith was elicited not by some refined discourse but by the straightforward narrative of Jesus' death as God's saving event (cf. Gal. 3:1). Of course, the very passage that we are reading here illustrates Paul's quite considerable rhetorical skill; still, he insists that it was the kerygmatic content of his preaching, not the manner of presentation, that won the Corinthians to the gospel.

The word *crucified* (1 Cor. 2:2) is a perfect passive participle in the Greek (the same as in 1:23); the perfect tense describes actions completed in the past whose effects continue into the present. Thus, when Paul summarizes the content of the gospel as "Christ crucified," he is identifying Jesus Christ as the one whose identity *remains* stamped by the cross. The cross has not been canceled out by the resurrection; rather, to know even the risen Jesus is to know him precisely as *the crucified one*. Any other account of his identity is not the gospel.

Paul's own personal bearing mirrored his message. His self-presentation was not like that of the esteemed and confident Greek orators; rather, his weakness and fear corresponded to his foolish proclamation of a crucified messiah. We know from 2 Corinthians 10:10 that some rival preachers regarded Paul as being an unimpressive figure: "For they say, 'His letters are weighty and strong, but his bodily presence is weak, and his speech contemptible.' " Interestingly, the words *weak* and *contemptible* are two of the words that Paul uses

35

in 1 Corinthians 1:27–28 to describe the vehicles that God has chosen to shame the strong and privileged. (The NRSV translates the latter in 1:28 as "despised.") So, Paul did not fit the popular stereotype of the dynamic orator, and he did not employ artful rhetoric—so he says—to sway his hearers. Why? Because he wanted his preaching strategy to be consistent with "the word of the cross," with the workings of a God who refuses to play games of power and prestige on human terms.

The result is that the efficacy of the preached word depends not on superficial packaging but solely on the power of God to make the word fruitful. The "demonstration of the spirit and of power" (v. 4) probably refers to miraculous events, such as healings and outpourings of prophecy, that accompanied Paul's missionary preaching (cf. 2 Cor. 12:12, "signs and wonders and mighty works"; Gal. 3:5; "God suppl[ies] you with the Spirit and work[s] miracles among you"). By referring to such evidence, Paul runs the risk of appealing to some of the very criteria that he has tried to avoid: signs and power. His point, however, is that such remarkable events were certainly not engineered or manipulated by the forcefulness of his preaching. They can only have been the work of God. The same applies to the blossoming of faith among the Corinthians; it is an indication of God's powerful presence, for it is certainly not produced by the attractiveness of the message or the messenger. The theme of the whole section (1:18—2:5) is restated one last time in 2:5, which creates an effective *inclusio* with 1:18: The reason that Paul avoided sophisticated rhetoric was so that the Corinthians' faith would be based "not on human wisdom but on the power of God." This closes the circle of the argument and closes the door one final time on the Corinthians' infatuation with wisdom.

REFLECTIONS FOR TEACHERS AND PREACHERS

This passage is foundational for understanding Paul's message and grasping the teaching that he will give throughout this letter. It is worthwhile, therefore, to reflect at some length about how 1 Corinthians 1:18—2:5 might shape our teaching and preaching of the gospel. I would call attention to six implications of this text.

1. *Paul's message focuses on the cross.* We should ponder seriously what implications this might have for our own preaching, if we take Paul as a model.

It would mean, first of all, that we must recover and emphasize the *apocalyptic* significance of the death of Jesus. Notice that in this passage Paul says nothing about blood atonement or forgiveness of sins as the meaning of the cross. Rather, the cross marks God's intervention to destroy the old age and bring the new into being.

Next, preaching that focuses on the cross in a Pauline fashion must emphasize that the death of Jesus is *God's act* for our salvation. All the weight of proclamation must fall on what God has done, not on how we respond to God. The only reference to faith in the passage is in its final sentence (2:5), which insists that faith rests "on the power of God." We have become so accustomed to anthropocentric preaching and theology that we hardly know how to talk in theocentric terms, but this text insists that we must—and models how we might do it. The preacher should note how often God is the subject of the verbs in this passage (especially in 1:18–31), both explicitly and implicitly: God destroys and saves, God made them foolish, God decided, God chose, God is the source of your life in Christ Jesus.

Finally, preaching that focuses on the cross will not be comforting and cheerful. Such preaching will take the full measure of human depravity and meditate deeply on the radical character of God's solution. No upbeat self-help message here! This kind of preaching may sound foreboding, but in an age when we are surrounded on all sides by sugar-coated public relations hype and superficial gladness, the honest preaching of the cross will strike a responsive chord deep in the human heart. We want to be told the truth about our desperate situation; indeed, only when that truth is told can the depth of God's grace be rightly grasped.

2. *Paul's message confronts human boasting.* Where do we confront boasting in the church in our time? Where the church is infested by flagwaving nationalism or denominational chauvinism, "boasting" has corrupted our common life. Paul's own words are also pertinent to individuals who think of themselves more highly than they ought to (cf. Rom. 12:3). There is, however, a less obvious way that Paul's assault on boasting might address us. We should recall that the Corinthian targets of Paul's critique were those who boasted of wisdom, which was linked closely with rhetorical eloquence. In our increasingly postliterate age, rhetorical eloquence of a classical sort is no longer highly valued, but self-presentation is. Image has become everything. This phenomenon is closely analogous to the ancient Hellenistic obsession with rhetorical self-presentation. Thus, anywhere we find the church infatuated with impressive individual leaders, Paul's critique of boasting becomes relevant. It is God who should receive glory, not forceful charismatic leaders. Wherever we find Christian faith presented in slick, high-tech, high-gloss images, as though it were a product to be marketed, we should ask ourselves immediately whether the gospel that is being proclaimed here is the word of the cross or whether it is some form of human boasting through image manipulation.

37

3. *The meaning of "wisdom" is controlled by "Christ crucified."*
This word of warning applies both to scholars who may be tempted to
idolize learning for its own sake and to those whose celebration of
sophia tacitly becomes a form of human self-affirmation. Wisdom is a
dangerous category and it can be employed rightly within the grammar
of Christian theology only when it is grounded firmly within the canonical narrative whose climax is the death of Jesus.

4. *The word of the cross creates a countercultural world for those
who are called.* Because God has confounded the wisdom of this world
and shown it to be foolish, Christians must see the world differently
and live in light of the wisdom of God. (This should not be confused
with Thoreau's "marching to the beat of a different drummer," which
implies merely individualistic and idiosyncratic behavior.) When people tell us that we must be "responsible" or "realistic," or act in ways
that will be "effective," we should be wary and ask whose wisdom,
whose rationality is being urged upon us. Is it God's? To whose power
are we deferring in the choices we make day in and day out? Preachers and teachers will want to work carefully to help their congregations
engage in critical discernment about such questions.

This point also means that Christian apologetics, if it can be done
at all, cannot proceed in such a way that we identify the culture's questions and then provide satisfying Christian "answers" (cf. Paul Tillich's
"method of correlation"). In fact, according to Paul, neither Jews nor
Greeks will get the answers they seek. What we have to offer instead is
the story of Jesus. To believe that story is to find one's whole life re-
framed, one's questions radically reformulated. Therefore, much of
the work of Christian apologetics will be to say to people, "No, you are
asking the wrong questions, looking for the wrong thing."

5. *The social composition of the church should be a sign of God's
election of the foolish, the weak, the low and despised.* We should look
around our congregations on Sunday. If we see too many of the educated, the powerful, and the wealthy and too few of the poor, we should
ask ourselves whether we have somehow gone astray from God's purpose, distorted the gospel of the cross, and fallen into captivity to human wisdom. Paul does not exactly condemn education, power, and
wealth in this passage, but merely suggests that God has made it foolish and irrelevant and gathered a community around different norms.

6. *The Old Testament texts in 1 Corinthians 1:19 and 1:31 are
heard as God's word addressed directly to the Christian community.*
38 The readers of this letter should learn to understand themselves within
the larger story of God's dealing with Israel. If the Corinthians had
done that rightly, they would have recognized that their excitement

about wisdom must be tempered by the prophetic word of judgment. Paul is trying to reshape the thinking of the Corinthian Christians in such a way that they will discover their own identity as heirs of Scripture and find themselves addressed by it. We will see this hermeneutical strategy employed again and again in the letter. Here we simply note it for the first time and suggest that teachers and preachers might want to begin pondering how to enable our hearers similarly to live increasingly within the world of the biblical story and to hear themselves addressed by God's word to Israel.

The Revised Common Lectionary never links Isaiah 29:13–14 or Jeremiah 9:23–24 or 1 Samuel 2:1–10 with 1 Corinthians 1:18—2:5. Thus, anyone preaching on this passage from the epistle must do the work of creating the linkage, either by drawing the relevant Old Testament passages into the sermon or, perhaps better, simply substituting one of these texts for the designated Old Testament reading. The lectionary should not be treated as sacrosanct. If we follow the lines of reflection suggested by Paul's own discussion, we should explore the Old Testament allusions that he has carefully woven into his argument.

2:6—3:4
Wisdom for the Mature

The argument suddenly shifts direction in this section. After insisting that he preaches nothing but the cross and that any other message would replace the power of God with human wisdom, Paul suddenly starts talking about a secret wisdom for the mature. What is going on here? Has Paul forgotten what he just said? Is he contradicting himself? Is he backtracking and qualifying his position? Is 1 Corinthians 2:6–16 a bit of incongruous material inserted into the text by a later editor? Scholars have puzzled over the passage, and it is by any account one of the most difficult in the letter.

The best explanation is that Paul moves here into an ironic mode, adopting some of the Corinthians' religious vocabulary in order to beat them at their own game and at same time to show how ridiculous the game is. He takes up the problematical language of the Corinthian wisdom-enthusiasts (wisdom, spiritual, mature, etc.), and trumps their boasting by speaking of a secret hidden wisdom which he does after all reveal to those who are ready to listen. That wisdom is, however, nothing other than the cross!

39

Irony is the most dangerous of rhetorical devices, because it employs semantic misdirection; the author relies upon the audience to pick up the clues that what is meant is not exactly what is said. Thus, the risk of misunderstanding is great: Readers who are not tuned in to the situation of author and audience may miss the clues and drastically misread the text. The most famous example of this is the public outcry that attended the publication of Jonathan Swift's "A Modest Proposal," when readers failed to recognize that Swift's "proposal"—that the problems of famine and overpopulation in Ireland could be solved by selling Irish babies to be eaten—was a piece of political satire. A similar hermeneutical misfortune has often befallen this passage, as verses 6–16—wrenched out of their context—have served as a classic proof-text for Gnostics, elitists, and enthusiasts who want to assert their possession of a spiritual insight exalted above that of their fellow Christians. Of course, that is exactly what Paul's Corinthian problem children were claiming!

To read the clues rightly in this passage, we must begin by anchoring our interpretation in five fundamental observations. Only if we keep these points constantly in mind will we appreciate what Paul is really doing in this section of the letter.

1. Paul has already explicitly and unambiguously defined the content of true divine wisdom: "Jews demand signs and Greeks desire wisdom, but we proclaim Christ crucified . . . Christ the power of God and the wisdom of God" (1:22–24). The *content* of the wisdom of God, which makes human wisdom look ridiculous, is precisely the cross.

2. Therefore, the discourse in 2:6–16 has to be read as ironic. This sort of ironic reversal can be shown to be characteristic of Paul's style. Paul would completely undercut his own position (1:18—2:5) if he really did mean to dangle some sort of esoteric wisdom other than the cross before his readers. (The theory that 2:6–16 is an interpolation becomes unnecessary when we perceive the biting irony of the passage.)

3. The positive categories that Paul uses to explicate this "wisdom" are not philosophical but apocalyptic in character: "this age," "hidden mystery," "decreed before the ages," "glory," "revealed," and so forth. Thus, the emphasis remains on God's revelatory initiative rather than on human capacities of knowing.

4. The distinctions made in the passage between those who do and do not know the mystery are not distinctions between two kinds of Christians; rather, they are distinctions between Christians (who have received the Spirit of God) and those who belong to the old age (who have not).

5. The meaning of "spiritual maturity" is defined, with a final ironic twist, in 3:1–4: those who are mature act in love rather than in jealousy and quarreling. Authentic wisdom is thus characterized by unity and humility rather than by special knowledge or rhetorical skill.

When we anchor our reading of the text in these points, the force of Paul's rebuttal to the Corinthians becomes clear, and we will not drift away into naive Gnosticism. Here, as throughout the letter, we can follow the argument only if we read it in big chunks, locating 2:6–16 within the unfolding logic of the larger unit and noting thematic links to the surrounding context. The following outline illustrates how this logic works:

> 1:10–17 Appeal for unity.
> 1:18—2:5 The word of the cross, foolishness to the world, is the true wisdom of God.
> Christian preaching must begin and end with the cross.
> 2:6—3:4 Wisdom for the mature:
> We preach *God's* wisdom (i.e., Christ crucified)(2:6).
> This was hidden from the powerful, as Scripture foretold (2:7–9).
> God has revealed this wisdom (Christ crucified) to us through the Spirit (2:10–13).
> This is foolishness to the natural mind, but we can discern all things because we have the mind (=spirit) of Christ (2:14–16).
> If you were really mature in the wisdom of God (Christ crucified), you would be unified in love, not divided (3:1–4).

The final verses of the section bring Paul back to his original theme: unity within the church. The whole intervening discussion of the cross and wisdom has prepared the theological groundwork for the more explicit exhortations that Paul will develop in the remainder of chapters 3 and 4. Let us now turn to some closer observations about the content of the argument in 2:6—3:4.

God Reveals the Hidden Wisdom of the Cross through the Spirit (2:6–16)

At 2:6, Paul pivots sharply on the word "wisdom," which is highlighted by the word order of Paul's Greek: "*Sophia,* however, we do speak among the mature. . . . " Is it wisdom you want? All right, he says, let's talk wisdom. This strategy of ironic reversal, abruptly coopting a term which has been previously the opposition's keynote, is a characteristic Pauline argumentative move. Consider the following examples.

In Philippians 3:2–6, Paul starts out with a polemical warning against those who urge circumcision of Gentile Christians; yet before the paragraph is through, he has claimed that "it is *we* [i.e., Christians] who are the circumcision." He insists that no confidence should be put in the flesh, yet before the paragraph is through, he pivots about and says, "As a matter of fact, I have confidence in the flesh. [The NRSV's words *reason for* confidence do not appear in the Greek text.] If any others think they can trust in the flesh, I can all the more."

Or, for a more fully developed example, consider the "fool's speech" in 2 Corinthians 11:1—12:10: "Since many boast according to the flesh, I will also boast" (11:18). Do the opponents boast of visions and revelations? Paul could as well—as a matter of fact, he knows somebody who was caught up into the third heaven—but he chooses instead to boast of suffering and weakness.

These two examples are directly pertinent because both of them involve Paul's response to "boasting," just as in 1 Corinthians. In both cases, he says in effect, "I can play your game and top you." Furthermore, if we keep reading, we find that in both cases his own "boasting" leads back to defining his own identity exclusively in terms of conformity to Christ's suffering, weakness, and death: in other words, *the cross.* In 1 Corinthians 2:6—3:4, we have a similar instance of Paul's ironic appropriation of the opponents' language for very different ends.

We have already seen that *sophia* is one of the slogan-words of the Corinthians, and in 2:6 we encounter another one: "the mature" (*teleioi*). This is a term which also appears frequently in the writings of Philo of Alexandria to describe those who have arrived at an advanced stage of spiritual insight and perfection. Presumably, the Corinthian wisdom-enthusiasts described themselves in this way, in contrast to the *nēpioi*, the "infants" or novices of lesser spiritual attainment. Paul has not yet sprung the rhetorical trap that his proud readers will encounter in 3:1—finding themselves excluded from the ranks of the *teleioi*—but here in 2:6 he is preparing the ground for it. They have apparently complained that Paul was not much of a teacher, because he did not instruct them in the niceties of wisdom. He responds that, as a matter of fact, he actually does teach wisdom *among the mature.* The Corinthians can draw their own conclusion. (For a very interesting example of the use of this term in the LXX, see Wisd. 9:6: "For even one who is perfect [*teleios*] among human beings will be regarded as nothing without the wisdom [*sophia*] that comes from you.") For Paul, being *teleios,* being a spiritual grown-up, is defined in terms of concern for upbuilding the community (1 Cor. 14:20), in terms of submission to God's will for service in community (Rom. 12:2—see the context), and in terms of pressing on toward conformity to the example of Jesus (Phil. 3:15; cf. Col. 1:28; Eph. 4:13).

Paul hastens to add that the wisdom he teaches is not "of this age or of the rulers of this age who are being brought to nothing." In other words, Paul's wisdom belongs to the new creation, not the old. This is straightforwardly apocalyptic language. The true divine wisdom is an eschatological wisdom that belongs to the new age inaugurated by the cross. This wisdom is not attainable through philosophical speculation or ascetic disciplines or any other human exertion; rather, it is "God's wisdom," revealed through the death of Jesus and the preaching of the gospel (1:23–24). The "rulers of this age" are the wielders of power in this world: the wise, the powerful, and those of noble birth, who find the cross incomprehensible (1:26–28). Using one of his favorite apocalyptic verbs, Paul says that they are being "brought to nothing" (NRSV: "doomed to perish"). This is precisely the same verb that was used of the eminent power-wielders in 1:28, there rightly translated by the NRSV as "reduced to nothing." This parallel shows that it is God who is acting to destroy these rulers and to establish his sovereignty over the world. (For other significant uses of the same verb, see Rom. 6:6; 7:6;1 Cor. 6:13; 13:8–11; 15:24–26; 2 Cor. 3:7–11; Eph. 2:15; 2 Thess. 2:8; 2 Tim. 1:10).

Continuing to develop the apocalyptic dimensions of divine wisdom, Paul indicates in 2:7–9 that the wisdom of the cross was foreordained before the ages but hidden from the rulers of this age; therefore Paul's preaching of the cross is in the form of a "mystery" (cf. 4:1; Rom. 16:25; Col. 1:26–27; 2:2; Eph. 1:9–10) to those who can see only the power structures of the present age. This has nothing to do, as older commentators sometimes suggested, with Hellenistic mystery religions; Paul's language is indigenous to Jewish apocalyptic thought, where the "mysteries" concern the concealed will of God, which is to play itself out in the historical unfolding of the eschatological events of judgment and salvation. These mysteries are revealed to the elect though the mediation of the prophet or seer. (See, for example, Dan. 2:27–28: "No wise men, enchanters, magicians, or diviners can show to the king the mystery that the king is asking, but there is a God in heaven who reveals mysteries, and he has disclosed [through Daniel] to King Nebuchadnezzar what will happen at the end of days.") In the case of Paul's specifically Christian apocalyptic, God's purpose in decreeing this mysterious salvation through the cross was "for our glory" (2:7). Thus, the

43

concealed wisdom of the cross points, in a way that Paul does not explain here, to the future eschatological redemption, God's gracious bestowal of glory upon the elect people (cf. Rom. 8:17, 29–30; 2 Cor. 3:18; 4:17; Phil. 3:20–21).

There is nothing in the present passage to suggest that "the rulers of this age" (2:8) are demonic powers. This interpretation, sometimes advocated in light of Ephesians 6:12, is difficult to support in the undisputed Pauline letters. As already noted, the mention of "rulers" in 1 Corinthians 2:6 is directly linked to 1:26–28 and entirely understandable in relation to human authority figures, just as in Romans 13:1–7. Paul's point in 1 Corinthians 2:8 is straightforward and rhetorically telling: The human power-wielders were so completely clueless about God's way of working that they actually crucified the Lord of glory. Why, therefore, should we now pay attention to human notions of wisdom and power? (It is sometimes argued that Paul thinks of cosmic forces operating behind and through these human rulers, but the present passage does not develop such an idea; a sermon pursuing such themes would be moving on a tangent away from the text.) Thus, the reference to the crucifixion reminds us once again of the actual counterintuitive content of God's wisdom, Christ crucified, and at the same time continues to develop the ironic juxtaposition of God's ways and human ways.

All this, furthermore, confirms what God has intended and announced ahead of time in Scripture. The Scripture quotation in 2:9, however, creates a number of puzzling problems, because it does not conform exactly to any known Old Testament text. There are two possible explanations for the source of the quotation: either Paul was referring to Isaiah 64:4 (with perhaps an echo of Isa. 65:16) and quoting it very loosely from memory, or the quotation comes from an apocryphal source no longer extant. Several factors speak in favor of the Isaiah reference. Paul elsewhere employs the citation formula "as it is written" exclusively for quotations that come from texts belonging to the subsequently formalized canon of Hebrew Scripture; it is unlikely, though not impossible, that he would use this formula to cite a Christian apocalypse otherwise unknown to us. Secondly, Paul's letters contain numerous allusions to Isaiah, particularly its later chapters, which he read as a prefiguration of God's eschatological salvation of Gentiles along with Israel. An allusion to this section of Isaiah would fit the general context in 1 Corinthians 2 very well indeed. (Note, for instance, the fervent appeal "O that you would tear open the heavens and come down" in Isa. 64:1 and the prophecy of "new heavens and a new earth" in 65:17.) On the other hand, there are equally good reasons to think

44

that the quotation comes from a lost source. The syntax of the quotation fits Paul's sentence very awkwardly; if he were quoting Isaiah loosely from memory, he surely would have made the citation fit into his sentence better. Secondly, Origen, writing in the third century C.E., identified this quotation as coming from the Apocalypse of Elijah, a text now no longer extant. Finally, a very similar quotation turns up in the Gospel of Thomas as a saying attributed to Jesus: "Jesus said: I shall give you what no eye has seen and no ear has heard and no hand has touched and (what) has not entered the heart of man" (Gos. Thom. 17). Thomas is a second-century text and therefore certainly not the source of Paul's quotation, but it may bear witness independently to this tradition as coming from a source unrelated to Isaiah.

Whatever the source of the quotation, its sense is clear: God's way of bringing salvation to the world through the cross was hidden from all human understanding, but God had "prepared" this plan from before the foundation of the world for those who love him. It is perhaps significant that Paul brings *love* into view here: the Corinthians might have expected Paul to say that God has prepared all these things "for those who *know* him." For Paul, however, we relate to God not primarily through knowledge or wisdom, but through love. This is a theme to which Paul will return later in the letter.

In 1 Corinthians 2:10–13, Paul makes a very simple point: The hidden wisdom of God (Christ crucified) is revealed to us by the Spirit of God. How do we know the mystery, which Paul characterizes in verse 12 as "the things graciously given to us by God"? (The noun "gifts" [NRSV] does not appear in the Greek; Paul is not talking here about "spiritual gifts" like tongues and prophecy but about the gift of God's deliverance of the world through the cross.) We know it because we (i.e., all Christian believers, cf. 12:3b) have received God's Spirit, and God's Spirit alone discloses that the word of the cross is the truth about God. The logic of the passage depends on the widespread Hellenistic maxim that like knows like. Paul proposes an analogy: Just as no one knows the thoughts of an individual person except the person himself or herself, so also, "Only God knows and can communicate the truth about himself" (Barrett, 74). (The NRSV's attempt at inclusive language produces a dreadful mistranslation of v. 11: "For what human being knows *what is truly human* except the human spirit that is within?" Paul's point is not that the human spirit knows humanity in some generic way; rather, the specific individual thoughts and identity of a person are known only to the spirit of that person.) The conclusion of all this is summarized in 2:13: Paul and other Christians can speak now about the identity of God not because they have received advanced

45

philosophical instruction or lessons on rhetorical declamation but because they have been taught by the Spirit of God how to speak of God through the word of the cross. The obscure phrase "interpreting spiritual things to those who are spiritual," which could be translated in several different ways, should probably be understood as one more ironic dig at the self-styled Corinthian *pneumatikoi*: If you were really as spiritual as you think you are, Paul suggests, you would understand that our rhetorically unembellished speech about Christ crucified is the message that comes from the Spirit of God.

Another way to put Paul's point is that the truth about God is revealed not through philosophy but through prophecy, not through rhetoric but by revelation. The "deep things of God" (2:10; cf. Dan. 2:22) are not arcane Gnostic trivia; rather they are the secret saving purposes of God for the whole world, now laid bare by the Spirit's disclosure that the wisdom of God is made known through the cross.

The NRSV translation of verse 14 ("Those who are unspiritual do not receive the gifts of God's Spirit") again runs the risk of suggesting that Paul is talking here about "spiritual gifts" of the sort that he will discuss in chapters 12–14. In fact however, he writes, "The *psychikos* does not accept the things of God's Spirit." The point is that the natural human mind *rejects* the preaching of the gospel, because—Paul reminds us—it sounds like foolishness (*mōria* again, cf. 1:18, 23, 25, 27). The term *psychikoi* is difficult to translate properly; it refers to human beings living in their natural state apart from the Spirit of God and therefore unenlightened and blind to the truth. They just don't "get it." In other words, it refers to those who belong to the old age; it emphatically does not refer to less advanced Christians. When Paul says in verse 15 that "those who are spiritual . . . are themselves subject to no one else's scrutiny" (NRSV) he certainly does not mean that Christians who have the spirit are no longer subject to community discipline. Indeed, everything in this whole letter suggests exactly the opposite (cf. 14:32–33a and the entirety of Paul's admonitions to the community in 1 Cor. 5—6)! He means, rather, that the person who has received God's Spirit has a privileged understanding of reality: she "discerns (*anakrinei*) all things but is herself discerned (*anakrinetai*) by no one." In other words, we understand what is going on in the world, but the world cannot understand us. The apparently startling last clause merely restates the point of verse 14, now referring not to the world's inability to understand the gospel, but to its incomprehension of those who have received the Spirit.

Once again Paul concludes a section of his argument with a clinching quote, this time from Isaiah 40:13 LXX. Isaiah's rhetorical question

46

"Who has known the mind of the Lord?" presumes a negative answer: "No one." Thus, on one level, the quotation reinforces Paul's point that the natural mind is incapable of understanding God's designs (cf. Rom. 11:34, quoting the same text). At the same time, however, the quotation also suggests a second, quite different point. The LXX phrase "mind (*nous*) of the Lord" translates the Hebrew phrase "spirit (*ruach*) of the Lord." Given the whole context, it is evident that Paul understands the terms "mind" and "spirit" to be synonymous. Because he also understands "the Lord" to be Jesus, and because Christians have received the Spirit, he can move forward to his final audacious claim: "We have the mind (=spirit) of Christ." Therefore, in a real sense, it *has* been given to us to know the mind of the Lord. Who has known the mind of the Lord? Answer: We who have received the Spirit know it, because we, unlike the world, have the mind of Christ. This formulation restates in more striking language what was already explained in verses 10–13.

Here it certainly sounds as though Paul has fallen into the insidious trap of trying to outdo the elitist boasters. But in order to understand rightly what it means to have the mind of Christ, we must remember who "Christ" is for Paul: the crucified one. To have the mind of the Lord is to participate in the pattern of the cross (cf. Phil. 2:1–11), for the wisdom of God is manifest definitively in the death of Jesus. Consequently, the privileged spiritual knowledge of which Paul speaks should result in the renunciation of all privilege, all boasting and quarreling. Wolfgang Schrage summarizes the implications of the whole passage aptly:

> The Spirit that teaches understanding to the Christians is not some kind of spirit of field, forest, and meadow, nor is it a natural magic potency that produces enthusiasm; rather, it is the spirit of the crucified Christ. Thus, this spirit is to be measured by the cross, and it is therefore unavoidably a critic of all self-directed wisdom and likewise of all elite wisdom.
>
> (Schrage, 267)

The fact that the Corinthian wisdom-enthusiasts are so dramatically failing to live according to "the mind of Christ" leads Paul on to the next devastating step in his argument.

People of the Flesh (3:1–4)

In contrast to the convoluted argument of the preceding section, Paul now speaks directly and clearly, though still with some overtones of irony, to the Corinthian situation. Consequently, this section requires considerably less exegetical comment.

47

The Corinthians have reproached Paul for failing to provide sufficiently advanced instruction in wisdom. Paul replies with a direct shot at their self-proclaimed status as *pneumatikoi*: "I could not speak to you as spiritual people, but rather as people of the flesh, as infants in Christ." The metaphors used here (adults vs. infants and solid food vs. milk) are stock language in relation to philosophical and religious instruction throughout the ancient world. The assumption is that spiritual progress can be graded and that a different sort of curriculum is appropriate to each level of maturity. Thus, Paul is not coining fresh categories in order to classify the relative spiritual maturity of his readers; rather, he is turning the tables on the spirit-enthusiasts, placing them at the bottom of their own scale of religious achievement rather than at the top, where they suppose themselves to belong. They consider themselves mature and spiritual, but Paul replies with a putdown: sorry, you remain immature and fleshly. How can he say that of them? His answer demonstrates how dramatically he wants to redefine their understanding of spirituality: "For as long as there is jealousy and quarreling among you, are you not of the flesh, and behaving [literally "walking"] according to human inclinations?" (v. 3).

The word translated here as "jealousy" (*zēlos*) can also mean "zeal" of a religious sort. Paul says of himself that he persecuted the church with zeal (*kata zēlos*, Phil. 3:6; cf. Gal. 1:14), and he also uses the same term to describe the religious enthusiasm of his Jewish kinsmen, whose unbelief he laments: "I can testify that they have a zeal for God (*zēlon theou*), but it is not enlightened" (Rom. 10:2). Similarly, the Corinthians may well have been motivated by religious zeal; we do them an injustice if we suppose that they were merely squabbling jealously over petty matters. The factions in the community were caused—at least to some extent—by serious questions of theological understanding and religious practice. How do we attain divine wisdom? What actions constitute idolatry? What sexual norms should be observed in marriage? How should manifestations of the Spirit function in worship? What is the meaning of resurrection? These are the sorts of issues that were splitting the church, and the different groups were no doubt zealous in their defense of their convictions. Paul insists, however, that when such matters produce "quarreling" (*eris*) it is a sign that the contending factions are not truly spiritual but "of the flesh."

Being "of the flesh" does not mean, as the Corinthian wisdom-enthusiasts supposed, lacking refined spiritual knowledge and experience. Nor does being "of the flesh" mean, as much of the subsequent Christian tradition has supposed, living in lust and sexual sin. No, for Paul, *being "of the flesh" means living in rivalry and disunity within the church.* This breathtaking assertion shatters and reshapes the whole scale of values on which the Corinthians are asked to measure themselves. If the Corinthians accept this new scale that Paul has proposed, they cannot deny that they fall at the immature end, for they have indeed aligned themselves with the party slogans that Paul quotes back at them: "I belong to Paul" or "I belong to Apollos." Thus Paul artfully brings his long reflection on the cross, the Spirit, and wisdom back to the issue that launched the letter: the problem of divisions in the church.

In light of the intervening discussion, we now know Paul's diagnosis of the problem that causes these divisions: The Corinthians are continuing to judge and act in accordance with the standards of "this age." This leads inevitably to the recapitulation within the church of the world's boasting and power struggles. Paul delivers a splash of cold water on their faces, which were burning with what they supposed to be spiritual ardor. "Wake up," he says. "Stop fighting with each other; you are acting like spoiled babies, not like people who have received the Spirit of God."

When we read the passage this way, we see that it would be a grave mistake to use 3:1–2a as if it provided a Pauline warrant for ranking individuals within the church on a scale of spiritual advancement. Paul is using the Corinthians' own elitist language ironically to execute a reversal of perspective—a reversal homologous with what God has done to "the wise" through the cross—to shake the Corinthians out of their infatuation with elitist spiritual experience. Thus, by the time we arrive at verse 4, we see that Paul has brought the "wisdom of the cross" powerfully to bear as a critique of his Corinthian readers.

REFLECTIONS FOR TEACHERS AND PREACHERS

Spiritual elitism of one sort or another is a perennial problem in the church. First Corinthians is our earliest example of a careful pastoral response to this problem, but the latter part of chapter 2 is subject to the possibility of serious misunderstanding. The preacher working with this text must take great care to illuminate the *irony* of Paul's response and to show how the message of the cross destroys spiritual elitism at the roots. Otherwise, this text may feed spiritual pride rather than deflate it. One way to make sure the message gets through is to insist on reading 3:1–4 as part of the pericope, even if the lectionary decrees otherwise. Only in these verses will Paul's point come through unambiguously to the congregation: The real measure of spiritual maturity is unity and peace in the community.

Elitism can take many different forms. Some will boast in spiritual

49

gifts, some in scholarly knowledge, some in doctrinal correctness or moral uprightness or proper political concerns. The most insidiously divisive forms of elitism will be precisely those that are most "spiritual" in motivation and manifestation. Wherever such apparently spiritual concerns fracture the community into special-interest caucuses or lead people into self-absorption with their own spirituality, the word of the cross needs to be spoken to recall the community to "the mind of Christ." Our teaching and preaching must ensure that talk about the mind of Christ is never severed from the passion story, from the model of Christ crucified.

In our time, there is much fascination both inside and outside the church with "spirituality," but much of it is individualistically focused and aimed at promoting selfish forms of personal well-being and contentment. Paul shows us how to address such concerns by insisting that the Spirit of God reveals the truth about things through the story of the *cross*, and that people who are animated by God's strange wisdom will seek unity within the community of faith.

Preachers and teachers handling this passage might consider how to encourage their congregations to claim for themselves the audacious but foundational truth that "we have the mind of Christ." Although, on the face of it, this sounds scandalously bold, there is no reason for the church to exist if it is not true. Thus, the interpreter of this text might well ask the congregation what discernments and actions would ensue if we really took this claim seriously. Linking 1 Corinthians 2:16 with Philippians 2:1–13 will facilitate such reflection.

One possible consequence of the congregation's putting "the mind of Christ" into action will be that the rulers of this age will react with hostility and violence against the church. In light of 1 Corinthians 2:6–8, we should not find this a surprising development. Those who live in light of the wisdom of God will appear foolish and even threatening to those with a vested interest in the status quo arrangements of power in this age. Beyond the story of Jesus' death, the stories of most of the saints exemplify this same truth, down to and including Dietrich Bonhoeffer, Martin Luther King, Jr., and Oscar Romero.

Finally, the interpreter of this text must once again grapple with the apocalyptic horizons of Paul's gospel. This is a message about God's plan from before the ages to bring God's people through the present time of conflict to eschatological glory. Only in that frame of reference does the cross make sense, and only in that frame of reference will the divisions in the church be seen in their proper light. It is God who is at work through the Spirit to reveal this eschatological truth in and through our common life.

50

3:5–23
The Community and Its Leaders
Belong to God

Having brought the discussion back around to the problem of factions in Corinth that align themselves with the names of various leaders (3:3–4), Paul now turns to confront the controversies in the community more directly. (As we shall see in 1 Cor. 4, however, he has not quite yet laid all his cards on the table.) His main line of argument in chapter 3 no longer focuses on the cross. Instead, he relentlessly emphasizes that the church belongs to God: God brought it into being, and God will judge it. The human instruments that God has used to raise up the church are merely servants of God's larger purpose. Therefore it is foolish for the Corinthians to choose sides and pit one leader against another. Indeed, it is worse than foolish: it is destructive and dangerous. Those who build with arrogance and false wisdom are compromising the integrity and holiness of God's plan for bringing the gospel to the world. Thus, they are courting God's wrath and judgment.

This section is structured around three metaphors for the church: the church as God's field (vv. 5–9), the church as God's building (vv. 10–15), and the church as God's temple (vv. 16–17). Paul moves fluidly from one metaphor to the next to make related but different points about the identity of the Corinthian church and its leaders. The final part of the chapter (vv. 18–23) first recapitulates the earlier teaching about wisdom, folly, and boasting and then concludes with a powerful affirmation that not only the church and its leaders but everything else in creation finally belongs to God.

Throughout this chapter, two fundamental points must be kept clearly in view. First, Paul thinks of the church not as an institution with a hierarchy and a certain formal structure but as a concrete community of people in a particular locality. (In fact, though "church" will be used in this exposition as a convenient shorthand, Paul does not actually use the word "church" in this chapter; of course, he does use the word frequently elsewhere in the letter.) Thus, when he says, for example, "you are God's temple," he is referring not to a building but to the gathered people of God. Second, Paul's metaphors all refer to the community viewed *corporately*: the building that is built by the apostles and tested by fire is not the spiritual life of the individual believer, but the church community as a whole. The latter point may be especially hard for some Protestant congregations to keep in focus, because the tradition

51

of individualistic reading is so entrenched. But if this point is not grasped firmly, Paul's whole meaning will be missed.

Paul and Apollos as God's Field Hands (3:5–9)

Paul demonstrates the futility of rallying around different leaders by using himself and Apollos as illustrations. The rhetorical questions of verse 5 ("What then is Apollos? What is Paul?") are answered immediately and straightforwardly: They are servants (*diakonoi*) who have been assigned various chores by God. In this case, as Paul develops the image, they are field hands given the task of planting and cultivating a crop. This passage shows that *diakonos* was not yet for Paul a technical term for a particular office in the church ("deacon"); here it is a simple metaphor. The fact that their designated chores were slightly different is of no consequence. Paul, who arrived on the scene first, planted the church in Corinth, and Apollos, who came later, watered the crop, but each of them was simply doing the task assigned by God. Thus neither one of them amounts to anything in his own right (v. 7a), because their efforts would be of no avail apart from the direction and empowerment of God. The field hands can do only what they are told to do, but they are utterly powerless to make the seed come to life: that is God's mysterious power. Paul highlights this point by stating it twice (vv. 6, 7). It is God who makes the word of gospel take root and spring up into a living community of faith. (Anticipating Paul's shift to the "building" metaphor, we might recall the opening words of Psalm 127: "Unless the Lord builds the house, those who build it labor in vain.")

Paul's reason for pursuing this line of reasoning is made clear in verse 8a: the efforts of the different servants are collaborative. The NRSV's statement that they "have a common purpose" is a periphrastic translation of the Greek: "The one who plants and the one who waters *are one.*" This means, of course, not that they are the same person but that their efforts are complementary parts of a single agricultural project. Therefore, to play one off against the other is ridiculous. Both are necessary: without the waterer, the crop would die; without the planter, there would be no crop to water.

Paul's way of elaborating the analogy does subtly remind the Corinthians that it was he whose preaching first founded the community; they first "came to believe" through him. Paul does not want them to lose sight of that fact (cf. 4:15). His present purpose, however, is to stress the *synergistic* relation of the different apostolic workers; indeed, he calls himself and Apollos God's *synergoi,* "coworkers" (3:9).

This does not mean here (in contrast to 2 Cor. 6:1) that he and Apollos are coworkers *with* God; rather, as the whole burden of the passage would suggest, they are fellow workers together *under* the authority of God, belonging to God. And the church, to complete the metaphor, is God's field. (Here we should perhaps hear an echo of the familiar Old Testament image of Israel as God's vineyard, e.g., Isa. 5:1–7). What matters is the fruitful cultivation of the harvest.

It is easy to give lip service to this principle, but hard to live out its practical implications in the church. Too often clergy, rather than working cooperatively to cultivate God's field, become embroiled in turf battles. The same thing is true of other workers in the church. We all want to be sure that no one else interferes with our little patch of the field, that things are done just precisely our way. And so the field becomes endlessly subdivided into unproductive subsistence plots. Perhaps there is no more vivid symbol of this foolish and tragic failure of cooperation than the Church of the Holy Sepulchre in Jerusalem, which today is divided up into different sections under the jurisdictions of the different Christian groups that want to claim a piece of the purportedly holy place: Greek Orthodox, Armenian Orthodox, Roman Catholic, Ethiopian Orthodox, and so forth.

Paul is saying to his readers, then and now, "No, don't you understand that the whole field belongs to God and that we are called to work together to bring in the eschatological harvest? Individual leaders are insignificant; they are just field hands."

Our Construction Work Will Be Tested by Fire (3:10–15)

With the final words of verse 9, Paul shifts to a new metaphor. "You are God's building." This allows him to direct attention to a new focal concern: the urgency of constructing the church with integrity. In this new metaphor, Paul compares himself to a head building contractor who has carefully laid the foundation of a building and then let out the rest of the work to subcontractors. If their work is not "up to code," or if they fail to use suitable materials, there will be dire consequences.

We might think of what happens in California earthquakes. Some buildings that have been properly constructed to withstand the shocks remain standing, while others that have not been built according to sound principles of seismic engineering come tumbling down, with sometimes tragic results. Rather than earthquake, Paul uses the image of fire, a traditional Old Testament image for God's judgment, but his point is the same: A cataclysm is coming that is going to test the structural

53

integrity of our construction work, so we should build with great care. Our building should not be hasty, nor just for show; we must build our community solidly from the ground up in a way that is designed to endure.

Paul's own argument here is carefully constructed. He compares himself to a "wise" (*sophos*) master builder (v. 10). In discourses about trades and arts, the term *sophos* quite commonly means "skilled"; however, the term takes on a special double sense in the present context. Paul is both the *skilled* artisan and the *wise* teacher who lays down the one foundation that is truly in accordance with God's wisdom rather than the wisdom of the world. Again, we see that he is contrasting himself ironically to the Corinthian devotees of wisdom.

Paul's foundation-laying was "according to the grace of God given to me." By this he means that his apostleship is commissioned by God (cf. Rom. 1:5): His apostolic work is itself a manifestation of God's grace for the community. Precisely for that reason, a warning must be sounded for his successors: "Let each one take care how he builds." (The NRSV, supplying the word "choose," which does not appear in the Greek, muffles the note of warning in this sentence.) Shoddy workmanship on top of the sound apostolic foundation is not to be tolerated. Sometimes commentators speculate that the reference to "someone else" who is building on Paul's foundation (v. 10) points to a single specific individual who is the hidden target of Paul's warning. This hypothesis is possible but unnecessary and unilluminating, since the identity of the other builder would remain unknown to us. In any case, Paul immediately formulates his admonition in general terms: "Let *each one* take care." Consequently, it is better to read this section as a general warning to all who teach or exercise leadership in the church.

Next, Paul explicitly articulates what was implicit in his use of the image of laying a foundation: The one foundation is Jesus Christ. If we recall what Paul has already said about Christ as the content of his foundational preaching (1:23; 2:2), we will recognize that it is Jesus Christ *crucified* who is the foundation of the church. The superstructure of the building (the church) must conform to the pattern of that foundation. Otherwise it will be crooked and unstable. Similarly, no one can expand this foundation by saying, "Let's add on a new wing founded on wisdom," or, "Let's build a new building on the foundation of scientific knowledge," or, "Our contemporary religious experience requires us to dismantle the foundation and reconstruct it in a different way." The fixed basis for the construction of the church is the kerygma of Christ crucified.

54

With that basis in place, Paul develops the hortatory point of his building metaphor in verses 12–15. Those contractors who employ inferior material will have the quality of their work exposed by the fire of God's judgment. "The Day" (v. 13) refers to the Day of the Lord, the day when God will examine and judge all human deeds and establish eschatological justice (cf. Rom. 2:5, 16; 13:12; 1 Cor. 1:8, 2 Cor. 1:14, Phil. 1:6, 10; 1 Thess. 5:2; for Old Testament background see Amos 5:18, 20; Mal. 4:1). Here again, the apocalyptic framework of Paul's thought is evident. The imagery of fire as a sign of God's judgment is deeply imbedded in the Old Testament and in Jewish apocalyptic traditions (cf. Dan. 7:9–10; 2 Peter 3:7). In Malachi 4:1–2a, for example, we read:

> See, the day is coming, burning like an oven, when all the arrogant and all evildoers will be stubble; the day that comes shall burn them up, says the Lord of hosts, so that it will leave them neither root nor branch. But for you who revere my name the sun of righteousness shall rise, with healing in its wings.

Paul's vision of final judgment is completely consonant with this tradition, with the single exception that here he is applying the image of judgment by fire not to the fate of individuals but to the ecclesiological construction work done by different church leaders. As Robertson and Plummer (64) rightly observe about 1 Corinthians 3:12–15, there is not "the remotest reference to the state of the soul between death and judgment." Nor is there any reflection here on the purifying effect of fire. Paul is talking not about purgatory for individual souls but about the final divine testing of the solidity of the church as constructed by various apostolic laborers.

The six different building materials, perhaps arranged in descending order of value (3:12), have no special significance beyond the fact that the last three are combustible and the first three are not. Paul does not develop the meaning of these different materials allegorically; a sermon that pursued the strategy of assigning some distinct spritual significance to each item in the list would be indulging in sheer fancy. Paul's point is that some leaders are building with valuable fireproof material (the gospel of Christ crucified) and others are building with ephemeral fluff (the fads of human wisdom) that will be consumed by flames in God's coming building inspection.

The motif of "reward" and "loss" in verses 14–15 creates difficulties for many interpreters, because it seems to be at odds with Paul's doctrine of justification by faith rather than by works. If salvation is solely through God's grace, how can Paul also speak of rewards and punishments based on the quality of the work of individuals? Several observations about this problem are in order. First of all, Paul held his doctrine of justification

55

alongside a continuing belief that God will judge the deeds of individuals (2 Cor. 5:10; Rom. 2:6–10). We must take care to examine what Paul actually thought rather than to impose upon him a theological abstraction about the meaning of *sola fide*. Secondly—and more importantly for the present passage—we must remember that Paul is not talking about the fate of individual souls at the final judgment but about God's scrutiny of the building work of different preachers and leaders. Paul did in fact have a distinct notion of special eschatological rewards for apostolic work (cf. 1 Cor. 9:15–18, 23, 27; Phil. 2:16). The doctrine of justification by faith is clearly distinguishable from this idea, as 1 Corinthians 3:15 suggests: The incompetent subcontractor will be saved (though barely) even though his work is burned up. Finally, the words translated "receive a reward" and "suffer loss" in the NRSV would be better understood as references to wages paid to workers and fines imposed on builders who do inadequate work; in other words, in these verses Paul is still developing the metaphor of construction work. Precisely this same language has been found in ancient Greek inscriptions dealing with penalties to be imposed on contractors who do inferior work or fail to meet their obligations. Keeping this in mind, we should translate as follows:

> The fire will test what sort of work each subcontractor has done. If the work that anyone has built on the foundation survives, he will receive his pay; but if the work of anyone is burned up, he will be fined; the subcontractor will be saved, but only as through fire.

A dramatic example of such consequences for careless builders occurred after the major southern California earthquake of 1994, in which an apartment building in Northridge, California, collapsed and killed sixteen people. The builders were subsequently taken to court and required to pay a settlement of more than a million dollars to the plaintiffs in a lawsuit alleging wrongful death. That is the kind of thing Paul has in mind. Those whose preaching and teaching fail to build solid community are responsible for loss and injury to many, and God will hold them accountable. If they are nonetheless finally spared and saved as individuals, it will be only by God's miraculous grace: They will be like "a brand snatched from the fire" (Amos 4:11).

The Church as God's Temple (3:16–17)

Paul's third metaphor may be understood as a development of the previous one. The community is not just any building but in fact *the Temple of God*, the place where God's Spirit dwells. It is crucial for interpreters of this text to understand that the verb and the second person pronoun in verse 16 are plural: "Do you not know that you [*plural*] are the Temple of God and that God's Spirit dwells in you [*plural*]?" The image here is of the Spirit dwelling not in the individual Christian (cf. 6:19) but in the gathered community. In focusing on the church, this metaphor is fully consistent with the other metaphors in chapter 3.

The Corinthians, hearing this language, might well have thought first of the many pagan temples in their own city, such as the temple of Apollo. But when Paul speaks of God's Spirit dwelling in a temple, he surely does not mean just any random gods and temples of the pagan world. He can be thinking of only one thing: the Spirit of the God of Israel in the Temple at Jerusalem. This role of the Temple as the dwelling place of God is now imaginatively claimed for the church.

In order to grasp the full audacity of this claim, we must remember that when Paul wrote to the Corinthians the Temple in Jerusalem was still standing and active. For Jews like Paul, the Jerusalem temple had been understood as the central locus of the divine presence in the world. Thus, when Paul now transfers this claim to the community of predominantly Gentile Christians in Corinth, he is making a world-shattering hermeneutical move, decentering the sacred space of Judaism (cf. John 4:21–24). How can Paul possibly assert that the church has replaced the Temple? He believes that the Spirit of God is present in the community and that the community is now the place where praise and worship are rightly offered up to God. The Spirit of God no longer can be localized in a sacred building: it is to be found in the gathered community of God's elect people in Christ.

Although this is a remarkable imaginative transformation of Judaism's symbolic world, we now know that such thinking was not utterly unique to the early Christians; the members of the Qumran community also understood themselves to be the temple of God—at least provisionally during their exile in the wilderness until right temple worship according to their interpretation of the Law could be restored (see, e.g., 1QS 8:5–10). At Qumran the use of this metaphor was prompted by a protest against the corruption of the Jerusalem temple and by the belief that the rigorous holiness of the covenanters could "atone for the land," by offering figurative sacrifices of obedient deeds (cf. Rom. 12:1–2; for the metaphor of the church as a temple offering spiritual sacrifices, see also 1 Pet. 2:4–5). Paul, however, employs the metaphor for slightly different purposes. He speaks of the community as temple *not because of what the members of the community are doing* (offering sacrifices of one sort or another) but *because the Holy Spirit is present in the community*: the community is the place where God resides (cf. 2 Cor. 6:16; Eph. 2:21–22).

Paul interestingly takes it for granted that the Corinthians will

57

accept his image of their community as the place where God dwells. (This is an assumption which preachers and teachers today should not make casually; we will return to this point below.) For the present, Paul has another point to make: if the church is the dwelling place of God, then God will surely deal severely with those who corrupt or damage it (3:17). Those who split the community are offending God and calling down God's judgment on their own heads. God's temple, he emphasizes, is *holy*: that is, it is set apart for the service of God. Those who turn the temple/community into a playground for their own arrogance and spritual vanity are solemnly warned: "If anyone destroys God's temple, God will destroy that person." Paul then ends the section by driving home the image one more time: "You [*plural*] are that temple."

The stakes are high: God has chosen to be present in the world in and through a specific community of human beings. The task of apostles and church leaders is to construct that community on the foundation of Jesus Christ in such a way that the Holy Spirit will be rightly worshiped and manifested; and as Paul has already hinted (3:1–4), the Spirit is to be manifested in the community's unity and harmony. This is no light matter. Those who damage the unity of the community are interfering with God's chosen mode of presence, and they will certainly incur judgment. We should probably make a distinction between those who build with inappropriate materials (vv. 12–15) and those who actively destroy the community (v. 17), though the line between these actions is perilously thin. One is saved, though with singed eyebrows, while the other is destroyed. Paul's call to his readers, however, is to avoid both of these fates by building soundly on the gospel of Jesus Christ and forswearing pretentious and divisive claims to elite spritual knowledge.

Reprise and Summary: All Belongs to God (3:18–23)

In the conclusion of 1 Corinthians 3, Paul reprises the themes that he has developed in the letter up to this point. The themes of wisdom and folly are revisited in 3:18–21a, with a couple of new twists. This time, rather than merely making descriptive statements about what God has done to confound the purveyors of human wisdom, Paul pointedly summons his readers to examine themselves and respond: "If you think that you are wise in this age, you should become fools so that you may become wise" (v. 18). Here, he says in effect, is a self-diagnostic test: Do you think that you are wise in this age? If so, this message is for you. In order to become wise, you are going to have to give up your "wisdom."

This appeal bears a superficial resemblance to Socrates's well-known interpretation of the saying of the Delphic oracle: "This one of you, O

58

human beings, is wisest, who, like Socrates, recognizes that he is in truth of no account in respect to wisdom" (Plato, *Apology* 23B). Indeed, this entire section of the *Apology* provides very interesting background for Paul's rhetorical treatment of wisdom throughout the opening chapters of 1 Corinthians. Paul, however, unlike Socrates, is not merely calling for epistemological humility and the cultivation of an inquiring mind. Instead, he is calling his readers to take upon themselves the obedience of faith. Paul's particular application of the logic of the cross to wisdom and knowledge parallels the call of Jesus: "If any want to become my followers, let them deny themselves and take up their cross and follow me. For those who want to save their life will lose it, and those who lose their life for my sake, and for the sake of the gospel, will save it" (Mark 8:34–35). In the same way, those who cling to the world's wisdom will lose it, and those who surrender their "wisdom" for the sake of the gospel will find God's wisdom.

Paul once again appeals to Scripture in verses 19–20 to demonstrate the futility of human wisdom. This time, however, rather than repeating any of the texts he cited earlier (1:19; 1:31; 2:9; 2:16) he adduces two completely different texts (Job 5:12–13 and Ps. 94:11)—thereby heightening the impact of his assault on wisdom by suggesting the wider range of Scripture's witness in support of his case.

The passage from Job is taken from the first speech of Eliphaz the Temanite. There is no evidence that Paul is paying any attention to the larger literary structure of Job, in which Eliphaz's words are discounted as facile counsel; instead, Paul cites them here as an authoritative disclosure of the truth about God's debunking of human wisdom. The immediate context of the quotation, however, does resonate with the themes of reversal and the mystery of divine mercy that Paul has introduced in 1 Corinthians 1:18—2:16:

> As for me, I would seek God,
>   and to God I would commit my cause.
> He does great things and unsearchable,
>   marvelous things without number. . . .
> He sets on high those who are lowly,
>   and those who mourn are lifted to safety.
> He frustrates the devices of the crafty,
>   so that their hands achieve no success.
> *He takes the wise in their own craftiness;*
>   and the schemes of the wily are brought to a quick end. . . .
> But he saves the needy from the sword of their mouth,
>   from the hand of the mighty.
> So the poor have hope,
>   and injustice shuts its mouth.

(Job 5:8–9, 11–13, 15–16, emphasis added)

59

Paul does not develop any of these ideas at this point—to do so would divert him from his immediate aim of providing a pithy recapitulation of his argument—but these echoes of Job may be heard in Paul's later treatment of the weak and the strong at Corinth, and in his response to inequities at the celebration of the Lord's Supper (1 Cor. 11:17–34). The preacher who wanted to explore this connection would do well to note that Job 5:8–16 sets up an opposition between "the wise" and "the poor," suggesting—no doubt aptly for the Corinthian situation—that the conflict over "wisdom" has a socioeconomic dimension.

Similar themes appear also in Psalm 94, which is an extended prayer for God to overthrow wicked oppressors and to vindicate the righteous. In his use of this psalm, Paul seems to be reaching just a bit, because he has to alter the quotation by supplying the key word "wise," which appears neither in the Septuagint nor in the Hebrew text of Psalm 94:11. It is not hard, however, to see what drew his attention to the passage, for Psalm 94:8 reads, "Understand, O dullest of the people; fools, when will you be wise?" That Paul knew the larger context of the psalm is evident (should anyone doubt it) from the fact that he quotes a different verse of it (Ps. 94:14) in Romans 11:2. Thus, given the linkage of "fools" and "wise" in the psalm, it is not surprising that Paul sees its reference to the futility of human thoughts as one more testimony to the emptiness of *sophia*.

The lesson of all this is then restated in 1 Corinthians 3:21a: "Thus, let no one boast in human beings." The NRSV helpfully makes the connection to 3:5–9 more explicit: "let no one boast about human leaders." The word *leaders* is not in the Greek text, but that is what Paul means. This sort of boasting is, of course, precisely the opposite of boasting in the Lord (1:31). This is a succinct summary of the burden of the whole argument up to this point; Paul has artfully reminded his readers of the major points of his exhortation.

We might expect the chapter to end at this point, but Paul instead offers a final rhetorical flourish in verses 21b–23. In order to appreciate the impact of this conclusion, we need to know that it was a universal maxim of Greco-Roman popular philosophy—particularly among the Cynics and Stoics—that "the wise man possesses all things." For example, the great Roman orator Cicero, describing the philosophy of the Stoics, writes as follows: "Then, how dignified, how lofty, how consistent is the character of the Wise Man as they depict it! ... Rightly will he be said to own all things, who alone knows how to use all things" (*De Finibus* 3.22.75). Or again, Paul's contemporary Seneca repeatedly quotes the dictum that "all things belong to the wise man," and devotes a long discussion to refuting objections to this claim (*De Beneficiis*

7.3.2–7.4.3). So when Paul declares, "All things are yours" (1 Cor. 3:21b), he appears to be making a major concession to the Corinthians' self-identification as *sophoi*. By now, however, we will not be surprised to discover that the concession is tactical and ironic. Paul continues, "all things are yours, whether Paul or Apollos or Cephas." If you are really wise, Paul suggests, why are you saying "I belong to Paul" and so on? In fact, Paul and all those other leaders should belong to you! Then, after just a slight pause to let that thrust sink in, Paul expands the list of things that belong to the Corinthians: not just the leaders, but the world or life or death or things present or things to come! If you are really wise, Paul reiterates in verse 22, "all belong to you," just as the philosophers say. Now a longer pause for effect, and then the last devastating twist: "And you belong to Christ, and Christ belongs to God."

Those at Corinth who boast in their possession of an exalted wisdom that claims to lift them above the rabble and give them possession of all things are making one fatal error: they are leaving God out of their assessment. But Paul insists that all things are God's, including the church—God's field, God's building, God's temple. Insofar as the wise at Corinth belong to Jesus Christ, they must acknowledge that they do not even belong to themselves. They, like Paul and Apollos, are servants of a common master who owns them all. God is sovereign over all creation and all time. The sooner that truth sinks in, the sooner they will begin to live in the real world rather than in the utopian fantasy of their own wisdom.

REFLECTIONS FOR TEACHERS AND PREACHERS

Interpreters of this passage would do well to begin by using the text as a mirror to see whether they find their own reflection in it. Paul's call to self-scrutiny should be taken with the utmost seriousness. Our habit of thinking of ministry as a "profession" is likely to produce serious distortions in our conception of the church and our role within it. Are we using the church as though it were ours, or as though it were an instrument for the advancement of our own careers or causes? If so, we need to be reminded that the church belongs to God, and that it is *God's* project, not ours. Are we treating church-building as a business or a competitive sport? If so, we are boasting in something other than the gospel. (I have been to enough United Methodist Conference meetings to know that this temptation is not merely hypothetical, and I suspect that the same is true in other ecclesial communities). Are we proud of our superior learning and intellectual ability? If so, we had better prepare ourselves to be shown foolish by God. Are we trying to

61

build the church with clever management techniques and psychological insights? If so, we need to be reminded that no foundation can be laid other than Jesus Christ and that currently "relevant" building materials may quickly be shown to be ephemeral. Before trying to preach on this passage, in other words, the interpreter should linger long over it, listening for the divine word of judgment on him- or herself.

Having done that, however, we need to ask how this text can become a word for congregations as well. This is, after all, part of Paul's letter to the Corinthian church as a whole, not just to the leaders. What does this part of the Corinthians' mail have to say to our churches?

First of all, the whole church must be reminded that the church is God's project. This has several implications, but prominent among them is that we cannot define the aims or agenda of the church. That has already been done for us in Jesus Christ. Our pet projects and jealously guarded areas of special responsibility within the community are only chores assigned us by God. We could with no advance notice receive different orders or be required to turn our task over to someone else, just as Paul had to turn the "watering" of the Corinthian church over to Apollos and others. Whether it is the church school program or the soup kitchen or the choir or the budget committee or the planning of worship, we cannot claim ownership of any part of the church's ministry. God is in charge, and that is likely to mean that the church will grow and change in ways impossible to determine ahead of time. If we resist that and try to maintain personal control we may divide the community and incur the judgment of which Paul warns.

Second, the passage contains an urgent call for the unity of the church. All our denominational and intradenominational divisions are in the last analysis simply silly; where squabbles persist, it is a sure sign that we are putting human wisdom and human boasting in the way of God's design to build a unified community. We are acting as though the various churches were franchise operations like McDonald's and Burger King and Wendy's, each hustling for a market share. But by dividing God's building we are endangering its capacity to stand. Anyone preaching on this text should ask the congregation to sing the hymn "The Church's One Foundation" and insist on singing, not omitting, the verse that laments the state of the church: "by schisms rent asunder, by heresies distressed." Bible study groups discussing this passage should be encouraged to reflect on direct and practical ways of working toward Christian unity within and among churches.

62

Third, the congregation should be invited to reflect on the image of the church as the temple in which God's spirit dwells. This is for Paul not merely a casual metaphor; it is an experiential reality. What would it mean for our communities to think of themselves in these terms? (a) It would mean that we urgently need to gather to experience God's presence. (b) It would mean that we are called to reflect seriously on how to be a *holy* community. This is an idea that many church members at the end of the twentieth century find distinctly unsettling. But if it really is true that the Spirit of God is present in our midst, we must ask how our lives should be ordered to give reverent honor and glory to God. The very fact that such language may sound strange to our ears—as perhaps it did to the Corinthians—is a measure of how profoundly we need to rethink our lives in light of the gospel. Just as the Corinthians had to be resocialized into the new symbolic world of the gospel, so it is with us as well. (c) Finally, to understand our community as the temple in which the Spirit of God lives would encourage us to open ourselves to the possibility of manifestations of the Spirit in our midst. As we shall see in later chapters, such manifestations proved problematical for the Corinthians; this problem will be dealt with at the appropriate point in the text, but let us simply observe for now that problematical manifestations of the Spirit are better than *no* manifestations. Because the church has become so rigid and has squeezed out the life of the Spirit, we now find people in Western culture searching about outside the church in all manner of specious speculations and occult practices, seeking to get in touch with some reality that transcends our closed and boring rationalistic vision of reality. This is a bitter and strange denouement for a community, the church, whose powerful evangelistic appeal in its time of origin was grounded in its experience of the living presence of God outside the channels of institutional religion. God is still present in our midst. We should loosen up and let God's power work among us.

Fourth, this text speaks a word of judgment on those whose actions compromise the church's integrity or destroy its unity. Our resistance to hearing and preaching about God's judgment is comically symbolized by the fact that lectionary committees have decided to recommend that when this passage is read in worship, verses 12–15 should be omitted! (We will encounter this same phenomenon with other judgment passages later in the letter.) This is irresponsible avoidance of the message of the text. The cure for abuse of the text is not avoidance but better exegesis. Teachers and preachers should read and deal with the full passage, making clear that it is *not* about "purgatory" or about individuals but about the church's structural wholeness; at the same time, we should emphasize that the passage portrays a God who will not tolerate pride and divisiveness. Judgment and grace are inseparable elements of the whole biblical message. Without the reality of judgment, there would be no grace at all, but only benign divine indifference.

63

Fifth and last, the passage's conclusion points again to the cosmic scope of the gospel message. The God whom we worship rightly claims us because he is the creator and Lord of the universe. Because we are in Christ, we participate in the reality of God's dominion and therefore are set free from anxiety and petty scrambling for human approval. Paul and Apollos and Cephas here (v. 22) symbolize any group allegiances that trick us into groveling around before human authorities or trying to manipulate people into joining our party. We all belong to God; if we believed that and acted on it, it would simplify our lives enormously—and, at the same time, heal our divisions.

4:1–21
Direct Confrontation with Corinthian Boasters

Up until this point, much of Paul's discourse has been artfully indirect, employing metaphors and irony to provoke the Corinthians to rethink their position. In chapter 4, however, he takes off the wraps and confronts them bluntly on two points: their presumptuous judging of Paul himself (vv. 1–5) and their arrogant boasting of their own wisdom and status (vv. 6–13). In the final sentences that bring this first major unit of the letter to a close, he adopts a warmer tone as a father appealing to his children (vv. 14–17) but then concludes with a stern warning to those at Corinth who may be inclined to resist his authority (vv. 18–21).

The common lectionary omits much of this material (vv. 6–21), perhaps for some or all of the following reasons: in this passage, the apostle addresses the congregation in a sarcastic, scolding tone; portrays the authentic Christian life as one of deprivation and suffering; employs patriarchal rhetoric to assert his own authority; immodestly calls his readers to imitate him; and threatens those who refuse with violent punishment (the "stick" of v. 21). This is not winsome material. On the whole, we tend to like Paul better when he is being less confrontational. The Corinthians may have felt the same way. Nonetheless, we should read this chapter carefully to see what word it contains for us. There are times when the church needs to hear a message of tough prophetic confrontation; this text might help us discern whether this is such a time.

Servants Are to Be Judged Only by Their Lord (4:1–5)

Paul reintroduces the servant metaphor here (cf. 3:5), but now with a different purpose. In 3:5–9, his point was that God's servants are all serving a single common purpose; in 4:1–5, however, his point is that he and the other apostles, as God's servants, are *accountable* to no one but God. The thing that matters is not whether they are winning popularity contests among the Corinthians but whether they are trustworthy (*pistos*, 4:2), that is, whether they are following their master's instructions. Thus, their status as servants sets them free from having to court favor in the church. This may seem paradoxical to us, but within the social world of Paul's time, his point was perfectly understandable: Servants or slaves of powerful masters often enjoyed positions of considerable delegated authority, being charged with major administrative responsibility for affairs of the household. Paul's image of the steward (*oikonomos*, 4:1) evokes this picture of the slave-in-charge. (In a world where there are no longer slaves in charge of big households, we might think analogically of the foreman in charge of a construction crew or the chief of staff in the White House.) The same picture of the trustworthy servant appears in a parable of Jesus: "Who then is the faithful (*pistos*) and prudent manager (*oikonomos*) whom his master will put in charge of his slaves, to give them their allowance of food at the proper time? Blessed is that slave whom his master will find at work when he arrives" (Luke 12:42–43). To be a "servant *of Christ*" (1 Cor. 4:1) is, in Paul's symbolic world, a position of privilege and authority. Thus, Paul uses this image to assert his independence from the Corinthians' judgments of him and his exclusive accountability to the Lord.

What does Paul mean when he says that he has been entrusted with stewardship of the mysteries of God? This refers to nothing other than the gospel message itself (cf. 2:1,7), the secret wisdom of God that has decreed salvation for the world through the death and resurrection of Jesus. In later letters and later in the Pauline tradition, this language is applied especially to the theme of the inclusion of the Gentiles within God's saving mercy (e.g., Rom. 16:25–27; Eph. 3:1–13; Col. 1:26–27), but there is no indication of this particular nuance in 1 Corinthians 4:1. Here it is simply a rephrasing of what Paul has already said in chapter 2 about his apostolic commission to proclaim the hidden wisdom of Christ crucified.

Because this is his commission, he counts it a trivial matter to be judged by the Corinthians (v. 3). This is our first unambiguous indication

65

that the Corinthians are in fact second-guessing Paul's apostolic labors and questioning his authority (cf. 9:3). Like callers to a radio talk show, they have nothing better to do than to rate Paul's performance and to compare him to other preachers. "Judged" is not exactly the right translation of the verb (*anakrinein*) in verse 3; it means something more like "examined" or "scrutinized," as in 2:15, where the same word previously appeared. (This may show that in chapter 2 Paul was already in veiled fashion scolding the Corinthians for criticizing him.) Paul brushes aside their criticism; indeed, the interrogation of any human court is of no consequence to him. There is an implicit contrast here between the insignificant human assessment of Paul's work and the all-important final judgment of God (3:13); the contrast is made explicit in 4:5.

Indeed, Paul says, he does not even judge himself: His own self-assessment is no more important than the Corinthians' criticism of him. This attitude contrasts in a fascinating way with Seneca's account of his practice of self-scrutiny at the end of each day:

> Can anything be more excellent than this practice of thoroughly sifting the whole day? And how delightful the sleep that follows this self-examination—how tranquil it is, how deep and untroubled, when the soul has either praised or admonished itself, and when this secret examiner and critic of self has given report of its own character! I avail myself of this privilege, and every day I plead my cause before the bar of self.
>
> (*De Ira* 3.36.2–3)

If in fact the Corinthians were entranced by Stoic "wisdom," it is possible that they have been encouraged to engage in the sort of self-examination that Seneca recommends as a way of disciplining the emotions and developing character. Paul, by contrast, would regard such detailed self-assessment as fruitless navel-gazing; even if one's own conscience is totally clean, that proves nothing, for our human capacity for rationalization and self-deception is boundless. The only judgment that counts for anything is the judgment of God, which will come soon enough.

This passage provides evidence that Paul—contrary to popular conceptions—was not haunted by guilt or the consciousness of his own sin; he can say "I am not aware of anything against myself" (v. 4; cf. Phil. 3:6b). But that is of no consequence, for "I am not thereby acquitted [the verb here is the same one ordinarily translated in Paul's letters as "justified"]. It is *the Lord* [not you!] who examines me [the same verb that was used in 4:3]." The use of the term "Lord" points to Christ as the agent of judgment, while at the same time continuing the metaphor of verses 1–2: *kyrios* is both a title for Christ and the ordinary word that means "master" of a servant. Paul is a servant of Christ the Lord/master, and therefore it is only the Lord who can evaluate his work. (The same metaphor is used again in Rom. 14:4: "Who are you to pass judgment on servants of another? It is before their own lord that they stand or fall.") Paul is in effect saying to the Corinthians, "Back off! It is none of your business to give me a job performance evaluation."

The evaluation will take place at the coming again of the Lord; therefore, the Corinthians are warned not to "pronounce judgment before the time" (1 Cor. 4:5). Here, as the NRSV rightly suggests, the verb *krinete* refers to the act of pronouncing a verdict, rather than simply examining a defendant. If the Corinthians pronounce judgment on Paul, they are not only being presumptuous but also acting prematurely. (This passage cannot mean, however, that the Corinthians are to abandon appropriate means of community discipline: see, e.g., 5:12; 6:5). Here is another expression of Paul's "eschatological reservation," his insistence that we respect the not-yet-completed character of God's judging and saving action. Human beings are impatient and want to rush ahead to conclusions, but Paul keeps saying over and over again in this letter, "No, we are not there yet." The Lord *will* come, and that certainty looms over all human action, but until he does come to bring the truth to light and to "disclose the purposes of the heart" (cf. Rom. 2:16), we must wait to see what the end will be. There is no indication here that the Corinthians actually suppose that the last judgment has already occurred; Paul's point is simply that they have arrogated to themselves the right to pass judgment on his work in a way that is inappropriate to their position and impossible for any human being on this side of the *parousia*. As C. K. Barrett notes (104), the most important words in the final sentence of the paragraph are the first and last: *then* (not now) each one will receive commendation *from God* (not from human judges). The business of praise and blame belongs to God.

Puffed-Up Corinthians and Suffering Apostle (4:6–13)

Having developed a series of metaphors for understanding the identity of the church and its relation to Paul and other leaders (3:5—4:5), Paul now shifts into a mode of literal explanation. No longer does he speak through figures; he explicitly discloses what he has been aiming at and confronts the Corinthians with the charge of behaving arrogantly. "The argument has reached the moment of truth" (Fee, 166).

Regrettably, the key transitional sentence (v. 6) contains several

67

obscurities that have caused many readers to get bogged down and miss what Paul is saying. Presumably, the meaning was perfectly clear to the Corinthians; our problem is that we lack information that was taken for granted by Paul and his original readers. It is possible, however, to form a definite understanding of Paul's meaning through a careful reading of the passage. Let us consider each of the clauses of this crucial sentence in turn.

"*I have applied all this to Apollos and myself for your benefit, brothers and sisters. . . .*" What does "all this" include? Because of the reference to Apollos, we can confidently assume that Paul means to refer back to the argument at least from 3:5 onwards. It is possible, however, that the reference of "all this" (literally, "these things") could be even wider, extending back into chapter 1 where Paul and Apollos are first mentioned (1:12). Although Apollos is not mentioned again until 3:5, Paul certainly uses himself as an example in chapter 2, an example of what it means to boast in the Lord rather than in human wisdom. He is now going to draw together the major lesson of his whole argument up to this point.

Next, what does Paul mean by saying that he has "applied" the whole discussion to Apollos and himself? The verb translated as "applied" (*metaschēmatizein*: its root meaning is "transformed," as in Phil. 3:21) is a technical term used in rhetoric to describe the device of making covert allusion through the use of figurative language to disguise the writer's meaning. (Note the use of this same verb, meaning "to disguise," in 2 Cor. 11:13–15.) In other words, by speaking about himself and Apollos, Paul has been speaking metaphorically; in truth, he is driving at something else entirely. This is a critical point. It means that we will utterly misunderstand Paul's argument if we think that the real problem at Corinth was a power struggle between Apollos and Paul. Everything Paul has said indicates in fact that the relationship between Apollos and himself is harmonious. Nor is there the slightest evidence in the context that Paul perceives any conflict with Cephas or his adherents. What Paul has in mind is explained quite straightforwardly in the rest of the paragraph.

". . . *so that you may learn through us the meaning of the saying, 'Nothing beyond what is written.'*" Commentators agree that "Nothing beyond what is written" is some sort of slogan or maxim that Paul assumes his readers will recognize, but there is no consensus about what the slogan means. Conzelmann (86) declares it "unintelligible," and there have been various speculative proposals for amending the text. In the present context, however, despite the puzzlement of the commentators, there can be little reasonable doubt about what Paul has in mind. The phrase "what is written" in Paul always refers to Scripture, and the present sentence is no exception. Paul has prominently spotlighted six Scripture quotations in the first three chapters of the letter (1:19, 31; 2:9, 16; 3:19, 20). In the case of the first two and the last two, the application of the texts is explicitly spelled out: No boasting in human beings. First Corinthians 3:21a links the two quotations in chapter 3 back to the quotations in chapter 1. As we have seen, the wider Old Testament context of each of these quotations reinforces the theme of divine reversal: God confounds the wise, the strong, and the prosperous and raises up the simple, the weak, and the poor. Furthermore, the two quotations in chapter 2, though they are not explicit admonitions against boasting, reinforce the same theme by juxtaposing God's gracious ways to all human understanding. The cumulative force of these citations is unmistakable: the witness of Scripture places a strict limit on human pride and calls for trust in God alone. What would it mean to go "beyond" (*hyper*) this witness of Scripture? It would mean, quite simply, to boast in human wisdom by supposing that we are, as it were, smarter than God. (Cf. Rom. 12:3: "For by the grace given to me I say to everyone among you not to think of yourself more highly [*hyperphronein*] than you ought to think.") The last clause of 1 Corinthians 4:6 confirms this interpretation.

"*. . . so that none of you will be puffed up in favor of one against another.*" The problem at Corinth is internal rivalry within the community, fostered by prideful claims about the possession of wisdom and rhetorical skill. The verb "puffed up," a vivid image to describe the Corinthians' problem with excessive self-esteem, appears here for the first time in the letter; we will meet it again in 4:18–19; 5:2; 8:1; and 13:4. (In the last two cases, the image is set in opposition to love). In Paul's view those who are puffed up should be pricked and deflated by the witness of Scripture. Throughout the opening chapters of the letter, he has spoken with studied indirection about Apollos and himself as examples of authentic collaborative service, boasting only in the Lord, as Scripture teaches. The Corinthians should take the hint and "learn through us" what it means to live in accordance with Scripture. But just in case they have missed the point, Paul now makes it explicit (4:6–7): Stop boasting and competing with each other.

The rhetorical questions in verse 7 ought to have a devastating impact on the wisdom-boasters. The first question means, in effect, "Who do you think you are, anyway?" (Fee, 171). The last two questions point up the absurdity of *boasting* (again reinforcing the connection with 1:26–31 and 3:19–21a) about anything, because all that we have is a gift of God. To claim credit for wisdom or any kind of spritual insight is

69

both absurd and ungrateful, for all that we have is solely God's gracious doing. The privileged are often those who, as the saying goes, "were born on third base and think they hit a triple." This is just as insidious an illusion in the realm of spiritual and intellectual things as it is in the realm of material wealth.

Just in case his readers have not been sufficiently chastened by the questions of verse 7, Paul now turns to withering sarcasm in verse 8 and begins an extended comparison between himself and the "wise" at Corinth (vv. 8–13). In contrast to the lowly apostle and apart from him, they "already" are filled and rich and have become "kings." On the basis of the adverb "already," many interpreters have argued that the Corinthian error was based on "overrealized eschatology," a belief that the kingdom of God had already arrived in all its fullness and that they were living already in a state of eschatological blessedness, like angels in heaven. It is by no means clear, however, that the present passage provides evidence for such a view. Certainly the Corinthians (or at least some of them) were suffering from an excess of pride and self-satisfaction, but there are other ways to arrive at such a state besides having an accelerated apocalyptic timetable. Indeed, most of the evidence of the letter suggests that the Corinthian problem was almost exactly the reverse: They *lacked* any definite eschatology, with the result that they were heedless of God's future judgment of their actions. It is far more likely that their "boasting" was caused not by an excess of eschatological enthusiasm but by their infatuation with popular philosophical notions of how the wise person can transcend the ordinary limitations of human existence. After all, throughout the letter up to this point Paul has chided them for inappropriate understandings of "wisdom," which, as we have seen, is linked with philosophy and rhetoric.

Let us consider Paul's derisive description of the Corinthians in verse 8. Where would they get the idea that they are already rich and that they reign as kings? Many ancient sources indicate that precisely these claims were made by Cynic and Stoic philosophers. Their wisdom sets them free from attachment to things and therefore makes them in effect rulers of all things. According to Epictetus, the true Cynic can say, "Who, when he lays eyes upon me, does not feel that he is seeing his king and master?" (*Diss.* 3.22.49). Plutarch takes a somewhat more skeptical view of such claims: "But some think the Stoics are jesting when they hear that in their sect the wise man (*sophos*) is termed not only prudent and just and brave, but also an orator, a poet, a general, a rich man, and a king; and then they count themselves worthy of all these titles, and if they fail to get them, are vexed" (*De*

Tranq. An. 472A). This comment reveals that the Stoics were commonly understood to make about themselves precisely the claims that Paul imputes to the Corinthian *sophoi*. Thus, the most natural inference is that Paul is scolding the Corinthians for adopting an inflated self-understanding based on a philosophy alien to the gospel. This certainly does not mean that the Corinthians had *consciously* rejected the gospel in favor of Stoicism; more likely they were creating an uncritical mixture of ideas, or even arguing that Christianity was the true wisdom that enabled them to attain the aims of the philosophers—just as Philo of Alexandria was arguing in this same era that the law of Moses was the epitome of philosophical truth.

If that is correct, then the Corinthian errors are less consciously "theological" than we often suppose. Rather, their difficulty is that they are uncritically perpetuating the norms and values of the pagan culture around them. It is *Paul* who diagnoses the situation and redescribes it in theological categories. It is *Paul* who keeps introducing apocalyptic language into the argument. The eschatological framework is his way of getting critical leverage on the Corinthian boasting, as he tries to encourage them to understand themselves in terms of an apocalyptic narrative that locates present existence in between the cross and the *parousia*.

This rather lengthy explanation is necessary in order to make a simple but crucial point: Pastors and teachers in our time have the same task that Paul had. We must analyze the ways in which our congregations are linking the gospel with the beliefs and aspirations of the surrounding culture and—where this is being done in inappropriate ways—provide sharply focused critiques and alternatives. Paul models what every pastor must do; he encounters people in a given cultural situation and tries to get them to reshape their lives in light of the gospel by reframing the story within which they live and move. (See "Reflections for Teachers and Preachers," below, for further comment.)

The alternative that Paul offers the Corinthians is his own way of life, set in antithesis to theirs. In contrast to the Corinthian self-designation as conquering kings, Paul offers the image of himself and the other apostles as prisoners sentenced to death. The image is taken from the well-known practice of the Roman "triumph," in which the victorious general would parade through the streets in a chariot, with the leaders of the defeated army trailing along in the rear of the procession, to be "exhibited" and humiliated as a public "spectacle" (4:9) on their way to imprisonment or execution (cf. also 2 Cor. 2:14). One could hardly imagine an image more antithetical to the Stoic conception of the philosopher as strong, free, and self-sufficient. It is a stunning image, not least because Paul suggests that it is *God* who has won the victory and made a spectacle of the apostolic prisoners. The Corinthians, by contrast, fancy themselves as leaders of the procession, victorious kings who therefore, Paul suggests, are *not* subject to the authority of God.

The Corinthians are wise, strong, and held in honor, whereas the apostles are fools, weak, and held in disrepute. The echoes of 1:26–31 are clearly audible here. Paul is saying that his manner of life is consonant with the cross, while the Corinthians aspire to a lifestyle that is a de facto repudiation of the cross.

The description of apostolic suffering (4:11–13) is one of several such lists in the Corinthian correspondence (2 Cor. 4:7–12; 6:4–5; 11:23–29; 12:10; cf. Rom 8:35–36). Paul regards these experiences not merely as misfortunes or trials to be surmounted but as identifying marks of the authenticity of his apostleship, because they manifest his conformity to Christ's sufferings. The reference to blessing in response to reviling is surely modeled on his understanding of Jesus' example (Rom. 15:3), if not on a reminiscence of the teaching of Jesus (Luke 6:28; cf. Rom. 12:14). Some features of the list are conventional (hunger, thirst, poor clothing, homelessness), but some are quite specific to Paul's own situation and to the matters at issue between him and the Corinthian church. For example, when Paul emphasizes at the beginning and end of the list that he suffers these hardships "to the present hour" and "to this very day," he is undoubtedly contrasting his experience to the Corinthians, who have "already" become full and rich. The reference to being beaten should be compared to his autobiographical remarks in 2 Corinthians 11:24–25. His reference to working with his own hands (cf. Act 18:3) is related to his refusal to accept financial support from the Corinthians, a fact that led to difficulties and misunderstandings (cf. 9:4–18 and 2 Cor. 11:7–9; 12:13–17). It is not entirely clear why Paul refused financial support, but it may have had something to do with his desire to remain independent and—just as important—to distinguish himself from popular philosophers who charged fees for their services or became attached to wealthy patrons. Certainly his manual labor marked him as a person of relatively low social status, a fact which seems to have been displeasing, perhaps even embarrassing, to some of the Corinthians. See the commentary on chapter 9, below, for further discussion of this issue.

The strong language of 4:13b ("rubbish of the world, the dregs of all things") should not be underplayed. Paul is saying in the strongest possible terms that to be a follower of Christ is to share his destiny of being scorned and rejected by the world. There is no direct allusion here

72

to Isaiah 53, but Paul's vision of the Christian life agrees with Isaiah's picture of the Servant as "despised and rejected . . . a man of suffering and acquainted with infirmity" (Isa. 53:3). In a sense, Paul is throwing down the gauntlet for his readers. If you really want to belong to Christ, he says, look at me: this is where it leads, this is what it looks like. This is a powerful word for the church in our time. To belong to Christ is not a way of assuring success or a trouble-free life; quite the opposite. Paul had a successful life *before* he was called by God to his apostolic vocation; to become a proclaimer of Christ crucified meant giving all that up (cf. Phil. 3:4–11). The image of the suffering apostle should be held clearly before our eyes, and then we should ask ourselves: Are we sure we want to belong to Christ and share his way?

Fatherly Admonition to Paul's Corinthian Children (4:14–17)

Paul's tone changes abruptly in verse 14. Having scolded his readers devastatingly, he reaches out to embrace them as his "beloved children." When he says that he is not trying to shame them, he means that his aim is not to disgrace them but to correct their behavior. This image of fatherly correction is deeply imbedded in Israel's wisdom tradition: It is the role of the father to reprove and chasten his children to bring them into the disciplined way of knowledge and obedience (e.g., Prov. 3:11–12; 13:24; 19:18). The "rod" that Paul brandishes in 4:21 (not a "whip," as in NIV), is the "rod of correction" that the Old Testament sages believed a father should use to drive away folly from the heart of the immature (Prov. 22:15; 23:13–14). Thus, even if Paul has had to use severe rhetoric, his severity has had a fatherly purpose, and he now seeks to reassure the Corinthians that he is acting out of love and concern for them. His hope is that they will recognize the error of their ways and accept the welcoming gesture that he offers in verses 14–15.

His claim to be their "father" is yet another reference to his role as the founder of the community: "in Christ Jesus I became your father through the gospel" (v. 15). As the evangelist who originally brought the gospel to Corinth, he brought the community into existence; thus, he has a unique relationship to them that can never be supplanted by other teachers, no matter how many they might have. Actually, Paul does not use the word "teachers" here; the NRSV's translation ("guardians") rightly makes the point that Paul's word *paidagōgoi* refers not to teachers but to slaves charged with supervising children (cf. the different metaphorical use of this term in Gal. 3:24).

73

Paul's appeal that the Corinthians should imitate him (v. 16) is directly based upon his claim to have fathered them. The idea is that if the children want to grow into greater maturity they should observe and follow the ways of the parent. Though this exhortation strikes some modern readers as manipulative and arrogant, it is based on an unimpeachable truth about the development of character: People learn from role models. At this juncture in the life of their community, the Corinthians are in particularly urgent need of a good role model. Recognizing this, Paul has sent Timothy to Corinth to remind the Corinthians of what the Christian life is supposed to look like in the flesh. Even though Paul himself is unable to return promptly to Corinth (16:8–9), sending Timothy is the next best thing, because Timothy is "my beloved and faithful [*pistos*, cf. 4:2] child in the Lord." As a faithful child, Timothy has modeled himself on Paul, so that he can "remind you of my ways in Christ Jesus as I teach them everywhere in every church."

We must remember that the church at Corinth is a church with no established Christian tradition, no members who have been believers longer than about three years at the most, no written gospels, and no authoritative Torah to regulate behavior. They are being forced to invent the Christian life as they go, and they are obviously having some trouble doing so. Under these circumstances, a living visible example of how to "walk" in the ways of the gospel is indispensible. Paul offers himself as such an example, appealing to their memory of him, and promises the coming of Timothy as a surrogate example. When we understand the exhortation to "become imitators of me" in light of this situation, it makes perfect sense. Paul characteristically insists that the meaning of the gospel must be embodied; the obedience of faith comes into focus only as we see it lived. (Notice that Timothy is being sent not just to teach right doctrine but to exemplify Paul's "ways in Christ.") This is true not just in the situation of the new mission church at Corinth, but still today. Paul's words are a challenge to us not only to take his example seriously but to become, like Timothy, faithful disciples who can model for others the meaning of the gospel.

One other observation is important here. When Paul calls his hearers to imitate the father figure, he is employing a traditional patriarchal image. Yet, as Dale Martin has observed, "He uses patriarchal rhetoric to make an anti-patriarchal point" (Martin, *Slavery as Salvation*, 142). He is calling on the strong and wise Corinthians to become weak, to renounce their positions of privilege. Paul himself as the "father" has modeled the way of renouncing power and comfort for the sake of the gospel. Thus, Paul's use of this traditional motif is charged with paradox and creative energy that seeks to overturn the status quo rather than underwrite it.

74

A Final Warning to the Boasters (4:18–21)

Given the present turmoil and division in the Corinthian community, however, Paul is not able to end this section of the letter on a kind and encouraging note. He has received discouraging reports (1:11) not only that the community is divided but also that some of the Corinthians, supposing that Paul is not coming back—he had, after all, by this time been gone for several years—have become "arrogant" (the same word that was translated "puffed up" in 4:6). We have already seen that their arrogance is based on their pretensions to possess wisdom, but there is also a clear suggestion here that they are explicitly repudiating Paul's authority. Presumably they have gained new ideas from other sources that they regard as being more spiritually sophisticated and rhetorically polished. In a breathtakingly bold conclusion to this section of the letter, Paul calls their bluff and threatens unnamed but ominous consequences if they persist in their rebellion against his authority. When he arrives, there will be a showdown: He will "find out not the rhetoric [*logon*] of these puffed-up ones but their power." The contrast is exactly the same as in 2:4–5—on one side rhetorical artistry, on the other the *power* of God. Clearly this is not an empty threat. Paul believes himself invested with God's authority in such a way that he has "divine power to destroy strongholds . . . and every proud obstacle raised up against the knowledge of God" (2 Cor. 10:4–5). This at least means that he will expose the superficiality and falsehood of the arrogant Corinthian arguments. It probably means more than that, however, for "the kingdom of God consists not in rhetoric but in power" (1 Cor. 4:20). Presumably Paul expects that if necessary God will unleash some manifestation of the power of the Spirit that will humble the arrogant ones. (One thinks, for example, of the story of Elijah's triumph over the prophets of Baal [1 Kings 18:20–40], a story that Paul elsewhere connects to his own apostolic vocation [Rom 11:2–4]). Paul's coming to disclose the truth about the Corinthian claims is also described, interestingly, in terms that anticipate and parallel the final coming of Christ in judgment.

Paul's use of the phrase "kingdom of God" is relatively infrequent. His choice of this terminology in 1 Corinthians 4:20 may be dictated in part by his desire to present a polemical rejoinder to the Corinthians' talk about already reigning as kings (4:8). If so, the force of verse 20 would be to reassert that God alone is king, and that God's kingdom operates in a way very different from what the Corinthian boasters imagine. Lest we suppose that Paul understands the kingdom of God exclusively in terms of threat, however, we might well remember also

Romans 14:17: "the kingdom of God is . . . righteousness and peace and joy in the Holy Spirit."

Paul concludes this section of the letter, then, by placing the choice back in the hands of the Corinthians. If they continue on their present course of boasting and resisting Paul's authority, he will be forced to administer stern discipline when he appears in Corinth; on the other hand, if they acknowledge his authority and repent of their boasting, he will be able to come with gentleness. By sending this letter ahead, he is giving them fair warning and allowing them time to get their affairs in order. Much will depend, then, on how they react to the more specific directives that he is going to give them in the rest of the letter.

Paul has at last brought to a close the opening section of the letter. He has exhorted the Corinthians in numerous ways to turn away from their boasting in human wisdom and to seek to be reunified in the service of the one God to whom they all belong, who is ultimately their one judge. In the chapters that follow, he will seek to build on the foundation of these opening chapters in a way that will decisively reshape the community's understanding of its identity in Christ—and, therefore, its behavior.

REFLECTIONS FOR TEACHERS AND PREACHERS

Each of the three subsections of chapter 4 bears an important message for the church in our time. Our reading of this daunting passage has opened up several issues that teachers and preachers should explore with their congregations.

Authority and Judgment. First of all, the portrayal of authority and judgment in 4:1–5 offers us a desperately needed vision of authentic leadership in the church. Too often leaders in the church have mimicked the vacillating style of politicians who constantly have to take polls to find out what to say and do. The church, however, is not a democracy: Christian leaders are accountable to another authority. What is required is faithfulness to God, with or without the support of popular opinion in the church. It is all too easy for the members of a congregation to fall into the habit of thinking of the pastor as *their* employee. This danger is of course greater in some church polities than in others, but it is subtly present in all communities. (That is almost certainly one of the reasons that Paul refused to accept financial support from the Corinthians [9:3–18]: he did not want to be "owned" by them.) The church leader who is called to be a servant of Christ must look to God's final judgment and approval, even if it requires him or her to swim against the tide of opinion. The church, moreover, must respect this

76

calling and refrain from judging by worldly standards of success and respectability those who do the work of ministry. The teacher working with this text could ask the group to reflect about ways in which the church scrutinizes and constrains its leaders. Do our job-evaluation techniques for ministers assist or undermine our leaders in doing the work of the gospel? The leaders themselves might take the text as an occasion to ponder for whom they are really working: Has the leader's provisional accountability to the board that signs the paycheck eclipsed or even compromised his or her faithfulness to God? Authentic leadership will occur only when the pastor or teacher, like Paul, operates as a "servant of Christ" who is free to speak unpopular truth. (This of course does not mean that Christian leaders should be autocratic or unreceptive to hearing what God might say through other members of the church; the balance that Paul strikes within 1 Corinthians as a whole provides a useful model of authoritative leadership that still takes seriously the ministry of the whole community. But these themes will be treated later; see the commentary on chapters 12–14 below.) This text might be linked to the story of the centurion in Matthew 8:5–13 who can recognize and exercise authority because he is "a man under authority." Similarly, we will be able to minister effectively only when we act out of a clear understanding that our primary accountability is to the authority of God.

A corollary of this first point is that our general cultural fascination with self-scrutiny and self-assessment can become a fruitless diversion from our primary responsibilities. We are inundated by magazines with "rate yourself" quizzes and by best-selling books that urge us to self-improvement through this or that technique of raising our self-consciousness. But Paul's message to the church at Corinth is that self-assessment is trivial, because it is the judgment of God that matters. This is a healthy corrective for our time.

Reframing Cultural Norms. A second major set of issues is posed by Paul's critical reframing of cultural norms in 4:6–13. His specific critique is aimed at a popularized version of the Stoic ideals of self-sufficiency and self-determination. Certainly there are times and places where our proclamation must still encounter the lineal descendants of these ancient philosophical tendencies; wherever that is the case, Paul's response will prove directly relevant and powerful: We are radically dependent on God's grace (v. 7), and our lives—in this time between the times—must be conformed to the pattern of the cross (vv. 9–13).

At the same time, however, we must remember *why* Paul is attacking the Corinthian version of wisdom: It has splintered the community of faith. Thus, if we want to read the Corinthian letter as a letter to ourselves as well, we must ask what forces are splintering the community of the church today, what their philosophical underpinnings are, and how those underpinnings are to be critiqued by the gospel. When we put the issue in these terms, different problems will come into focus. The prevailing "philosophy" of Western culture at the end of the twentieth century is not Stoicism but *hedonism*. We are coaxed and conditioned by powerful persuasive forces on all sides (advertising, popular entertainment, political rhetoric) to believe that the highest good is the pursuit of individual pleasure. This is still self-determination, but of a very different sort from what the Stoics envisioned. The crasser manifestations of this cultural tendency are easy to spot and criticize: rampant materialism, disregard for the needs of the poor, and a bankrupt liberal individualism that attends only to the freedoms of the individual and ignores the concerns of the community. Where we see such signs around us, those who are "puffed up" by material wealth and personal autonomy must be confronted with the gospel of Christ crucified.

Yet hedonism has infiltrated and corrupted the church in subtler ways also. In attitudes about sexual behavior (a topic that will be treated in the commentary on subsequent chapters of 1 Corinthians) or even in our understanding of "ministry," we have come to think that the purpose of the church's ministry is to make people feel good and comfortable. First Corinthians 4 poses a severe challenge to such an understanding of the gospel. Recently I read a report from a Clinical Pastoral Education supervisor evaluating the fitness of a certain candidate for ministry. The supervisor was extremely critical of her. Why? Because she was so excessively self-giving, focusing only on the needs of others and not paying sufficient attention to "caring for herself." I could not help wondering how that supervisor would have evaluated Paul on the basis of his self-report in 4:11–13. The current worldly wisdom teaches us to look out for ourselves, to make ourselves secure and comfortable, and worst of all to interpret "ministry" as helping other people to achieve the same condition. Paul's message poses a severe challenge to such thinking.

Other interpreters may see in their communities different signs of the church's cultural captivity and compromise. For example, one could argue that the uncritical perpetuation of *patriarchy* is another cultural phenomenon that divides the church by causing male holders of power and privilege to be "puffed up" and to dominate and belittle others in the community. Wherever this is true, Paul's message of the cross calls those who enjoy power, privilege, and honor to surrender them and to be conformed to Christ.

How can we see clearly enough to formulate such critical responses to our culture's corruption of authentic Christian community? First Corinthians 4 offers three major criteria to keep us from getting fooled by the power-illusions of the present age: the eschatological reservation, Scripture, and the apostolic example of suffering. The eschatological reservation insists that the world's present way of seeing power and value is distorted and that we must await God's final setting-right of all things while trusting the truth of a gospel that offers power in weakness. Scripture stands as a word from God that challenges our pride and blocks us from going beyond what is written (v. 6); of course, for Paul, "what is written" also must be interpreted with the aid of the Spirit in light of the cross. Finally, the apostolic example of suffering gives experiential concreteness to the word of the cross, showing that the death of Jesus, while surely a vicarious atonement for the sins of the world, is also a model of the life of faithfulness in the world. According to 1 Corinthians 4, all our discernments about the life of our community must be formed in light of these three criteria.

Thus far I have spoken as though we are to take on the "apostle" role in this passage and to pronounce criticism on those who confuse the gospel with the regnant cultural systems of our day. But of course if we are to read this letter to the Corinthians as a letter also to us, we must feel the force of Paul's critique on our own lives. Many of us are filled and rich. Whether we boast in that or not, we must at least ask ourselves whether Paul is talking directly to us in 1 Corinthians 4:8–13. If so, we must wonder whether our proclamation of the gospel can have any credibility unless, like Paul, we respond to the call of God by living a visibly alternative lifestyle that bears prophetic witness against a culture of self-satisfaction.

Ways in Christ. The final set of issues raised by our text has to do specifically with the modeling of our "ways in Christ." The teacher or preacher might encourage the congregation to reflect on who our models are. If not Paul or Timothy, to whom do we look to embody the practical meaning of being in Christ? At the same time, how are we modeling the gospel for our own children and for others less experienced in the life of faith? If it is true that the kingdom of God does not consist in talk but in power, that power should be made evident in our lives and—as Paul would in the end insist—in the life of a community unified in humble gratitude for what we have received from God.

A Call for Community Discipline

1 CORINTHIANS 5:1—6:20

Paul now begins to address specific problems in the conduct of the Corinthian community, reacting to alarming reports that have reached him, presumably either through "Chloe's people" (1 Cor. 1:11) or through Stephanas, Fortunatus, and Achaicus (16:17). In 1 Corinthians 5—6 Paul calls the Corinthians to discipline church members whose actions compromise the holiness of the community. As we interpret this section of the letter, we must remind ourselves again and again that Paul's primary concern is not the sin of individuals but the health and integrity of the church as a corporate body. Those who commit sexual sins or pursue litigation against their brothers and sisters in the faith are doing damage not only to themselves but also to the community; consequently, the community must act to preserve its unity and its identity as the sanctified people of God (cf. 1:2).

This section of the letter provides striking evidence that Paul thinks of the Corinthian church, composed predominantly of Gentile converts, as belonging to God's covenant community; they bear the same moral responsibilities given to Israel in Scripture. This emphasis on the church as covenant community may appear strange to readers formed in the traditions of Western individualism, but unless we keep this aspect of Paul's concern clearly in focus, we will find it impossible to comprehend either his specific counsel to the Corinthians or the urgency with which he presses this counsel upon them.

5:1–13
"Drive Out the Wicked Person from among You"

The first problem that Paul highlights is the case of a man in the Corinthian church who is living in a sexual relationship with "his father's wife"—not his own mother but a subsequent wife of his father. (From Paul's scanty description there is no way of knowing whether

80

the father had died or divorced this second wife; the Corinthians of course knew the particulars of the matter.) As commentators universally note, the woman surely was not a member of the community of believers; otherwise, she too would have been subject to the disciplinary action that Paul orders in verses 2–5 and 11–13. Horrified by this relationship, Paul labels it *porneia* (sexual misconduct) "of a kind that is not found even among the Gentiles" (5:1).

The word *ethnē*, translated by NRSV and most English versions as "pagans," is Paul's normal word for "Gentiles" (i.e., non-Jews). His use of this term here offers a fascinating hint that he thinks of the Gentile converts at Corinth as Gentiles no longer (cf. 12:2, 13; Gal. 3:28). Now that they are in Christ, they belong to the covenant people of God, and their behavior should reflect that new status.

In this case, however, the offending church member is not only failing to live up to the standard of holiness to which Christ's people are called; he is doing something that "even Gentiles" would find reprehensible. Cicero offers an especially vivid account of a case similar to the present one, though—for reasons related to the particular case—he places the moral blame on the woman involved rather than the man:

> And so mother-in-law marries son-in-law, with none to bless, none to sanction the union, and amid nought but general foreboding. Oh! to think of the woman's sin, unbelievable, unheard of in all experience save for this single instance! To think of her wicked passion, unbridled, untamed! To think that she did not quail, if not before the vengeance of Heaven [Latin *vim deorum*, "the power of the gods"], or the scandal among men, at least before the night itself with its wedding torches, the threshold of the bridal chamber, her daughter's bridal bed, or even the walls themselves which had witnessed that other union. The madness of passion broke through and laid low every obstacle: lust triumphed over modesty, wantonness over scruple, madness over sense.
>
> *Pro Cluentio* 5.14–6.15

This passage certainly lends credence to Paul's claim that Gentiles would find such incestuous alliances objectionable.

Paul's considerably less vivid description of the woman involved in the Corinthian scandal as "his father's wife," however, also has its own particular rhetorical force, for it echoes the Scriptural prohibition of such relationships: "Cursed be anyone who lies with his father's wife" (Deut. 27:20; cf. Lev. 18:8; 20:11). Thus, the behavior of the incestuous man is a direct violation of God's covenant norms for Israel. As we shall see, this fact is pertinent to understanding Paul's directive to the community to expel the offender. Before examining his specific instructions about how to deal with this man, however, we must consider the theological framework within which these instructions are given.

81

The most startling aspect of Paul's response is that he does not merely condemn the perpetrator of this unseemly affair; instead, he scolds the community *as a whole* for their complicity in the matter: "And you [plural] are arrogant ["puffed up," the same word that we have already encountered in 4:6, 18]! Should you not rather have mourned, so that he who has done this would have been removed from among you? . . . Your boasting is not a good thing" (5:2, 6a). It is difficult to say whether Paul means that the Corinthians are boasting in spite of the immoral man's conduct or because of it. In the latter case, they would be flaunting their new freedom in Christ by celebrating this man's particular act of defying conventional mores (this would explain why in 5:6a Paul uses the noun *kauchēma* ["a boast"] rather than *kauchēsis* ["boasting"]); this is not as far-fetched as it might sound, for in this same section of the letter Paul chides them for trumpeting that "all things are lawful for me" (6:12). In the former case, on the other hand, they would be heedlessly boasting in their own spirituality and wisdom while tolerantly ignoring a flagrant moral violation in their midst. Either way, Paul insists that the community has moral responsibility for the conduct of its members and that the conduct of the individual members (even private conduct between "consenting adults") affects the life of the whole community. Later in the letter, Paul will explain this truth by using the image of the "body of Christ": "If one member suffers, all suffer together with it; if one member is honored, all rejoice together" (12:26). Here in 1 Corinthians 5, however, Paul simply assumes the reality of *corporate responsibility.*

This way of thinking has deep roots in Scripture. The paradigmatic story is the account of how the one man Achan brought the Lord's disfavor upon all Israel by his secretive act of claiming forbidden booty from the destroyed city of Jericho (Joshua 7). This is not, however, an isolated case of such theological thinking. The Holiness Code of Leviticus stipulates that those who commit various sexual offenses must be "cut off from their people"; otherwise the land will "vomit out" the people of Israel as a whole (e.g., Lev. 18:24–30; 20:22–24). The covenant blessings and curses of Deuteronomy 28 apply not just to the fate of individuals who obey or disobey the Law but to the nation as a whole. This helps us to understand more clearly why Ezra "mourned" over the faithlessness of the exiles (Ezra 10:6; the LXX uses the same verb that Paul employs when he says the Corinthians should have mourned over the offense in their midst [1 Cor. 5:2]) and why the great prayers of national confession in Ezra 9:6–15; Nehemiah 9:6–37; and Daniel 9:4–19 all assume the reality of corporate guilt and the hope of corporate redemption.

Paul's understanding of the church belongs to this scriptural tradition. "No man is an island," as the poet John Donne perceived; all in Christ's church are bound together closely, responsible for one another, and profoundly affected by one another's actions. Paul pictures this reality by using the proverbial image (cf. Gal. 5:9; Mark 8:15; Matt. 16:6, 11–12; Luke 12:1) of the corrupting influence of leaven: "Do you not know that a little leaven [not 'yeast,' as in NRSV and NIV] leavens the whole lump of dough? Clean out the old leaven so that you may be a new lump" (5:6b–7). The image provides an explanation for Paul's directive of expulsion: Allowing the offender to remain in the church will contaminate the whole community, which is conceived as a single lump of dough. When Paul says to clean out the old leaven, he is not telling the individuals at Corinth to clean up their individual lives; rather, he is repeating in symbolic language the instruction of verses 2–5 to purify the community by expelling the offender.

This symbolic language is drawn from the heart of Israel's story, the celebration of the Passover commemorating the Israelites' liberation from bondage in the land of Egypt. Paul assumes not only that his Corinthian readers will understand this symbolism but also that they will identify metaphorically with Israel. Christ, as the Passover lamb, has already been sacrificed (cf. Exod. 12:3–7), so the time is at hand for the Corinthians to carry out the other major part of the festival, searching out and removing all "leaven" (symbolizing the wrongdoer) from their household (Exod. 12:15). It is important to be clear about the function of the Passover lamb. This is not a sacrifice to atone for sin; rather, it symbolizes the setting apart of Israel as a distinct people delivered from slavery by God's power. "And when your children ask you, 'What do you mean by this observance?' you shall say, 'It is the passover sacrifice to the Lord, for he passed over the houses of the Israelites in Egypt, when he struck down the Egyptians but spared our houses' " (Exod. 12:26–27). The blood of the lamb on the doorposts of the houses marks Israel out as a distinct people under God's protection, spared from the power of destruction at work in the world outside. In the same way, Paul's metaphor suggests, the blood of Christ marks the Corinthians as a distinct people.

It is against this background that we must understand Paul's directions to the Corinthians in verses 3–5. These verses contain several translation difficulties, but their overall import is clear enough: The Corinthians are to gather as a community and take solemn action to exclude the incestuous man from the church. While the Corinthians have been ignoring the problem, Paul has "already pronounced judgment," and he expects them to follow suit.

There is some ambiguity about how the prepositional phrase "in the name of the Lord Jesus" (v. 4) fits into the sentence. We could translate either "I have already pronounced judgment in the name of the Lord Jesus on the man who has done such a thing," as in the NRSV text, or "I have already pronounced judgment on the man who has done such a thing in the name of the Lord Jesus," as in the NRSV footnote. The latter interpretation would fit well with the hypothesis that the Corinthians were actually boasting about this man's freedom from ordinary sexual constraints: the man would be explicitly claiming in the name of Jesus to be beyond the jurisdiction of merely human moral laws. (NIV adopts a third interpretation of the sentence, taking "in the name of the Lord Jesus" with the verb "assembled," but the Greek word order makes this reading less likely.)

Paul thinks of the church's action of expulsion not merely as a judicial proceeding; rather, the community is to assemble—probably for worship—and act in the realm of the Spirit "with the power of our Lord Jesus." Furthermore, Paul says that his own spirit will be present with them. This should not be read in a weak, merely psychological sense. In some mysterious way he believes that his spirit will actually be there with the community, efficaciously participating in their solemn action. We should never forget that Paul had strong mystical experiences and convictions, even though he was not inclined to talk much about them. If he could be "caught up to the third heaven" (2 Cor. 12:2), it would not be difficult to imagine that he could think of himself as being transported "in spirit" from Ephesus (1 Cor. 16:8) to Corinth to take part in some mysterious but real way in the church's crucial disciplinary action. Paul's major point, though, is that the gathered community itself is invested with the power of the risen Jesus to declare this offender no longer a member of the covenant community. This sort of community action may be compared to the teaching of Jesus in Matthew 18:15–20: After due attempts to call the sinful member to repentance, the community is expel him or her (cf. also Titus 3:10). The community is given the authority to "bind and loose," i.e. to exercise community discipline, because Jesus himself is present where his people are present in his name. If all this sounds a bit spooky to Christians at the end of the twentieth century, it is a salutary reminder that this letter is not addressed to post-Enlightenment rationalists; instead, it is addressed to a community that understood itself as living and moving in a world where the power of the Spirit was a daily experienced reality.

84

Perhaps the most puzzling part of the passage is found in verse 5: "hand this man over to Satan for the destruction of the flesh, so that his spirit [literally, "the spirit"] might be saved in the day of the Lord."

Although there may be an echo here of Job 2:4–6, in which God gives Job over to the power of Satan to "touch his bone and flesh," the situation is not closely parallel: Job is not being disciplined for any sin, and there is no sense in which Job's suffering either purifies the community or promotes his own salvation. Thus, the faint echo of Job does not give us much help in understanding the passage. There are three major problems to be resolved in interpreting Paul's command. What does it mean to "hand this man over to Satan?" Does "flesh" refer to the literal physical body or the "sinful nature" (NIV) of the man? And is the purpose of the action remedial, hoping to induce the man's repentance? These problems interlock with one another.

The best explanation of the "handing over to Satan" is suggested by the Passover metaphor (vv. 6–8). By excluding the incestuous man from the community, the church places him outside the sphere of God's redemptive protection. He is no longer inside the house (cf. 3:9, "God's building") whose doorposts are covered by the blood of Jesus. He is therefore hung out to dry in the realm of Satan ("the god of this world," 2 Cor. 4:4), exposed to the destructive powers of the world (cf. the reference to "the destroyer" in Exod. 12:23). We may remember that Paul has already spoken of those outside the community of faith as "those who are being destroyed" (1 Cor. 1:18). Probably Paul did not expect the community to perform a ceremony explicitly cursing the man; rather, delivering him to Satan is a vivid metaphor for the *effect* of explusion from the church. The parallel passage in 1 Timothy 1:20 should be understood in the same way. The closest analogy in the Pauline corpus to this notion of Satan as destroyer is found in 2 Thessalonians 2:9–10, which speaks of the powerful working of Satan to deceive "those who are being destroyed" (again, cf. 1 Cor. 1:18).

But what did Paul expect as the concrete result of this consignment to Satan? Did he expect the physical suffering and death of the excommunicated offender? Or does the expression "destruction of the flesh" refer to a process of purifying him of his fleshly desires, perhaps through shaming him into repentance? And does Paul think that this "destruction," whatever it entails, will somehow bring about the man's eschatological salvation? Some interpreters have suggested that Paul has no interest whatever in the final fate of the man, and that the sentence should be understood to mean: "Deliver such a one to Satan for the destruction of the flesh [i.e., the evil], in order that the Spirit [present in the community] might be saved [i.e., preserved] for the day of the Lord." This reading has much to commend it, for it preserves a single-minded focus on the well-being of the church, which is Paul's central concern in verses 2 and 6–13. Nowhere else, however, does

85

Paul speak of "the Spirit" as needing to be "saved"; given his consistent use of the verb "save" to refer to the eschatogical deliverance of human beings (to cite only the examples in 1 Cor., see 1:18; 1:21; 3:15; 7:16; 9:22; 10:33; 15:2), it is more likely that Paul actually does conceive of the community's discipline as leading somehow to the repentance and restoration of the sinner. In that case "the flesh" would refer—as in 1 Corinthians 3:3; Romans 7:5, 18, 25; 8:3–8; Galatians 5:13, 19, 24—to the rebellious human nature opposed to God. The meaning of the "destruction of the flesh," then, must be interpreted in light of what Paul declares in Galatians 5:24: "Those who belong to Christ Jesus have crucified the flesh with its passions and desires." Paul hopes that the community's censure and expulsion of the incestuous man will lead to this result: his fleshly passions and desires will be put to death. Thus, the eschatological fate of this man, after undergoing discipline and repentance, will be salvation.

Even if 2 Corinthians 2:5–11 refers to a case different from that of the incestuous man, it demonstrates Paul's belief that stern community discipline can lead to transformation and reintegration into the life of the community: "This punishment by the majority is enough for such a person; so now instead you should forgive and console him, so that he may not be overwhelmed by excessive sorrow." (Cf. 2 Cor. 7:10: "Godly grief produces a repentance that leads to salvation.") Likewise, the other major New Testament passages on community discipline envision forgiveness and reconciliation as the ultimate goal of the community's action; for example, Matthew 18:15–20 is followed by the teaching on forgiveness in Matthew 18:21–35 (cf. also Gal. 6:1). In all these cases, however, it is clear that forgiveness *does not take the place of* discipline; rather, it *follows* clear community discipline and authentic repentance.

In verses 6–8, Paul returns the focus to the community's spiritual state. Rather than boasting as they do (cf. 4:7), they should recognize where they really stand in the unfolding story of God's redemptive action. Because they are being liberated from captivity through the death of Jesus, they should act like Israel on the night of Passover: clean out the old leaven and gather together for the feast that celebrates their deliverance. It is possible, though hardly certain, that Paul here is foreshadowing the discussion of the Lord's Supper that will follow later in the letter (11:17–34), particularly since that passage also deals with the theme of judgment in the community (11:27–32). In the present context, however, the Passover imagery is not primarily eucharistic; rather, it points to the necessity of community discipline and purity.

The final paragraph of this section (vv. 9–13) makes an important distinction between the church's dealings with insiders and outsiders. Paul is not calling for the church at Corinth to withdraw from all contact with their pagan neighbors, like the Qumran covenanters withdrawing to live in the wilderness near the Dead Sea to avoid defilement. The holiness of the church is a matter of its internal discipline and integrity, not of its separateness from the world. This point may have been misunderstood by some at Corinth. Thus, Paul now writes to clarify what he had said in an earlier letter (now lost to us, though some have suggested that a fragment of it might be preserved in 2 Cor. 6:14—7:1). When Paul had told them "not to associate with sexually immoral persons" (*pornoi*, cf. *porneia* in 5:1), he meant members of the community, not outsiders. Verse 10 offers a wry commentary on the moral condition of society as a whole: In order to avoid contact with *pornoi* and the greedy and robbers and idolaters, you would have to leave the world altogether! (cf. Rom. 1:18–32). The fact that Paul regards this suggestion as self-evidently ridiculous shows that his vision for the church is not isolationist. His communities live and work in the midst of the thriving cities of the Hellenistic Mediterranean world, seeking to live as a prophetic counterculture in the midst of an unbelieving world. His concern is that the church must truly be a counterculture, rather than becoming indistinguishable from the world around it. That is why he instructs the Corinthian church "not to associate with anyone who bears the name of brother or sister" if that person is bringing discredit to the "family" name through immoral conduct. They are to "not even eat with such a one" (v. 11), for table fellowship with nominal Christians living immoral lives would seriously blur the identity of the church as God's holy people. Paul expresses no objection to eating with sinners out in the world; rather, he is concerned about the discipline and symbolic integrity of the church as an alternative society in a world of idolatry and misconduct. God will judge the outsiders; the responsibility of the church is to exercise discipline over its own members (vv. 12–13a).

The list of sins requiring exclusion from the church's fellowship in 5:11 looks at first glance like a generic catalogue of vices. Brian Rosner (*Paul, Scripture and Ethics*, 69) has persuasively suggested, however, that the six items in Paul's list are closely correlated with six passages in Deuteronomy that call for the penalty of death, followed by the exact exclusion formula that Paul quotes in 5:13b: "So you shall drive out the evil person from among you." (Paul's citation of the formulation follows the Septuagint rather than the Hebrew text; he changes the verb from a future indicative to an aorist imperative, thus making it clear that he is reading Deuteronomy as a word of command addressed to his Corinthian readers.) The parallels may be lined up as follows:

87

1 Corinthians 5:11	*Deuteronomy*
sexually immoral	promiscuity, adultery (22:21–22, 30)
greedy	(no parallel, but paired with "robbers" in 1 Cor. 5:9)
idolater	idolatry (13:1–5; 17:2–7)
reviler	malicious false testimony (19:16–19)
drunkard	rebellious drunken son (21:18–21)
robber	kidnaping, slave-trading (24:7; LXX uses the noun *kleptēs*, "thief")

If Paul is implicitly following the outline of these Deuteronomic exclusion texts, he has moved sexual immorality to the beginning of the list because of the immediate problem in Corinth. The term "greedy," the anomalous element in Paul's list, may be placed second because it prefigures the next issue that Paul is going to confront: Corinthians taking one another to court over financial matters (6:1–11). The last four items in the list follow the canonical order of occurrence in Deuteronomy. Rosner admits that the actual terminology in Paul's vice list is not derived directly from Deuteronomy, but the correspondences are nonetheless suggestive.

Paul seems to have translated and transferred the basic disciplinary norms of Israel's covenant community over onto the church at Corinth. The word of command, "Drive out the evil person from among you," is presented as a word spoken directly to the Corinthians. There is no appeal here to analogy ("Just as God told Israel to drive out the evil person, so you should do the same"); rather, Paul in effect addresses the Gentile Corinthians *as* Israel. God's word to Israel has become God's word directly to them. The scriptural command with which Paul closes the chapter culminates his treatment of the incest problem and discloses the fundamental theological basis for his directions to the Corinthians. Sinful behavior of this sort cannot be allowed to corrupt God's elect covenant community.

REFLECTIONS FOR TEACHERS AND PREACHERS

This part of the Corinthians' mail deals in a confrontational way with an embarrassing local incident in ancient Corinth; thus, it may not be immediately apparent how this text can be God's word for us. For that reason, no doubt, the Revised Common Lectionary omits it entirely except for a snippet (vv. 6b–8) taken out of context to be read on Easter evening. No one who hears the Scripture only through the lectionary readings would ever learn that Paul had castigated the Corinthian church for tolerating an incestuous member in their midst. Yet there is much for us to gain by reflecting theologically on this passage as a word for Christians at the end of the twentieth century.

First of all, the passage emphatically calls the church to claim its identity as a people with a distinct character and mission, a counter-cultural prophetic community. Within such a community, the members are called to take active responsibility for one another's lives and spiritual wholeness. In 1 Corinthians 5, we encounter a vision of the church not as one voluntary association among many, but as the covenant people of God; to be *inside* this community is to find life, and to be *outside* is to be in the realm of death. Paul would have agreed with Cyprian's dictum that there is no salvation outside the church—not because God pronounces damnation on non-Christians, but because, in the midst of a self-destructive and perishing world, ultimate wholeness is to be found only in the community rescued by God through Jesus Christ. To abandon such a community—or to be expelled from it—is like jumping ship, or being thrown overboard, in the midst of a storm. The church must recover its lively sense of vocation as a people set apart for God's service and living in a way that exemplifies fidelity and grace (cf. Matt. 5:13–16; 1 Peter 2:9–10).

Second, within such a community, discipline is necessary. This is the most fundamental challenge of 1 Corinthians 5 to the church today. Churches that have grown up in the intensely private and individualistic ethos of Western culture find Paul's call for corporate accountability disturbing. Our beloved canon within the canon has become Matthew 7:1: "Do not judge, so that you may not be judged," which we misinterpret to mean, "I won't judge you if you won't judge me. (This saying of Jesus actually means, of course, "Do not harbor private judgment against your neighbor so that you may not be judged ultimately *by God.*") This Matthean text is an important warning against hypocritical self-righteousness, but it does not in any way preclude the church's corporate responsibility, as sketched here in 1 Corinthians 5, for disciplining members who flagrantly violate the will of the God for the community. The fact that the church so rarely exercises this disciplinary function is a sign of its unfaithfulness. Our failure to do so is often justified in the name of enlightened tolerance of differences, but in fact "tolerance" can become a euphemism for indifference and lack of moral courage.

Let us speak in terms of specific examples. Only very recently has the church begun to acknowledge instances of sexual abuse of women and children by church leaders and members. The example of 1

89

Corinthians 5 should encourage us to name such violations for what they are and to exercise swift and severe discipline upon the offenders. Insofar as the church has failed in the past to deal forthrightly with such matters, it has been complicit in a conspiracy of silence. We ought rather to have mourned and removed from our midst those who have done such things. We may hope, as Paul did, that our disciplinary actions might have a transforming and healing effect for the offender, but it is certain that no healing is possible at all without clear public confrontation of the offense. We have somehow deluded ourselves into believing that the "caring" thing to do is to be infinitely nonjudgmental and inclusive. This is quite simply a demonic lie, for it allows terrible cancerous abuses to continue unchecked in the community. Do we not know that a little cancer corrupts the whole body? Surgery is necessary; clean out the cancer so that the body may be whole.

Of course, it would be wrong to limit our concern to sexual offenses against the community; this example comes readily to mind only because it happens to be a sexual offense that Paul addresses in Corinth. It is important to recognize, however, that five of Paul's six examples of sins that require community exclusion (v. 11) have nothing to do with sex. It will be a great day when the church finds the moral courage also to confront and discipline the greedy, idolaters, and perpetrators of violence.

Third, the community that exercises such disciplinary authority is a community acquainted with spiritual power, "the power of our Lord Jesus" (v. 4). There is a self-perpetuating feedback loop between our failure to discipline our communities and our timidity about the life and manifestations of the Holy Spirit in our midst. If we took more seriously the promise of Jesus' actual presence in our assemblies (Matt. 18:20), we might be more likely to follow his teaching about how to deal with sinners in our midst (Matt. 18:15–19). It is by no means clear that Paul even knew about this teaching of Jesus—he does not allude to it here—but his conviction about the presence of the Lord in the church was sufficient to authorize his insistence on community discipline.

Fourth, the Passover image in the center of this text is richly generative for our theological reflection. It suggests, first of all, that we must learn or relearn to understand our identity as heirs of the legacy of Israel. We can "celebrate the feast" rightly only if we understand what this feast meant and means to the Jewish people who observe the Passover in commemoration of their liberation from bondage in Egypt (Exodus 12). (This means, among other things, that Christian congregations should seek to enter mutually respectful dialogue with their Jewish neighbors and to learn all they can about the roots of their common tradition.) To repeat what was said above, the Passover festival has nothing to do with atonement for sin and everything to do with deliverance from the powers of oppression. This fact has wide-ranging implications for the way we think about Christology and about our own communal identity. In the church we are protected from destruction by Christ's death, set free from the power that held us captive, and sent out on a journey toward a promise. Paul does not develop all these implications of his metaphor here in 1 Corinthians 5:6–8, but they lie waiting to be explored in our theological reflection and preaching. The one implication that Paul does develop in this passage is that the church must be distinguished from its destructive cultural environment, so that those who disobey God's commands must be placed outside the protective household of faith.

Finally, we should take careful note of the way in which Paul treats Deuteronomy as a word spoken to the Corinthian church. A number of factors in the letter suggest that the Corinthians did not understand themselves to be either addressed by or bound to Scripture. Paul had to try to teach them not to go "beyond what is written" (4:6) because they were so self-assured in their wisdom that they believed themselves to be above and beyond the limitations and norms of God's written word to Israel. The immoral man at Corinth either did not know or did not care that Deuteronomy forbids a man to "lie with his father's wife" (Deut. 27:20) or to marry her (22:30). For him, his own experience of freedom in Christ was sufficient to assure him that what he was doing was either right or, at least, of no moral significance. Old covenant commandments in the Bible and old moral standards of his own Greco-Roman culture meant nothing to him, for "in the name of Jesus" he had transcended such fleshly hangups. It is easy to see how this attitude could have arisen in the context of the hybrid Christian-Cynic/Stoic "wisdom" that was flourishing in Corinth (see the discussion of 1 Corinthians 4, above), and, as we have noted, this also explains why some of the other Corinthians might have been "boasting" about this affair, celebrating the transgressor as a hero of Christian freedom. Paul punctures this puffed-up balloon of philosophical-theological speculation by insisting that with respect to the scriptural moral norms, the rules of the game have not changed. Deuteronomy still speaks—as it was designed to do (cf. Deuteronomy 26)—to subsequent generations of the people of God and still calls them to walk in his ways and obey him. There could be no more effective way to make this point than the way Paul does it: by placing at the climax of the chapter (5:13b) a direct quotation from Deuteronomy 22:21 that addresses the Corinthians as God's covenant people and commands them to act to preserve the integrity of their covenant relationship to him: "Drive out the evil person from among you."

How does all this pertain to us? In our time, too, we have within the church people claiming that their newly attained enlightenment or wisdom sets them free *precisely as Christians* to disregard the teachings of Scripture and tradition on moral issues (not just sexual conduct but other matters as well, such as possessions and the use of violence). They boast in their liberated transgression of what they regard as outmoded norms. What would Paul say to the church today? Should we not rather mourn? Does not Scripture continue to speak directly to us?

6:1–11
Legal Disputes Should Be Handled within the Community

In the first part of 1 Corinthians 6, Paul addresses the report that some of the Corinthian Christians are pursuing legal action against other members of the church. Paul's comments give us very little information, but the disputes seem to concern matters of civil law: he refers to the cases as dealing with everyday matters (*biōtika*, vv. 3–4: NRSV catches the right meaning by translating "ordinary matters," while NIV's "things of this life" is an unfortunate paraphrase that suggests that Christians should be concerned only about things of the next life; this is far from Paul's present point). The reference in verses 7–8 to being "defrauded" suggest that the disputes have arisen over economic issues.

Why is Paul so disturbed about this report? (Notice, in contrast to 4:14, that he *is* now trying to bring the Corinthians to feel shame [6:5] about what they are doing.) While many Christian readers today would share Paul's outrage about the case of incest (5:1–5), lawsuits may seem to belong to a different category altogether. Every law court in the Western world has for centuries seen Christians bringing suit against one another; it seems a normal way of settling disputes and doing business. Thus, Paul's indignant reaction (6:1–8) may appear to us—as perhaps it did to the Corinthians—to be exaggerated. We may also be surprised that Paul has placed this discussion in between two units that deal primarily with issues of sexual morality (5:1–13 and 6:12–20). How does this section fit into the context of chapters 5 and 6? And why does Paul find the litigious behavior of the Corinthians so scandalous?

The two questions have a single answer: Paul is upset with the

Corinthians because they are failing to act as a community, failing to take responsibility for one another. Just as they have failed to discipline the incestuous man, so they are failing to take responsibility for settling their own disputes; consequently they are taking their legal cases before unbelievers (6:6), whom Paul calls "the unrighteous" (6:1). In other words, they are going through the normal channels of the civil courts in Roman Corinth. The judges in such courts are "unrighteous" (*adikoi*) in the sense that they do not belong to God's covenant community. Thus when the Corinthian Christians take one another to court, they are declaring primary allegiance to the pagan culture of Corinth rather than to the community of faith. This action breaks down the boundaries of the church and damages its unity.

Let the point be registered clearly: In 1 Corinthians 6:1–11 Paul has not really changed the subject from the topic of chapter 5. In both cases the problem is "a failure of the church to be the church" (Fee, 230). That is the fundamental issue of these two chapters of the letter. He is summoning his Corinthian readers to a conversion of the imagination, calling them to understand themselves first and foremost as "the saints" (vv. 1–2; cf. 1:2)—that is, the eschatological people of God, called out of their previous social world, like Israel out of Egypt. That means that they are now bound together as a people in a way that requires them to modify their former ways of life.

Recent research on the court systems of the Roman empire has shown that there was a strong systemic bias in favor of higher-status litigants. The overwhelming majority of civil cases were brought by the wealthy and powerful against people of lesser status and means. The judges themselves were members of the privileged classes and would ordinarily give preference to the testimony of their social peers against the testimony of those of lower rank; furthermore, those of high standing had the funds to hire professional rhetors to argue their cases and, if necessary, to bribe the judges. In consequence, a character in the *Satyricon* of Petronius complains as follows: "Of what avail are laws to be where money rules alone, and the poor suitor can never succeed? . . . So a lawsuit is nothing more than a public auction, and the knightly juror who sits listening to the case approves, with the record of his vote, something bought" (*Satyricon*, 14). Certainly Corinth, an important commercial and administrative center, was no exception to this general picture. Dio Chrysostom notes that Corinth, especially around the time of the Isthmian Games, was full of "lawyers innumerable perverting judgment" (*Or.* 8.9). (These references from Alan C. Mitchell, "Rich and Poor in the Courts of Corinth," 562–86).

Thus, in all likelihood, the members of the Corinthian church who were initiating civil proceedings against their fellow Christians were among the more privileged and powerful members of the community, whereas the defendants in such suits were likely to be the poorer members. This is consistent with a pattern that emerges elsewhere in the letter (see especially 11:17–34): the wealthier Corinthians were "shaming" those in the church who were of lower status and lesser means. This background information—none of which had to be explained to the original readers—helps us to interpret Paul's stern rebuke to the litigators: "When any of you has a grievance against another, do you *dare* to take it to court before the unrighteous [pagan high-status Corinthian judges, who will be biased in favor of the wealthy] instead of taking it before the saints? . . . I say this to your shame" (6:1, 5a).

Paul tries to show the scandalous absurdity of this practice by reframing the present situation in light of the eschatological reality. He draws on the idea, standard in Jewish and early Christian apocalyptic texts, that God's elect will have a part in the judgment of the world and in ruling it in the age to come (Dan. 7:18, 22; Wisd. Sol. 3:8; Matt. 19:28; Luke 22:30; Rev. 3:21). Paul's matter-of-fact statement that "we are to judge angels" (v. 3) is, however, unprecedented: perhaps this is an inference from his conviction that all things are ultimately to be subjected to Christ (1 Cor. 15:24–28), so that those who are "in Christ" will be placed over even the angels. In any case, his immediate aim is to highlight the ridiculous contrast between the church's glorious eschatological destiny and its present failure to exercise jurisdiction over minor property disputes: "And if the world is to be judged by you, are you incompetent to try trivial cases?" (6:2b).

In such matters, he asks incredulously, "do you appoint as judges those who are despised [NRSV, have no standing] in the church?" (v. 4). The NIV interpretation of this verse takes the phrase to refer to low-status Christians and reads the sentence as an imperative rather than a rhetorical question: "Therefore, if you have disputes about such matters, appoint as judges even men of little account in the church!" Such a statement, however, would reinforce precisely the class distinctions that Paul is seeking to overcome. Therefore, the NRSV interpretation is to be preferred, even though its rendering of *tous exouthenēmenous* as "those who have no standing" is too mild: the word means "those who are *despised*." Those who are "despised in the church" are the unrighteous pagan judges; whatever their social standing in the world, in the church their honored position is worth nothing (cf. 1:26–31).

94

Paul's sly rhetorical question in verse 5b is intended to deflate the puffed-up Corinthians: "Can it be that there is no *sophos* among you who is able to decide between one brother and another?" The question is the more devastating if—as is likely—those who are pressing legal disputes are precisely the same upper-class members of the community who claim to possess an exalted philosophical wisdom. Paul's question is, "If you people are so 'wise,' why can't you even settle your differences among yourselves rather than going to outside authorities?" Their recourse to outside arbitration proves the point that they are not what they claim to be.

Worst of all, however, is the fact that such litigation pits "brother . . . against brother" (v. 6), as rightly in the NIV. Once again the NRSV's effort to achieve inclusivity by using "believer," rather than "brother," loses the point that Paul regards the community of faith as God's *family*. The Corinthians are shamefully taking family disputes out into the streets, as it were, thereby bringing the whole family into disrepute. Paul insists that this must stop. If necessary, the Corinthians should appoint for themselves judges (as Israel did, cf. Deut. 1:9–17; 16:18–20) to settle internal disputes (cf. 1 Cor. 5:12). This would be in accordance with the normal practice of *Jewish* communities in the Diaspora, which established their own court systems and sought to avoid the Gentile courts. At least this way of handling disputes would keep problems within the jurisdiction of the community rather than disgracefully playing out their arguments in front of outsiders.

Even such an arrangement, however, would be from Paul's point of view a concession, for "to have lawsuits at all with one another is already a defeat for you" (v. 7). There are no winners: the whole church loses, and the individuals involved lose, even if they win their cases. Why? Because by fighting it out in the law courts, they become the perpetrators of wrongdoing. "You yourselves wrong and defraud—and brothers at that." The Corinthians wrong (*adikein*) one another and thus become just like the *adikoi*, the unrighteous pagans. It would be far better to suffer economic injustice than to seek legal restitution, better to be wronged than to do wrong (vv. 7–8).

Although many comentators see here an allusion to the teaching of Jesus, there are no direct points of contact with the language of Matthew 5:38–42. If Paul had known this teaching of Jesus, it would have served his purpose to quote it (cf. 7:10); the fact that he does not do so suggests that he probably did not know it. There is, however, a very strong echo here of the well-known teaching of Socrates as reported by Plato: "If it were necessary either to do wrong or to suffer it, I should choose to suffer rather than do it" (*Gorgias* 469C and passim, using exactly the verbs that Paul employs in 1 Cor. 6:7–8, *adikein* and *adikeisthai*). This maxim is repeated by philosophers such as Epictetus and Musonius Rufus; the latter actually wrote a treatise arguing that

95

the philosopher should never prosecute anyone for personal injury, not only because it is disgraceful to inflict wrong on another person but also because the Stoic should never concede having been harmed by anyone in the first place. Thus, Paul's rhetorical move in verses 7–8 implicitly accuses the Corinthians one more time of failing to act like true *sophoi*; once again we see him turning their own philosophical categories against them, beating them at their own game.

This does not at all mean that Paul is merely playing rhetorical games. His point is quite a serious one: those in the church are called to act righteously and to put behind them the self-asserting, injurious ways of the world. He formulates this idea in general terms in verses 9–11: "Wrongdoers [*adikoi* again] will not inherit the kingdom of God" (v. 9). Again the eschatological perspective frames Paul's argument. While they jostle each other for economic status and advantage, the Corinthians wrong and defraud, acting just like the unrighteous outsiders who will ultimately incur the much greater loss of not "inheriting" God's kingdom. The inheritance metaphor is common in Paul (with reference to "the kingdom of God," see 15:50; Gal. 5:21; cf. also Gal. 3:29—4:7; Rom. 8:17). Here, however, it makes a subtle point about the particular problem of lawsuits in the Corinthian church: By grasping for material advantage now, the Corinthians are jeopardizing their far greater reward in the coming age.

Yet Paul's argument is not a threat, nor is it finally based on an appeal to cost-benefit analysis; his point is not merely that they should refrain from litigation because it compromises their own long-term interests. Rather, he insists that such conduct is fundamentally inconsistent with their true identity in Christ. As baptized members of the church, they have been transferred into a new reality and given a new identity under the Lordship of Jesus Christ. Conduct such as suing one another is incongruous with this new corporate identity, and it should therefore be stopped. This is an excellent example of a pattern of moral reasoning that we encounter repeatedly in Paul: the indicative (you *are* in Christ) precedes and grounds the imperative (therefore *act* accordingly).

Legal disputes are, to be sure, only one characteristic of life lived under the destructive power of the old age. Paul fills in the content of the general term "wrongdoers" by giving a list of other types of people who will not inherit the kingdom (6:9b–10). The list repeats the six offenses already set forth in 5:11 as requiring exclusion from the community (fornicators, idolaters, the greedy, drunkards, revilers, robbers) and adds four more categories. Two of these (adulterers and thieves) require no comment because they merely expand or restate the

Deuteronomic prescriptions (Deut. 22:21–22; 24:7) and are closely related to "fornicators" and "robbers," respectively. The other two terms, however—"male prostitutes, sodomites" (NRSV)—introduce a new twist.

There has been much scholarly debate recently over the proper interpretation of these words. The first term (*malakoi*) means literally "soft ones." It could sometimes refer to male prostitutes—particularly young boys who were the passive partners in pederastic relationships—but it is not the ordinary word for such persons, and it could have a broader sense, such as "sissies" or "dandies." The second word (*arsenokoitai*), however, is a general term for men who engage in same-sex intercourse. Although the word *arsenokoitēs* appears nowhere in Greek literature prior to Paul's use of it, it is evidently a rendering into Greek of the standard rabbinic term for "one who lies with a male [as with a woman]" (Lev. 18:22; 20:13). (Despite recent challenges to this interpretation, the meaning is confirmed by the evidence of *Sibylline Oracles* 2.73.) Paul here repeats the standard Jewish condemnation of homosexual conduct. (For slightly more extended comment on the matter, see Rom. 1:24–27; cf. also Tim. 1:10.) Though this offense does not appear in the community-exclusion texts of Deuteronomy, it is labeled by Leviticus 20:13 as an "abomination" requiring the penalty of death. Thus, it is not surprising that Paul would link it with the other items in his previous list (5:11), all of which also, according to the Old Testament, required the offender to be executed. (As we have seen, Paul—in keeping with Jewish practice of his day—had reinterpreted these texts to require banishment from the community rather than literal capital punishment.)

We should remember, however, that Paul's present purpose in 1 Corinthians 6 is not to set up new rules for sexual behavior but to chastise the Corinthians for taking each other to court. All the items in the list of verses 9–10 are merely illustrations of what the Corinthians *used to be* prior to their coming into the church. But a life-transforming change has occurred: "you were washed, you were sanctified, and you were justified in the name of the Lord Jesus Christ and in the Spirit of our God" (v. 11). In light of this transformation, they ought to stop acting like *adikoi* by taking their property disputes into courts where the powerful can take advantage of the less influential members of the community. Unless we keep this basic aim of the argument in view, our reading of and preaching on this text will become severely out of focus.

Paul alludes here to their baptism ("you were washed"), which he understands as a sign of their transference into the sphere of Christ's lordship. They have been cleansed from their past sinful behavior and set apart for God's service ("sanctified," cf. 1:2) as members of God's

97

covenant people ("justified"). The three verbs in verse 11 do not point to three sequential experiences in a pilgrimage of faith; rather, they are three descriptions of the one fundamental transformation that has occurred for those who now belong to Christ. The climactic verb "justified" rounds out the whole unit with a deft wordplay that is lost in most English translations: "You used to be unjust (*adikoi*); . . . but you were justified (*edikaiōthēte*)." Since they have been justified—made members of God's family—they must stop wronging (*adikeite*, v. 8) one another by going to court before the *adikoi* (v. 1).

REFLECTIONS FOR TEACHERS AND PREACHERS

First Corinthians 6:9–11 has provided the launching pad for countless moralistic sermons that decry the types of sinners listed here. In fact, however, the preacher who zeroes in on Paul's vice list has placed the homiletical accent emphatically in the wrong spot. The concern of the passage as a whole is threefold: to call the Corinthians to act as a community, to condemn litigation as an instrument of injustice, and to assert the transformed identity of the baptized. Let us reflect briefly on each of these points.

1. *Acting as a community.* The Corinthians' legal disputes betray and jeopardize the solidarity of the community in Christ: that is the fundamental reason for Paul's indignation. More important than any private property is the unity of the church. Paul calls again for a conversion of the imagination. The Corinthians are to stop seeing themselves as participants in the "normal" social and economic structures of their city and to imagine themselves instead as members of the eschatological people of God, acting corporately in a way that will prefigure and proclaim the kingdom of God. Whatever decisions are made about economic affairs ought to be made by the church acting together, and in making such decisions, the church should remember that they are the saints who will be called upon ultimately to participate in God's righteous judgment of the world. In reframing the Corinthians' civil disputes in this way, Paul is asking a great deal of them. He is seeking to resocialize them into a new way of doing business, a new community consciousness.

This text asks no less of us. We, no less than the Corinthians, participate in conventional legal and economic structures that are foreign to Paul's gospel-centered community vision. The task of the teacher or preacher is to articulate the analogies between our situation and the Corinthian practices. In what ways are we as Christians deferring to outside authorities to shape our business and legal affairs? In what ways are we asserting private economic rights that may ignore or fracture the larger interests of the community of faith? The answers to such questions will have to be found in each local situation, but their impact on the church is potentially devastating. In a culture shaped profoundly by the values of individualistic materialism, we should find in Paul's scolding of the Corinthians a challenge to examine ourselves. Are we conducting our affairs in a way that shows clearly—to ourselves and to others—that our primary loyalty is to the family of God's people?

In some places, churches have begun to sponsor programs for the mediation of disputes outside the legal system. Such conflict resolution programs seek to achieve not only out-of-court settlements but also reconciliation between the quarreling parties. This sort of creative initiative is deeply consonant with the call of 1 Corinthians 6:1–11 to the church.

2. *Condemnation of injustice.* When we read this section of the letter against the background of what we know about the judicial system of the time, we recognize that Paul is concerned not only about the unity of the community but also about the potential for the abuse of the poor by the privileged. This is not made very explicit in the passage, because Paul does not give any details about the cases he has in mind. Nonetheless, the Corinthians would have known perfectly well what he was talking about. The telltale indicator appears in verse 8: "But you yourselves wrong and defraud—and believers at that." Some of the Corinthians are using the civil courts as an instrument of injustice, unfairly taking advantage of those who are not able to defend themselves.

We might ask ourselves whether matters have changed fundamentally in our time. Money still talks. The wealthy can still hire high-powered lawyers to argue their cases and exert disproportionate influence on the legal process. Our cities are riddled, no less than Corinth, with "lawyers innumerable perverting judgment." Insofar as Christians are complicit in this process, Paul's words can be heard as addressed to us also: "I say this to your shame."

The passage is, after all, addressed specifically to the problem of Christians taking Christians to court. To use this text—as is often done—primarily to condemn one of the other classes of sinners in Paul's vice list (such as "fornicators" or "homosexuals") is a strange per-version of Paul's message. Faithful attention to 1 Corinthians 6:1–11 will lead us to reflect primarily upon whether we as a community are harboring and even tacitly approving "the greedy." The question is so uncomfortable that we may be relieved—though not surprised—to find the passage conveniently omitted from our lectionaries.

3. *The transformed identity of the baptized.* The right way to handle

99

1 Corinthians 6:9–11 is to place the emphasis where Paul does: on the fact that God has already acted to transform the identity of those who are in Christ. It is possible, though not certain, that verse 11 echoes the actual language of the baptismal ceremony (note the implicit trinitarian structure of the formula: "in the name of *the Lord Jesus Christ* and in *the Spirit of our God*"). In any case, Paul emphasizes that those who are baptized into the community of faith have been transferred out of one mode of existence into another. The believer is to leave behind the behaviors characteristic of that old mode just as the butterfly leaves behind the cocoon and the habits of caterpillar life. Now—washed, sanctified, justified—baptized Christians are set into a new reality, not by some act of will or commitment but by the gracious action of a loving God.

The interpreter of this passage should seek to guide the members of the congregation in reflection about their baptismal identity. A more extensive discussion of the same theme may be found in Romans 6, but 1 Corinthians 6 contains sufficient clues to provoke much helpful discussion of this matter. To be "washed" suggests that we are cleansed and forgiven for what is past. To be "sanctified" is to be set apart for God's service (cf. 1:2, 30; 3:17). To be "justified" (cf. 1:30) is to be placed in right relation to God within the community of God's people. Paul is convinced that these affirmations remain true of the Corinthians even though some of their present actions seem to contradict the new identity that God has given them in Christ. Similarly, our pastoral task is to enable the congregation to receive and act upon this God-given identity. The art of living faithfully as Christians is to live imaginatively and practically on the basis of these truths about ourselves.

As we have already seen, this new identity in Christ will entail a break not only with our individual past sinful behaviors but also with our community's past cultural patterns and assumptions. Having explained this point, the teacher working with this passage may want to write two headings on the blackboard: "We used to be . . ." and "But now we are . . ." Students or members of the congregation could then be encouraged to brainstorm about how to complete these sentences in ways that extend the range of examples given by Paul. (For example, "We used be trained by the media to think of ourselves as 'consumers,' but now we are sharers of the good things that God gives us." Or, "We used to be racists, but now we are part of God's family, made up of all races and tongues.") This is, however, a dangerous exercise if it is taken seriously, for it will call the class or congregation to act upon the transformations that they identify. To be baptized into Christ is to enter a reality in which the factors that used to give us status, security, and identity no longer count (cf. Phil. 3:4b–16) and we find our identity in Christ alone. Once we understand that, we may have to give up not only lawsuits but many other things as well.

6:12–20
"Glorify God in Your Body"

The idea of giving up their personal prerogatives was objectionable to many of the Corinthians. Indeed, their conception of "wisdom" placed great emphasis on personal freedom. Their watchword was, "I am free to do anything." This was their justification for numerous practices that Paul found troubling. In the final part of chapter 6, therefore, he attacks the roots of their community-destroying insistence upon autonomy. The argument is a little difficult to follow, because Paul here adopts the *diatribe* style, in which he constructs an imaginary dialogue between himself and his Corinthian hearers. To understand the line of argument, we must reconstruct the different voices in this imaginary conversation.

"I am free to do anything" must have been a favorite slogan of the Corinthians. (This is the translation of NEB, which nicely catches the force of the saying; the emphasis lies not on what is *legally* allowable but on the sovereign authority of the individual over all external constraints.) Paul quotes this saying back at them both here and in relation to the idol-meat controversy in 10:23—in both cases, in order to qualify it substantially. In light of the evidence we have already seen of Stoic-Cynic tendencies in the thinking of the Corinthian *sophoi*, we should understand that this slogan declares a philosophically-informed autonomy: The enlightened wise person is free to do anything he or she chooses. This is consistent with the idea that the *sophos* is a "king" to whom all things belong (see the discussion of 3:21–23 and 4:8, above). The precise slogan "I am free to do anything" is not found in contemporary philosophical writings, but in Epictetus there are numerous passages that discuss the freedom of the philosopher, using exactly the same verb that Paul cites here. It is likely that the Corinthians have drawn upon this philosophical tradition to create a slogan expressing their radical understanding of freedom in Christ.

The inspiration for this idea may well have come originally from Paul himself (cf. 9:1, 19); at least, many of the "wise" Corinthians might have supposed that Paul would agree with their slogan. Was he not the great apostle of freedom from the rules of the Jewish Law? He preached

God's unconditional grace, did he not? In light of this theological understanding, surely all the old scruples and prohibitions must fall away into insignificance. The wise and enlightened person knows, like Paul, that "nothing is unclean in itself" (Rom. 14:14). Therefore, they reasoned, we are free to do whatever we want with a clear conscience.

The case of the incestuous man (1 Cor. 5:1–13) may have represented an extreme instance of such thinking, but Paul's forceful argument in 6:12–20 suggests that he has heard reports of a similar attitude among many of the Corinthians with regard to matters of sexual conduct. Apparently some of them were going to prostitutes and contending that such conduct was harmless. To the modern reader, this may seem surprising, but we must remember that the social world of the ancient Corinthians differed greatly from ours. Prostitution was not only legal; it was a widely accepted social convention. "The sexual latitude allowed to men by Greek public opinion was virtually unrestricted. Sexual relations of males with both boys and harlots were generally tolerated" (Talbert, 32). Thus, the Corinthian men who frequented prostitutes were not asserting some unheard-of new freedom; they were merely insisting on their right to continue participating in a pleasurable activity that was entirely normal within their own culture.

In order to counter this attitude, Paul opens the next section of the argument by quoting a series of three Corinthian slogans, each followed by his own counterslogan in rebuttal (6:12–14).

Corinthians:	*Paul:*
"All things are lawful for me."	But not all things are beneficial.
"All things are lawful for me."	But I will not be dominated by anything.
"Food is meant for the stomach	The body is meant (not for fornication but) for the Lord,
and the stomach for food.	and the Lord for the body
And God will destroy	And God raised
both one and the other."	the Lord and will also raise us by his power.

There is some guesswork involved in reconstructing this dialogue, because the ancient Greek manuscripts do not use quotation marks. The translator must decide where Paul is quoting a slogan and where he is offering his own rejoinder. For example, many translations take the words "and God will destroy both one and the other" as Paul's own words. The precise parallelism of the structure outlined above, however, suggests strongly that it is the Corinthians, not Paul, who contend that God will destroy the merely physical elements of the self. Indeed, a moment's reflection will show that this has to be the correct way to interpret the passage, for the idea that the physical body is unimportant is precisely the point that Paul is trying to refute.

Paul insists, both here and in 1 Corinthians 15, that the body is created by God as a good part of creation and that God will redeem the body through resurrection. If Paul agreed (as in NRSV and NEB) with the slogan that "Food is meant for the stomach and the stomach for food" and added that God would destroy both, he would be playing right into the hands of the Corinthian dualistic argument. The Corinthian *sophoi*, seeing the body as transient and trivial, have concluded that it makes no difference what we do with our bodies. If we are hungry, we should eat; if we are desirous of sexual gratification, we should seek it. None of this makes any difference, they say, because it concerns only external physical matters, which are of no lasting significance.

In light of this analysis of the dialogue, let us examine Paul's three responses to the Corinthian slogans. In his first rejoinder to the slogan "I am free to do anything," Paul cleverly rebuts the *sophoi* by using another philosophical term: not all things are beneficial (*sympherei*). Even apart from any specifically Christian reasons, Paul suggests, the extreme Corinthian position is simply bad philosophy: the wise person will not act in self-indulgent ways but will seek to act in accordance with an enlightened understanding of what is good. Johannes Weiss (159) comments that "here Paul strikes the Greek freedom-enthusiasts with their own weapon." In Paul's other uses of the verb *sympherein* in 1 Corinthians (10:23; 12:7), he is clearly talking about what is beneficial for the community, not just the individual. Here in 1 Corinthians 6:12, however, this statement could be heard by the Corinthians in individualistic terms, as the NEB rendering indicates: "'I am free to do anything,' you say. Yes, but not everything is for *my* good."

Paul then restates their slogan and offers a second rejoinder: "I will not be dominated by anything." This too sounds like a Stoic argument: the wise person will not surrender control to anything or anyone. The danger is particularly great that the person seeking to exercise freedom through promiscuous sexual activity will end up as a slave to passion. The verb translated "dominated" here is the same one that appears in

103

7:4, where husband and wife are said to "have authority" over one another's bodies: by using this term Paul may be suggesting subtly that the "wise" Corinthians who go to prostitutes are in effect surrendering control over themselves to the prostitutes. Once again, then, this response is an ironic put-down of the pretentious claims of the *sophoi*.

Paul's most emphatic rebuttal, however, is reserved for the slogan about "food for the stomach." The Corinthians themselves must have been using this argument about food analogically to justify their sexual freedom. That is why Paul's response ignores the issue of food (an issue that he will treat later in response to their specific questions) and targets the problem of fornication. No longer here does he toy around with the philosophical categories of the "wise"; instead, he appeals to the primary language of Christian confession. The body belongs to the Lord Jesus, and God has confirmed his concern for the body by raising the Lord Jesus; this act of power declares God's ultimate promise to raise us also (cf. Rom. 8:11 and 1 Corinthians 15 in its entirety). No one who understands the fundamental content of the *kērygma* can suppose that our bodies are irrelevant. The body is not simply a husk to be cast off in the next life; the gospel of Jesus Christ proclaims that we are to be redeemed body, soul, and spirit (cf. 1 Thess. 5:23–24; Rom. 8:23). Salvation can never be understood as escape from the physical world or as the flight of the soul to heaven. Rather, the resurrection of the *body* is an integral element of the Christian story. Those who live within that story, then, should understand that what they do with their bodies in the present time is a matter of urgent concern.

Having emphatically asserted that God's raising of Jesus validates the physical body, Paul begins (6:15–17) to explore the implications of his statement that "the body is for the Lord." This means that our bodies *belong to* the Lord Jesus. Those who are in Christ have been united with him in a relationship of intimate union ("one spirit with him," v. 17) that is analogous to—but even deeper than—sexual union. (Note that Paul describes union with Christ in v. 17 with the same verb that he had used in v. 16 to describe union with a prostitute.) This means that our physical bodies no longer belong to us; they belong instead to Christ, in a manner analogous to the belonging of the bodies of husband and wife to one another (cf. 7:4; 2 Cor. 11:2; Eph. 5:22–33). The man who has sexual intercourse with a prostitute is therefore not only committing an act of infidelity to Christ but also taking something that belongs to Christ (his own body) and linking it to the sphere of the unholy. Contemplating this blasphemous prospect, Paul asks rhetorically, "Should I therefore take the members of Christ and make them members of a prostitute?" (No one can ever accuse Paul of being a

104

timid theological thinker; this is a bold metaphor carried through forcefully to its conclusion.) His response is an emphatic, "Never!"

The whole argument presupposes that sexual intercourse cannot be understood merely as a momentary act that satisfies a transient natural urge. Instead, it creates a mysterious but real and enduring union between man and woman. In support of this claim, Paul cites Genesis 2:24: "The two shall be one flesh." The union of a member of the church with a prostitute is disastrous for the Christian community precisely because it creates a real bonding with her; therefore it creates an unholy bond between the Lord's members and the sinful world. The result is both defilement and confusion.

In light of this explanation, Paul concludes with an emphatic imperative: "Flee fornication!" There is a possible echo here of the story of Joseph's fleeing from Potiphar's wife (Gen. 39:12), which became proverbial in Jewish tradition for resistance to the lure of sexual immorality (see *T.Jos.* 2–10; cf. *T. Reub.* 5:5). If Paul intends this echo, however, he does nothing to develop it thematically. His immediate goal is to urge the Corinthians in the strongest possible terms to cease the practice of patronizing prostitutes.

A new subsection begins in 6:18b, but it is difficult to know what to make of the first sentence in this unit: "Every sin that a person commits is outside the body." There are two possible ways to interpret this puzzling remark. The first way is to take it as the first half of a comparison that asserts fornication to be somehow worse than all other sins, or at least more body-related. This is the option adopted by the NIV: "All *other* sins a man commits are outside his body, but he who sins sexually sins against his own body." The word *other* is not in the Greek text; this interpretation assumes that Paul has expressed himself imprecisely. The other possible interpretation is to take this sentence as one more quotation of a Corinthian slogan in the imagined diatribal dialogue:

Paul: Flee fornication!
Corinthians [*objecting*]: [But why?] Every sin a person commits is
                          outside the body.
Paul: But the fornicator sins against his own body.

According to this reading, the Corinthian slogan means, "The body has nothing to do with sin" (Murphy-O'Connor, "Corinthian Slogans," 391–96). This fits well indeed into the context, where the Corinthian *sophoi* are arguing that bodily actions are of no significance. All things considered, the latter interpretation is to be preferred, even though there is no clear syntactical indication in the text of a quotation.

105

Either way, Paul's own position is clear: The fornicator not only defiles the church by linking Christ with a prostitute (vv. 15–17) but also sins against his own body (not "the body itself," as in NRSV). His action damages not only the community but also himself. Such damage is tragic, for the individual body of the Christian is "a temple of the Holy Spirit within you," a place where God's Spirit resides (v. 19; cf. Rom. 8:11). Elsewhere, as we have seen, Paul uses the "temple" image for the church as a corporate whole (1 Cor. 3:16–17; cf. 2 Cor. 6:16; Eph. 2:19–22). Here he dramatically transfers this metaphor to the individual. Just as the church should be kept holy through the exercise of community discipline, so the individual body should be kept as a disciplined holy vessel, fit for the indwelling Spirit. Paul takes some pains, however, to emphasize that the Spirit is a gift ("which you have from God"). Once again here Paul's moral exhortation moves from indicative to imperative. He does *not* say, "Keep your body holy so that God might give you the Spirit." Rather, he says, in effect, "Because the Holy Spirit *already* dwells in you, you should keep your body from fornication." Anyone preaching on this text should take care to respect this line of logic.

The unit closes with a return to the idea that our bodies are not our own property which we may use according to our own autonomous designs. "Do you not know . . . that you are not your own?" (v. 19). Paul insists that we have been placed under the ownership of the Lord. By his death, Jesus has paid the terrible price to ransom us from bondage to the powers of sin and death; consequently, we now belong to him and not to ourselves, for "you were bought with a price" (v. 20a). The metaphorical picture is of the purchase of slaves by a new master; compare Romans 6:18, "you, having been set free from sin, have become slaves of righteousness." A similar idea will appear in a different context in the next chapter of 1 Corinthians: "[W]hoever was free when called is a slave of Christ. You were bought with a price" (7:22b–23a).

The key idea for Paul's argument at the end of chapter 6 is not a particular theory about the mechanism of atonement, but the affirmation that we belong to God and not to ourselves (cf. Rom. 14:7–9). From this fundamental theological truth follows the closing exhortation: "Therefore glorify God in your body." That is Paul's climactic argument against fornication with prostitutes: our bodies, which belong to God, should be used in ways that bring glory to God, not disrepute. It is by no means a question of individual freedom, as the Corinthian slogan asserted. The distance between the Corinthian *sophoi* and Paul may be measured precisely by the distance between 6:12 and 6:20. They say "I am free to do anything"; Paul says "Glorify God in your

106

body." Their argument focuses on the rights and freedoms of the individual; Paul's focuses on the devotion and service owed to God.

Paul does not call upon the church to expel the men who have been visiting prostitutes. Instead, he provides an alternative theological vision and calls upon them to cease this behavior. It is crucial to recognize, however, that he does not treat fornication as belonging to the sphere of merely private morality. It damages the community as a whole, and it can be corrected only if the Corinthian *sophoi* come to understand their bodies as "members of Christ." As the rest of the letter unfolds, we will see that "the body of Christ" is a major Pauline image for the church (10:16–17; 12:12–31). Paul does not yet develop the ecclesial implications of the "body" metaphor in 1 Corinthians 6:15–17, but he provides the necessary groundwork. The implication of the argument in 6:12–20 is that the Corinthians who claim the freedom to do anything must stop acting as free agents and submit their moral discernment to Paul's apostolic teaching and to the discernment and discipline of the community as a whole. If the argument of 1 Corinthians 5:1—6:11 summons the whole church to take responsibility for moral discipline in the community, the concluding piece of the argument in 6:12–20 is the necessary complement: it summons individuals to the moral humility of recognizing themselves to be subject to the lordship of Christ. With that recognition, they will be forced to abandon their provocative pose of moral autonomy and to return into the discipline and nurture of the community.

REFLECTIONS FOR TEACHERS AND PREACHERS

As in ancient Corinth, so in the church today, we hear a chorus of voices declaring, "I am free to do anything." Paul's vigorous rebuttal to the Corinthians may carry an important word for us, as we listen in on his response and reflect on the ethical issues that confront us in our own time.

As we have seen, in 1 Corinthians 6:12–20 Paul weaves together three different arguments against the Corinthians who would justify going to prostitutes: an argument based on resurrection of the body (6:13–14), an argument based on the body as a temple for the presence of the Holy Spirit (6:18–19), and an argument based on the Lord's rightful ownership of the body (6:15–17, 20). The shifts from one argument to the other are abrupt and potentially confusing, but in the end the three lines of thought are complementary. Though few Christians today would argue in defense of prostitution, Paul's three lines of theological argument address us just as urgently as they did the Corinthians.

1. *The resurrection of the body.* This fundamental aspect of the Christian *kērygma* often gets lost in the popular piety of the church. Even though we recite the article of the Apostles' Creed that says, "I believe in the resurrection of the body," many Christians imagine their future hope in disembodied terms. Singing beloved gospel hymns like "I'll Fly Away," they expect their "souls" to "go to heaven" when they die. It hardly ever occurs to anyone that this is a major modification—indeed, a betrayal—of the New Testament's eschatological hope for God's redemption of the creation and of our bodies. (This issue will be discussed in much more detail in 1 Corinthians 15.) Paul regards the resurrection of the body as a crucial underpinning of Christian moral teaching. God has joined the spiritual and the physical, and they cannot be put asunder. Because "God raised the Lord and will also raise us by his power," we cannot act as though our actions in the body are of no moral significance. The resurrection reconfirms the Creator's love for the creation. Therefore, *the body matters.* To misuse the body is to hold the creator in contempt.

Christians today are probably less inclined than were Paul's Greek converts to slip into forms of dualism that denigrate the physical body. (If anything, we may be subject to the opposite error of idolizing the body and supposing that *only* the present physical world matters.) Nonetheless, we may need to remind ourselves and our hearers that our bodily actions stand under the eschatological judgment of God and that we should therefore use our bodies in ways that point towards the wholeness for which we hope in the resurrection. If we could learn to think of our bodies as bodies with a future, we might be more careful about what we do with them now. This would have important implications not only for sexual morality but also for other issues such as health care and ecological responsibility.

2. *The body as temple.* In a culture where there is no temple, no holy place that is reverenced as the singular dwelling place of God, it will be hard to recover the power of this Pauline metaphor. Nonetheless, it may be worth trying. Sex education in the church might begin by seeking to cultivate a deep awareness of the indwelling presence of God. An authentic reverence for the reality of the Holy Spirit's presence in our bodies might facilitate the recovery of the Bible's powerful categories of holiness and purity as meaningful norms for our sexual practices. Could the teaching of such reverence within the church help to overcome the growing cultural tendency to accept premarital and extramarital sexual relations as normal and inevitable? Whether or not such teaching proves effective is in one sense not our business. Our

task is to bear witness to the truth we are given and leave the results to the working of God's Spirit. Certainly the destructive forces arrayed against our teaching are no greater than those with which Paul had to contend in seeking to reshape the moral imagination of his Corinthian readers.

3. *The body is the Lord's.* This is the argument that most directly challenges us today. Once we confess that we are not our own, that we have been bought with a price, all talk of sexual autonomy becomes nonsense. We are not free to do anything we like, not free to invent our own standards, not free to behave as moral "free agents." We are bound to a relationship of obedient faithfulness to Christ.

It is striking that Paul's argument against extramarital sex in 1 Corinthians 6:12–20 never mentions the issue of infidelity to a spouse. Perhaps the specific fornicators he had in mind were not married, but another explanation seem likelier: he regards sexual promiscuity not primarily as an offense against any human relationship but, most fundamentally, as a sin against God. The union with a prostitute violates the believer's prior bond with Christ.

In Western culture today, by contrast, most discourse about issues of sexual and reproductive ethics is dominated by post-Enlightenment categories that sound eerily like a reprise of the Corinthian slogans: "rights," "freedom of choice," "self-determination," "autonomy." Even within the church, such language is rarely questioned by any of the factions into which our churches are divided. So, for example, the discussion of abortion becomes polarized into a debate over "the *right* to choose" versus "the *right* to life." How might our contemporary debates change if we would stop shouting such slogans for a while and listen to Paul? *Do you not know that you are not your own? For you were bought with a price; therefore glorify God in your body.* Such an approach would of course not settle questions about legislation in the secular world, but it might change the texture of debate within the church. The task of the preacher or teacher is to reframe the questions in ways more faithfully responsive to Paul's vision for the community. We need to learn anew how to talk about sexual issues—and other moral matters—as people who belong to the Lord, people whose moral decisions are shaped not by personal preference or expediency but by the desire to glorify God in our bodies.

With his appeal to the Corinthians to glorify God in their bodies, Paul concludes his call for community discipline (5:1—6:20). The first six chapters of the letter have built a theological foundation for the pastoral task that follows: Paul must now address questions that the Corinthians have posed in a letter to him.

Responses to Contested Issues in Corinth

1 CORINTHIANS 7:1—15:58

With the beginning of chapter 7, Paul makes a major structural transition in the letter, as he turns to address issues that have been raised explicitly by the Corinthians in a letter to him: "Now concerning the matters about which you wrote . . ." (v. 1a). Presumably, their letter was delivered to Paul in Ephesus by three representatives of the church: Stephanus, Fortunatus, and Achaicus (16:8, 17). Some of the content of the Corinthians' letter may be inferred from Paul's responses.

It is conventional to suppose that each time Paul uses the phrase "now concerning *x*," he is introducing a topic about which the Corinthians have asked him a question. If so, their letter raised the following issues:

> sex, marriage, and divorce (7:1)
> virgins (7:25)
> idol meat (8:1)
> spiritual gifts (12:1)
> the collection for the saints (16:1)
> Apollos's travel plans (16:12)

It is by no means certain, however, that so much weight can be placed on the simple expression "now concerning" (*peri de*); it is a standard phrase used by Paul and other writers of his time to introduce a new topic.

We can be certain that Paul is responding to the Corinthians' written concerns in chapter 7 (sex) and in chapters 8—10 (idol meat). Chapter 11, however, seems to introduce matters that were not posed directly by the Corinthians (see especially 11:18, where Paul again refers to what he has heard about them from other sources). When the phrase "now concerning" reappears in 12:1, this is perhaps a signal that he is returning (after some digression in chapter 11) to address their questions again, in which case chapters 12—14 (concerning spiritual gifts) also constitute an answer to some points in their letter. The way that Paul approaches the issue of resurrection of the dead in chapter 15, however, suggests that here he is once again reacting to reports about the Corinthians rather than

110

to direct queries from them. The two passages in chapter 16 are so cursory that it is hard to tell whether Paul is responding here to issues raised by the Corinthians, or whether he is summarily finishing up the list of matters that he himself wants to mention.

In any case, it is striking that Paul takes up the Corinthians' concerns only after writing the lengthy discussion of chapters 1—6, in which he calls for unity, reasserts his authority, forcefully scolds the community, and calls them to new standards of holiness and community discipline. Plainly, he is not content to allow the Corinthians' concerns to set the agenda. He addresses their questions only after carefully rebuilding the foundation upon which he believes answers must be based. This strategy allows him, as we shall see, to reframe the issues; he calls repeatedly for the Corinthian community to be re-socialized into a pattern shaped by the gospel of the cross and illuminated by the eschatological setting of the church between the cross and the final day of the Lord. Teachers and preachers may find Paul's example instructive: It is not necessarily wise to begin "where the people are." The teacher who does so may find it impossible to move the students to any other place. Of course, the students' questions must be engaged—as Paul's example also shows—but that engagement will be most fruitful if the groundwork of the gospel has first been laid out clearly.

7:1–40
Sex and Marriage
at the Turn of the Ages

Paul's discussion of sex and marriage in this chapter has been widely misunderstood in the history of the church, with tragic consequences. Therefore, the teacher or preacher working with this text may have to clear away many misconceptions. The view is widespread that Paul despised women and thought sex was dirty or defiling. In fact, as we shall see, this is a grossly inaccurate caricature of Paul's teaching. When we read this passage carefully, five crucial findings come into focus:

1. Paul is not writing a general treatise on marriage; rather, he is responding to a specific set of issues and questions posed in the Corinthians' letter to him.

2. The slogan "It is well for a man not to touch a woman" comes not from Paul himself but from the Corinthians.
3. There is no trace in this passage of contempt for women or of the idea that sexual intercourse within marriage is sinful.
4. Paul's teachings demonstrate a remarkable vision of mutuality between man and woman in the marriage relationship.
5. Paul's advice on the topic of sex and marriage is strongly conditioned by his belief that the day of the Lord is coming very soon.

These points will be demonstrated more fully in the discussion that follows.

In order to see how the discussion is structured, it will be useful to begin within an overall outline of chapter 7 before taking up each section in turn.

Counsel for Corinthians in various marital statuses (1–16)
  For the married: maintain sexual relations (1–7)
  For widowers and widows: stay unmarried (8–9)
  For Christian married couples: no divorce (10–11)
General rule: remain as you were when called (17–24)
  Analogy of circumcision/uncircumcision (18–19)
  Analogy of slavery/freedom (21–23)
Counsel for engaged couples (25–38)
  In view of the present necessity, stay as you are (25–28)
  Reasons for this advice (29–35)
    The form of this world is passing away (29–31)
    Freedom to serve the Lord without distraction (32–35)
    Freedom to marry or not, as they choose (36–38)
Reprise: Counsel for wives and widows (39–40)
  Woman bound to husband, but may remarry if he dies (39)
  More blessed to remain unmarried (40)

As this outline indicates, the consistent tendency of Paul's advice is to urge his readers to remain in whatever condition they find themselves. Those who are married should remain married and continue to fulfill all their marital obligations; those who are unmarried are encouraged to remain in that state. What this outline does not show, however, is the flexibility and openness of Paul's counsel. He continues to hold open a space for the Corinthians—particularly those who are not already married—to exercise their own discernment about how best to serve God, whether in the married or the unmarried state.

This is the one place in the letter where, hearing only one side of the conversation, we have to guess what the people on the other side of the conversation were actually saying and doing. Because we do not have that information (for example, who were the "virgins"?), many of Paul's comments are difficult to interpret. Nonetheless, the general direction of his advice is clear. It is not possible here to explain in detail all the exegetical decisions that lie behind the present exposition. Readers interested in the exegetical details are encouraged to consult more technical critical commentaries, especially Fee (266–357), whose analysis of the issues is particularly helpful.

1. Counsel for Corinthians in Various Marital Statuses

The first issue from the Corinthians' letter that Paul tackles is this: May Christians continue to consummate marriages, or is it more appropriate for people who have received the Holy Spirit to live celibate lives? We have already seen in chapter 6 that Paul frequently adopts an interactive style of argumentation, in which he quotes a slogan expressing the point of view of his readers and then rebuts or qualifies it (6:12–14, perhaps 6:18). This pattern is clearly evident in 7:1, as the NRSV translators have indicated: "Now concerning the things about which you wrote: 'It is well for a man not to touch a woman.'" The quoted material is probably a direct citation from the Corinthians' letter, or at least a pithy summary of one of its main points. Paul does not entirely reject this slogan, but he strongly qualifies its implications in the following verses. (For similar patterns of a quotation followed by Paul's rebuttal, see also 8:1 and 10:23.) Paul does think that a life of singleness or celibacy is a good thing (7:8–9, 27, 32–35, 40). Nonetheless, he disagrees strongly with some inferences that the Corinthians have drawn from this position.

For the married: maintain sexual relations (7:1–7)

The key to understanding this opening section of the chapter lies in the first two verses. In the Corinthian slogan, the expression, "to *touch* a woman" (7:1) is a common euphemism meaning "to have sexual intercourse with a woman." This expression is never used to mean "to marry," as the NIV misleadingly translates it. Likewise, the language in verse 2, "Let each man *have* his own wife and let each woman *have* her own husband" does not mean that those who are unmarried should find spouses; that in fact is the exact opposite of the advice that Paul gives to the unmarried in this chapter (vv. 8, 27, 38)! Instead, the verb "to have" in this context means—just as it can also in English—to enjoy

113

sexual possession of another person. (For example, this is the same Greek verb used in 5:1: literally, "for a man *to have* his father's wife.") What, then, does verse 2 mean? The text makes sense only when we recognize that Paul is speaking here not to the unmarried, but to the already married. He is telling married couples that they ought to continue to have sexual relations with one another. This interpretation is decisively confirmed when we read verses 3–4: Paul reiterates the point in unmistakable terms, insisting that each partner possesses the body of the other.

The logic of these opening verses, then, is as follows. It is all very well in principle to abstain from sexual intercourse, as the Corinthians have suggested, but Paul insists that couples who are already married should not try to renounce their sex life, because of the danger that one of the partners might be tempted outside the marriage into fornication (v. 2).

All this may seem rather puzzling to the modern reader. Is this advice really necessary? Do married couples need to be told to keep having sexual intercourse? Do the Corinthians need to write a letter to Paul to clarify this issue? The answer to these questions, in fact, is yes. Some of the Corinthians may very well have concluded that sexuality was part of a "fleshly" unspiritual existence and that persons in Christ ought to renounce such base physical pleasures in order to "be holy in body and spirit" (cf. 7:34).

This sort of asceticism was "in the air" in ancient Mediterranean culture. The Stoic and Cynic philosophical schools—whose thought, as we have seen, significantly influenced the Corinthians—debated whether a philosopher should marry or whether the unmarried state was more conducive to the pursuit of wisdom. In Greek popular religion, virginity and sexual purity were often associated with those set aside for the service of the gods, particularly for women who were prophets—the priestess of the oracle at Delphi, for example. In Paul's day, even Judaism, which classically had celebrated procreation as the duty of everyone, developed ascetic movements such as the Essenes and the Therapeutae about whom Philo of Alexandria wrote glowingly. Difficult as it may be for many at the end of the twentieth century to appreciate, sexual abstinence was widely viewed as a means to personal wholeness and religious power.

At the same time, there were ascetic impulses afoot within early Christianity itself. How were the Corinthians to interpret the baptismal proclamation, which they probably would have learned from Paul, that in Christ "there is no longer male and female" (Gal. 3:28)? If tradition about the teaching of Jesus were circulating in their church,

114

would they have heard that Jesus had said, "Those who belong to this age marry and are given in marriage; but those who are considered worthy of a place in that age and in the resurrection from the dead neither marry nor are given in marriage . . . they are like angels" (Luke 20:34–35, 36)? And what conclusion were they to draw from the fact that Paul himself—their founding apostle—had been conspicuously unmarried (cf. 1 Cor. 7:8; 9:5)? We must remember that the Corinthians had no past Christian tradition to look to for guidelines about how to interpret such things; they were inventing the Christian life as they went, trying to work out the implications of the gospel for refashioning their lives.

We know from other early Christian writings that some groups within the church did seek to practice radical forms of asceticism. In Colossians 2:20–23 we find Paul opposing false teachers who say "Do not handle [the same verb translated as *touch* in 1 Cor. 7:1], do not taste, do not touch." Such rules, he insists, "have indeed an appearance of wisdom (*sophia*) in promoting self-imposed piety, humility, and severe treatment of the body, but they are of no value in checking self-indulgence." Similarly, 1 Timothy 4:3 polemicizes against those who "forbid marriage and demand abstinence from foods."

Under these circumstances, and under the influence of cultural forces that associated holiness and wisdom with celibacy, it is hardly surprising that some of the Corinthians might have decided that the ordinary married life was incompatible with their new spiritual identity in Christ. This is the situation that seems to lie behind 1 Corinthians 7. Some of the members of the Corinthian church had decided that celibacy was necessary; even some of those who were married were attempting to renounce sex. Some interpreters of 1 Corinthians have suggested that sexual abstinence might have been especially appealing to some of the women in the community, who were functioning as prophets in the church and finding a new sphere of power and freedom outside the traditional restraints of domestic life. Abstinence from sexual intercourse also would give women freedom from pregnancy and the responsibilities of caring for children. At the same time, however, the formulation of the Corinthian slogan (v. 1b: "It is well for *a man* not to touch a woman") suggests that it was the *men* in the community who were urging the renunciation of sexual relations. Probably the call to asceticism found a sympathetic hearing among some members of both sexes in the Corinthian church.

In any case, this development would have proven difficult for some members of the church who suddenly found themselves deprived of sexual companionship. They found their spouses withdrawing

115

from the physical relationship or perhaps even separating from the marriage altogether (cf. 7:10–11) in the interests of holiness. Perhaps this is part of the reason that some of the Corinthian Christians were going to prostitutes (6:15–16).

Against this background, Paul's response to the Corinthians in 1 Corinthians 7:1–7 comes with clarity and force: No, he says, those who are married must not declare a moratorium on sexual relations! "The husband should give to his wife her conjugal rights, and likewise the wife to her husband" (v. 3). The first reason for this was already suggested in verse 2: "because of cases of sexual immorality." The spouse who "deprives" his or her partner of sexual intimacy may be preparing the conditions for Satan to tempt the partner into *porneia* because of the difficulty of self-control (cf. v. 5). And, as Paul has already explained at length, *porneia* is damaging to the community of faith as a whole.

But Paul now goes on in verse 4 to offer a second reason more profoundly related to the character of marriage itself: "For the wife does not have authority over her own body, but the husband does." This was a commonplace view in the ancient world. Paul's next sentence, however, must have struck many first-century hearers as extraordinary: "likewise, the husband does not have authority over his own body, but the wife does." Here Paul articulates a view of marriage that stands as a challenge to views ancient and modern alike. The marriage partners are neither placed in a hierarchical relation with one over the other nor set apart as autonomous units each doing what he or she pleases. Instead, the relationship of marriage is one of *mutual submission*, each partner having authority over the other. Regrettably, Paul does not pause to develop the wider implications of this remarkable idea. His immediate concern is focused on the problem at Corinth: in marriage, he insists, there is to be no unilateral withdrawal—nor even a mutually negotiated withdrawal!—from regular sexual intercourse.

In verse 5, however, he does offer one concession to the Corinthians' desire to seek special spiritual disciplines. Temporary short-term abstinence is permissible *if* it is undertaken "by agreement" (the Greek *ek symphōnou* means literally "with a common voice"—notice the etymological root of the English word "symphony") of husband and wife together. The purpose of such an arrangement is to allow the partners to devote themselves to prayer, but Paul is insistent that they must come together again after the fixed time, in order to avoid the danger of temptation. This allowance for temporary abstinence is the "concession" to which Paul refers in verse 6, though he makes it clear that he is not at all commanding such a practice.

In light of these observations, we can see how disastrously misinterpreted this passage has been by much of the Christian tradition. The time-honored reading of this text sees Paul as grudgingly permitting marriage itself as a distasteful concession to the lusts of the flesh. In fact, however, it is some of the Corinthians who are seeking to renounce marriage and sexual intercourse, and it is Paul who insists in a robustly realistic way that sexual relations within marriage are normal and necessary.

To be sure, Paul himself is unmarried and—by his own account—in control of his own sexual impulses, so that he does not need the physical satisfaction of marriage. Even though he says in verse 7 that he wants everyone to be "as I myself am," he simultaneously recognizes that different people have different gifts and that not everyone is called by God to celibacy. This statement may imply that marriage itself is also a gift (*charisma*) from God, though Paul does not say so explicitly.

In light of these exegetical observations, we can clarify the meaning of the passage by constructing a paraphrase, filling in some of the silent assumptions and gaps in the conversation. The words in italics are supplied as explanatory expansions to show how Paul's advice seeks to address the particular issues raised by the Corinthians.

> (1) Now I will respond to the matters about which you wrote. *You propose that, for the sake of holiness and purity, married couples should abstain from sexual intercourse. As you say,* "It is a fine thing for a man not to touch a woman." (2) But—*since that is unrealistic*—let each husband have sexual intercourse with his own wife, and let each wife have sexual intercourse with her own husband. (3) *Marriage creates a mutual obligation for a couple to satisfy one another's needs; therefore,* let the husband give the wife what he owes her, and likewise let the wife give what she owes to her husband. (4) For the wife does not rule her own body; the husband does. Likewise, the husband does not rule his own body; the wife does. (5) Do not deprive one another, unless you decide—in harmony with one another—to abstain from intercourse for a time so that *both of* you can devote yourselves to prayer. But *(when the time is up)* come together again, so that Satan will not be able to tempt you. (6) I am not commanding this *practice of temporary abstinence*; rather, I am saying this as a concession *to your proposal [see v. 1, above].* (7) I wish that everyone could be *in control of sexual desire* like me. *Obviously, however, that is not the case.* But each person has his or her own gift (*charisma*) from God: *if not celibacy, then something else,* one in one way and another in some other way.

When the passage is read in this way, the true emphases of Paul's pastoral advice are brought more clearly into view.

One question must be raised about this historical reconstruction, however: How is this account of the situation related to the problems addressed in chapters 5 and 6, where the Corinthians' problem seems to be an excess of sexual free expression rather than a withdrawal into asceticism? Two mutually reinforcing answers may be given.

First, we know already from the letter that the Corinthian community was divided into factions (1:10–17; 3:1–4). If the debate over abstention from certain foods was a cause of division in the community, as we learn in chapters 8—10 it was, it is not unreasonable to suppose that differences over sexual practices might also have been among the causes of division, though Paul says nothing in 1 Corinthians 7 to indicate this explicitly. This might well explain, however, why the Corinthians had raised this issue prominently in their letter. Paul's teaching in chapters 5—7 would, then, address different factions sequentially: first those who believe themselves free to do whatever they want with their bodies, then those who believe that their bodies should be kept from all sexual contact. In response to both groups, Paul offers a single consistent position: celibacy is good, sex within marriage is good, and *porneia* is a disaster for the community. By affirming the rightness and necessity of sexual love in marriage—and only there— Paul rejects the extreme positions on both sides.

Second, it is a sad truth of human nature that hyperspirituality can often lead, paradoxically, to a backlash of fleshly indulgence. This truth is impressed upon us each time we see another headline about a television evangelist or church leader whose sexual misadventures have been exposed to the light—and all of us have seen more than enough such headlines in recent years to make us grieve deeply. Paul's directives in 1 Corinthians 7:1–7 take the measure of this sober reality. There is an inner spiritual connection between these apparently antithetical claims and behaviors at Corinth. Those who say "I am free to do anything" and those who say "I must abstain from everything" are equally setting themselves outside their God-given creaturely limitations. The attempt to escape our finitude—whether one way or the other—is bound to fail and send us crashing down. That is why Paul gives simple earthy counsel; husbands and wives should cling together and fulfill one another's needs.

For widowers and widows: stay unmarried (7:8–9)

Next, Paul addresses a different group within the community: "the unmarried and the widows." The word "unmarried" (*agamoi*) is used here to refer specifically to widowers, not in a generic fashion to include all those who are not married. (Paul's advice to other classes of non-married persons—the divorced and the not-yet-married—is given separately in vv. 11 and 25–38). Thus, this counsel, like most of the

118

other directives in the chapter, is carefully balanced and directed equally to men and women: in this case, men and women who have lost a spouse to death. Apparently Paul classes himself within this group, telling them that it is well for them to remain "as I am," i.e., unmarried. This is the only hint in Paul's letters that he might once have been married—as would have been normal, indeed virtually mandatory, for a Jewish man of his time who was devoted to the study of Torah (Acts 22:3; Gal. 1:14; Phil. 3:4–6; cf. the later rabbinic teaching that "He who is twenty years old and not yet married spends all of his days in sin" [*b. Qidd.* 29b]). Paul's marital history and status, whatever it may have been, was no doubt known to the Corinthians; consequently, he need offer no further explanation here. His purpose is simply to advise widows and widowers to remain as they are (note the contrast to 1 Tim. 5:14).

This counsel is accompanied, however, by an important qualifier urging them to seek remarriage "if they are not practicing self-control." Here again the specter of *porneia* looms in the background. Paul is concerned that widowers or widows might find themselves lured into illicit sexual activity (perhaps with prostitutes or in extramarital affairs). Those who feel the compulsion of sexual desire should marry, "for it is better to marry than to burn." Almost all modern translations correctly interpret the last verb to refer to the "burning" of sexual passion, rather than the flames of God's judgment; for example, in NRSV, "It is better to marry than to be aflame with passion." This is another statement that is often read as though Paul were damning marriage with faint praise. It must be kept in mind here, however, that Paul is specifically addressing the widowed, not everyone, and that his teaching on this question is far more flexible and permissive than the position of the anti-sex faction at Corinth, who were undoubtedly insisting that it was forbidden for the widowed to remarry.

For Christian married couples: no divorce (7:10–11)

Paul now turns his attention back to married couples within the church. If continuing sexual relations are mandatory for Christian husbands and wives, might some of them seek an escape route into celibacy by means of divorce? Had this perhaps already been occurring in Corinth? Or had the issue of divorce arisen for other, more ordinary, reasons? Whether prompted by a concrete instance or not, Paul articulates a general norm in verses 10–11: Christian wives and husbands should not divorce one another.

In contrast to the counsel of verses 8–9, this teaching is not merely advice: it is commanded by the Lord himself. This is one of the very

119

few places that Paul appeals explicitly to a teaching of Jesus in support of a directive to his churches (see also 9:14 and perhaps 1 Thess. 4:15–17). Although the wording here is different from that found in the Gospels, Paul is certainly alluding to the tradition that Jesus had forbidden divorce (Mark 10:2–12; Matt. 5:31–32; Matt. 19:3–12; Luke 16:18), an unusual stance more stringent than anything found either in Judaism or in Greco-Roman culture. In Judaism, only the husband had the prerogative of divorce, but in the Roman world women also had the right to initiate divorce. The fact that Paul uses different verbs to describe the action of the wife ("separate") and the husband ("divorce") probably reflects his Jewish background and sensibilities, but there is no difference in the legal or practical effect of the action: the modern distinction between "separation" and "divorce" is not in view here, and Paul's formulation in verse 13 does recognize the woman's legal right to divorce her husband—though he is urging Christian women not to exercise it.

Interestingly, Paul not only repeats the teaching of Jesus but also reckons with the possibility that some within the community may not obey it. In verse 11a, therefore, he adds his own proviso to the Lord's commandment: If the wife does terminate the marriage, she is to remain single (*agamos*) unless she is reconciled to her husband. Paul does not explicitly state the reciprocal commandment (that a husband who divorces his wife must remain single or be reconciled to his wife), but in view of the symmetry of Paul's teachings for men and women throughout the chapter, this norm should be assumed as implicit in Paul's directive. The reasoning behind this ruling is probably the same as the reason articulated in Mark 10:11–12: divorcing one spouse to marry another is nothing other than a legalized form of adultery. Paul says nothing here, however, about whether the spouse who has been abandoned is free to remarry. The major concern of his pastoral counsel is to prevent either partner from *initiating* divorce.

Perhaps surprisingly, Paul does not call upon the community to expel or discipline persons who go against this teaching of the Lord by divorcing their partners. Presumably, they are allowed remain in the community, with the proviso that they are not to marry again.

For Christians married to unbelievers: stay in the marriage (7:12–16)

Next Paul must confront an issue not envisioned by the teaching of Jesus: mixed marriages in which a believer is married to an unbeliever. Jesus was addressing a Jewish audience, and his prohibition of divorce assumed that both husband and wife were part of the covenant

120

people of God. Paul's Gentile mission, however, had created a very different set of circumstances. What about those situations in which one partner in a marriage hears the gospel and becomes a convert to the new faith, while the other remains an unbeliever (*apistos*)? Can such a marriage continue? Surely, some of the Corinthians must have argued, in such a marriage the believer is defiled by sexual contact with the pagan spouse. Surely a Christian must break off intimate attachment with an unbeliever who lives in the realm of darkness and lawlessness. (For a powerful expression of the theology behind such sentiments, see the odd fragment in 2 Cor. 6:14—7:1).

Paul's response to this problem is bold and surprising in several ways. First, speaking on his own authority ("I say—I and not the Lord"), he offers an amendment to Jesus' unconditional prohibition of divorce. (Paul shows no sign of knowing the Matthean exception clause that permits divorce in cases of *porneia* [Matt. 5:32; 19:9]; that seems to have been a later adaptation of the tradition.) Paul makes a point of distinguishing his own ruling—one is tempted to say his own *halakah*—from Jesus' commandment, but nonetheless offers it for the guidance of the Corinthians. The believer should stay with the unbelieving spouse as long as the unbeliever is willing to maintain the marriage, but if the unbeliever desires to terminate the marriage, the believer is no longer bound to the marriage commitment. Once again Paul is careful to state this ruling in a way that applies symmetrically to men and women in the church. The striking thing here is the way in which Paul exercises the freedom to adapt the Lord's teaching to new circumstances.

In taking this stance, Paul rejects the assumption—an assumption congenial to his own pharisaic background—that the pure person is defiled by contact with the unclean. Instead, he argues, "the unbelieving husband is made holy through his wife, and the unbelieving wife is made holy through her husband." Holiness is, as it were, contagious. This extraordinary affirmation declares the power of God to work through the believer to claim and transform the spouse and children (v. 14). The logic here is exactly the reverse of the logic of defilement that Paul has used earlier in the argument (union with a prostitute defiles Christ, 6:15–17; bad leaven leavens the whole lump of dough, 5:6). Here, Paul reverses the metaphor and asserts that, within the family at least, holiness is more powerful than impurity; compare this to Romans 11:16: "If the part of the dough offered as first fruits is holy, then the whole batch is holy."

The somewhat ambiguous final sentence of this unit (1 Cor. 7:16) is probably to be understood as encouragement to the believing partner to stay in the marriage even if there is no evidence of the unbeliever's receptiveness to the gospel. As one whose own life had undergone a dramatic reversal—from persecutor of the church to apostle—Paul knows that we should never underestimate the power of God's grace to redeem and transform even the unlikeliest people (cf. 15:8–11).

The situation that Paul addresses here must have arisen with some frequency in Corinth and elsewhere in the early church. The spouse who joined the Christian movement would often be perceived as having joined a bizarre sect of people venerating a crucified criminal. It is not hard to imagine that many pagan spouses might have found their Christian spouses' new religious practices and companions to be embarrassing, or even intolerable. In such cases, Paul says, let the unbeliever go if he or she wishes, for "it is to peace that God has called you" (7:15b). The believer's fundamental loyalty is to the new family of God. At the same time, Paul's openness to maintaining mixed marriages must have seemed like a puzzling compromise to those at Corinth who were pressing the community to adopt radical ascetic standards. Paul is walking on a tightrope here, maintaining a delicate balance between the radically new character of the community of faith and its continuing existence within the sphere of worldly commitments. Marriage is one of those commitments that remains in force, and it is to be seen not merely as a burdensome obligation but as a sphere in which God's holiness and transforming power may operate. Thus, Paul's view of marriage, even marriage to an unbeliever, is hope-filled.

General Rule: Remain as You Were When Called (7:17–24)

Paul now pauses to reflect more generally on the guiding principle behind his advice on marriage. In this short section, he repeats three times the maxim that believers should remain in the condition in which they were called—their position in life at the time they first accepted the preaching of the good news about Christ. The section has the structure of a club sandwich: in between the three-layered repetition of the maxim (vv. 17, 20, 24), he inserts two illustrative analogies, implicitly comparing the married/unmarried distinction to the circumcised/uncircumcised (vv. 18–19) and slave/free distinctions (vv. 21–23). All these distinctions, he declares, are unimportant before God.

There is no indication that circumcision and slavery were contested issues at Corinth. Paul is merely using these as parallel illustrations to support his counsel that the Corinthians should not seek to change their marital status. It is surely more than coincidental that

122

these two illustrations, combined with the surrounding discussion of sex in the Christian life, parallel precisely the three elements in Paul's baptismal catechesis:

> As many of you were baptized into Christ have clothed
> yourselves with Christ.
> There is no longer Jew or Greek   [cf. 1 Cor. 7:18–19]
> there is no longer slave or free,   [cf. 1 Cor. 7:21–23]
> there is no longer male and female;   [cf. the rest of 1 Cor. 7]
> for all of you are one in Christ Jesus.
>   (Gal. 3:27–28)

These binary polarities provide the basic categories for Paul's perception of the human condition, but even such basic markers of human identity have been rendered meaningless in light of the gospel. First Corinthians 7 can be read, therefore, as Paul's own explication of Galatians 3:28. Some of the Corinthians thought that "no male and female" obliged them to give up sex; to the contrary, Paul declares that the gospel is meant to set us free from anxiety about such distinctions and to call us to find our identity in Christ rather than in gender. Marriage, like ethnicity and social status, belongs now to the category of *adiaphora*: matters that fundamentally make no difference. On this basis, Paul articulates a very simple rule: Do not try to change your position.

In view of Paul's strong proclamation elsewhere of the world-transforming power of the gospel (cf. 2 Cor. 5:16–21), this may seem like a disappointingly conservative account of the social implications of the new life in Christ. We must remember, however, that Paul writes under the conviction that "the present form of this world is passing away" (1 Cor. 7:31b). To scramble for new social positions is like rearranging the deck chairs on the *Titanic*: it is a pointless exercise that only generates anxiety. His immediate pastoral concern is to set his readers free for wholehearted service of God wherever they find themselves located in the present time. The maxim "Let each of you remain in the condition in which you were called" means, in effect, "Bloom where you are planted; don't worry about trying to become something you are not." When we consider that Paul's immediate application of this advice to the Corinthian situation was to dissuade the Corinthians from abandoning their marital commitments, we can see that there may be more wisdom in such counsel than in utopian schemes for breaking free from human limitations. At the same time, the application of Paul's maxim requires discernment and the ability to know when exceptions are appropriate, as his discussion throughout this chapter indicates.

123

Each of Paul's two illustrative analogies calls for brief comment.

Paul's conviction that "circumcision is nothing, and uncircumcision is nothing" (v. 19) would have shocked his Jewish contemporaries, but it was integral to his vision for the church. He saw the church as a community that transcended ethnic boundaries in order to unite Jew and Gentile as one new people serving one God. More shocking still, however, is the punchline of Paul's declaration: What matters is neither circumcision nor uncircumcision; what matters is "obeying the commandments of God" (v. 19). But circumcision *is* one of the commandments of God (Gen. 17:9–14)! If obeying the commandments is crucial, how can circumcision be unimportant? Since the present argument is not dealing with the problem of Jewish identity, Paul offers no explanation here. His statement presupposes that the Law is to be read anew through a different hermeneutical lens, since Christ is the *telos* of the Law. (These ideas are more fully developed in Romans, especially Rom. 2:25–29; 8:1–4; 10:1–13; 13:8–10.) The Gentile Corinthians, perhaps already instructed about such matters by Paul, would have acknowledged the force of this argument. Coming to be a member of Christ's people had not required them to change their ethnic status by becoming Jewish proselytes. Similarly, Paul suggests, there is no reason for them to change their marital status.

The second illustration (vv. 21–23) will strike many readers as far more problematical, because it urges Christian slaves to remain contentedly in their slave status. This is the point where the "conservatism" of Paul's teaching most clearly seems to play into the hands of oppressive social forces. Before rushing to judgment, however, we must consider what is known about ancient slavery and observe how Paul is using the illustration in his argument. First, slavery in the ancient Greco-Roman world was a pervasive institution, but it was not invariably perceived as oppressive. American readers instinctively think of slavery as it was practiced in the antebellum South, but the ancient reality was more complicated. Dale Martin's book *Slavery as Salvation* has shown that slavery provided for many people not only economic security, but also upward social mobility. To be the slave of a powerful master could be an honorable station, and slaves were sometimes highly educated and entrusted with major administrative responsibility. (See the discussion of 4:1–5, above.) That is why "slave of Christ" (7:22) could be an honorable designation, suggesting a position of some authority. Of course, some slaves were treated badly, and many sought emancipation when possible, sometimes through saving up money to buy their way out of slavery. The emancipated slave was still not a freeborn citizen, but a "freedman" (*apeleutheros*), who often remained attached to the service of his or her former master. Many of the early

Christian converts came from these lower ranks of society, being either slaves or former slaves. Indeed, as Wayne Meeks has suggested in *The First Urban Christians*, the Christian movement may have appealed especially to people of low social status who were nonetheless relatively well-educated or economically successful.

Against this background, let us observe how Paul is using this language rhetorically. His first move is to say that those who were slaves when called by God should not "be concerned about it." The explanation for this is given in 7:22–23 in a way that recalls the status reversal proclaimed in 1:26–29. Paul repeats the "bought with a price" metaphor (7:23) that he had used already in 6:20: Through his death Christ has paid the price to redeem those whom he has called. The result of this transaction is a reversal of relative status within Christ's household. The slave becomes "a freed person [*apeleutheros*] belonging to the Lord," whereas the one who was free (*eleutheros*) when called becomes a "slave of Christ" (v. 22); thus, the former slave is accorded the higher rank. All, regardless of wordly social status, are now under the authority of Christ. Thus, Paul insists that those who have been "bought" out of slavery by Christ's death should not "become slaves of human masters." He may intend in part a literal sense here ("Do not change your status by selling yourself into slavery"), but he certainly means also that they should live their lives, whatever their outward station, as people devoted to the service of Christ.

Where such language is deployed, the symbolic world of the ancient slave system has been dramatically destabilized. Paul expected the sociopolitical order of his day to be swept away in the immediate future by God's eschatological judgment. When that did not occur, however, the metaphorical reversals of the present passage could only serve to undermine the system from within and to prepare the way for the withering away of slavery as a social institution in later Christian civilization.

This brings us, however, up against the one sentence in this passage that we have so far not confronted. The traditional interpretation of 7:21b is—surprisingly—represented in the NRSV translation: "Even if you can gain your freedom, make use of your present condition [slavery] now more than ever." The translation of this sentence is a difficult problem, but for many reasons, the interpretation of the RSV, NIV, NEB, JB, and NRSV footnote is to be preferred: "Were you a slave when you were called? Do not let that trouble you; but if a chance of liberty should come, take it" (NEB). This reading fits the pattern we have already seen throughout the chapter, in which Paul first tells the Corinthians to remain as they are but then allows exceptions for various reasons

125

(cf. vv. 8–9, 10–11, 12–15, 26–28). The exception here is, of course, the slave's opportunity to gain freedom. Paul's point is not to insist that people *must* remain in their present status, even to the extent of refusing emancipation (such a refusal would have been legally impossible, in any case); rather, his point—to say it one more time—is to reassure his readers that they should not be troubled about their present social location and that they should focus their attention on serving God, wherever they stand in the social order.

The purpose of all this, let us remember, is to function as an analogy in support of Paul's argument that the married should not abandon their marriages and that the unmarried should not necessarily be urgently seeking partners. For many readers at the end of the twentieth century, the analogy may be more opaque and troubling than the point it is supposed to explain, but presumably Paul's original audience in Corinth would have found it relatively clear and reassuring. Regardless of our evaluation of this particular argument, we can understand Paul's basic advice: relax and "remain with God" (7:24) wherever you find yourself.

Counsel for Engaged Couples: Remain as You Are (7:25–38)

In 7:25, Paul takes up another point from the Corinthian letter: "Now concerning virgins." It is notoriously difficult to determine from Paul's response exactly who the people were that the Corinthians designated as virgins, and what question the Corinthian letter may have posed about them. The following interpretation, which is supported by all major modern translations except JB, seems to make the best sense of the evidence: the virgins are young women who are betrothed but not yet married to men in the church. The question raised by the Corinthians is whether young people in this situation may go ahead and marry or whether as Christians they are now obliged to remain unmarried. Paul's answer to this question is completely consistent with the pattern we have seen in all the other cases in this chapter: it is better for them to remain as they are (in this case, unmarried), but if they choose to marry, that is no sin. The conclusion of the unit (v. 38) sums up Paul's position nicely: "He who marries his fiancée [literally, "virgin"] does well; and he who refrains from marriage does better." The decision is left to the persons involved, with some encouragement from the apostle to stay unmarried if they are able to choose that course freely and decisively (v. 37). (Interestingly, in vv. 36–38 Paul discusses the problem exclusively from the male point of view, and the decision of whether to marry is presented as the man's unilateral decision. This is one place where the careful symmetry of his treatment breaks down.)

Many of the traditional complications for interpreting this passage are created when 7:2 is misread as a command from Paul to the unmarried, because his advice there would then seem to contradict what he says in verses 26–27 and 36–38. When verses 1–7 are understood as directed to married couples, as in the commentary above, the difficulty is resolved. We see that Paul first begins to address those who have not yet been married only in verse 25.

For our purposes, though, the interesting thing about this passage is not so much Paul's particular advice, which by this time should be predictable, but the reasons that he gives for it. Why should the unmarried remain unmarried? Paul offers two interrelated reasons: the present order of the world is going to pass away in the very near future, and marriage presents many distractions that may hinder service to the Lord. Let us consider each of these reasons in turn.

First, "the appointed time has grown short" (v. 29a). Paul expects the return of the Lord and the judgment of the world within the very near future. As he says in Romans 13:11–12, "Salvation is nearer to us now than when we became believers; the night is far gone, the day is near." This powerful apocalyptic expectation should shape the thought and action of believers in decisive ways. Because the time is foreshortened, ordinary temporal matters dwindle in significance or—to speak more precisely—assume the significance that is properly theirs in the light of God's eschatological judgment. That is why Christians should live as if the end were at hand (vv. 29b–31a), not investing themselves inappropriately in issues and affairs that belong to the old age. When Paul says "let even those who have wives be as though they had none" (v. 29), he cannot be telling married Christians to renounce sex, for he has explicitly given the opposite advice in verses 1–7; rather, he means that they should live out their marriages with a watchful awareness that the present order of things is not ultimate. Similarly, Paul cannot be telling the Corinthians not to mourn and rejoice (v. 30ab; cf. Rom. 12:15; 1 Cor. 12:26); rather, he means that even in the midst of mourning and rejoicing they must recognize that the day is coming when God will wipe away all tears and joy will be complete. And "when the complete comes, the partial will come to an end" (13:10). The same logic applies to possessions and financial transactions (vv. 30c–31a). Christians should live as people who know that all these things have at best penultimate significance; knowing that, we can take whatever may

127

come with equanimity. (For a late but interesting parallel to this passage, see 2 Esdras 16:40–48).

Thus, even though these phrases sound like a recommendation of Stoic apathy, Paul's reasoning is very different from that of the Stoics. The Stoics sought to cultivate an imperious detachment from all things, based on internal strength of character and on the conviction that all events are ordered by providence. Paul's teaching of detachment is based instead on the conviction that the future is impinging upon the present; consequently, "the present form of this world is passing away" (v. 31b). Under such circumstances, it simply looks illogical to undertake long-term commitments such as marriage.

At the same time, the unfolding eschatological scenario may impose particular hardships on the people of God. Paul's reference to "the present crisis" (v. 26) may point to the conventional apocalyptic idea that suffering will come upon the elect in the last times (cf. Mark 13:3–23 and parallels; see below, however, for further discussion of this phrase). Paul seems to believe that Christians will be better prepared to face these trials if they are single rather than married. (It is striking that neither here nor anywhere else does Paul mention children as the fruit of marriage or as a possible hindrance during a time of eschatological trial; however, cf. Mark 13:17.)

These thoughts lead to the second reason that Paul offers for single people to remain unmarried: "those who marry will experience distress in the flesh, and I would spare you that" (v. 28b). What Paul has in mind here is not made explicit: Pain in childbearing for the woman? The cares and sorrows of raising a family? One senses that Paul is speaking here from some sad personal experience, but the text offers us no information about what he means. It is clear, however, that he thinks marriage will bring complications and responsibilities that will prevent believers from serving the Lord without distraction (*aperispastōs*). At best, marriage will produce divided interests, because the married Christian (rightly) must consider how to please the spouse rather than concentrating singlemindedly on pleasing God (vv. 32–35). Thus, Paul tells his readers, his advice is not designed "to keep [them] on a tight rein" (NEB, literally "to throw a noose upon you") but to set them free for unhindered service to God. This argument bears a striking similarity to a passage in which Epictetus argues that the Cynic philosopher should avoid marriage:

128

But in such an order of things as the present, which is like that of a battle-field, it is a question, perhaps, if the Cynic ought not to be free from distraction [*aperispaston*], wholly devoted to the service of God, free to go about among men, not tied down by the private duties of men, nor involved in relationships which he cannot violate and still maintain his role as a good and excellent man, whereas, on the other hand, if he observes them, he will destroy the scout and messenger of the gods, that he is.

(Diss. 3.22.69)

Paul's thinking runs parallel to what we see in Epictetus. The potential danger of marriage is that it will hinder the Christian's singleminded devotion to the mission of the church, which Paul here calls "the affairs of the Lord." It is this concern about *freedom for mission* that motivates Paul's hesitation about the advisability of marriage.

In light of this point, we may reconsider the meaning of v. 26: "I think that, in view of *the present necessity*, it is well for you to remain as you are" (author's translation). The italicized phrase is usually understood to refer to the eschatological sufferings that Paul expects to come upon the church. Another meaning, however, fits the context better. The translation "impending crisis" (NRSV) is simply wrong: the participle *enestōsan* refers to present, not future, events (cf. 3:22, where the same word refers to "things present" *in contrast to* "things to come"). The more difficult question concerns the meaning of the noun *anagkē*. This is usually interpreted to refer to some sort of suffering or (as in NRSV) "crisis." The ordinary meaning of the word, however, is "necessity" or "urgency." An illuminating illustration is given by Paul's use of the same word just a few paragraphs later: "[N]ecessity [*anagkē*] is laid upon me; yea, woe is unto me if I do not preach the gospel!" (9:16, KJV). In light of this usage, it seems probable that the "present necessity" to which he refers in 7:26 is the urgent imperative of proclaiming the gospel and doing the work of the Lord in the short time that remains. This interpretation links verse 26 with verses 32–35 and explains more clearly why Paul regards celibacy as preferable to marriage: It frees the time and attention and energy of believers for the crucial work that is to be done in the precious short time before the *parousia*.

Reprise: Counsel for Wives and Widows (7:39–40)

The brief final section adds nothing substantively new to the counsel that Paul has already given. It merely reiterates some of the things he has previously said, with particular application to the situation of the wife. She is "bound as long as her husband lives": in other words, no divorce (cf. vv. 10–11). She may remarry after his death if she wishes, but Paul thinks she is "more blessed" if she chooses to follow Paul's maxim of remaining as she is (cf. vv. 8–9). The fact that Paul's closing summary focuses on this issue suggests that the Corinthians' letter may have explicitly targeted the problem of remarriage for widows.

The final sentence of the chapter is intriguing. How are we to read its tone? Recognizing that Paul chides the Corinthians throughout much of the letter for prideful claims about their special knowledge and possession of the Spirit, one wonders whether there is a little sting in this pronouncement: "[Oh, you think that your opinions about sex are given to you by the Spirit? Well,] I think that I *too* have the Spirit of God." Through much of this chapter, Paul has avoided confrontational rhetoric, but he ends his treatment of the Corinthian questions about sex and marriage with a pointed reminder that, if they are really interested in being guided by the Spirit, they would do well to listen to his advice.

REFLECTIONS FOR TEACHERS AND PREACHERS

For the church today issues of sex, marriage, and divorce top the list of controversial problems. Precisely because Paul's response to the Corinthians reframes these issues in categories that appear strange to us, we have much to learn as we ponder his counsel. Numerous books could be (and have been) written on the themes of this chapter, but we must confine ourselves here to a brief list of reflections on the theological and ethical issues raised by our reading of 1 Corinthians 7.

1. *The tone and texture of normative reflection.* In contrast to other places where he makes unequivocal pronouncements (e.g., 5:3–5; 6:1–8), here Paul moves much more cautiously. He carefully distinguishes his own teachings and opinions from the command of the Lord and repeatedly invites the Corinthians to join him in the task of moral discernment. What does it mean for us to acknowledge as Scripture a text that says, "I have no command of the Lord, but I give my opinion as one who by the Lord's mercy is trustworthy" (7:25)? Paul's way of presenting his advice encourages the Corinthians to weigh it seriously but to make their own decision, entering with him into the process of discerning God's will. He offers them not a packaged pronouncement, but an invitation to reflection. On some issues where he believes the will of God to be unambiguous, he issues clear directives (vv. 2–4, 10–11, 39a), but on many other issues throughout the chapter he leaves room for the church to exercise judgment and for individuals to discern their own calling. Thus, he models a welcome alternative to much contemporary debate in the church, which often seems to be characterized by strident dogmatism on one side and shrugging relativism on the other. Paul's ethical reflection in this chapter is firm but open-textured.

2. *Mutual submission in marriage.* As we observed in verses 3–4, Paul offers a paradigm-shattering vision of marriage as a relationship in which the partners are bonded together in submission to one another, each committed to meet the other's needs. In the ancient world, this vision posed a challenge to the prevalent patriachal picture of the husband as master of the wife; in our world, it poses a challenge to the prevalent picture of the sexual autonomy of each individual. Any congregation that begins to reflect seriously on the implications of this Pauline model for marriage will find themselves forced to reevaluate many of their assumptions and habits. In our time, no less than in first-century Corinth, the church has unthinkingly absorbed many assumptions about sex and marriage that are simply "in the air" in our culture—disseminated in our case through television, movies, magazines, and self-help books. Grappling seriously with Paul's alternative vision may help us begin to identify the false images of sex and marriage that surround us.

3. *The purpose of sexual intercourse in marriage.* One very strange development in the history of Christian doctrine is the Roman Catholic Church's later espousal of the nonbiblical idea that the purpose of marital intercourse is primarily for procreation. Nothing could be further from Paul's view. He never mentions procreation at all, but he argues strongly that partners in marriage should satisfy one another's desires. This approach takes very seriously the reality and power of the human sexual drive—and the danger of sin and self-deception when that reality is denied. Of course, Paul offers here nothing like a comprehensive treatise on the purpose of marriage. He says nothing about love and companionship, nothing about bearing and raising children; there was no reason for him to discuss these matters, because he was responding to a specific question from the Corinthians. Therefore, anyone seeking to articulate a rounded theological view of marriage will address many topics that Paul ignores here. But in no case should Christian teaching ignore Paul's fundamental insight that *one* of the good purposes of marriage is to provide sexual satisfaction for husband and wife together.

4. *Divorce and remarriage.* By alluding to the teaching of Jesus and reaffirming his strong prohibition of divorce, Paul subscribes to the view—more fully articulated in the Gospels of Mark and Matthew—that marriage is an aspect of Christian discipleship. To acknowledge that Jesus is Lord is to enter the reconciling power of God's kingdom, where forgiveness and healing should dissolve the alienation that leads to divorce. When we insist on the seriousness of marriage as a binding covenant commitment, we order our lives in the church in a

way that reflects the love of God, a love that overcomes all faithlessness. At the same time, however, Paul's discussion of this issue leaves open the sad possibility that members of the church may exercise their legal option of divorce. If that happens, they are not to be excluded from the fellowship of God's people; if anything, their need for the community will be even greater in such circumstances. Furthermore, Paul's judgment in the case of the believer married to an unbeliever shows that the church may need to exercise flexible moral discernment in particular cases not sufficiently dealt with by the command of the Lord. This has significant implications for our thinking about the problem of remarriage after divorce. Paul does not tell us, for example, whether the believer whose unbelieving spouse chooses to separate is then free to remarry. (This is, of course, the one case where Roman Catholic tradition *has* allowed remarriage.) That question remained on the agenda for the Corinthians' own discernment. If remarriage is allowable in that case, might there be others as well, such as in cases of abuse or abandonment of one spouse by the other? The teaching of Paul and the gospels clearly excludes divorce and remarriage as a legal strategy for serial polygamy. But this still leaves many questions unresolved, and Paul's careful reflection about the issues addressed in verses 10–16 offers a model of how our thinking about such matters might proceed.

5. *The power and lure of holiness.* Paul's pronouncement that the believing partner sanctifies the unbeliever marks a revolution in religious consciousness, the same revolution that began when Jesus had table fellowship with sinners and tax collectors and prostitutes. The claim of 7:14 is that the power of holiness is so encompassing that it can draw the unholy into its field of force and transform it. The hope of 7:16 is that the lure of holiness will be manifest through members of the community of faith in such a way that their unbelieving spouses will be drawn to the truth and love of God. The logic of this way of conceptualizing holiness can be extended to many situations other than marriage relationships; it suggests metaphorically a broader truth about the vocation of the church in the world.

6. *The dignity and value of singleness.* One of the most important messages of this text for the church is that the single life has dignity and value before God. Most Protestant churches, historically in reaction against the Catholic imposition of mandatory clerical celibacy, have come to regard the unmarried state as aberrant and unhealthy. This tendency has been reinforced by powerful forces in popular culture that insinuate the idea that human wholeness is possible only through sexual relationships. Here the great Catholic tradition offers another

132

way, and 1 Corinthians 7 insists that we take a serious look at it. Paul argues that for many people it is *better* to remain unmarried—not because sex is dirty or wrong, but because the single life allows Christians the freedom and flexibility to serve God without distraction. This line of theological reflection merits sustained reflection. What would it mean for Christians to learn to think about their choices between marriage and singleness within the framework of the church's mission to carry the gospel to the world? It would mean, at the very least, that our conversation in the church about these matters would begin to pose a serious challenge to Western culture's frantic idolatry of sexual gratification as a primary end of human existence.

7. *Rethinking the eschatological story.* The most problematical aspect of Paul's counsel on sex and marriage is that it presupposes a version of the world-story in which Paul's generation expected to see the coming of the day of the Lord. Living in the same story more than nineteen hundred years later, we know that Paul's expectation of the imminent *parousia* was wrong. Now what? How does that fact affect the validity of his advice that Christians should "remain in the condition in which [they] were called"? The exegetical discussion above has tried to suggest some of the positive theological consequences of living in the framework of imminent expectation. Two points in particular stand out. First, Paul's eschatological framework enables us to look to the future in trust and hope, knowing that our salvation depends not on our success in restructuring the world but on the vast mercy and justice of God. The second point is a corollary of the first: we can disregard the various roles assigned us by society, finding our identity in Christ rather than in affiliations of ethnic group or gender or social class. Insofar as we grasp these truths, we will walk more gracefully though the conflicts, hassles, and disappointments of mundane reality. Furthermore, we may even be empowered to act more boldly and confidently to represent God's truth in a recalcitrant world.

Nonetheless, I say—I and not Paul—that some rethinking and renarration of the story is necessary. If Paul had known certainly that all of the "virgins" whom he was advising would go to their graves without witnessing the coming of the Lord, would he so strongly have advised them to remain as they were? He does, after all, describe his opinion on this subject as precisely that: his opinion, rather than revealed knowledge. This chapter, perhaps more than any other in the New Testament, actively *invites* us into the process of rethinking and moral deliberation. Insofar as Paul's clear preference for celibacy is based on the assumption that "the form of this world is passing away," we must make some adjustments to account for our changed historical

133

perspective. One such adjustment would be to tip the balance a bit more clearly in favor of seeing marriage, for many, as a constructive calling or gift from God, while still holding onto the equal validity of singleness as a call for others. Another adjustment, which the church has already made historically, is to rethink the question of slavery not just as a matter of individual calling but as a form of social ordering that contradicts the symbolic logic of the gospel. (I have suggested above that this judgment is already present—if only in embryonic form—in Paul's own proclamation: "You were bought with a price; do not become slaves of human masters.") The important point is that such adjustments are not only necessary if we are to read the Corinthians' mail as Scripture for us—they are also actually called for by the text itself. To retell the story, now with more chapters, and to ponder the implications of that retelling for our decisions about sex and marriage is not to reject the authority of 1 Corinthians; rather, it is to remain faithful to Paul's vision for making moral judgments "in view of the present necessity" under the guidance of the Spirit.

8:1—11:1
Idol Meat

Paul now takes up another issue from the Corinthians' letter to him: the problem of "food sacrificed to idols" (*eidōlothyta*). There was some controversy among the Corinthian Christians whether it was permissible to eat meat from animals used in pagan sacrifices. We might expect Paul to give a simple and clear-cut answer to this problem, for elsewhere in the New Testament there is a flat prohibition against eating such idol meat. This is one of the few fundamental restrictions imposed upon Gentile converts by the decree of the apostolic council at Jerusalem (Acts 15:28–29; see also *Didache* 6.3). The only other mention of the problem in the New Testament occurs in the letters to the seven churches in Revelation, where eating idol meat is linked with fornication; the churches of Pergamum and Thyatira are castigated for tolerating such practices (Rev. 2:14, 20). Of course, the fact that such a polemic was necessary shows that the issue was a live one in the churches of Asia Minor near the end of the first century.

134   In contrast to these other brief New Testament references, Paul does not render a simple judgment; instead he launches into a long and complex argument (8:1—11:1). Indeed, the argument is so complicated

that many readers have found it internally contradictory. In 8:1–13 and 10:23–30, Paul seems to hold that idol meat is actually harmless, while nonetheless encouraging the enlightened to abstain for the sake of other people's scruples. In 10:14–22, however, he seems to prohibit any contact with idol meat: "You cannot partake of the table of the Lord and the table of demons" (v. 21b). How do these different parts of the argument fit together, if at all? And how is the long section defending Paul's refusal of financial support (9:1–27) related to any of this? Some critics have suggested that these chapters do not hang together and must be fragments of different letters. This theory is, however, unnecessary, for the argument does make sense when we read it as a whole. One key to following Paul's argument is to recognize that he is primarily addressing the problem of sacrificial food consumed *in the temple of the pagan god* (8:10; 10:14, 21). That must have been the primary issue raised by the Corinthians' letter. Only in 10:25–30 does he discuss other situations: meat sold in the market and served in private homes.

There are actually four movements in Paul's treatment of the idol meat problem:

1. First movement: Knowledge puffs up; love builds up (8:1–13)
2. Second movement: The apostolic example of renouncing rights (9:1–27)
3. Third movement: Warning against idolatry (10:1–22)
4. Conclusion: Use your freedom for the glory of God (10:23—11:1)

Our exposition will treat each of these four sections in turn, but in order to appreciate the force of the argument, we must hear it in its entirety. If we take any one piece in isolation, we will not have a rounded picture of Paul's response.

The very fact that Paul crafts such an elaborate argument concerning idol meat shows that it was a major issue in the church at Corinth. Even though this may appear to be an obscure problem from our point of view, we should take this section of the letter seriously and try to understand what was at stake. Idol meat was a hot-button issue in Corinth because it dramatized three much larger concerns: the problem of boundaries between the church and pagan culture, the strained relationship between different social classes in the community, and the relation between knowledge and love as the foundation of the church's life. As we explore these chapters, we shall see how these problems come to expression in the text.

135

Knowledge Puffs Up, but Love Builds Up (8:1–13)

As in chapter 7, Paul introduces the topic with a brief quotation recapping the content of what the Corinthians had written, followed by his own pithy corrective response.

Corinthians: "All of us possess knowledge."
Paul: Knowledge puffs up, but love builds up.

The conversational diatribe style continues throughout this section, as Paul reflects the Corinthians' views back to them (vv. 1, 4, 8) and replies in counterpoint, seeking to provoke them to reexamine their understanding of the gospel. The "presenting problem" is a conflict in Corinth: Are Christians free to eat meat from animals slaughtered in pagan cultic rituals? Paul's discussion of the problem suggests that the issue had arisen particularly because some Corinthian Christians were attending feasts held in the pagan temples, where meat was served to all present (v. 10).

Their justification for this practice may be reconstructed from Paul's remarks here. As enlightened Christians, they possess "knowledge" (*gnōsis*) that there is only one god and that pagan idols are nothing other than lifeless statues, having no power to help or harm anyone (v. 4). Furthermore, they also have the "knowledge"—in accord with Paul's own teaching—that food is spiritually insignificant (v. 8). Just as Gentiles need not seek God's approval by keeping Jewish dietary laws, so also they need not worry about the source of the meat they eat. Those Christians who fear defilement from idol meat are simply ignorant and superstitious. The strong Christian, armed with the appropriate *gnōsis*, can go without compunction to the pagan temple and eat whatever is offered there; indeed, doing so may be a way to demonstrate one's spiritual maturity and freedom. The Corinthians who advocated this position may actually have argued that their more scrupulous brothers and sisters—the "weak," as the Corinthian letter called them—should try to build up the strength of their own consciences by attending such ceremonies and eating the idol meat. If they would only do that, they would see that no harm comes of it, and their consciousness would be raised. The Corinthian letter probably appealed to Paul to set the record straight by encouraging the weak to overcome their qualms and enter the world of spiritual freedom enjoyed by those who possess *gnōsis*.

Furthermore, as Gerd Theissen has argued, there may have been a socioeconomic aspect to the argument about idol food. Feasts held in temples were common events in the daily life of a Greco-Roman city.

136

For example, the sanctuary of Asclepius in Corinth comprised both an area for cultic sacrifice and several dining rooms that opened onto a pleasant public courtyard. The wealthier Corinthians would have been invited to meals in such places as a regular part of their social life, to celebrate birthdays, weddings, healings attributed to the god, or other important occasions. Examples of such invitations have been preserved. For example: "Herais asks you to dine in the room of the Serapheion (=Asclepieion) at a banquet of the Lord Seraphis tomorrow the 11th from the 9th hour" (cited in Murphy-O'Connor, *St. Paul's Corinth*, 164; for discussion of the archaeological evidence, see 161–65). For those few Corinthian Christians who were among the wealthier class (cf. 1:26–29), their public and professional duties virtually required the networking that occurred through attending and sponsoring such events. To eat the sacrificial meat served on such occasions was simple social courtesy; to refuse to share in the meal would be an affront to the host. At the same time, the specifically religious connotations of the act might not have seemed particularly important. Within the social circle of the poorer Corinthians, on the other hand, such meat-eating would not have been commonplace. Meat was not an ordinary part of their diet; it may have been accessible only at certain public religious festivals where there was a general distribution of meat. Consequently, the wealthy and powerful, who also had the most advanced education, would take the eating of meat in stride and readily accept the view that it was a matter of spiritual indifference; at the same time, however, the poor might regard meat as laden with "numinous" religious connotations (see Theissen, 121–43). Thus, the distinction between "the weak" and those with "knowledge" may have fallen, at least to some extent, along socioeconomic lines.

In view of all this, Paul's response must have come as a shock to the *gnōsis* group in Corinth. Rather than taking sides in the dispute, Paul seizes the occasion to challenge those with "knowledge" to reconsider their actions on the basis of very different standards. He provisionally accepts the slogan that all have knowledge (v. 1; but see v. 7); nevertheless, he immediately suggests that knowledge is defective if it fails to build up the community in love. Knowledge "puffs up." Paul has already used this vivid metaphorical verb several times in the letter, urging the Corinthians not to be "puffed up in favor of one against another" (4:6), warning them not to be puffed up against his own apostolic authority (4:18–19), and castigating them for being puffed up about (or in spite of) the case of incest in their midst (5:2). Here in 8:1 the cause of this prideful puffing up is stated explicitly for the first time: *gnōsis* can lead to arrogance.

Paul's use of this word does not mean that there were Gnostics at Corinth. Gnosticism as a formal religious movement, with its dualistic cosmology and elaborately developed speculative teachings, did not emerge until the second century; Paul's letter gives no hint of confronting the Gnostic heresies that later Christian writers such as Irenaeus battled. Among the Corinthians of Paul's day, we see only incipient tendencies, the seeds that later sprouted into Gnosticism. Prominent among these tendencies was a spiritual elitism that separated the church into different classes based on the possession of "knowledge." Those in the know could feel superior to others who lacked their privileged perspective. In fact, they could imagine themselves as being saved through their own intellectual and spiritual capacities, rather than by God's grace alone.

In sharp contrast to this "soteriology of knowledge" (Theissen, 135), Paul insists that what really matters is *love*, which builds up the community (8:1b). Paradoxically, those who boast in their own exalted knowledge demonstrate precisely by that boasting that they do not yet "know as [they] ought to know" (v. 2, NIV). Implied here is that the one who knows rightly will love the brothers and sisters in the community. Paul, however, goes on to make a different point: "anyone who loves God is known by him" (v. 3). We would expect Paul to say, "anyone who loves God knows God truly," but the reversal of subject and object in the last clause of the verse expresses a truth close to the heart of Paul's theology: The initiative in salvation comes from God, not from us. It is God who loves first, God who elects us and delivers us from the power of sin and death. Therefore what counts is not so much our knowledge of God as God's knowledge of us. That is the syntax of salvation. The dominance of this syntax in Paul's thought is shown in Galatians 4:9, when he commits an error of theological grammar and stops to correct himself in midsentence: "Now, however, that you have come to know God, or rather to be known by God. . . ." Anyone who understands that the logic of the gospel depends on God's initiative will not become puffed up by the possession of knowledge. Thus, the first three verses of chapter 8 establish Paul's basic critique of the Corinthian *gnōsis*-boasters who think their knowledge permits them to eat idol meat: they have misconstrued the faith by interpreting it as a special sort of knowledge that elevates them above others. Paul insists on the priority of love over knowledge.

With this point made, Paul begins again to address the idol meat problem about which the Corinthians had written. Again he quotes slogans from the Corinthian letter: "no idol in the world really exists," and "there is no God but one" (v. 4). Both slogans are consistent with the standard preaching of Hellenistic Judaism and early Christianity, which proclaimed the one God and decried the worship of idols. Thus, even more clearly than in the previous cases, these slogans express a theological perspective with which Paul does not disagree; his quarrel is with the Corinthians' *application* of the slogans. Because the idol has no real existence, they contend, idol worship is a meaningless gesture. Therefore, if Christians find it socially advantageous to eat idol meat, what difference does it make?

Before challenging this argument, Paul affirms its theological premises and expands upon them in a way that will serve the purposes of his counterargument. There are many "so-called gods" (v. 5); anyone who walked through the city of Corinth and observed the ubiquitous shrines and statues of the gods could hardly avoid recognizing that "in fact there are many gods and many lords" (v. 5). Paul's use of the dismissive adjective "so-called" shows that he does not believe these figures to be real gods. Verse 5 simply acknowledges the empirical fact that the world is teeming with representations of such entities and with their worshipers. Is there a distinction between "gods" and "lords?" Perhaps the gods are the traditional deities of the Greco-Roman pantheon, whereas the lords (*kyrioi*) are the figures venerated in mystery cults and religions more recently imported from the eastern empire. (The latter category also implicitly includes the figure of Caesar, who was venerated as *kyrios* in the imperial cult.) By mentioning both categories, Paul deftly prepares the way for the two-part confessional formula of verse 6, which contrasts the *many* gods and lords to the *one* God and *one* Lord whom Christians worship.

This confessional acclamation in verse 6 is in all likelihood another quotation, this time not of the Corinthians' letter but of a hymn or creed that the Corinthians would have recognized as an authoritative statement of the content of Christian faith. Printed editions of the Greek New Testament highlight the structural balance of this confessional fragment in a way that most English translations do not. The following literal translation displays the parallelism:

> One God, the Father,
> From whom are all things and we for him,
> And one Lord, Jesus Christ,
> through whom are all things and we through him.

The final phrase may not mean "through whom we exist" (NRSV, JB), but rather something like "we through him [go to God]." This would preserve the parallelism with the second line of the formula, which encompasses both origin and destination; thus, the last line of the confession acclaims Jesus Christ as the agent of both creation and eschatological redemption.

We should hear in this confession a significant echo of the *Shema* (Deut. 6:4), the great proclamation of Israel's faith:

Hear, O Israel;
The Lord our God,
The Lord is one.

Paul's present interest is not to reflect about christological problems or to explain the relation of Jesus Christ to God the Father. Still, we may observe in passing that the early Christian confession cited in verse 6 takes the extraordinarily bold step of identifying "the Lord Jesus" with "the Lord" acclaimed in the *Shema*, while still insisting that "for us there is one God." Paul and other early Christians have reshaped Israel's faith in such a way that Jesus is now acclaimed as Lord within the framework of monotheism. It is a great pity that Paul's surviving letters nowhere take up this paradox as a topic for extended discussion.

Why, then, does Paul quote this confessional statement? First of all, he is establishing firm common ground with his readers, who will enthusiastically share in the monotheistic affirmation of verses 5–6. At the same time, however, by bringing this formula into play, he has subtly broadened the theological basis on which the discussion of idol meat must occur. Christian thought about this problem must start neither from an abstract doctrine of monotheism nor from a theoretical statement that "gods" do not really exist; rather, Christian thought begins from a confession that binds us specifically to the one God of Israel and declares our personal union with and allegiance to this one God. We exist "for him," not for our own purposes. To the extent that this confession of the one God echoes the *Shema*, we should also hear the echo of that text's call to "love the Lord your God with all your heart and with all your soul and with all your might" (Deut. 6:5). (Indeed, the reference in 1 Cor. 8:3 to *loving* God—which seems to fit awkwardly into the context—suggests that Paul already had the *Shema* in mind a few sentences earlier.) All of this has a direct bearing on the question of idol meat: this one God of Israel is "a jealous God" who is well known to have no tolerance for idolatry. At this point in the argument, however, Paul is content to let that suggestion reverberate in the background; he will bring it directly into the foreground in chapter 10.

140

Paul turns instead to press the question of how the actions of the *gnōsis*-advocates will affect other members of the community. That is the burden of the remainder of the chapter (vv. 7–13). First he poses a challenge to the premise of the Corinthian slogan that "we *all* possess knowledge." In fact, he insists, not everyone in the community shares this exalted knowledge. Some members of the fledgling church are so accustomed to thinking of the idols as real that they cannot eat the idol meat without conjuring up the whole symbolic world of idol worship; they are dragged back into that world and so "defiled" (v. 7). (This shows, by the way, that "the weak" about whom Paul writes here are not Jewish Christians but Gentile converts from paganism; they are the ones who would be "accustomed to idols.") This may show their weakness, Paul allows for the sake of argument, but that is nonetheless the truth of the situation. Those who are saying "we *all* possess knowledge" are ignoring or excluding those in the community who do not share their opinion.

In Paul's imagined dialogue, this elicits a protest from the Corinthian interlocutors, who say, "Food will not bring us close to God" (v. 8a; see NRSV). Neither eating nor abstaining has any effect, either positive or negative (v. 8b). This is simply a restatement of their "knowledge." Again, Paul does not disagree, but their response misses the point that he is trying to make. He states that point in some detail in verses 9–12. His rejoinder to the slogan of verse 8 is articulated concisely in verse 9: "But take care that this liberty [*exousia*] of yours does not somehow become a stumbling block to the weak." The word *exousia* is a loaded word which will become a major theme of chapter 9. The ordinary meaning of the word is "authority"; it is etymologically related to the verb *exestin* that appeared in the Corinthian slogan, "I am free to do anything" (6:12). The precise nuance of *exousia* here is something like this: it does not refer to an externally granted permission to eat idol meat; rather, it refers to the internal strength and authority to do whatever one pleases, to transcend mundane limitations. Thus, as Paul is using it here, it is closely correlated with "knowledge" and "wisdom." Those Corinthians who eat the idol meat claim to do so by virtue of their own sovereign *exousia*, their philosophically formed strength of character. Paul somewhat wryly warns that those who seek to flex their spiritual muscles ("this *exousia of yours*") in this way should watch out to see what effect it will have on others around them. (Cf. Matt. 18:6–7, in which Jesus warns sternly against placing "a stumbling block before one of these little ones who believe in me.")

Verses 10–12 offer a specific description of how Paul imagines the possible damage inflicted on the community by those who want to eat the idol meat. The weak will see the *gnōsis*-boasters eating *in the temple of an idol* and be influenced, contrary to their own consciences, to participate in the same practice (v. 10). This is a very important statement, 141 because it shows that Paul's primary concern here is not the consumption of meat sold in the marketplace (cf. 10:25–26); rather, he is worried about having weak Christians drawn back into the temple, into the powerful world of the pagan cult, which was, we must always remember, the dominant symbolic world in which the Corinthian Christians lived. In verse 11 Paul states the dire consequence of such cultural compromise: The weak will be "destroyed." This language should not be watered down. The concern is not that the weak will be *offended* by the actions of the *gnōsis*-boasters; Paul's concern is, rather, that they will become alienated from Christ and fall away from the sphere of God's saving power, being sucked back into their former way of life.

Paul presents this horrifying possibility with biting irony: "So, the weak one is destroyed by your *gnōsis*, the brother for whom Christ died." If the Corinthians will only pause to ponder this picture seriously, the contrast is stunning: Christ gave up his life for this "brother" (or sister: again, Paul's point is to emphasize the *family* tie between the strong and the weak in Christ)—Christ died for this person, and you can't even change your diet? On one side we have the Son of God who died for us "while we were still weak" (Rom. 5:6); on the other side we have the *gnōsis*-flexers who are so fixated on exercising their own freedom that they are willing to trample on the weak and jeopardize their very salvation. This is not only to injure the community but also to "sin against Christ" (v. 12) by scorning and undoing his saving work. The picture is reminiscent of Matthew's great parable of the last judgment, in which it is revealed that whatever was done to "the least of these my brothers [and sisters]" was in effect done for—or against—Christ himself (Matt. 25:31–46).

Paul concludes this unit by declaring his own resolution in this matter. "Therefore, if food causes my brother [or sister] to fall, I will never eat meat, so that I may not cause my brother [or sister] to fall." Interestingly, the word "meat" in this sentence is the generic word for animal flesh, not the specific term "idol meat" that has occurred previously in the passage. Paul is willing to forego not only the specific practice of eating idol food but also the eating of meat altogether if that is necessary to protect the weak from stumbling. The effect of this policy, of course, is that it places Paul himself de facto among the ranks of the weak (9:22; cf. Rom 15:1). This was hinted at earlier in the letter, when, in another powerfully ironic passage, Paul contrasted himself to the Corinthian *sophoi*: "We are weak, but you are strong" (4:10). Thus, 1 Corinthians 8 must be read as a compelling invitation to the "strong" Corinthians to come over and join Paul at table with the weak. This invitation is far more urgent than any invitation to savor meat with their rich friends in the respectable world of Corinthian society.

REFLECTIONS FOR TEACHERS AND PREACHERS

The interpreter of 1 Corinthians 8 must help the congregation to see the specific matter of idol meat as a trigger issue that poses larger problems of perennial concern to the church. To read the Corinthians' mail as a letter to us, we must consider what contemporary issues present our churches with temptations and conflicts analogous to those presented to ancient first-generation Christians by the pagan temples in their midst. Our reflections about this matter may be grouped under four headings.

1. *Boundaries between church and culture.* Can Christians fit into the social world of their surrounding culture? Or must they withdraw altogether from "normal" social practices that represent participation in symbolic orders alien to the gospel? Where are the lines to be drawn between acceptable accommodation to the realities of the culture and unacceptable compromise? Questions such as these always arise for the church in a missionary setting (such as first-century Corinth) where the gospel encounters a new cultural context. Converts to the faith must work out how to reorder their lives in obedience to Christ, discerning which old customs may be continued and which must be left behind. For example, Korean students have reported to me that 1 Corinthians 8 reminds them of disputes in their own churches about whether Christians must abandon traditional meals venerating ancestors. Some see these traditions as harmless honoring of the memory of family members; others see them as a form of idolatry.

But such problems are hardly confined to churches in non-Western cultures. Similar questions must also be posed to Christian churches that have grown comfortably familiar with their cultural setting. As the world becomes increasingly secular and pluralistic, we find ourselves in a situation more like that of the first-century Christians, having to rethink our allegiances in fundamental ways. First Corinthians 8 encourages us to shine a spotlight on our own social networks to see whether perhaps we are unwittingly eating in the temples of the idols that surround us. One obvious point of conflict might arise with regard to the participation of church members in clubs and fraternal orders outside the church: Masons, Shriners, Eastern Star, and so forth. What kinds of commitment, religious or quasireligious, is required or implied by participation in such groups? One student recently told me that she had been asked by some members of her church to join a women's group called The Daughters of Isis! After some reflection, she

143

decided that as a Christian she could not associate herself with such a group. That seems a fairly clear-cut case, but what about other societies and subcultures that claim our loyalties—college fraternities and sororities, the American Civil Liberties Union, the National Rifle Association, and so forth? Paul's words to the Corinthians should cause us to look closely at all such external attachments and ask whether they are really consistent with our allegiance to Jesus Christ as Lord.

Indeed, the exclusive lordship of Jesus stands as a challenge to many arrangements that we take for granted. If Jesus is Lord, then Caesar is not, and any form of nationalism can turn into a form of idolatry. If we display national flags in our churches, are we leading the weak to lose sight of the distinctiveness of Christian discipleship and to confuse faith with patriotism? Perhaps the most insidious form of idolatry for churches in the United States is the idolatry of materialism. In the name of freedom and individual rights, Christians enmesh themselves in economic practices that draw their loyalty from Christ and divide the community of faith by disregarding the poor.

The fundamental question underlying all these issues is whether monotheistic faith by definition sanctions pluralism (as the *gnōsis* group at Corinth contended) or whether monotheistic faith requires exclusivity, expressed in clear separation from the symbolic world of pagan culture (as the weak contended). In chapter 8, Paul has not yet given an answer to this question, but he has called those who possess "knowledge" to attend respectfully to the concerns of the weak.

2. *Class divisions in the church.* Paul does not confront this problem directly in 1 Corinthians 8, but by reading between the lines we have seen that the idol meat problem had a socioeconomic dimension. Having recognized this, we might look again at the disputes in our own congregations and denominations and ask whether there is also a similar economic substratum to our quarrels. If so, we might ponder the fact that Paul places the onus for flexibility on those with more education and economic resources. To the dismay of the "strong" at Corinth, he refuses to take their side against the weak; instead, he calls the strong to surrender what they understand as their legitimate prerogatives for the sake of the weak. What would it mean for us to do likewise?

Furthermore, this text calls Christians who have many possessions to beware of easy rationalizations that treat the world of everyday affairs as religiously neutral, thereby permitting them to continue enjoying their privileged lives. Theissen (136) tellingly describes the position of the high-status Corinthians: "The world is rejected in a theoretical way in order to profit from it in a practical way—the usual verbal radicalism of the affluent."

3. *Love trumps knowledge.* The central message of this chapter is a simple one: Love is more important than knowledge. Paul calls for a shift from *gnōsis* to *agapē* as the ordering principle for Christian discernment and conduct. Rather than asserting rights and privileges, we are to shape our actions toward edification of our brothers and sisters in the community of faith. In so doing, we will be following the example of Christ, who died for the weak (v. 11), and also the example of Paul, who is willing to renounce all meat in order to keep his brothers and sisters from stumbling (v. 13). The *gnōsis*-boasters frame their decisions and actions in terms of their own *exousia*, looking to the cultivation of their own spiritual freedom and sophistication as their highest end; Paul calls them instead to look to the cultivation of loving community as the goal of Christian action. Every congregation will profit from looking at themselves in the mirror of 1 Corinthians 8 and asking whether there are ways in which they are using knowledge as a weapon rather than as an instrument of love. Whether Bible-thumping certainty about revealed truth, or serene confidence in the latest scientific findings, or passionate discernment of the "right" social causes, any "knowledge" that divides the community and causes the knowledgeable ones to despise those who are ignorant or uncertain is not being used in the service of God.

4. *The danger of destruction through idolatry.* The "stumbling block principle" is often erroneously invoked to place limits on the behavior of some Christians whose conduct offends other Christians with stricter behavioral standards. For example, it is argued that if drinking alcohol or dancing or dressing in certain ways might cause offense to more scrupulous church members, we are obligated to avoid such behaviors for the sake of the "weaker brother's conscience." The effect of such reasoning is to hold the entire Christian community hostage to the standards of the most narrow-minded and legalistic members of the church. Clearly, this is not what Paul intended. He is concerned in 1 Corinthians 8 about weaker believers being "destroyed" by being drawn away from the church and back into idol worship. Therefore, in applying this text analogically to our time, we should be careful to frame analogies only to those situations in which the boundary-defying actions of the "strong" might actually jeopardize the faith and salvation of others by leading the weak to *emulate* high-risk behaviors. Framing the analogy in this way will significantly limit the number of situations to which the text is directly relevant.

A corollary of this point, however, is that idolatry *can* actually lead to destruction. This was denied by the *gnōsis* group at Corinth, but Paul solemnly warns of the danger in dabbling with idolatrous practices.

The seductive lure of idolatry is real, and the destructive power of the pagan world is real. Members of the church who are drawn away from God will suffer irreparable loss. If we are tempted to be casual about dalliances with the idols that rule our culture's symbolic world (primarily the gods of wealth, military power, and self-gratification), we would do well to reread 1 Corinthians 8 and consider the possible risks for those among us who are seeking to escape the pull of these forces. Our first concern should be to preserve the symbolic integrity of the church in such a way that weaker members will be protected from these destructive temptations.

The Apostolic Example of Renouncing Rights (9:1–27)

Chapter 9 looks like the beginning of a long digression. Paul begins defending his apostolic practices, particularly his refusal to accept financial support from the Corinthians, and the problem of idol meat seems to drop from view until 10:19. In fact, however, while reading chapter 9 we must keep the wider context in view. Paul has not by any means left behind the problem of food sacrificed to idols; rather, he is taking a new tack, reframing the perspective from which the Corinthians should view the problem. The indirect approach of chapter 9 is particularly artful, because it allows Paul to kill two birds with one stone: his direct treatment of one subsidiary problem (his means of financial support) also functions implicitly in the service of his larger argument about food, idolatry, and the requirements of love.

In order to see how this argument works, we need to have the map in our minds before we start walking through it. In chapter 8, Paul calls upon the strong at Corinth to limit their freedom for the sake of the weak. In the last verse of that chapter, he points to himself as an example: he will never eat meat if it causes his brothers and sisters to fall. The strong may regard this self-limitation as preposterous. After all, if Paul is a real apostle, surely he should be the boss and tell other people how to behave. His policy of deferring to the superstitious scruples of his most ignorant converts has led some of the Corinthians to question the authenticity of his apostleship. Paul seems to them simply cowardly and duplicitous, sometimes willing to eat meat among the strong but timidly caving in to the dietary restrictions of the weak on other occasions. This sort of behavior casts doubt on the legitimacy of Paul's claim to be an apostle.

The doubt is reinforced by Paul's practice of supporting himself by working as a tentmaker (Acts 18:1–3). This sort of menial labor is surely unworthy of a true apostle. Other Christian preachers who have come to Corinth (Apollos? Cephas?) have acted more like respectable philosophical teachers by accepting financial support from wealthy members of the congregation. Paul's slavish pursuit of a low-status occupation, taken together with his vacillating inability to take a consistently "strong" line on the freedom to eat, has suggested a disturbing conclusion to the Corinthians: perhaps Paul is not really a legitimate apostle at all. If he were legitimate, surely he would act in ways more dignified and more demonstrative of his own authority.

It is important to remember that Paul did not fit readily into any recognizable job description within the culture of the Corinthians. There was no established model for "Christian ministers." Nor were there existing institutions such as universities or church denominations to employ or sanction teachers and preachers. Paul was simply a freelance missionary. The Corinthians would most naturally have compared him to the rhetoricians and philosophers familiar within their world. Ronald F. Hock (50–65) has explained that within this cultural setting there was an ongoing debate about the appropriate means of economic support for a philosopher. Four basic models were advocated, each with its distinctive drawbacks. The philosopher could charge fees for his teaching, as the Sophists did; they were often accused of greed and manipulating their pupils. Alternatively, the philosopher could be supported by a wealthy patron, as the "resident intellectual" in the patron's household, often with the task of educating the family's children; such a role entailed an obvious loss of independence, for the philosopher would be tied to the purse strings of the patron. A third option, notoriously practiced by the Cynics, was to beg on the streets; for obvious reasons this was widely perceived as eccentric and demeaning. The final option was for the philosopher to work at a trade in order to support himself; this had the disadvantages of low social status and of consuming time and energy for mundane matters. At least, however, working for a living preserved the philosopher's independence from control by other people.

Paul decided early in his apostolic career to follow the fourth of these models, working with his own hands to earn his living (cf. 1 Thess. 2:5–10; 2 Thess. 3:7–9)—supplemented by occasional unsought gifts from some of his churches, particularly the church in Philippi (cf. Phil. 4:10–20; 2 Cor. 11:9b). This was a relatively unusual choice (the first two options were by far the most common), and the Corinthian correspondence shows that it proved controversial. In 2 Corinthians we find Paul addressing the issue in explicit terms:

> Did I commit a sin by humbling myself so that you might be exalted, because I proclaimed God's good news to you free of charge? I robbed other churches by accepting support from them in order to serve you. And when I was with you and was in need, I did not burden anyone, for my needs were supplied by the friends who came from Macedonia. So I refrained and will continue to refrain from burdening you in any way. . . . How have you been worse off than the other churches, except that I myself did not burden you? Forgive me this wrong!
>
> (2 Cor. 11:7–9; 12:13)

By the time Paul wrote these words, the criticism of his refusal to accept support from the Corinthians had escalated into a major issue. In 1 Corinthians 9, by contrast, we hear him responding to the first rumblings of a criticism that only later erupted in full force. Clearly, his self-defense (*apologia*, 9:3) did not succeed in defusing the issue.

The argument has two phases. In verses 1–14 he argues that he is a real apostle and therefore has every right to receive financial support from the Corinthians. Then in verses 15–23 he explains that he has renounced these legitimate rights "for the sake of the gospel" by offering the gospel free of charge and identifying with lower-status members of the community. Thus, by choosing "not to make full use of my rights [*exousia*] in the gospel" (v. 18), Paul confirms rather than denies his apostolic mission.

At the same time, Paul's self-description serves as a model for the conduct that he is urging upon the strong: like him, they should be willing to surrender their *exousia* for the sake of the weak in order to promote the gospel. This is not explicitly stated until the very conclusion of the larger argument (10:32—11:1), but it is clearly implied by the thematic links between chapters 8 and 9 (*exousia* in 8:9 and throughout chapter 9; the example of Paul in 8:13, taken together with 9:12 and 9:22). We may be sure that, whether they liked what Paul had to say or not, the Corinthians would have seen what he was driving at. The argument targets those members of the Corinthian church who enjoy greater wealth and social prestige, who also are most enamored of their freedom to do what they like: to them, Paul says, in effect, "No, for the sake of the gospel you must exercise self-restraint. You must discipline yourself for the sake of the greater good of building up the community in love." That is why the athletic metaphors are introduced at the end of chapter 9: just as the athlete in training exercises self-discipline, so Christians are called to discipline themselves for the work at hand. By sandwiching chapter 9 in between chapters 8 and 10, Paul causes his readers to think about the idol meat issue in light of the apostolic example and vice versa.

148

Those who try to read chapter 9 as a defense of Paul's apostleship unrelated to the idol food problem have great difficulty explaining how verses 24–27 fit into the defense. The presence of this material at the end of the chapter shows clearly that the purpose of the unit as a whole is hortatory rather than apologetic. Paul is presenting his own pattern of renouncing rights as exemplary and calling the Corinthian *gnōsis*-boasters to follow suit. Thus, we see that 1 Corinthians 9 is an artful piece of rhetoric that accomplishes two purposes simultaneously: explaining Paul's controversial renunciation of his rights and suggesting that renunciation as a model to be imitated. With this map in hand, let us turn to a closer reading of some of the details.

Paul's right to receive support (9:1–14)

The opening of chapter 9 should be heard as a direct reflex of the conclusion of chapter 8. In 8:13, Paul articulates his principle of self-limitation for the sake of the weak. Recognizing that this will appear objectionable to his strong readers, he anticipates the objection with a rhetorical question: "Am I not free?" That is, is he not free to eat what he wants? This question touches off a volley of rhetorical questions, all formulated to expect a positive answer: of course Paul is a free apostle. His apostleship is validated not only by his having encountered the risen Lord Jesus but also by his founding of the Corinthian church. Even if "others" (no explanation of their identity is given here) may challenge the legitimacy of Paul's ministry, the Corinthians themselves can hardly do that, for their existence as a Christian community is dependent on Paul's work in their midst. That is the sense in which the Corinthian church itself is a "seal" of Paul's apostleship, an external mark signifying the authenticity of the message (vv. 1–2; cf. 2 Cor. 3:1–3).

In verse 3 Paul openly declares that he is now replying to those who presume to scrutinize his apostolic work. The sentence addresses not a hypothetical possibility but a situation that Paul regards as a present reality (NIV: "This is my defense to those who sit in judgment of me"). The Corinthians' letter has indicated that they are in fact passing judgment upon him. This formulation recalls an earlier statement in the letter using the same verb: "But with me it is a small thing that I should be judged by you or by any human court" (4:3). In that context, Paul brushed aside the scrutiny of the Corinthians by declaring himself accountable to God alone; as we shall see, the present passage will make a similar point (cf. vv. 16–17). In chapter 4, there was a suggestion that the Corinthians were judging Paul for his lack of rhetorically polished wisdom; here in chapter 9, the points in dispute seem to

149

be related to his lifestyle and his means of self-support. Although Paul takes up the issues in different places, they are not unrelated. In both cases, he is being unfavorably compared to the Corinthians' ideal image of the true wise man.

Paul begins his defense with another salvo of rhetorical questions. The first of these (v. 4) might refer either to his right as a free person to eat and drink what he likes, or to his right to receive support from the churches. The former fits the foregoing context, but the latter points in the direction of the succeeding argument (vv. 6–14). The ambiguity of the question allows it to work on both levels, smoothing the transition from one phase of the argument to the next (Barrett, 202).

The key word here is *exousia*: "Do we not have have the right/authority [*exousia*] to eat and drink?" The Corinthians, hearing their own buzzword thrown back at them and emphasized by its threefold repetition in verses 4–6, should remember 8:9: "Take care lest this *exousia* of yours does not somehow become a stumbling block to the weak." In principle, Paul has the right to eat what he wants, to be accompanied by a wife like the other apostles, and to be supported financially by the churches that he has founded. Yet, as the Corinthians already know, he does not do any of these things. Therefore, the very posing of the questions suggests the important distinction between having a right and exercising it; the fact that Paul *chooses* not to do these things does not mean that he lacks the *authority* to do them.

The reference to the wives of "the other apostles and the brothers of the Lord and Cephas" shows that the apostles and other early Christian leaders were normally married—a fact that surely causes some embarrassment to those Christian traditions that later came to insist upon clerical celibacy. Paul's point in verse 5, however, is not that apostles have the right to marry; rather, he is saying that they have the right to receive support from the churches for their wives to accompany them in their travels. "The brothers of the Lord" refers to the natural siblings of Jesus, who apparently overcame their initial skepticism (Mark 3:31–35) and became leaders of the early Christian movement (cf. Acts 1:14). James the brother of the Lord particularly emerged as a prominent figure in the Jerusalem church (Acts 12:17; 15:13–21; 21:18). The singling out of Cephas for special mention here suggests once again that partisans of Cephas may have been among those at Corinth who fomented opposition to Paul (cf. 1 Cor. 1:12; 3:22).

With verse 6, Paul at last focuses clearly on the issue that is most troublesome at present for his relationship with the Corinthians: financial support. The normal pattern is that apostles are supported by their churches; Paul and his former mentor and associate Barnabas

150

(Acts 4:36–37; 9:26–28; 11:19–26; 15:36–41) are the exceptions to the rule. To show that this is an anomaly Paul spins out three analogies, still in the interrogative mode, in verse 7: Don't soldiers and vinegrowers and shepherds all get their livelihood from their work? Likewise, it is implied, proclaimers of the Word should be sustained by their own flock of followers.

The argument, which began by citing the precedent of other Christian leaders (vv. 5–6) and then added common-sense analogies (v. 7), turns next to the authority of Scripture: even the Law supports Paul's case that he has a right to be financially sustained by the church (vv. 8–11). How so? Paul cites Deuteronomy 25:4: "You shall not muzzle an ox while it is treading out the grain." This is often cited as an example of arbitrary prooftexting on Paul's part, but closer observation demonstrates a more complex hermeneutical strategy at play here. First of all, Paul is operating with an explicitly stated hermeneutical principle that God is really concerned about human beings, not oxen, and that the text should be read accordingly (vv. 9–10). Second, a careful look at the context of Deuteronomy 25:4 lends some credence to Paul's claim about this particular text. The surrounding laws in Deuteronomy 24 and 25 (especially Deut. 24:6–7, 10–22; 25:1–3) almost all serve to promote dignity and justice for human beings; the one verse about the threshing ox sits oddly in this context. It is not surprising that Paul would have read this verse also as suggesting something about justice in human economic affairs. Third, once one allows the figurative reading of Deuteronomy 25:4, it functions as an elegant metaphor for just the point that Paul wants to make: the ox being driven around and around the threshing floor should not be cruelly restrained from eating the food that his own labor is making available. Since he is doing the work, the ox should be allowed to eat; so, too, with apostles. Finally—a point rarely appreciated by interpreters of 1 Corinthians—Paul is not just claiming that the biblical verse applies to human laborers in general; rather, "It was indeed written *for our sake*," that is, for the sake of the church in Paul's own time. The first person plural pronoun of verse 10 ("written for *our* sake) has the same implied antecedent as the first person plural pronoun of verse 11: Paul and his associates in ministry. "If *we* have sown spiritual things among you, is it a big thing if *we* reap material things among you?" (v. 11). Thus, Paul claims that the text addresses the church of his own time directly, in an oracular fashion, metaphorically instructing them to provide financial support for Paul and other apostles. This is for Paul not a derived sense of the text, but its fundamental meaning, now eschatologically disclosed. (On this hermeneutical strategy, see Hays, *Echoes*, 165–68).

151

The conclusion of the argument so far is drawn in verse 12a: Paul has a stronger claim than anyone on a fair share of the crop (cf. v. 10).

In the latter part of verse 12, Paul at last tips his hand about the point to which he has been building up throughout the chapter: despite all the above arguments establishing his right to receive support, he has made no use of this *exousia*. Why? Because he does not want to "put an obstacle in the way of the gospel." The echo here of the "stumbling block" image of 8:9, 13 is unmistakable. For reasons not yet explained, Paul believes that accepting financial support from the Corinthians would create barriers for his work of proclamation; since that is his pre-eminent concern, he takes no money.

The argument could end there, but Paul doubles back and adduces still two more arguments warranting his right to receive support. The first (v. 13) is the analogy of the priests in the temple getting a share of the sacrificial meat—a particularly vivid image in light of the issue under discussion in chapters 8–10. And finally, dropped in almost as though it were an afterthought, is the trump card of the whole argument: Jesus himself commanded that proclaimers of the gospel should get their living by the gospel. Here we see what a skilled rhetorician Paul was: He has saved his knockdown argument for last, yet he introduces it without fanfare or elaboration, allowing the point to carry its own considerable weight. Paul does not actually quote the saying of Jesus, but he probably has in mind the tradition preserved in Luke 10:7 as part of the commissioning of the seventy to proclaim the kingdom of God: "The laborer is worthy of his wages" (cf. Matt. 10:10). (Interestingly, 1 Tim. 5:17–18 quotes this same saying alongside Deut. 25:4 to teach that elders who rule well in the church should get "double honor," i.e., extra pay.)

The apostolic model: Paul's renunciation of rights (9:15–23)

After all this buildup, one would suppose that the logical conclusion would be for Paul to demand that the Corinthians ante up the money they rightfully ought to give him, but in fact, as he has already indicated, this is the exact opposite of his intention. Verse 15 is the dramatic climax and pivot-point of the chapter. Not only has Paul not made any use of these impressively attested rights, he would rather die than . . . than what? The sentence in the Greek sputters to a halt. Then Paul blurts that no one will deprive him of his "boast." The meaning of this somewhat opaque statement is explained in the following highly compressed sentences (vv. 16–18). Despite all the impressive reasons for receiving support, including the command of the Lord, Paul will take no money because he cannot claim to be working voluntarily as an apostle. Therefore, unlike the sophists, he can receive no fees in payment for services rendered. His service is rendered to God, not willingly (!) but because he has been "entrusted with a commission." The language here suggests once again the image of the slave as steward (cf. 4:1–4). Paul preaches because "necessity" (*anagkē;* NRSV "obligation"; cf. 7:26 and my comments on that text, above) has been laid upon him by God. (We might recall the image of Jeremiah, for whom the prophetic word is "something like a burning fire shut up in my bones," Jer. 20:9.) He has no choice but to proclaim the gospel. Therefore, his "reward" is, paradoxically, to make the gospel available to others "free of charge" (v. 18; cf. his caustic description of other preachers as "peddlers of God's Word," 2 Cor. 2:17), thereby not making use of his rights. In what sense is this a "reward"? Gordon Fee's comment on the passage captures the sense of Paul's claim: "In offering the 'free' gospel 'free of charge' his own ministry becomes a living paradigm of the gospel itself" (421). His renunciation of rights allows him to share in the pattern of Christ's own sacrificial action and thereby paradoxically to share in the lifegiving blessings of God.

If all this is a bit difficult, the argument becomes much clearer in verses 19–23: everything that Paul does is aimed at winning as many people as possible to the gospel. He will adapt his behavior (not his message!) in whatever way necessary to achieve that end. As Margaret Mitchell has observed (*Paul and the Rhetoric of Reconciliation,* 130–34), Paul represents himself here as a conciliator, seeking to overcome cultural and ethnic divisions in order to bring people of all sorts into the one community of faith. In order to do this, he has made himself—a free man—into "a slave to all" (v. 19; cf. 2 Cor. 4:5). Notice that this is exactly what Paul had said happens to free persons when they are called: they become "slaves of Christ" (7:22b). Paul's slavery to Christ is expressed in the form of submitting himself in various ways to the cultural structures and limitations of the people he hopes to reach with the gospel.

Paul gives four examples of his adaptive behavior in verses 20–22, the first three having to do with Jew/Gentile issues. In verse 20, he makes the remarkable statement that to Jews he became "*as* a Jew." Since Paul was in fact a Jew, this formulation shows how radically he conceives the claim that in Christ he is "free with respect to all," that is, in a position transcending all cultural allegiances. To relate to Jews as a fellow Jew (cf. Acts 21:17–26) is for Paul now seen as an act of accommodation! The second example may be nothing other than a restatement of the first, though it is sometimes suggested that this formulation might include the slightly wider circle of Gentile god-fearers

153

who observed the provisions of Jewish Law. Perhaps the main value of this second example is that it allows Paul to interject parenthetically that he is not himself under the Law, even though his "strong" critics may accuse him of acting as though he were.

The third example (v. 21) refers clearly to Paul's ministry to Gentiles, his fundamental apostolic mission (Gal. 1:15–16; Rom 1:5). This sentence states clearly what is abundantly apparent from many other bits of evidence: Paul not only resisted the imposition of Jewish Law on Gentiles but also himself adopted a casual attitude about Law observance (kosher laws, etc.) when he was among Gentiles. The real bite of the sentence comes in the play on words in Paul's parenthetical qualifying remark: even though he became "as one outside the law [*anomos*]," he himself is not lawless (*anomos*) toward God but is "under Christ's law [*ennomos Christou*]." The precise nuance of this last phrase is not easy to pin down, but the general sense is clear: being free from the Law does not mean that Paul runs wild with self-indulgence—a word pointedly spoken to Corinthians who are proclaiming, "I am free to do anything." Instead, he lives with a powerful sense of obligation to God, defined now by his relationship to Christ. By using the expression "under Christ's law" (cf. Gal. 6:2) Paul does not mean that he has acquired a new legal code of commandments to obey (such as the teachings of Jesus); rather, he is asserting that the pattern of Christ's self-sacrificial death on a cross has now become the normative pattern for his own existence. This idea is expressed here in compact formulaic fashion; for further elaboration, see 2 Corinthians 4:10–12; Galatians 2:19–20; Philippians 2:5–8; 3:10–11; and especially 1 Corinthians 11:1, which is the culminating appeal of the present argument.

The first three examples, however, have merely served to prepare the way for the fourth and decisive illustration of Paul's willingness to adapt his actions in the interest of gospel: "To the weak I became weak, so that I might win the weak." (v. 22a). This statement is the immediate goal of Paul's exposition. How can we tell? There are two decisive clues: there is no counterbalancing statement saying that to the strong he became strong, and—most tellingly—he does not say, "I became *as* the weak," but rather, "*I became weak*." This is not a matter of pretending or mere analogy. Paul actually took on the lifestyle and condition of the weak. In the context of 1 Corinthians 1–10, that means two things: he accepted for himself their strictures against eating idol meat, and he lowered himself to the social status of the weak by refusing the patronage of the rich and becoming a manual laborer. (The reader of this letter may recall that the "weak" were grouped with the "low and despised" in contrast to the "strong" and "those of noble birth" in

154

1:26–29). While these actions may have seemed puzzling and even de-meaning to the "strong" higher-class Corinthians, Paul understands this action as a necessary means to win more people over to the gospel (v. 22). Indeed, though the thought remains only hinted rather than ex-pressed here, this self-lowering is homologous with the law/pattern of Christ, who also became a slave (cf. Phil. 2:6–8) in obedience to God. Paul understands this movement as embodying the basic logic of the Christian life. The point is concisely expressed in Galatians 5:13–14: "For you were called to freedom, brothers and sisters; only do not use your freedom as an opportunity for self-indulgence, but through love become slaves to one another." That is the same message that Paul of-fers to the "strong" in 1 Corinthians 9, not as a direct exhortation, but by way of his own personal example. He is inviting the "strong" to see in his own self-enslaving action a call upon their own lives as well.

Sometimes it is suggested that "the weak" in 9:22 cannot refer to the weak Christians at Corinth, because Paul speaks here of "winning" or "saving" them. Therefore, it is alleged, he must be referring to non-believers. This is, however, to make too sharp a distinction, as though Paul thought his converts were already "saved" as soon as they pro-fessed faith. We should remember that in 1:18 Paul referred to him-self and other members of the believing community as those "who *are being* saved." For Paul, conversion is a process of having one's life re-shaped in the likeness of Christ, and salvation is the eschatological end for which we hope. The weak Christians, as we have already seen in chapter 8, are in danger—in Paul's view—of falling away from Christ and therefore not being saved (see also the illustration in 10:1–13). Thus, his continuing identification with the weak aims not only to gain converts but also to strengthen their adherence to the community and to help them along the path to salvation.

Self-discipline for the sake of the gospel (9:24–27)

In the final paragraph of chapter 9, Paul, while continuing to refer to himself as an example, also for the first time in this chapter explic-itly exhorts the Corinthians: they are to be like athletes in training to win the race. The Christian life is not an orgy of self-gratification but a disciplined life focused on things that really matter ultimately (not run-ning aimlessly, v. 26). Unlike some of Paul's other metaphors, this one requires little explanation for readers today, who know well the sacri-fices and discipline required of athletes. Paul's use of this imagery is in-spired by the Isthmian Games, the great athletic festival held at Corinth every two years; the Corinthians would find Paul's depictions of the runner and the boxer familiar, vivid, and compelling. Even his

155

reference to the athlete's "perishable wreath" (v. 25) is illuminated by the fact that the victory wreath at the Isthmian Games was made of withered celery (Murphy-O'Connor, *St. Paul's Corinth*, 17, 101). Paul is saying, "If these athletes push themselves to the limit in training to win that pathetic crown of withered vegetables, how much more should we maintain self-discipline for the sake of an imperishable crown?"

We should take care here not to lose the thread of Paul's argument and slip into thinking of spiritual discipline in an individualistic way. The self-control to which Paul is calling the "strong" is precisely the discipline of giving up their privileges *for the sake of others in the community*. They are to exercise self-discipline by giving up their rights to certain foods—and perhaps some of their privileged social status as well. This is a minor consideration, Paul suggests, in contrast to the prize set before us.

One other point may also require clarification. Throughout this letter, Paul resists the Corinthians' tendency to deprecate the body, and the present passage is no exception. While Paul speaks of "punishing" and "enslaving" his body in order to avoid being disqualified (v. 27), the interpreter may need to explain that the body is not the enemy of the spiritual life; rather, it is the *instrument* of that life. The athletic metaphor continues to govern the sense of verse 27: the "punishment" of the body refers to grueling training for the contest, seeking to bring the body to peak efficiency. To "enslave" the body means, in this context, to devote it unreservedly to God's service through service to others (cf. 9:19), not to practice self-denial for its own sake.

REFLECTIONS FOR TEACHERS AND PREACHERS

Because 1 Corinthians 9 falls in the middle of an extended argument, the preacher working with a passage from this chapter should be careful to set the text in its appropriate context. Some help in this regard is provided by the Revised Common Lectionary, which appoints readings from 8:1–13; 9:16–23; and 9:24–27 for the Fourth, Fifth, and Sixth Sundays after the Epiphany in Year B. Thus, when preaching on either of the lessons from chapter 9, the preacher will want to refer back repeatedly to chapter 8 in order to make clear that Paul's vision for "becoming all things to all people" (9:22) and his call for disciplined self-control (9:24–27) stand in service of building up the community in love. (Because the epistle readings here in the lectionary are sequential, they do not correlate thematically with the other appointed readings.) Regrettably, the reading of 10:1–13 is placed during Lent of Year C, and 10:14—11:1 is omitted from the lectionary altogether. Thus, the preacher who wants the congregation to think through the entirety of Paul's argument would have to abandon the lectionary temporarily or, alternatively, deal with the text in study groups outside of worship.

Because we are considering just one movement in a more complex discussion, it may be wise to reserve most of our reflections for the end of the matter (see below on 10:23—11:1). Nonetheless, by the time we reach the conclusion of chapter 9, several issues have been brought more clearly into focus.

1. *Financial support of Christian ministers.* Paul makes it abundantly clear that the church ought to provide for the financial needs of those who preach the gospel (vv. 4–14). At the same time, his own example of renouncing such support from the Corinthians (vv. 12b, 15–18) raises a number of interesting possibilities. Is it possible that we have arrived at a moment in the life of the church where salaried ministers have become so domesticated by "patronage" that they are no longer able to preach the gospel effectively? Are they, like some servile household philosophers of the ancient world, rendered excessively dependent on those who provide for them? Paul's model of tentmaking self-support poses an alternative that might be worthy of consideration in some circumstances. Certainly Paul's strategy was not required of apostles and other preachers in the first century church, nor should it be mandatory now. But anyone whose vocation is to proclaim the gospel should stop and ask from time to time, "Who is footing the bill for me to do this, and what implications does that have for the content and integrity of my ministry?" Or again, "Have I become the house chaplain for the wealthy members of my congregation to the detriment of the less affluent?"

2. *Downward mobility.* By emphasizing his identification with "the weak," Paul declares to his Corinthian readers a "preferential option for the poor." Rather than acting like a strong, free, well-educated citizen, Paul understands his vocation to require self-lowering actions: restricting his diet and doing menial labor. Implicitly, such choices are for Paul part of what it means to be "under Christ's law" (v. 21): his life responds to and recapitulates the life-pattern of Christ who gave his life for the weak (cf. 8:11; Rom. 5:6). This sort of downward mobility is not a model for apostles only; all who are in Christ are called to share it. It is hard to avoid the conclusion that 1 Corinthians 9 should speak most powerfully and disturbingly to Christians in situations of ease and privilege. What would it mean for us to embrace Paul's determination to do everything for the sake of the gospel (v. 23), to let that consideration shape all our vocational and economic choices?

157

3. *Getting free from "rights."* Perhaps the most striking element

of this chapter for American Christians is its studied indifference to the "rights" of the individual. Without ever denying that he could claim various rights, Paul exemplifies instead a freedom that relinquishes rights for the sake of others (v. 19). True Christian freedom is exercised in service. By contrast, the Corinthians who insist on exercising their right to do whatever they like have become paradoxically captive to the agenda of their own *exousia*: they are not free to act in the interest of their brothers and sisters. To put it bluntly, 1 Corinthians 9 suggests that if we find ourselves campaigning on the party platform of defending our own rights and privileges, we have lost sight of the gospel.

4. *Training for victory.* Several years ago when the Duke University men's basketball team won back-to-back national championships, there was a popular T-shirt on campus. The front read, "You can talk the game, but can you play the game?" On the back, above the school logo, in large letters was printed the slogan, "We can play." That is the challenge that Paul poses to his readers—and to himself—in verses 24–27: can we play the game? Rather than just talking about the gospel, we are called to pay the price of sacrifice and discipline in order to *play* the game rightly and thus to win the prize. The high level of discipline and skill required of competitive athletes provides us with a compelling metaphor that suggests what might be required. That is one reason the Olympic Games remain perpetually fascinating for us: we are captivated by the dedication that these women and men devote to the pursuit of the gold medal. What about our own dedication to the gospel? Is it comparably rigorous, or are we flabby, armchair spectators? The question must be asked.

It is a pity that the athletic contests at the Isthmian Games were all individual competitions, for when Paul says, "only one receives the prize," he does not mean that Christians are to be in competition with one another—indeed, as we have seen, he means exactly the opposite: they should strive for excellence by subordinating their individual freedom to the good of others. If Paul had known about team sports, they would have given him a richer metaphor to make his point: team players must couple rigorous training with restraint of individual egos for the sake of the team's success. Teachers and preachers might want to pose the challenge to their own home team, the local congregation: Can we play the game? Are we willing to undergo disciplined training for the sake of the gospel? And can we exercise self-control for the sake of others on the team? To pose such questions is Paul's aim in 1 Corinthians 9.

158

Warning against Idolatry (10:1–22)

As we begin reading 1 Corinthians 10, it is important to recall the situation that Paul is addressing. The letter from the Corinthians has appealed for Paul's support of an enlightened understanding that idols are meaningless. Some of the Corinthians are attending meals and festivities in the temples of pagan gods, just as they had done before becoming Christians. In their view, this is merely a normal aspect of social life in their culture. Such activities entail no spiritual danger, they argue, because they have *knowledge*: knowledge that there is only one God, knowledge that sets them free from the petty rules and restrictions of ordinary religious life. Perhaps they are also arguing that, having participated in the mysteries of baptism and the Lord's Supper, they have passed into a zone of spiritual blessedness that makes them immune to any harm from associating with pagan worship. If they are sharers in the table of the Lord, receiving there the elements that Ignatius of Antioch later called "the medicine of immortality," what possible difference can it make if they accept friendly invitations to other meals that just happen to be located in the shrine of some imaginary god?

Paul's first response to this situation in chapter 8 was to raise a concern for weaker members of the community who might be led astray, by the example of the strong, to fall back into idol-worship. The *knowledge* of the strong might prove the spiritual undoing of the weak. Chapter 9 then indirectly summons the strong to follow Paul's example of surrendering rights for the sake of others: in this case, foregoing the eating of food offered to idols. In chapter 10, however, the argument takes a new turn. Paul now contends that there is another equally compelling reason to avoid dining in the presence of idols: the Corinthians who attend these temple meals are not only endangering the weak but also putting themselves in spiritual peril. By casually participating in idolatrous practices, they are putting Christ to the test (v. 9) and provoking the Lord to jealousy (v. 22). The dangerous folly of such actions is shown by the story of Israel in the wilderness (vv. 1–11), which serves as the basis for the emphatic admonition of 10:14: "Flee from the worship of idols."

Paul's use of Israel's story is crucial to his case: the God with whom we have to do, he insists, is not merely some abstract divine principle that sets us free from polytheistic superstition. The God with whom we have to do is the God of Israel, a jealous God who sternly condemns idol-worship and punishes all who dare to dabble in it. The Corinthians

159

who lightly flit about to temples, supposing themselves impervious to harm, are courting destruction.

That is the broad framework of Paul's argument. Let us now look more closely at some of its details in 10:1–22.

When Paul begins to retell the story of Israel in the wilderness, he refers to the Israelites in the wilderness as "our fathers" (v. 1; NRSV's "ancestors" is for the sake of inclusivity). It may seem odd that Paul would describe the Israelites in this way in a letter addressed to the predominantly Gentile congregation at Corinth, who of course are not the physical descendants of Israel, but Paul's language reveals something essential about his understanding of the church. His Gentile converts, he believes, have been grafted into the covenant people (cf. Rom. 11:17–24) in such a way that they belong to Israel (cf. Gal. 6:16). Thus, the story of Israel is for the Gentile Corinthians not somebody else's story; it is the story of their own authentic spiritual ancestors. Whether the Corinthians were used to thinking of themselves in this way is doubtful, but Paul is trying to teach them to think in these terms; "I do not want you to be unaware, brothers and sisters."

The linkage is strengthened by the bold metaphorical correspondences that Paul sketches in verses 1–4. Just as the Corinthians have left behind their pagan past through baptism into Christ, so also the Israelites after leaving Egypt were "baptized into Moses in the cloud [Exod. 13:12–22; Ps. 78:14; 105:39] and in the sea [Exod. 14:21–22; Ps. 78:13]"; the two elements correspond to Spirit and water in Christian baptism. Just as the Corinthians receive spiritual food and drink at the Lord's Supper (cf. *Didache* 10.3), so also the Israelites were given spiritual food and drink in the wilderness: manna (Exod. 16:1–36; Ps. 78:23–29) and water from the rock (Exod. 17:1–7; Num. 20:2–13; Ps. 78:15–16). To make the correspondence complete, Paul goes so far as to suggest that Christ was present with Israel in their wanderings: the rock from which they drank "was Christ" (v. 4). Thus, in every respect Israel enjoyed the grace and presence of God.

The interpreter should not make the mistake of supposing that the Old Testament itself interprets these events as sacramental symbols or that Jewish tradition before Paul had conceived of these events as figurative foreshadowings of future realities. For example, the expression "baptized into Moses" is nowhere to be found in Jewish sources; Paul has coined the phrase on the basis of Christian language. He is thinking metaphorically, perceiving illuminating likenesses between dissimilar entities. The assertorial weight of these metaphors is relatively slight; they should not be pressed too hard either as historical claims or doctrinal statements. For example, to insist that Israel *really* had

160

"sacraments" would be to fall into a stultifying literalism; Paul is reading Israel's story through the lens of the church's experience and discovering figurations of God's grace.

These observations apply also to the statement that "the rock was Christ." The legend that the rock, or well, had followed Israel in its travels through the desert is amply documented in rabbinic tradition; Paul is our earliest witness to this embellishment of the biblical narrative, but the offhanded way that he refers to "the spiritual rock that followed them" suggests that the tradition (attested also in the first century by Pseudo-Philo, *Biblical Antiquities* 11.15) was already familiar to his readers. We also have evidence that, before Paul's day, the provision of water for Israel in the wilderness was attributed to divine Wisdom (Wisd. Sol. 11:4), and that Philo, Paul's near contemporary in Alexandria, allegorically identified the rock itself as the wisdom of God: "For the flinty rock is the wisdom of God [*hē sophia tou theou*], which he marked off highest and chiefest from his powers, and from which he satisfies the thirsty souls that love God" (*Leg. All.* 2.86). With such ideas in the air, it is not difficult to see how Paul might have hit upon the notion of identifying the rock metaphorically with Christ, since the transference of the attributes of divine Wisdom to Christ was already a common interpretive practice in early Christianity (cf. 1 Cor. 1:30). One more factor that may have influenced Paul's identification of Christ with the rock is that the Hebrew text of Deuteronomy 32, a passage central to Paul's thinking in this chapter (cf. comments on vv. 20, 22, below), repeatedly ascribes to God the title "the Rock" (Deut. 32:4, 15, 18, 30, 31); perhaps Paul, rereading this text through Christian lenses, saw here a hidden christological reference. In any case, the parallel from Philo shows that such readings were possible in the Hellenistic Judaism of Paul's time and, simultaneously, that such language is clearly figurative. The metaphorical identification should not be pressed too hard, as though preachers should solemnly seek to determine whether Christ was igneous, metamorphic, or sedimentary.

The important point in verses 1–4 is that Israel—whose legacy the Corinthians have inherited—experienced powerful spiritual signs of God's favor and sustaining power. Paul's summary narration highlights the fact that these signs were given to all the Israelites: the word "all" appears five times in these verses (a single sentence in the Greek). *All* were "baptized," and *all* enjoyed the blessings of spiritual food and drink. And yet, despite these signs of grace, "God was not pleased with *most of* them, and they were struck down in the wilderness" (v. 5). The verb "struck down" conveys the vivid and appalling image of the bodies of the Israelites strewn across the desert sand (see NEB). With that

161

sobering note, Paul begins to develop the hortatory application of Israel's story to the situation of his Corinthian readers: Just because you have received spiritual blessings, he says, do not suppose that you are exempt from God's judgment.

In verses 6 and 11 Paul articulates the hermeneutical basis for this reading of the story. "These things [the events of the exodus] became types [*typoi*] of us, so that we might not desire evil as they did" (v. 6, au. trans.). The word *typoi* is often translated in a broadly interpretive manner as "warnings," but its root sense refers to a "mold" or "pattern" (cf. Rom. 5:14: Adam is a *typos* of Christ). Paul is claiming that the biblical events happened as prefigurations of the situation in which he and his Christian readers now find themselves. To be sure, his point in verses 6–12 is that they should take warning from this alarming pattern of correspondence. This is repeated in verse 11: "These things happened to them to serve as an example [*typikōs*, literally 'typologically'], and they were written down to instruct us, on whom the ends of the ages have come." The arrogant idolatry of the Israelites and the terrifying punishments imposed upon them by God actually foreshadow the perilous situation of the Corinthian church in the present time: anyone with eyes to see should learn the appropriate lessons.

Paul reads Scripture in the conviction that its narratives and prophecies all point to his own time; the church lives in the exhilarating moment in which all of God's past dealings with Israel and the world have come to their climactic point. When Paul says that "the ends of the ages [note the plural of both nouns] have come," he is referring to the eschatological point of collision between the old age and the new. That point of collision is precisely "upon us": the church stands in the crucial moment in which a bright new light is shed upon everything past, particularly everything in Scripture. From the privileged perspective of the new eschatological situation in Christ, Paul rereads the Old Testament stories and finds that they speak in direct and compelling ways about himself and his churches, and he concludes that God has ordered these past events "for our instruction." (For further discussion of Paul's hermeneutical strategies, see Hays, *Echoes*.)

Next, the way in which the wilderness story ought to instruct the Corinthians is explicitly spelled out with a number of references to the Pentateuchal narrative. Paul has already explained in verse 6 that the purpose of the scriptural story is (literally) "that we might not be cravers [*epithymētas*] of evil, just as they also craved [*epethymēsan*]." The emphasis here on "craving" suggests an allusion to Numbers 11, in which the Israelites' craving for *meat* (Num. 11:4) kindles God's anger against them and causes "a very great plague" to fall upon them

(Num. 11:33). Although the connection remains only implicit in the argument, the echo of Numbers 11 sounds ominously for those Corinthians who desire to eat the meat sacrificed to idols. In verses 7–10, Paul exhorts his readers four times not to repeat the mistakes of Israel, pointing more directly to four specific offenses. In each case, he carefully notes that these sins were committed not by all of the Israelites but by "some of them." The fourfold repetition of this phrase stands in contrast to the emphasis on God's graciousness to *all* the Israelites in verses 1–4. *All* received good things from God; *some of them* defied God and were destroyed.

The first of these four exhortations targets the central theme of the passage as a whole: "Do not become idolaters as some of them did" (v. 7a). The grave sin of the wilderness generation was their worship of the golden calf, even after they had experienced God's mighty deliverance from slavery in Egypt; this story presents a telling analogy for Paul's argument that Christians should not become implicated in idol worship. His reference to the golden calf story is accomplished by the one explicit scriptural quotation in this unit: "as it is written, 'The people sat down to eat and drink, and they rose up to play' " (v. 7b, quoting Exod. 32:6). This brief excerpt from Exodus 32 does not explicitly mention the idol worship, but the quotation works powerfully for any reader who recognizes its source: it immediately follows the narration of the people's offering of sacrifices to the golden calf made by Aaron. In the context of Exodus 32, the verb "play" refers to the revelry and dancing surrounding the worship of the calf; some commentators also see an allusion here to sexual misconduct (cf. 1 Cor. 10:8), which is often in Jewish tradition linked to idolatry.

Paul has no doubt selected this one verse from the Exodus passage precisely because its reference to eating and drinking reinforces the themes of his exhortation in 1 Corinthians 10. There are two ways of understanding the function of the first part of the quotation ("the people sat down to eat and drink") within Paul's argument. The eating and drinking could refer to the Israelites' eating and drinking the spiritual food and drink provided by God (vv. 1–4). In that case, the point of verse 7 would be to emphasize their appalling ingratitude: "Even though they ate and drank the spiritual nourishment that God provided, nonetheless they rose up to commit idolatry." The advantage of this interpretation is that it permits us to see the whole of verses 1–12 as structured upon this single quotation. Alternatively, the eating and drinking of verse 7 could refer not to their consumption of God-given food and drink but to their feasting in the presence of the idol. In that case, the point of verse 7 would be to emphasize that participation in the idol feast leads on to other immoral behavior. "They ate and drank before the golden calf and rose up to commit other offenses against God." There are two major advantages of this second interpretation: it is in keeping with the contextual meaning of the sentence in Exodus 32 (unlike the first interpretation), and it relates directly to the problem that Paul is addressing in 1 Corinthians 10:1–22—eating sacrificed meat in a pagan temple. All things considered, the second reading is to be preferred. By quoting Exodus 32:6, Paul deftly identifies the "eating" of the temple food with the act of idolatry that brought God's wrath upon Israel.

The second exhortation (v. 8) is also aimed directly at the Corinthians' misdoings. As we have already seen, "sexual immorality" is a major concern of Paul's correspondence with them (5:1–13; 6:12–20; 7:2–5). In this case, Paul alludes to the warning precedent of Numbers 25:1–9. The opening verses of this passage illustrate the conventional linkage between fornication and idolatry and, at the same time, demonstrate its pertinence to the theme of eating in the presence of idols: "While Israel was staying at Shittim, the people began to have sexual relations with the women of Moab. *These invited the people to the sacrifices of their gods, and the people ate and bowed down to their gods.* Thus Israel yoked itself to the Baal of Peor, and the Lord's anger was kindled against Israel" (Num. 25:1–3, emphasis added). The Septuagint rendering of verse 2 makes the passage even more striking in relation to Paul's concerns. Instead of "gods," the Septuagint uses the word "idols"; furthermore, it also says, "the people ate *of their sacrifices.*" The Israelites at Shittim were doing precisely what the Corinthians are claiming the "right" to do now. The Lord's anger at such actions produced a terrible plague that killed 24,000 people (Num. 25:9). (Paul's figure of 23,000 has long puzzled commentators; apparently he was alluding to the story from memory and just got the number wrong; the exact number is not important for the point he is making.)

The third exhortation (v. 9) alludes to the story of Num. 21:4–9. Once again, food is the issue, though here there is no direct reference to idolatry. The sin seems to be primarily the sin of complaining against God: "The people spoke against God and against Moses, 'Why have you brought us up out of Egypt to die in the wilderness? For there is no food and no water, and we detest this miserable food' " (Num. 21:5). This time the punishment takes the form of poisonous serpents. Psalm 78:18 may provide a link to Paul's interpretation of the story, because it speaks of the people putting God to the test by their desire for food: "They tested God in their heart by demanding the food they craved." But why does Paul say, "We must not put *Christ* to the test, as some of them did" (1 Cor. 10:9, NRSV)? (The NIV, following a different Greek text, reads "test *the Lord*"; however, the reading adopted by the NRSV is clearly the more difficult and therefore more likely to be original.) The likeliest explanation for this odd turn of expression is that Paul is thinking primarily of the action of the Corinthians in the present time: they are putting *Christ* to the test by attending pagan temples and participating in the idol meals. That is what Paul insists must not be done. The formula, "as some of them did," already established in verses 7 and 8, is repeated for the sake of rhetorical parallelism, even though the Israelites in the wilderness were not, strictly speaking, putting Christ to the test (but cf. 10:4).

The final exhortation in this series (v. 10) is the most difficult to connect to a specific Old Testament text and also the most difficult to relate to any known behavior of the Corinthians. The best guess is that Paul is thinking of Numbers 14, in which the people complain against Moses and Aaron and desire to return to Egypt (14:2–4). There is no mention here of "the destroyer" (1 Cor. 10:10; cf. Exod. 12:23), but the passage concludes with God's definitive pronouncement that all of the current generation of Israelites except Joshua and Caleb will fall in the wilderness and not be allowed to enter the promised land (Num. 14:28–38). This punishment is decreed precisely in light of their "complaining": in 14:27, God says to Moses and Aaron, "How long shall this wicked congregation complain against me? I have heard the complaints of the Israelites, which they complain against me." How is this related to the problems at Corinth? Perhaps Paul thinks of their criticisms of him as analogous to Israel's complaints against Moses; this might be pertinent to the idol meat problem if the Corinthian letter had expressed complaints against Paul's "weak" restrictive policy on eating such meat. Alternatively, perhaps Paul concludes his exhortations with this one because it represents the most comprehensive judgment of God against the unfaithful people; here it is not merely a few thousand who are punished, but the whole nation. There is not enough information given in the text to make a confident decision about whether Paul's final illustration is specifically related to the controversies at Corinth or whether it is simply a general homiletical remark based on the wilderness narratives.

In either case, Paul's heaping up of examples from the Pentateuchal narratives has demonstrated emphatically that God is not to be trifled with. Those who defy God's authority by flirting with idolatry and "craving" idol-tinged food will suffer catastrophic consequences. The moral of these tales is stated in a preliminary way in verse 12: "So if you think you are standing, watch out that you do not fall." The

165

Corinthian *gnōsis*-boasters are confident in their own *exousia*, their own power to stand against any temptations or dangers associated with the pagan temples. Paul, however, sternly warns that they should not be so cocky. The dire fate that befell "our fathers" may await them as well. The ultimate conclusion of this line of thought appears in the emphatic pronouncement of verse 14: "Therefore, my beloved, flee from the worship of idols." We have seen this verb "flee" once before in the letter: "Flee from fornication" (6:18a, weakly translated by the NRSV as "shun"). Paul's judgment on the Corinthians' desire to attend the temple feasts is finally just as uncompromising as his judgment on their desire to frequent houses of prostitution. The two practices are closely linked in Jewish tradition and in the rhetoric that Paul uses to reject both. Such behavior can only bring the community under God's judgment.

But how does 10:13 fit into this discussion? As a word of reassurance it sits awkwardly in the midst of a unit (vv. 1–22) that is otherwise full of stern warnings. The best explanation is that Paul is contrasting the "testing" that God allows to come to us (v. 13) with the very different dangers associated with our "testing" of God (v. 9). God provides a "way out" for those who are "overtaken" by the trials that all flesh is heir to. But those who put themselves in jeopardy by participating in idolatry are in a very different position and should not presume to have any guarantees of safety or salvation. That is why they must "flee" from idol worship as from a burning building. Thus, the word of reassurance in verse 13—which looks like a general maxim affirming the faithfulness of God to his people—is used here as part of Paul's larger prohibition of idolatry.

Sometimes 10:14–22 is treated as a separate pericope, but it really should not be so considered, for it continues to draw out the immediate practical implications of the wilderness story. After his forceful call for the Corinthians to flee from idolatry, Paul changes his tone somewhat in verse 15, but he is still pressing the same argument. Now he appeals to the Corinthians as "sensible people" (*phronimoi*) to judge the case that he is presenting (v. 15). In this apparently straightforward appeal, however, there is a note of irony, for the adjective "sensible" is probably another of the Corinthians' favorite self-descriptions. For evidence, note Paul's only other use of this word in the letter, where he sarcastically contrasts their "sensible" nature to his foolishness (4:10; cf. the even more caustic 2 Cor. 11:19). Apart from these passages, Paul's only other uses of the term are pejorative (Rom. 11:25; 12:16). Presumably, therefore, we should understand that in their letter the "knowing" Corinthians have described their liberal policy about sharing in temple meals as the "sensible," realistic position, in contrast to the hysterical sectarian extremism of the weak, who would forbid such eating. Paul ironically turns this language back on them: if they are really sensible they will be persuaded by the argument that follows in verses 16–21.

This argument holds up for comparison meals of three types: the Lord's Supper (vv. 16–17), Jewish meals in conjunction with sacrifice (v. 18), and meals at the table of a pagan god (vv. 19–21). What they have in common is this: Each meal creates a relation of *koinōnia* ("fellowship") among the participants and between the participants and the deity honored in the meal. Paul takes this as a commonplace interpretation of such cultic meals. Once the point is granted, his argument is nearly irrefutable: the God who demands exclusive allegiance will not tolerate cultic eating that establishes a bond with any other gods or powers.

Paul begins on ground shared with his readers by discussing the Lord's Supper first (vv. 16–17). There is no reason to think that the wording of these verses represents liturgical language actually used in the celebration. Paul is neither giving instructions about this aspect of the Corinthians' worship (cf. 11:17–34) nor describing the sequence of events in its celebration. Rather, he is stating certain assumptions about the significance of the Lord's Supper in order to argue *from* a shared interpretation of this meal *to* the point he wants to make about the temple meals. Thus, the fact that he mentions the cup before the bread in verse 16 (as also in *Didache* 9.1–4) is of no significance. We know from 11:23–26 that Paul's form of the Lord's Supper tradition places the bread first; he reverses the order of the elements in verse 16 only because he wants to elaborate on the significance of sharing the bread in verse 17.

The references to sharing in the blood and body of Christ in verse 16 have nothing to do with mysteriously ingesting Christ in the meal; rather, Paul means that the participants in the supper are brought into partnership or covenant (cf. 11:25) with Christ through sharing the meal. (For a comprehensive study of these issues, see Willis.) The Corinthians would find nothing surprising in Paul's words; he is articulating a commonly held understanding, perhaps even using traditional language. In the next verse, however, Paul goes on to highlight a corollary of the first point: because all the members of the community are brought together into covenant relation with Christ through eating the one bread, they become in effect one body; the eucharistic celebration creates not only *koinōnia* with Christ but also unity within the community. This point is not, strictly speaking, germane to the line

167

of thought in verses 16–21, but it prepares the way for Paul's subsequent appeal to his readers to act for the sake of others in the church (10:23–24; 10:31—11:1). Here again, as we have seen throughout the letter, Paul's concern for unity and peace in the community undergirds his exhortation.

In verse 18, Paul alludes briefly to the sacrificial practices of Israel. Not only do the priests eat the sacrificial meat (9:13; Lev. 7:6) but also all the people participate in eating the sacrifices and thus become "partners [koinōnoi] in the altar" (cf. Philo, *Spec. Leg.* 1.221). Probably Paul is thinking of the provisions for tithe offerings in Deuteronomy 14:22–26:

> In the presence of the LORD your God, in the place that he will choose as a dwelling for his name, you shall eat the tithe of your grain, your wine, and your oil, as well as the firstlings of your herd and flock, so that you may learn to fear the LORD your God always. . . . And you shall eat there in the presence of the LORD your God, you and your household rejoicing together.
>
> (Deut. 14:23, 26b)

This example shows that Paul is not thinking of some sort of mystical union affected through the meal—an idea foreign to the Old Testament. The meal is, however, to be eaten "in the presence of the Lord" as a sign of the covenant relationship between God and the people, a covenant that also binds the people together. The comments of Josephus on Jewish sacrifices are especially interesting in this context:

> Our sacrifices are not occasions for drunken self-indulgence—such practices are abhorrent to God—but for sobriety. At these sacrifices prayers for the welfare (sōtēria) of the community must take precedence of those for ourselves; for we are born for fellowship (koinōnia), and he who sets its claims above his private interests is specially acceptable (kecharismenos: "graced") to God.
>
> (Ap. 2.196)

Paul's first two examples have demonstrated that the community meal in the presence of God establishes a bond with the one who is worshiped by the community. Both of these examples pertain to the one true God. The case of the "knowing" Corinthians rests, however, on their assertion that the pagan gods are nothing but human fantasy (8:4) and that any activity in their temples is therefore nothing other than an empty gesture. No bond can be established with a god that does not exist. Thus, Paul's argument, which depends on establishing parallelism between the three meals in verses 16–21—Christian, Jewish, and pagan—threatens to break down unless he attributes real existence to the pagan gods. Seemingly the argument will work only if he

168

denies what he has already asserted in 8:4–6: that there is no God but one. In 10:19, then, he recognizes the problem he has created for himself: "What do I imply then? That food sacrificed to idols is anything, or that an idol is anything?"

His way out of this dilemma is through a Scripture quotation. Most English translations of verse 20 fail to make this point clear, but the NEB laudably bends over backward to make sure that readers follow what Paul is doing here: "No; but the sacrifices the heathen offer are offered (in the words of Scripture) 'to demons and to that which is not God'." The only thing wrong with this translation is that it follows some Greek manuscripts that supply "the heathen" as the subject of the action of offering sacrifice. In fact, a literal translation of the better Greek text would read as follows:

> What then am I saying?
> That idol meat is anything
> or that an idol is anything?
> [No,] but
> that what they sacrifice
> "they sacrifice to demons and not to God."

This distinction is important because in the source of Paul's quotation, Deuteronomy 32:17, it is *Israel*, not pagans, that is accused of sacrificing to demons. In this important passage from the Song of Moses—a text that Paul alludes to repeatedly (see, e.g., Rom. 10:19; 12:19; 15:10; as well as 1 Cor. 10:22)—Moses indicts Israel's unfaithfulness in turning to idolatry despite God's many blessings:

> They made him jealous with strange gods,
>   with abhorrent things they provoked him.
> *They sacrificed to demons, not God,*
>   to deities they had never known. . . .
> *They made me jealous with what is no god,*
>   provoked me with their idols.
>   (Deut. 32:16–17, 21, emphasis added)

This does, of course, imply that the sacrifices of pagans are likewise offered to demons, but Paul's real concern, like that of the Song of Moses, is that *God's own people* are becoming implicated in this "abhorrent" practice.

In any case, this quotation from Deuteronomy 32:17 provides the crucial missing piece in Paul's argument. While denying the real existence of pagan gods, Paul affirms the existence of a world of spiritual powers hostile to God, who are associated with pagan cultic practice (cf. 1 Cor. 8:5). Those who participate in the temple meals are becoming "partners [*koinōnoi*] with demons" (1 Cor. 10:20b); that is what Paul is trying to prevent at all costs. The alternatives are starkly posed in verse 21: the Corinthians must choose between the table of the Lord and the table of demons. It is impossible to be a sharer in both. Why? Because God will not permit it, as the Old Testament stories adduced in this chapter amply demonstrate. It is impossible to remain in covenant relation to God while forming entangling alliances with these evil inferior spiritual powers—which Paul believed to be entirely real.

Here the radically *exclusive* character of Israel's monotheistic faith becomes clear. In the ancient Mediterranean world, it was thoroughly commonplace for people to worship various gods and goddesses. Participating in cultic rites for one deity did not by any means preclude participating with equal piety in the rites for another; the pantheon was infinitely inclusive. Indeed, it was probably a good bet to worship several gods as a way of diversifying one's spiritual investments. The God of Israel, however, would tolerate none of this. Jews—and, later, Christians—puzzled and outraged their pagan neighbors by refusing, even for the sake of appearances, to venerate any god but one. The "knowing" Corinthians were seeking to work out some sort of "sensible" compromise on this matter, but Paul would have none of it.

Here again, we can sense the magnitude of the imaginative conversion that he was urging upon his readers, calling them out of the pluralistic religiosity of their culture into a rigorously exclusive symbolic world depicted by the fearful narratives of Exodus, Numbers, and Deuteronomy. Even those venturesome souls at Corinth who responded to Paul's preaching of the gospel and took the plunge into that world may not have realized fully at first what they were getting themselves into. They were not merely accepting a more refined system of philosophical truth that would allow them to relativize all particular religious practices and therefore to sample them as they chose, with lofty indifference; rather, they were entering a binding covenant relationship with a God who had given up his only Son for them and who demanded nothing less than total allegiance in return.

The conclusion of this unit (v. 22) echoes the passage from Deuteronomy one more time: "Or shall we provoke the Lord to jealousy?" Of course, by this time, the necessary answer to such a rhetorical question is clear. Those considering such a course ought to reread Deuteronomy 32 and some of the other stories to which Paul had alluded. Yet, some Corinthians may still dare to venture into the temples of idols and eat their sacrificial meat in order to display their own freedom and strength of character. Paul leaves the "strong" with a final ominous question: "Are we stronger than he?"

As we reach the end of this unit, one outstanding question remains: If Paul takes such an uncompromising stance against eating idol food in temples, why did he begin the discussion of the problem back in chapter 8 with a much milder appeal, asking the "knowing" Corinthians to act in loving consideration for the weak? The question has at least two answers.

First, the two arguments are complementary rather than antithetical. Both lead to the same conclusion: Do not go to the temple feasts. By beginning with the argument for building up the community in love, Paul seizes the occasion to teach the *gnōsis*-boasters a lesson they sorely need to learn. He wants them not only to stay out of the temples but also to see the Christian life in a radically different way: as he puts it in Phil 2:4, "Let each of you look not only to your own interests, but to the interests of others." If he had simply begun with the word of prohibition, he would not have been able to make this point so effectively.

The second possible answer, however, introduces further complications. Perhaps the Corinthian letter posed more than one aspect of the problem of "food offered to idols"; such meat was available not only at temple dinners but also in the public market—and, therefore, in private homes. Paul's arguments in 8:7–13 and 10:1–22 address the problem of idolatry in temples but not the question of whether the meat itself is forbidden in other settings. By appealing first, however, to concern for others Paul has also laid a foundation to address the latter problem as well. To that issue he will turn in the conclusion of the whole discussion, 10:23—11:1.

REFLECTIONS FOR TEACHERS AND PREACHERS

The message of 10:1–22 focuses with laser-like intensity on the warning of 10:14: "Flee from the worship of idols." Everything in the passage is constructed to support that urgent admonition. It is unfortunate, then, that when this text appears in the Revised Common Lectionary as the epistle reading for the Third Sunday in Lent during Year C, the prescribed reading ends in the middle of the pericope at 10:13, omitting the climactic warning. The preacher working with this text should surely extend the reading to include verse 14, if not verses 15–22 as well.

The other readings designated for this Sunday suggest some thematic linkages for the preacher who likes to explore intertextual correlations. Isaiah 55:1–9 begins with a call to come drink and eat; these motifs could be interwoven with the eating and drinking motifs in 1 Corinthians 10, contrasting Isaiah's gracious offer of divine sustenance to the temptations of eating idol food. The Gospel reading, Luke 13:1–9, which reflects on disasters that have befallen innocent victims, offers an interesting counterpoint to Paul's narration of the disasters that came upon Israel because of their idolatry; however, despite the differing causes of these misfortunes, Luke and Paul are in agreement that their readers should take such stories as a word of warning, an occasion for self-examination and repentance.

On the other hand, a strong case can be made that if the sermon is to be based primarily on 1 Corinthians 10:1–22, the Old Testament reading should be taken from either Exodus 32 or Deuteronomy 32. These texts, along with the narratives in Numbers, provide the background against which Paul is working.

Paul's argument in this passage is so forceful that it requires no artful exegesis to discern its fundamental themes. The following reflections may serve as a starting place for the interpreter seeking to read this chapter as though it were a letter to us.

1. *The danger of idolatry.* In a secularized world, we are in danger of recapitulating the Corinthians' error of supposing that there is no real danger of idolatry. If there really are no other gods, we tell ourselves, we can participate casually in whatever customs our culture may deem normal and "sensible." But 1 Corinthians 10:1–22 raises a warning flag and summons us to scrutinize our small compromises with the cultural systems around us. (See my reflections on the boundaries between church and culture at the end of chapter 8, above.) When we find ourselves in the face of some dubious invitation or opportunity saying, "No problem, I can handle it; I can be involved in this and still be a good Christian," we should pause and remember Paul's warnings to the strong at Corinth. There are two distinct dangers here: the idols have more power than we suppose to reshape us, and we are courting the judgment of God. We should heed Paul's warning not to put God to the test. Choices must be made, for we cannot partake of the table of the Lord and the table of demons.

There was a time when it was fashionable for biblical scholars and theologians—working in a cultural climate influenced by optimistic rationalism—to discount belief in "demons" as antiquated superstition. By the end of the twentieth century, however, anyone who does not believe in the power of evil afoot in the world is simply closing his or her eyes to the evidence of our times. The task for us is to discern where the demonic powers are inviting us into partnership with them and to flee resolutely. A hint: I suspect that in our time the powers have changed their strategy. Rather than seeking to lure us away from the table of the Lord through offering meat, they now invite us into "temples" where the chief activity is acquiring wealth by whatever means may be necessary.

2. *Worship creates koinōnia.* Paul's brief but suggestive remarks about the Lord's Supper highlight the fact that when we eat the bread and drink the cup together, we are bonded together in community with Christ and with one another. This is the positive counterreality set over against the danger of idolatry: authentic Christian worship draws us together around the table of the Lord in such a way that we become a covenant people, receiving the blessings of fellowship with God and sharing our lives with one another. In order to flee from idolatry we must order our lives so that this *koinōnia* becomes the focal point of our existence. Paul does not develop this theme extensively in chapter 10, but the teacher working with the text may want to invite students to reflect on what it means for us to be "one body" that participates in the body and blood of Christ. (This theme will, of course, receive further development in chapter 12.) In what ways do we see this reality in our congregational life? We might also want to ask what it costs us to enter this *koinōnia*; if the strong at Corinth obeyed Paul's teaching, it may have cost them their place in the respectable social circles of their city.

3. *Learning to see ourselves in Israel's story.* Paul creates a double-exposure effect between the wilderness generation and the Corinthian church. By speaking of Israel as "our fathers" and by reading the wilderness narrative as a typological prefiguration of the church's experience, Paul blurs the boundary between past and present and invites his readers to reimagine their lives as belonging to that story—in opposition to other models of self-understanding available in first-century Corinth. That is what all good narrative preaching aims to do. This passage should encourage us as preachers to let our metaphorical imagination work boldly as we seek to discover previously undiscerned correspondences between our world and the scriptural story. One of our fundamental pastoral tasks is to teach our congregations to find themselves in the stories of Israel and the early church, just as Paul sought to teach the Corinthians to find themselves in Israel's story. Is that difficult? Yes. Possible? Yes. Thinking typologically is a necessary survival skill for adult Christians. Our pedagogy has failed miserably to teach this skill because we have usually tried too hard to make the text "relevant." Rather than seeking to make the text relevant, Paul seeks to draw his readers *into* the text in such a way that its world reshapes the norms and decisions of the community in the present. That is the task of biblical preaching.

173

Conclusion: Use Your Freedom
for the Glory of God (10:23—11:1)

It remains for Paul to draw general conclusions and wrap up some loose ends left in his lengthy treatment of "food sacrificed to idols." Unfortunately, this concluding section is a bit muddled, because he is making two different points, and he swings back and forth between them in a potentially confusing way. Still, the two basic emphases are clear enough:

> Point A: All our actions should glorify God by seeking the benefit of others rather than ourselves.
> Point B: Within the framework of that principle, we are free to eat whatever we like with thankfulness.

The first point is the fundamental one, the guiding principle that has governed Paul's whole discussion of idol food. By pressing this principle he hopes to change the terms of the discourse at Corinth, to provide a new framework for moral judgment. This principle poses a fundamental challenge to those Corinthians who style themselves strong and wise: they should stop asserting their rights and start thinking of the interests of others in the community. On the second point, however, Paul agrees fundamentally with their judgment about the moral neutrality of food per se, and he affirms—contrary to the scruples of the weak—that outside the temple setting Christians can eat meat without worrying about its source.

This is a delicate balancing act, because Paul's position does not fit precisely into either of the opposing positions in the Corinthian debate. It is easy to see how each side might accuse him of inconsistency or lack of moral courage. Nonetheless, his position is a coherent one, however difficult it might be to put into practice in a community.

The structure of 10:23—11:1 is best understood when we see that Paul has nested point B within his general statement of point A, and that in the midst of discussing point B he inserts a qualification based on point A. This produces the following structure (see also Fee, 478):

A. Seek the benefit of others (23–24)
  B. Eat whatever you want (25–27)
    A^1. Exception: abstain for sake of the other's conscience (28–29a)
  B^1. Defense of freedom to eat (29b–30)
A^2. Do everything for the glory of God by seeking the benefit of others (10:31–11:1).

174

The greatest exegetical difficulty of the passage is to understand the transition from A^1 to B^1 within verse 29. The greatest practical difficulty in following Paul's advice is, of course, to understand when it is necessary to place limits on one's freedom for the sake of others.

Paul introduces the final section of his argument by quoting, once again, the slogan of the Corinthian *gnōsis* faction: "All things are lawful." First Corinthians 10:23 is almost a verbatim repetition of 6:12: the same slogan is quoted twice, followed by Paul's rejoinders. With the final clause of 10:23, however, Paul breaks the pattern of repetition. Instead of "I will not be dominated by anything" he writes, "not all things *build up*." Thus, he signals that he is reaching the conclusion of his treatment of idol food, which began in 8:1 with the declaration that "love *builds up*."

The full sense of 10:23b is rightly conveyed by the NEB: "'We are free to do anything,' but does everything help the building of the community?" Paul regularly uses the verb *oikodomein* ("to build up") and the noun *oikodomē* ("upbuilding, edification") to refer to loving actions that benefit the whole community (cf. 14:3–5, 12, 17, 26; Rom. 14:19; 15:2; 2 Cor. 12:19; 13:10; 1 Thess. 5:11) That he has this meaning in mind here is confirmed by 10:24, which directly states the principle he is trying to impress upon the headstrong Corinthians: "Do not seek your own advantage but that of the other." This principle—which, as we see at the end of the unit in 11:1, is based on the example of Christ—is fundamental to Paul's moral vision (cf. Phil. 2:4; Rom. 15:1–3). The application of this principle to the present situation has already been explained in 8:7–13: love should constrain the "knowing" Corinthians from eating in temples, because this action will jeopardize others in the community. Thus, verses 23–24 recapitulate the opening theme of the argument in chapter 8.

Having offered his readers that reminder, however, Paul now addresses a new problem not identified in the discussion heretofore. What about meat that is sold in the public market or served in private homes? Such meat often came from the temples or had been slaughtered by the pagan priests. Is such meat spiritually contaminated even if it is not eaten in a cultic context? (The question would be of concern primarily to the wealthier Corinthians; the poor could not ordinarily afford meat, nor would they be likely to be invited to private dinners where such delicacies were served.) Presumably the weak at Corinth were arguing for the position almost universally held elsewhere in orthodox early Christianity and in Judaism: such meat was still idol meat, and it must be forbidden. At this point, however, Paul emphatically declares his agreement with the strong: you can eat anything sold in the market (v. 25). As a warrant for this position, he quotes Psalm 24:1, affirming that the whole creation belongs to "the Lord" (v. 26). In the

175

psalm, "the Lord" of course means God, but Paul often reads Old Testament references to "the Lord" as pointing to Jesus. If that is how he understands Psalm 24:1, he would be claiming that Christian freedom to eat all foods is a consequence of the sovereignty of Jesus Christ over all creation (cf. Rom. 14:14).

Here is dramatic evidence of Paul's break with his past understanding of Judaism. He has become to the Gentiles "as one outside the Law" (9:21). As a zealous Jew, Paul would never have eaten marketplace meat unless he were certain it had been ritually slaughtered in accordance with kosher laws. Now, however, in his role as apostle to the Gentiles, Paul can write "I know and am persuaded in the Lord that nothing is unclean in itself" (Rom. 14:14). Therefore, he tells the Corinthians they are free to eat market meat without bothering to ask any questions about where it came from. To Jewish sensibilities, as well as to the weak at Corinth, such an attitude would have been shocking. This stance is, however, completely consistent with what we know of Paul's attitude towards the other identity-marking features of the Law, such as circumcision: They no longer mean anything (cf. 7:19). Thus, Paul gives license to Christians to eat as they please.

This license applies not only to their own private homes but also to social occasions, as long as they are not directly linked to pagan worship. In verse 27, he tells them they can eat whatever is served to them in the home of an unbeliever without conducting any inquiries about the source of the meat; it is not an issue of "conscience" (*syneidēsis*) at all. Paul views the church as open to interaction with the surrounding world; as he has suggested earlier in the letter, he does not want to prohibit social contacts and eating with unbelievers (5:9–13). All of this was no doubt gratifying to the higher-status members of the Corinthian church, who desired to maintain their social networks and business contacts insofar as possible.

Paul's policy of openness to social contact and eating with Gentiles was, as we know from other passages in the New Testament, a source of considerable controversy, and he took a great deal of criticism for it (e.g., Acts 21:21; Gal. 2:11–14). Probably we should see in verses 29b–30 his defensive reaction to such criticism. (Whether this sort of criticism actually came from the weak at Corinth or not is impossible to say.) The verbs in Paul's rhetorical questions here are simple present indicative verbs, indicating that someone is in fact judging and denouncing him for this behavior. (In 9:3, however, it appears that he is also being judged by some for his *lack* of freedom rather than for excessive exercise of freedom in such matters.) The reading proposed here, then, is that verses 29b–30 should be connected very closely with

176

verse 27, providing warrants for the freedom claimed "[E]at whatever is set before you without raising any question on the ground of conscience. . . . For why is my freedom judged by the conscience of another? If I partake with thanksgiving, why am I denounced because of that for which I give thanks?"

In the midst of all this, however, Paul does not want the Corinthians to forget about his concern for the weak in the community. Therefore, he constructs a hypothetical scenario in which a Christian dining in the house of an unbeliever is informed by someone else that the meat being served is *hierothyton*, "sacrificial meat." (The word appears for the first time here in these chapters; it is a neutral designation that pagans might use to describe the meat taken from the altar, in contrast to the pejorative term *eidōlothyton* ["idol meat"] that Paul had used in chapter 8 and in 10:19.) Under such circumstances, Paul says, the Christian should not eat the food for the sake of the other person's conscience (vv. 28–29a). This is a notoriously confusing passage because Paul's description is so sketchy. Who is the informant, and what motives are to be attributed to him or her? Is the informant a Christian? How is the other person's conscience affected by someone else's choice to eat or not to eat?

Without entering into all the minute exegetical details, the following explanation seems to make the best sense of this obscure passage. The informant—either another dinner guest or perhaps a household slave of the host—is a Christian who is among the "weak" faction of the church. The strong Christian's rejection of the food for the sake of the conscience of the weaker one would then be another example of the policy already recommended in 8:7–13, except that here there is no question of participation in temple worship. (Note, in contrast to chapter 8, that Paul says nothing here about the possible destruction of the weak informant.) The strong Christian simply chooses not to create an embarrassing moral dilemma for a fellow member of the church, who might feel pressured to eat the meat if his fellow Christian does.

The term *syneidēsis* ("conscience") is very difficult to translate properly into English. Here and elsewhere in 1 Corinthians 8–10 it seems to refer not to an inner moral sense of right and wrong but rather to the level of self-awareness or *moral confidence* possessed by an individual. It is probable that the "knowing" Corinthians made much of this term. In their view, the weak are weak precisely with respect to *syneidēsis*: lacking the requisite knowledge, they do not have a sufficiently formed moral character to eat freely without being riddled by qualms and guilt. Though Paul himself makes little use of this concept, he basically agrees with the "knowing" Corinthians. Thus, he insists

177

that own his freedom to eat should not be hamstrung by someone else's lower level of moral confidence (vv. 25–27, 29b–30); still, he recognizes that there are situations in which the loving thing to do is to forego that freedom temporarily in order to avoid causing problems for a brother or sister in the faith (vv. 28–29a). That is why he himself has adopted a policy of becoming "all things to all people" (9:22) for the sake of promoting his preaching of the gospel.

The sense of all this can be clarified by a paraphrastic rendering of verses 25–30:

> Eat everything sold in the meat market; you don't need to engage in any scrutiny for the sake of "conscience." For, as Scripture says, "The earth and its fullness belong to the Lord (Jesus)." If one of the unbelievers invites you to dinner and you want to go, eat everything that is put in front of you; you don't need to engage in any scrutiny for the sake of "conscience."
> (But if some weak brother or sister says to you, "This is sacrificial meat," then don't eat it, for the sake of the one who made an issue out of it and for the sake of conscience. I certainly don't mean your own conscience—I'm talking about the conscience of the other person.)
> As I say, you yourself don't need to engage in any scrutiny for the sake of "conscience," for why should my freedom be judged by the limited moral awareness of somebody else? If I partake with thanks, why am I denounced for the food over which I give thanks?

Again, it must be remembered that this discussion is framed within Paul's more fundamental call for believers to exercise their freedom by surrendering their own prerogatives if necessary for the sake of their brothers and sisters in the faith (10:23–24; 10:31—11:1).

This brief final movement of Paul's treatment of the idol food problem (10:23—11:1) is closely parallel in substance to the more clearly worked out discussion in Romans 14:1—15:13. The major differences are that the Romans passage says nothing specifically about idol meat, and—unlike 1 Corinthians—it explicitly calls the weak as well as the strong to practice mutual acceptance: "Those who eat must not despise those who abstain, and those who abstain must not pass judgment on those who eat" (Rom. 14:3). In 1 Corinthians 8:1—11:1, by contrast, all the burden for accommodation falls upon the strong.

Paul at last draws the general conclusion of his discussion of food offered to idols. In place of the slogan "All things are lawful for me" (10:23), Paul coins a counterslogan: "All things for the glory of God" (10:31). Thus, the movement of 10:23—11:1 runs closely parallel to the movement of 6:12–20, which began with "All things are lawful for me" and ended with "Glorify God in your body" (6:20). Once again we see Paul trying to move his readers from an anthropocentric view to a theocentric one, from an emphasis on rights to an emphasis on obedience and service. Eating, drinking, and all other activities are embraced by this comprehensive mandate. In light of the entire passage, we can infer that the glory of God is served when God's people serve one another and live in loving unity.

In verses 32–33 Paul once again holds himself up as an example (as he had done explicitly in 8:13 and implicitly in 9:19–23) of accommodating himself to others for their benefit (*symphoron*; cf. 10:23a: "not all things are beneficial [*sympherei*]"). The motive for his seeking to "give no offense" is so that as many people as possible can hear the gospel without impediment and be saved. Paul's closing recapitulation thereby explicitly recalls the argument in chapter 9, especially 9:22–23. There is a hidden difficulty in these verses, however, which should not be lost in the closing swoop of Paul's rhetoric. Is it in fact possible for him—or anyone—to "please everyone in everything"? Of course, the answer is no: to please the Greeks he has to live in a way that displeases the Jews, and vice versa. Paul's policy of accommodating himself to the standards of various reference groups will work only so long as those groups are not actually trying to live together. Alternatively, this strategy might work if everyone else within the church would adopt Paul's policy of evangelical flexibility so that all were willing to adapt themselves to one another and to the needs of the church's mission. That is a very big "if," but it is precisely the goal of Paul's exhortation. The climax of the section, therefore, is the invitation in 11:1 for the Corinthians to become imitators of Paul, as he himself imitates Christ.

It is regrettable that the chapter division (introduced centuries later) has caused many readers to miss the connection of 11:1 to the foregoing argument. In fact, the entire treatment of idol food (8:1—11:1) should be read in the light of this closing call for imitation. Paul has presented himself as exhibit A of giving up prerogatives in order to reach out to others (8:13, chapter 9 in its entirety, 10:33); furthermore, what has been implicit throughout is now at last made explicit: the fundamental pattern of self-emptying, on which Paul's own actions are based, is Christ. Paul concludes the section, leaving the word "Christ" hanging in the air, without explanation or elaboration. Perhaps he trusted that the Corinthians, having already heard what he had to say in 1:18—2:5 about Jesus Christ crucified, could work out the implication of this for their own lives. If we are less confident of the ability of our congregations to make the connections, we might refer to Phil. 2:1–3 for further elucidation.

179

Paul's summons to the church to imitate him (cf. Phil. 3:17; 4:9; Gal. 4:12; 2 Thess. 3:7–9) sounds like breathtaking immodesty, but in fact it reflects simple wisdom: we learn who we are and how to act only by the example of others (see the commentary on 4:16, above). Believing that his own life was in fact conformed to the self-sacrificial example of Christ, Paul was willing to offer himself as a role model. Here is a sobering challenge for all who preach the gospel: how many of us would be willing to present our own lives for inspection as models of Christ's self-giving love?

REFLECTIONS FOR TEACHERS AND PREACHERS

As we reflect back over Paul's argument about eating food offered to idols, we can hardly help observing that he has answered a simple question with remarkable theological complexity. First he rejects the original framework of the question and reframes the problem in terms of love rather than rights (8:1–13). Then he offers himself as an example of renouncing personal rights for the sake of making the gospel effective in the community—and along the way defends himself against criticisms of his refusal to accept patronage (9:1–27). Shifting ground, he narrates the Corinthian church into the world of Scripture and warns of the dangers of idolatry (10:1–22). Finally, in the last section (10:23—11:1), he dialectically balances freedom and servanthood and relocates the whole problem, in a final deft move, in relation to the imitation of Christ. By any standard this is a remarkable performance of pastoral theology.

Most of these themes have already been discussed in the foregoing sections. There are, however, two new elements in the conclusion that merit careful attention.

The first is Paul's affirmation of *Christian freedom* in matters that do not compromise the glory of God (vv. 25–27, 29b–30). This theme receives far less development here than in Galatians, but it provides an important concluding note in the present argument. We are not to suppose that the prohibition of eating in pagan temples is the first of a new set of laws that will bind the faithful into rigid separation from the world. Rather, as long as idolatry is avoided, Christians are free to receive God's created gifts with a relaxed openness that must have seemed heady indeed to Paul the ex-Pharisee. Our teaching and preaching should seek to recapture this exhilarating sense of thanksgiving for "the earth and its fullness." Of course, some Christian communities already emphasize this theme so one-sidedly that they are in danger of sliding into hedonism. But perhaps just as many churches have assumed a cramped, fearful posture, distrusting the tastes and smells and sights of God's world and drawing inward to avoid contamination. To such communities, Paul's counsel should come as a liberation: O, taste and see that the Lord is good.

The second element demanding further reflection is *the imitation of Christ* (11:1). For Paul, such imitation means one thing only: shaping our lives in accordance with the pattern of Jesus' self-sacrificing love. The imitation of Christ is, therefore, focused on the cross. This is precisely what the Corinthians were failing to perceive in their quest to affirm personal freedoms for themselves. Paul seeks throughout this section to impress upon them that life in the church is life in fellowship with those weak ones for whom Christ died (8:11). To live in such a fellowship is to find oneself called perpetually towards Jesus' example of costly service on behalf of others. This has always been a hard word for Jesus' followers to hear—from the time that Peter recoiled in shock from Jesus' prediction of his passion (Mark 8:31–38) to the present. Authentic preaching of the gospel must always seek to discern where we are summoned to lay down our lives for others. Sometimes the call will be to dramatic action, as it was for Dietrich Bonhoeffer, Martin Luther King, Jr., and Archbishop Oscar Romero. Sometimes, as in the case of Paul's directives to the prosperous Corinthians, the call will seem more modest: merely to surrender some privilege or mark of respectability for the sake of the church's wholeness. In either case, our identity as God's people is given its indelible character by its conformity to Christ's example: "For while we live, we are always being given up to death for Jesus' sake, so that the life of Jesus may be made visible in our mortal flesh" (2 Cor. 4:11). The brilliance of Paul's theological insight is to apply this paradigm to a seemingly unrelated mundane quarrel about what kind of meat can be consumed. Our task as interpreters is to discover how the same paradigm might reshape our thinking about the issues faced by our congregations today.

11:2—14:40
Community Worship

The next major block of the letter (chapters 11—14) turns to address several problems concerning the worship practices of the Corinthian community. The discussion of head coverings in 11:2–16 is apparently triggered by something in the Corinthians' letter to Paul; likewise, in chapters 12—14, Paul is responding to their comments or inquiries about spiritual manifestations in worship. In 11:17–34, on the other hand, he is reacting to secondhand reports (11:18) about divisions that occur in the community's celebration of the Lord's Supper. Paul has grouped these issues together because all of them pertain to the actions of the community gathered for prayer and worship. The structure of the unit may be outlined as follows:

Hairstyles and gender distinctions (11:2–16)
The Lord's Supper: Discerning the body (11:17–34)
Spiritual manifestations in worship (12:1—14:40)
    Varieties of gifts, but the same Spirit (12:1–31a)
    The preeminence of love (12:31b—13:13)
    Regulating spiritual gifts in worship (14:1–40)

Throughout this section of the letter, Paul's teaching is undergirded by his concern for the Corinthians to conduct themselves in worship in a manner that is orderly, dignified, motivated by love, and conducive to the common good. The Corinthians' tendency to see themselves as virtuoso spiritual soloists is nowhere more evident than in their behavior in worship: Paul recalls them repeatedly to perceiving worship as a *corporate* action of the community that requires complementary participation by all.

Hairstyles and Gender Distinctions (11:2–16)

In 11:2, Paul appears to be responding to something that the Corinthians have written in their letter: they have affirmed their loyalty to the traditions that Paul had handed on to them. From what follows, however, it seems that they have appealed to Paul's own teaching in order to argue for certain practices that seek to erase the distinctions between men and women in worship—practices of which Paul now expresses disapproval. Since we hear only Paul's side of the conversation, we are forced to do a certain amount of guesswork about what the Corinthians were saying. Perhaps they had written to him somewhat as follows:

> Dear Paul,
>
> We remember you fondly and wish that we could see you again. Some of us are trying hard to maintain the traditions you taught us, such as the tradition we learned at our baptism that in Christ there is no longer any distinction between male and female [cf. Gal. 3:27–28]. You would be glad to know that, when we come together for worship, the women in our community continue to play a role equal to the men, praying and prophesying freely in the assembly under the inspiration of the Spirit, just as they did when you were here

with us. But a dispute has now arisen on one point: some of the women, acting in the freedom and power of the Spirit, have begun to remove their head coverings and loose their hair when they prophesy, as a sign of their freedom in Christ. Some of the more timid and conservative members of the community have objected to this, thinking it unseemly and disgraceful for women to let their hair down in public. Most of us believe, however, that you would surely approve of this practice, for it is an outward and visible sign of the truth of the tradition we received from you. We would be grateful if you could comment directly on this matter in order to dispel any doubt about this point. We remain

Your devoted followers,
The church in Corinth

Paul's reply no doubt came as a surprise to the Corinthians. Rather than endorsing the freedom of the women to prophesy with unbound hair, he instructs them instead to maintain the discipline symbolized by head coverings. His reasoning is notoriously obscure, partly because we do not know precisely how to interpret some of the key terms in the argument and partly because the line of argument is—by any standard—labored and convoluted. In view of the uncertainty surrounding these matters, it is impossible to give a fully confident interpretation of the passage. It is possible, however, to identify some things that *are* clear about Paul's argument. The following points may be affirmed with confidence:

> Paul endorses the freedom of women to pray and prophesy in the assembly; the only question is what sort of headdress is appropriate for them while exercising this freedom.
>
> The patriarchal order of verses 3 and 7–9 is set in counterpoint with a vision of mutual interdependence of men and women "in the Lord" (vv. 11–12).
>
> The passage does not require *subordination* of women—even though some of Paul's arguments presuppose a hierarchical ordering—but a symbolic *distinction* between the sexes.
>
> The immediate concern of the passage is for the Corinthians to avoid bringing *shame* on the community.

These basic points should help us to keep our bearings as we work through the difficulties of the passage.

As we have already seen in chapter 7, some of the the Corinthians had enthusiastically embraced the early Christian tradition that in Christ there is no male and female, and they were seeking to transcend their sexuality. In keeping with this tendency, the Corinthian women who were removing their head coverings or letting their hair down in

183

worship were consciously discarding a traditional marker of gender distinction. The head covering—whatever it may have been—symbolized their femininity and simultaneously their inferior status as women. To throw off this covering was to throw off a symbol of confinement and to enter the realm of freedom and autonomy traditionally accorded only to men. As Robin Scroggs has pointed out, this symbolic function of the head covering is vividly expressed in the Hellenistic Jewish narrative *Joseph and Aseneth* (written sometime in the first century B.C.E. or the first or second century C.E.): after her conversion to Judaism, the young woman Aseneth is ordered by an angel to remove her head covering, "because you are a holy virgin today and your head is as that of a young man" (*Joseph and Aseneth* 15:1–2). The Corinthian women who rejected head coverings were giving expression to a similar claim of transformed spiritual status. Paul shares the view that women enjoy a new spiritual status in Christ; however, just as in chapter 7, he rejects some of the behavioral inferences that the Corinthians were drawing from this theological truth.

Paul comes at the Corinthians' question about head coverings indirectly, by first positing a hierarchical chain of being in verse 3 in which the word "head" (*kephalē*) is given a metaphorical sense. (Some interpreters have attempted to explain away the hierarchical implications of v. 3 by arguing that *kephalē* means "source" rather than "ruler." This is a possible meaning of the word, and it fits nicely with v. 8, in which Paul alludes to the Genesis story that describes the creation of woman out of man; however, in view of the whole shape of the argument, the patriarchal implications of v. 3 are undeniable. Even if Paul is thinking here primarily of man as the source of woman rather than authority over woman, this still serves as the warrant for a claim about his ontological preeminence over her, as vv. 7–9 show.) The argument about bare heads in worship is thereby placed within a symbolic framework different from the one the Corinthians had been presupposing. The covering or uncovering of the head is not merely a sign of individual freedom, Paul insists; rather, it signifies either respect or disrespect for one's superior in the hierarchy. Consequently, to display the literal head inappropriately attired in worship is to bring shame upon one's figurative "head" (vv. 4–5). If this seems odd to modern readers, we might well remember that analogous customs persist in our social world. For a man to show up at a formal dinner—or in church—wearing a baseball cap would be widely perceived as rude and irreverent. In ancient Mediterranean culture such a breach of etiquette would bring disgrace not only on the perpetrator of the act but also on the "head" to whom that person was responsible. Thus, one of Paul's concerns is that women who pray and prophesy with "uncovered" heads (v. 5) are in effect shaming the men of the congregation. (For men to cover their heads, he says, would also bring shame to Christ; since Paul focuses primarily on the behavior of the women, however, it appears that his comments about men's head coverings are purely hypothetical.)

In Greek there are no words equivalent to the English "husband" and "wife": the generic words for "man" (*anēr*) and "woman" (*gynē*) do double duty, and the context determines whether reference to a married couple is intended. In the present passage, however, the context does not give us much help. (The NRSV translates the words as "husband" and "wife" in v. 3, but as "man" and "woman" elsewhere the passage; this seems arbitrary. Most other translations employ the generic terms "man" and "woman" consistently throughout.) In the absence of any indicators to the contrary, it is preferable to understand Paul's directives here as applying to everyone in the community, married or unmarried: women should have covered heads in worship; men should not.

But what exactly is meant by "covered" and "uncovered" heads? And what precisely is it that Paul wants the women at Corinth to do? Traditionally his remarks have been understood to mandate that women should wear veils, and this interpretation continues to exert influence over English translations (e.g., NRSV, NEB, JB). The word for "veil," however, actually occurs nowhere in the passage. A more literal translation of verses 5–6, for example, is given by the NIV (emphasis added): "every women who prays or prophesies with her head *uncovered* shames her head—it is just as though her head were shaved. If a woman does not *cover* her head she should have her hair cut off; and if it is a disgrace for a woman to have her hair cut or shaved off, she should *cover* her head." In light of verses 13–15, in which Paul is clearly discussing hair, and in which he affirms that a woman's long hair is "given to her for a covering," some interpreters have suggested that the whole passage deals not with wearing a veil but with having the hair bound or unbound. To have the head "covered" would mean to have the hair tied up on top of the head rather than hanging loose.

This proposed interpretation makes excellent sense for a number of reasons. It was not the normal custom for women in Greek and Roman cultures to be veiled; thus, it is hard to see how their being unveiled in worship could be regarded as controversial or shameful. For women to have loose hair in public, however, *was* conventionally seen as shameful, a sign associated either with prostitutes or—perhaps worse from Paul's point of view—with women caught up in the ecstatic worship practices of the cults associated with Dionysius, Cybele, and Isis. Paul is concerned that the practice of Christian prophecy be sharply distinguished from the frenzied behavior of prophetesses in pagan worship (cf. 14:26–33, 37–40). The symbolic confusion introduced by women with loose, disheveled hair in the Christian assembly would therefore be, from Paul's point of view, shameful. If the women will not keep their hair bound up, he says, they should cut it off—an action which he regards as self-evidently disgraceful.

Thus, the argument in verses 4–6 is strictly an argument about honor and shame. The problem was that some of the Corinthian women were acting in ways that brought shame on the community by blurring the traditional lines of gender distinction and/or by appearing to act in a disgraceful or disorderly manner. Such conduct, Paul suggests, brings shame particularly on the men in the church, whose "headship" is discredited by the disorderly behavior of the women. The logic of Paul's advice depends upon unspoken and undefended (because "self-evident") assumptions about what is honorable and shameful behavior for men and women in first-century Greco-Roman culture. To pose analogous taboos for our culture, it would be as though Paul had written, "Men shouldn't come to church wearing dresses, and women shouldn't come to church topless." Whatever one may think about the ultimate theological validity of such judgments, they are at least understandable pastoral advice.

In verses 7–9, however, Paul raises the theological stakes by introducing a new line of argument based on his reading of the Genesis creation story. A man should not cover his head because man is created as "the image and glory of God" (Gen. 1:27), but woman is "the glory of man." Here, regrettably, Paul gets himself into a theological quagmire. Genesis 1:27 explicitly says that humankind is created "in the image of God . . . male and female he created them." Paul's interpretation of the text, however, seems to depend on a tradition—perhaps based on Genesis 2:7—that thinks of the male only as originally created in God's image. Furthermore, it is difficult to see how Genesis provides any support for the notion that woman is the "glory" of man (cf., however, 1 Esdr. 4:17: "Women . . . bring men glory"). On top of these difficulties, Paul fails to explain how any of this is directly relevant to the issue of head coverings. Perhaps he means that the man with uncovered head will *reflect* the glory of God by letting the divine image shine forth (cf. 2 Cor. 3:18). If so, this would then help explain why women should be covered: given Paul's assumption that woman is the glory of the *man*, her uncovered head would then inappropriately reflect the man's glory in the worship setting, deflecting attention from God's glory.

None of this, however, is actually stated in Paul's argument. He leaves his readers to infer the relevance of verse 7 to his present topic.

In verses 8–9, continuing to allude to Genesis, he adduces further reasons for the ontological priority of the male. The man was created first and the woman "out of" him (Gen. 2:21–23), and the woman was created for the man (Gen. 2:18), not the other way around. These exegetical observations provide further support for Paul's insistence that the symbolic distinctions between the genders must acknowledge the right hierarchical ordering between male and female (cf. v. 3).

Thus, verses 7–9 function to provide further reasons in support of the central imperative of the unit: "let her be covered" (v. 6). The covering of the woman with bound-up hair appropriately symbolizes her relation to the man within the order of creation; the unbinding of the hair effaces the created distinction between the sexes and somehow impugns the man's role as bearer of the image of God. Such arguments may appear unpersuasive and objectionable to modern readers, but there is no point in attempting to explain away what Paul actually wrote. (On the question of how we should deal with such texts hermeneutically in the church, see "Reflections for Teachers and Preachers," below.)

Lest the reader not be sufficiently confused already, Paul abruptly interjects a sentence that has remained almost completely bewildering to subsequent interpreters: "For this reason a woman ought to have authority upon her head, because of the angels" (v. 10). There are two very difficult problems here: what does the idiom "to have authority upon her head" mean, and what do "angels" have to do with the argument? With regard to the first question, it is easy to reject some of the answers that have traditionally been given. The word "authority" (*exousia*) does not mean "veil" (as in the RSV), nor is there any reason to think that Paul means a woman ought to have a symbol of being under authority on her head. The expression "to have authority" in Greek always means, just as it does in English, to exercise authority, not to submit to it. Consequently, two interpretations are plausible. On the one hand, the sentence might mean that a woman should wear her hair bound up as a symbol of her new authority in Christ to prophesy and pray in the assembly. This interpretation, however, seems incongruous with the context, and it is unclear how bound-up hair, which was the normal cultural custom, would serve to symbolize a new authoritative status for women. More likely, the expression should be translated "to have authority over *[epi]* her head" (for the expression "have authority over" cf. Rev. 11:6b; 14:18; 20:6) and understood to mean that the woman should take charge of her hair and keep it under control, that

187

is, bound up rather than loose. This interpretation is consonant with the specific directive that Paul has already given to women in verses 5–6. By telling the women to "take charge" of their own heads, Paul seeks to transform the symbolic connotations of the head covering: the bound hair becomes a fitting symbol of the self-control and orderliness that Paul desires for the community as a whole.

But what about the angels? Paul's fleeting reference to angels here is completely cryptic, because nothing else is said about them either before or after this comment. Among the many guesses proposed by commentators, two are worthy of mention. From antiquity, some interpreters have suggested that Paul regards the uncovered heads of woman as a sexual provocation to the angels, who might be tempted to mate with the women, as in Genesis 6:1–4. Surely, however, if Paul had intended to express this rather bizarre idea, he would have offered a somewhat fuller explanation. More likely is the hypothesis that Paul thinks of the angels as present with the worshiping community as guardians of order and as participants in the church's praise to God; parallels to this idea can be found in the Dead Sea Scrolls. Presumably, then, Paul means that the community ought to behave in a decorous manner because of the presence of these heavenly "dignitaries" in their midst. Whether he thinks the angels would be offended by the women's loose hair or whether he thinks the angels might in some way punish disorderly behavior is impossible to say; the text simply offers us too little to go on.

Having established guidelines for the appropriate distinctions between women and men in worship, Paul takes a completely different tack in verses 11–12 and actually reaffirms the theological convictions that had led the Corinthian women to discard their head coverings in the first place: even though social decorum requires women and men to maintain symbolic distinctions, and even though Paul contends that such distinctions have a basis in creation itself (vv. 3–9), nevertheless "in the Lord" things are different. Men and women live in mutual interdependence. This does not mean that the differences between the sexes are abolished; it does mean, however, that they are both radically dependent on God (v. 12b; cf. 8:6) and that they are called to live as complementary partners in Christ. These statements do not, as is sometimes claimed, contradict or revoke the position that Paul articulated in verses 3–10; rather, they render it more complex. The hierarchical order that Paul sketched in verses 3 and 7–9 is counterbalanced by other considerations. For example, the earlier statement that woman is "from man"—an exegetical remark based on Genesis 2—is now balanced by the argument that "man comes through woman" in

188

childbirth. The result is that Paul supports a *functional* equality of men and women in the church. Women are free to pray and prophesy and exercise leadership of all sorts through the guidance of the Spirit, so long as they maintain the external markers of gender difference, particularly with regard to head coverings.

In the final paragraph of this section, Paul briefly adduces two more considerations in support of his position: an argument from "nature" (vv. 13–15) and an argument from "custom" in the churches. The appeal to the Corinthians to judge for themselves (v. 13) is not really an open invitation to independent judgment; rather, it is a rhetorical gesture introducing a set of questions whose answers Paul regards as self-evident. "Nature" teaches, Paul avers, that long hair is shameful for men and glorious for women. The appeal to "nature" (*physis*) as a source of behavioral norms is characteristic of the Stoic and Cynic philosophers—and highly unusual in Paul. Thus, this is perhaps another case (cf. the comments above on 3:21–22 and 6:7) in which Paul points out, with a more than a trace of irony, that the philosophical wisdom on which the Corinthians pride themselves ought to lead them to behave differently. Paul's comments about the natural difference between the hair of men and women are closely parallel to the remarks of the philosopher Epictetus:

> Can anything be more useless than the hairs on a chin? Well, what then? Has not nature used even these in the most suitable way possible? Has she not by these means distinguished between the male and the female? . . . Wherefore, we ought to preserve the signs [*symbola*] which God has given; we ought not to throw them away; we ought not, so far as in us lies, to confuse the sexes which have been distinguished in this fashion.
>
> (*Diss.* 1.16.10, 14)

Of course, the Corinthians might well have regarded themselves as transcending the patterns of "nature" as it was commonly understood in their culture. By virtue of possessing the Spirit, they were able to know and do things beyond the capacity of ordinary mortals. Paul's appeal to the natural order—even if it seems to us to be nothing more than the invocation of a particular cultural code—was intended to bring them back down to earth and remind them that they were still living within the constraints of finitude while awaiting the return of the Lord. If that is the major burden of the argument in 11:2–16, the parallel to Paul's arguments about sex and marriage is strong indeed.

In the final sentence of the unit, Paul reckons with the possibility of continuing contentiousness from the Corinthians on this issue. Perhaps at some level he recognizes the weakness of his own rather

189

fragmented argument. His trump card, then, is to appeal to the custom of "the churches of God." Presumably he is referring here not only to his own mission churches but to other early Christian communities as well, including the Jewish-Christian communities that looked to Jerusalem as their spiritual leader. This final argument assumes that the Corinthians will recognize themselves as bound to respect the uniformity of practice in the other churches of the fledgling Christian movement. Whether this argument in fact carried any weight with the Corinthians or not, Paul seems to regard it as decisive: Even if they do not accept his other arguments, the Corinthians should conform their head-covering practices to those of the other churches, because they are called to be one with "all those who in every place call on the name of our Lord Jesus Christ" (1:2).

REFLECTIONS FOR TEACHERS AND PREACHERS

More than any other passage in this letter, 1 Corinthians 11:2–16 presents severe problems for the interpreter. The first principle that should be applied in our readings of this text is the principle of hermeneutical honesty: we should never pretend to understand more than we do. In the case of this passage, the teacher or preacher should be prepared to acknowledge that we can neither understand it entirely nor accept it entirely (the latter perhaps follows from the former). Telling the truth about such matters will do much to clear the air, and it may help members of our congregations recognize more clearly the great cultural distance between first-century Corinth and our world.

It will not do, however, to say that the text does not apply to us because it is "culturally conditioned," for all texts are culturally conditioned. The aim of Paul's letters is to reshape his churches into cultural patterns that he takes to be consistent with the gospel. The question that we must ask, then, as we wrestle with this text is whether Paul's directives are in fact persuasive on their own terms, whether he successfully mounts an argument consonant with his own fundamental theological vision. If not, the argument has no weight at all; if so, then we still have to make the second move of asking *how* his advice to the Corinthians might speak analogically to Christians in dramatically different cultural settings.

So, are Paul's arguments persuasive on their own terms? The picture here is complex. Insofar as Paul focuses on the created *distinction* between man and woman and places that distinction within a larger view of the complementarity of the sexes (vv. 11–12), his arguments make sense and are consistent with the theological vision that he articulates throughout the letter. His advice for men and women to maintain their traditional symbolic gender distinctions even in Christian worship is

190

one more expression of the "eschatological reservation" that he has articulated repeatedly: the community in Christ should remain in the condition in which they were called (7:17–24) while they await the coming of the Lord. Attempts to transcend or eradicate the symbols of gender difference are premature and presumptuous, for, as Talbert puts it, "Christians are not angels" (37). They continue to live in the world as persons with a specific gender identity, male or female.

On the other hand, insofar as he posits a *hierarchy* based on gender, Paul's argument becomes strained and begins to break down, as shown by his problematical exegesis of Genesis. If Genesis 1:27 provides the overarching framework within which Genesis 2 must be read, then in fact women as well as men are created in the image of God—as Genesis 1:27 indicates. In that case, the hierarchical chain of 1 Corinthians 11:3 and the argument for women's head coverings in verse 7 lose their validity.

The preacher who works from the Revised Common Lectionary will never have to deal with this text, but questions about it will certainly arise from time to time. Perhaps the best way to deal with it is in the context of a study group, where the various proposals for interpreting the text can be fully considered. In the context of such a study, several issues should be highlighted.

1. The created *distinction* between man and woman should be honored in the church. Symbolic "gender-bending" actions in which women and men seek to reject their specific sexual identities are a sign not of authentic spirituality but of an adolescent impatience with the world in which God has placed us. We are not disembodied spirits; consequently, spiritual maturity in Christ will lead us to become mature women and men in Christ. Our dress and outward appearance should appropriately reflect our gender identity; to blur these distinctions is to bring needless shame upon the community. In a time of rampant confusion about gender identity in our culture, Paul's teaching on this matter is timely for us. A healthy community needs men and women together (v. 11), not a group of people striving for sexless neutrality.

2. At the same time, the functional *equality* of men and women in worship and community leadership should be emphasized. Paul promulgates his teaching about head coverings for women not in order to restrict their participation in prayer and prophecy but rather to enable them to perform these activities with dignity, avoiding distractions for people whose cultural sensibilities were formed by the social conventions of the ancient Mediterranean world. Anyone who appeals to this passage to silence women or to deny them leadership roles in the church is flagrantly misusing the text. The gift of prophecy is "from God" (v. 12b), and Paul

191

assumes that women and men alike will exercise it freely. The churches
in our own time have begun to recover the long-suppressed power of
women's ministry and leadership in proclaiming the word of God. This is
a profoundly evangelical development, brought about by the work of the
Spirit; if Paul were present with us, he would celebrate it.

3. Any honest appraisal of 1 Corinthians 11:2–16 will require both
teacher and students to confront the patriarchal implications of verses 3
and 7–9. Such implications cannot be explained away by some technical
move, such as translating *kephalē* as "source," rather than "head," because the patriarchal assumptions are imbedded in the structure of
Paul's argument. There are various possible approaches to this problem.
One way is to demonstrate how patriarchal presuppositions have shaped
Paul's decision to read Genesis 1:27 through the lens of Genesis 2:7, and
to invite the class to consider other readings that might stand alongside
Paul's and provide a challenge to it. In other words, we must reconsider
how the doctrine of creation might lead us to conclusions about the re-
lation between male and female that are not precisely the same as Paul's.

Another strategy would be to begin with the clause "God is the
head of Christ" (v. 3) and to ask what such headship means concretely
within a trinitarian understanding of God. Paul, of course, did not have
an explicit doctrine of the Trinity, and he often appears to operate with
a subordinationist christology (cf. 15:28). If, however, we now read
11:3 through the lens of a theological tradition that affirms Christ's full
participation in the Godhead, then we must ask ourselves how this affects our understanding of the analogy between "God is the head of
Christ" and "man is the head of woman." The subsequently developed
orthodox doctrine of the Trinity actually works against the subordinationist implications of Paul's argument about men and women; it
presses us to rethink the way in which "in the Lord" men and women
participate together in a new identity that transcends notions of supe-
riority and inferiority. Such suggestions move us beyond simplistic arguments about whether Paul was right or wrong and enable us to
rethink more deeply the substantive theological issues raised by his
treatment of hairstyles in the worship of the Corinthian church.

The Lord's Supper: Discerning the Body (11:17–34)

Paul tactfully opened his discussion of worship practices by com-
mending the Corinthians for keeping the traditions that he had passed
on to them (11:2), but his approval is subject to severe qualifications,
as the next section of the letter shows (11:17–34). Paul has received
information that there are divisions in the community during their

celebration of the Lord's Supper (v. 18); consequently, he must rebuke them once again for their disunity and offer a stern corrective concerning their common worship meal.

The source of the report is unnamed, but probably the news of the Corinthians' disunity at table had been brought to Paul either by Chloe's people (1:11) or by Stephanas, Fortunatus, and Achaicus (16:17). Division in the community has been a consistent concern of the letter; therefore, we should not be surprised that their differences find expression in the celebration of the Lord's Supper, although the divisions here may not be precisely the same as the factions that Paul deplored in 1:10–17 and 3:1–4. In any case, the meal that should be the symbol and seal of their oneness has in fact become an occasion for some of them to shame others (11:21–22). Thus, their assembly for the common meal has actually become an occasion for them to "eat and drink judgment against themselves" (v. 29). That is why Paul says that "when you come together it is not for the better but for the worse" (v. 17).

The Revised Common Lectionary appoints 1 Corinthians 11:23–26 as the Epistle reading for Holy Thursday each year but never designates the full passage (vv. 17–34) for reading in worship. Consequently, many Christians may know that Paul retells the story of the institution of the Lord's Supper without having any sense of the context for the retelling. The teacher or preacher working with this text must therefore take care to highlight the specific situation to which Paul is speaking; only in this way will the congregation be challenged to reflect about how Paul uses the Lord's Supper tradition to address issues of inequality and conflict in the church. Two preliminary observations about the original historical setting will help to keep our reading of the passage in focus.

First, when Paul refers to the Lord's Supper at Corinth, he is not talking about a liturgical ritual celebrated in a church building. At this early date, there were no separate buildings for Christian worship. The Lord's Supper was an actual meal eaten by the community in a private home. Commentators sometimes refer to a distinction—documentable only later in church history—between "the *agapē*" (love-feast) and "the eucharist," but Paul makes no such distinction. Evidently, the sharing of the symbolic bread and cup of the Lord's Supper occurred as a part of a common meal; otherwise, the passage makes no sense. Christians accustomed to experiencing the Lord's Supper only as a ritual "in church," removed from a meal setting, will need to discipline their imaginations to keep this original setting in mind.

Second, the problem that Paul is addressing at Corinth is not (overtly) a problem of sacramental theology; rather, it is a problem of

193

social relations within the community. Paul's vision of community comes into conflict with the Corinthians' conventional social mores, which require distinctions of rank and status to be recognized at table: the more privileged members expect to receive more and better food than others. Paul regards this as a humiliation for the community and as an abuse of the Supper of the Lord, whose own example contradicts such status divisions. Paul appeals to the tradition of Jesus' institution of the meal in order to highlight Jesus' death and to remind the Corinthians that they are to remember him as they eat together; this memory should bring a halt to their selfish behavior.

With these points in mind, we can turn to a reading of the passage, which has three main parts. In the first part (vv. 17–22) Paul describes and deplores the behavior of the Corinthians. In the second part (vv. 23–26) he reminds them of the tradition of the institution of the Supper. Finally, in the third part (vv. 27–34) he draws inferences about the meaning of the tradition for reshaping their practices of sharing the meal.

Divisions at the Lord's Supper (11:17–22)

Verse 17 is set in deliberate counterpoint to verse 2: whereas Paul had commended them for keeping the traditions, he now announces clearly that he will *not* commend them in the remarks to follow. The problem concerns what happens when they gather for worship, as signaled by the fivefold repetition of the verb *synerchesthai* ("to come together") in this unit (vv. 17, 18, 20, 33, and 34). This verb has the same semantic ambiguity in Greek that it possesses in English: it can mean either "to assemble" for a meeting (the obvious primary sense here in 1 Cor. 11:17–34) or "to be united." Paul's rebuke to the Corinthians plays off this double sense of the term: when they come together as a church they paradoxically do not "come together" in unity and peace. Rather, their coming together merely makes things worse, because their schisms (*schismata*, as in 1:10) are the more clearly brought to light. By contrast, Aristotle had suggested that the coming together of citizens in the *polis* might promote the common good:

> For it is possible that the many, though not individually good men, yet when they *come together* may be better, not individually but collectively . . . for where there are many, each individual, it may be argued, has some portion of virtue and wisdom, and when they have *come together*, just as the multitude becomes a single man with many feet and many hands and many senses, so also it becomes one personality as regards the moral and intellectual faculties.
>
> (*Politics* 3.6.4)

194

Paul sees the opposite effect in the Corinthians' worship: rather than acting as one body when they meet, they are divided, and their disunity is damaging to all.

Paul's remark that he "partly" believes the report of divisions among them (v. 18, RSV) has sometimes led commentators to suggest that this passage cannot have belonged originally to the same letter as chapters 1—4, in which he has already emphatically scolded them for their factionalism. Such a hypothesis, however, overlooks the rhetorical intent of Paul's "mock disbelief": it is a way of implying that the Corinthians "have fallen way short of the norm of concord which is to be expected of them" (M. Mitchell, 153). It is perfectly clear from verses 20–22 that Paul does in fact believe the reports. His saying that he believes the report only "to some extent" (NRSV, NIV) is an indirect way of expressing his shock about what he has heard; the note of incredulity serves to heighten his characterization of the Corinthians' conduct as outrageous. (It is as though he had written, "I can't believe it! You couldn't possibly have done what they report, could you?")

In verse 19, however, there is a shift of tone, and Paul makes the sobering observation that it is "necessary"—presumably necessary in the divine plan—for there to be factions in the community in order to expose the distinction between those who are authentic members of God's people and those who are not. This idea, foreshadowing the theme of God's judgment that appears explicitly in verses 27–32, is rooted in Jewish apocalyptic soil. Apocalyptic texts frequently warn that times of trial will bring out the true colors of those who profess the faith (cf. Mark 4:14–20; 13:9–13). Those who are *dokimoi* (the ones "approved by God" [NIV] will stand the test, while those who are not will fall away or separate themselves from the community (cf. 1 John 2:19). Paul clearly does not welcome this splitting of the community, but he acknowledges its inevitability. By placing the fact of the community's divisions in an apocalyptic context, he emphasizes the gravity of the situation.

The specific nature of the problem is described in verses 20–22: When the church gathers for its communal meal, some of the Corinthians who have greater resources are feasting on their own food and wine, while others "who have nothing" are going hungry. As a result, Paul declares that—contrary to what they may suppose—what they are eating is not in fact "the Lord's Supper"; it is their own private meal (vv. 20–21).

This scenario no doubt seems strange to most readers in our time. It is hard for us to imagine how the wealthier Corinthians could possibly suppose such overt snubbing of the poor to be justified. In the

195

context of first-century Greco-Roman culture, however, the Corinthians probably understood their actions as entirely normal. In order to appreciate this point, we need to know more about the concrete setting of the meal and about the conventions for dinner parties in the Corinthians' cultural environment.

We must bear in mind that the Christian gatherings were held in private homes, not in large public spaces. Archaeological study of Roman houses from this period has shown that the dining room (*triclinium*) of a typical villa could accomodate only nine persons, who would recline at table for the meal. Other guests would have to sit or stand in the atrium, which might have provided space for another thirty to forty people (see Murphy-O'Connor, *St. Paul's Corinth*, 153–61). The host of such a gathering would, of course, be one of the wealthier members of the community. It is reasonable to assume, therefore, that the host's higher-status friends would be invited to dine in the *triclinium*, while lower-status members of the church (such as freedmen and slaves) would be placed in the larger space outside.

Furthermore, under such conditions it was not at all unusual for the higher-status guests in the dining room to be served better food and wine than the other guests—just as first-class passengers on an airliner receive much better food and service than others on the same plane. A number of surviving texts from this period testify to this custom among the Romans (and Corinth was, we must recall, a Roman colony). For example, Pliny the Younger describes his experience of dining as guest of a man who boasted of the "elegant economy" of his hospitality:

> The best dishes were set in front of himself and a select few, and cheap scraps of food before the rest of the company. He had even put the wine into tiny little flasks, divided into three categories, not with the idea of giving his guests the opportunity of choosing, but to make it impossible for them to refuse what they were given. One lot was intended for himself and for us, another for his lesser friends (all his friends are graded), and the third for his and our freedmen.

(*Letters* 2.6)

This is the sort of hospitality that was being provided to the church by the wealthier Corinthian Christians. They may have considered themselves patrons of the community because they were hosting the gatherings, but they were continuing to observe status distinctions in the fare that was served. Indeed, verses 21–22 suggest that, while consuming their own meals, they may have provided no food at all for "those who have nothing."

196

Some translations of verse 21 suggest that the problem was not so much a matter of social inequality as of bad manners: some people were eating up all the food before others arrived. For example, NIV gives a broad paraphrase: "each of you goes ahead without waiting for anybody else." Although the Greek verb *prolambanein*—here translated "go ahead without waiting"—might carry such a temporal sense ("to take beforehand"), it does not necessarily have this meaning. A simpler translation would be "For, when you eat, each one *consumes* his own supper." On this reading, the problem is not just that some are refusing to wait for others but also, more importantly, that they are eating their own private food without sharing it. This interpretation makes better sense in the context. (See further comments on v. 33, below.)

Paul regards such practices—however "normal" in respectable Roman culture—as an outrage. He does not deny the right of the more prosperous Corinthians to eat and drink however they like in their own homes (v. 22a), but he insists that the church's common meal should symbolize the unity of the community through equitable sharing of food at the meal. The Corinthians' present practice demonstrates "contempt" for the church and brings "shame" on the poor in the community (v. 22). This is a powerful indictment of the high-status members of the community who are disregarding the symbolic implications of their behavior for the community as a whole. Paul's exasperation with the status-conscious Corinthians is forcefully expressed in the latter part of verse 22, as he reiterates what he had said in verse 17: "In this matter I do not commend you!"

The Lord's Supper as proclamation of the Lord's death (11:23–26)

In response to this problem, Paul reminds the Corinthians of the tradition he had taught them about Jesus' last meal with his disciples (vv. 23–26). The language of "receiving" and "handing on" indicates clearly that Paul is referring here to early Christian tradition (see the identical language in 15:3; for the same terminology in rabbinic tradition, see *m. Abot* 1.1). He does not mean that he learned about the Lord's Supper in some unmediated experience of revelation (as in Gal. 1:11–12) but that he received it "from the Lord" in the sense that it was Jesus himself who originated the tradition of sharing the bread and cup as a sign of his death and of the new covenant. This passage shows clearly that Paul's original preaching and teaching included the narration of the events of Jesus' passion (cf. 1 Cor. 15:3–5; Gal. 3:1b). Even though there were no written Gospels in Paul's time, the telling of the story of Jesus' death and resurrection stood at the center of Christian

197

proclamation from the beginning. Paul is not giving the Corinthians new information here; rather, he is recalling to mind the story that he told them about the foundational redemptive event, a story that they themselves repeat—or *should* repeat—every time they gather at table.

Most translations fail to represent Paul's repetition of the verb *paradidōmi* ("hand on, hand over") in verse 23: "For I received from the Lord what I also *handed on* to you, that the Lord Jesus on the night when he was *handed over* took a loaf of bread. . . ." Usually the second instance of the verb in this verse is interpreted as a reference to Judas's handing over of Jesus to the authorities, and it is therefore translated as "betrayed." Although this is a possible interpretation, Paul's own usage of the same verb elsewhere suggests a different sense: Jesus was "handed over" (*paredothē*) to death *by God* "for our trespasses" (Rom. 4:25), and *God* "gave him up [*paredōken*] for all of us" (Rom. 8:32). If Paul is thinking along similar lines here, the meaning would be, "on the night when God handed the Lord Jesus over to death for our sake, he took a loaf of bread. . . ." All these formulations must be heard as echoes of the Septuagint's rendering of Isaiah 53:6 ("And the Lord *gave him up* [*paredōken*] for our sins") and 53:12b ("And he bore the sins of many, and on account of their iniquities he *was handed over* [*paradothē*]"). This is the background against which 1 Corinthians 11:23 must be understood. Even if the story of Jesus' betrayal was circulating in the early Christian tradition, Paul never mentions it. Instead, he consistently interprets Jesus' death as an act of obedience to the divine will—as foreshadowed in Isaiah 53—and at the same time as *God's own act* for the salvation of the world.

The specific form of the eucharistic tradition in 1 Corinthians 11:23–25 corresponds much more closely to the pattern found in the Gospel of Luke than to the tradition found in Mark and Matthew. A detailed study of the differences (for example, Paul and Luke place the cup after the meal) is of considerable interest for scholars interested in reconstructing the evolution of the eucharistic liturgy, but such close comparisons are unnecessary for understanding Paul's advice to the Corinthians. (For a convenient schematic comparison, see Fee, 546.) Paul's point rests not upon any particular "order of service" for the Lord's Supper but upon his overall interpretation of its significance.

The most striking feature of Paul's renarration of the tradition is the emphasis that he places upon *memory*: the church is twice instructed to "do this *in remembrance of me*." The precise interpretation of this phrase is much debated: is the church to perform these actions in order that *they* might remember Jesus, or in order that his memory might be kept alive in the sight of God? However one might speculate about what Jesus himself originally meant, it is clear that Paul thinks of the symbolic action as reminding the *church* of Jesus' death: the proclamation of Jesus' death (v. 26) occurs in and for the community of faith. This interpretation of "remembrance" is also consonant with readings that link the Lord's Supper with Passover: according to Exodus 12:14, Passover is to be "a day of remembrance for you," a day in which Israel recalls God's deliverance of his people from bondage. In the same way, the Lord's Supper is to be an occasion for the people of God to remember God's action of deliverance through Jesus' death.

The word "remembrance" (*anamnēsis*) is sometimes thought to suggest the actual making-present of the Lord through the representation of his body and blood in the eucharistic elements. Whatever value such a eucharistic theology may possess on other grounds, it is far removed from Paul's concerns here in the argument of 1 Corinthians. Indeed, according to verse 26, the Lord's Supper expresses precisely the opposite of the "real presence" of the Lord. It expresses, instead, the community's memory of his death in the interval between cross and *parousia*: "For as often as you eat this bread and drink the cup, you proclaim the Lord's death—until he comes" (punct. added). Thus, the meal acknowledges the *absence* of the Lord and mingles memory and hope, recalling his death and awaiting his coming again.

Thus, in Paul's rendering of the tradition, two closely linked themes stand out: the sharing of the Supper calls the community to think of Jesus' death for others, and that death is understood to initiate a new covenant (v. 25; cf. Jer. 31:31–34). To be in covenant relation with God is to belong to a covenant people bound together by responsibilities to God and to one another; the character of this new covenant should be shown forth in the sharing of the meal. The trouble with the Corinthians is that they are celebrating the Supper in a way that disregards this structure of covenant obligations and demonstrates an odd amnesia about Jesus' death. By showing contempt for those who have nothing, they are acting as though his death had not decisively changed the conditions of their relationship to one another. Paul therefore retells the story so as to spotlight the death of Jesus as the central meaning of the Supper. This is especially clear when we realize that his recounting of the tradition appears only in verses 23b–25 and that verse 26 is not a part of the tradition but Paul's own explanatory commentary on it. Thus, according to Paul's explanatory gloss, the meaning of the meal is the same as the fundamental message of Paul's preaching: Christ crucified (cf. 2:1–2).

199

The proclamation of the Lord's death occurs not just in preaching that accompanies the meal; rather, the community's sharing in the broken bread and the outpoured wine is itself an act of proclamation, an enacted parable that figures forth the death of Jesus "for us" and the community's common participation in the benefits of that death. That is why Paul says that what the Corinthians are doing in their common meals is *not* the Lord's Supper (v. 20). The problem is not that they are failing to say the right words but that their enactment of the word is deficient: their self-serving actions obscure the meaning of the Supper so thoroughly that it no longer points to Christ's death.

Call to discern the body (11:27–34)

Beginning in verse 27, Paul starts to draw conclusions and propose remedies. Unfortunately verses 27–28 have often been taken out of context and seriously misinterpreted: the statement in verse 27 about eating the bread and drinking the cup "unworthily" has often been misunderstood to mean that only the perfectly righteous can partake of the Lord's Supper, and the call for self-examination in verse 28 has been heard as a call for intense introspection. This is, however, a grave misreading. Paul's words must be understood in the context of the specific situation that he is addressing: The more affluent Corinthians are consuming their own food and shaming the poorer members (vv. 20–22). In this context, to eat the meal unworthily means to eat it in a way that provokes divisions (v. 18), with contemptuous disregard for the needs of others in the community. Paul's call to self-scrutiny (v. 28) must therefore be understood not as an invitation for the Corinthians to probe the inner recesses of their consciences but as a straightforward call to consider how their actions at the supper are affecting brothers and sisters in the church, the body of Christ.

That this is indeed Paul's concern is shown clearly by verse 29: "For all who eat and drink *without discerning the body* eat and drink judgment against themselves" (NRSV, emphasis added). "Discerning the body" here cannot mean "perceiving the real presence of Christ in the sacramental bread"; this would be a complete non sequitur in the argument. For Paul, "discerning the body" means recognizing the community of believers for what it really is: the one body of Christ. Paul has already used this image for the church in 10:16–17, and he will develop it at greater length in 12:12–31a. Those who are failing to "discern the body" are those who act selfishly, focusing on their own spirituality and exercising their own social privileges while remaining heedless of those who share with them in the new covenant inaugurated by the Lord's death.

200

Those who eat and drink in this selfish way, Paul declares, are "answerable for the body and blood of the Lord" (v. 27). What does he mean by this strange phrase? The later Christian tradition's devout fixation on the sacred character of the eucharistic elements has led to interpretations such as the paraphrase offered by the NEB: "guilty of desecrating the body and blood of the Lord." But this is to put the emphasis in the wrong place by focusing on the holiness of the eucharistic symbols per se. (Note that in v. 25 Paul avoids identifying the wine directly with the blood of Christ.) The problem is not desecration of the sacred elements but rather offense against Christ himself. The thought is similar to the idea expressed in 8:12: "When you sin against your brothers in this way . . ., you sin against Christ." By mistreating other members of the church, the Corinthians repeat the sort of sin that made the death of Christ necessary; they place themselves "among those who were responsible for the crucifixion, and not among those who by faith receive the fruit of it" (Barrett, 273). They are like the lapsed Christians decried in the letter to the Hebrews who continue to sin, who are "crucifying again the Son of God and are holding him up to contempt" (Heb. 6:6).

Those who behave in this way are courting disaster. Rather than finding grace at the Lord's table, they are bringing God's judgment on themselves (v. 29). Paul suggests that this judgment is already making itself felt in misfortunes of sickness and death that have befallen members of the community (v. 30; we have no additional information about the matters to which Paul refers here). Such events should be read as signs of God's displeasure and discipline, seeking to make the Corinthians recognize the error of their divisions; the purpose of this discipline is corrective, seeking to change the community's behavior so that they can avoid eschatological condemnation along with the unbelieving world (v. 32; on the theme of suffering as the disciplinary action of a loving God, see Heb. 12:5–6, quoting Prov. 3:11–12). If they could learn to make right discernments about their own community life— that is, if they could mend their divisions—they would not be subject in this way to the judgment of God (v. 31). This line of reasoning may be disturbing to many readers (see "Reflections for Teachers and Preachers," below), but Paul's judgment is unmistakably clear: the Corinthians have brought suffering on their community by their divisiveness.

One other possibility should be considered in interpreting these verses: Paul may be calling on the community as a whole to exercise disciplinary authority over those members who are abusing the common meal. In order to understand this point, it is necessary to trace the interplay of a series of etymologically related words for judgment that Paul uses in verses 29, 31–32:

> All who eat and drink without discerning (*diakrinōn*) the body
> eat and drink judgment (*krima*) against themselves. . . .
> But if we discerned (*diekrinomen*) ourselves,
> we would not be judged (*ekrinometha*).
> But when we are judged (*krinomenoi*) by the Lord, we are disciplined
> so that we might not be condemned (*katakrithōmen*) along with the world.

The verb *diakrinein* (to discern or judge) has already appeared prominently in Paul's discussion of internal community disputes earlier in the letter (6:5): "can it be that there is no one among you wise enough to decide (*diakrinai*) between one believer and another?" The same verb appears again in 14:29 to describe the community's activity of judging and regulating prophecy in their midst. In light of these parallels, we should perhaps understand 11:31 not just as a summons to individual self-judgment but rather as a call for the *community* to exercise self-regulatory judgment to bring greater order to the Lord's Supper by disciplining those who treat it as their own private dinner party. Where the church exercises such disciplinary discernment, God's judgment is averted; where the church fails to exercise discernment, God's judgment intervenes to prevent them from falling under final condemnation.

In any case, Paul draws his discussion of this matter to a close in verses 33–34 by giving specific practical directions. The meaning of verse 33 is not, however, entirely clear. There are two different possible readings, turning on the ambiguity of the verb *ekdechesthai* ("to wait for" or "to receive"). According to the interpretation found in most English translations and in most commentaries, Paul tells the Corinthians to wait for (*ekdechesthe*) one another when they assemble to eat. Those who are too impatient or too hungry to wait—presumably the wealthier Corinthians—are told to eat at home before the meeting (cf. v. 22a: "Do you not have homes to eat and drink in?") so that they will not shame the poor by gorging themselves on their private store of rich food in front of the whole assembly, perhaps before the poor have arrived. This interpretation has in its favor the fact that the verb *ekdechesthai* elsewhere in the New Testament consistently means "wait for," including Paul's only other use of it in 1 Corinthians 16:11.

On the other hand, as we have already noted, it appears in verses 21–22 that the problem lies not so much in the timing of the eating as in the unequal distribution of food. A second possibility, therefore, should be given consideration: Paul is telling the Corinthians not just to wait for one another but to *receive* one another as guests (cf. Rom. 15:7) when they come together. This meaning of *ekdechesthai*, though not found elsewhere in the New Testament, is well established in other

Greek sources (e.g., 3 Macc. 5:26 and Josephus, *Antiquities* 7.351). On this reading, Paul is calling the more affluent Corinthians not merely to preserve a public appearance of unity in the celebration of the Supper but actually to break down the barriers of social status and to receive the poorer members as guests in their homes, sharing their food with those who have none. This second interpretation of the passage provides a more satisfying solution to the problem sketched in verses 21–22, and it is therefore to be preferred.

Even so, Paul stops far short of calling for radical economic equality: the instruction in verse 34a to eat at home—even if this is only a stopgap solution until Paul can get to Corinth to straighten things out—presumes that the wealthy may continue to eat as they like in private. Gerd Theissen describes the implications of this solution accurately: "Within their own four walls they are to behave according to the norms of their social status, while at the Lord's Supper the norms of the congregation have absolute priority. Clearly this is a compromise" (Theissen, 164).

The last sentence of the unit is tantalizing for those of us who read, at a long historical distance, over the shoulders of the Corinthians: "About the other things I will give instructions when I come." What are the "other things?" We will never know. Paul had apparently started in verses 17–18 to deal with a list of matters in which he could not commend the Corinthians. His opening *prōton men*" ("to begin with") in verse 18 is not, however, followed by any additional items. Perhaps he decided that the other matters were too complicated to deal with in a letter, or perhaps he deemed them less important and able to be deferred until his arrival. Alternatively, perhaps verse 34b means that he will give them further instructions about the Lord's Supper or about issues of economic sharing when he returns to Corinth. In any case, we are left to wonder and to wish that we too could await the arrival of the apostle to explain things more fully.

REFLECTIONS FOR TEACHERS AND PREACHERS

Strangely, we are indebted to the Corinthians for messing up their celebration of the Lord's Supper. If they had not suffered divisions at the Lord's table, Paul would never have written to correct them, and we would know nothing about his teaching concerning the tradition and practice of the Lord's Supper. (And some New Testament scholars would undoubtedly insist that the Eucharist was unknown in the Pauline churches, since he does not mention it elsewhere in his surviving letters!) As it is, the Corinthians' trouble serves for our instruction: Paul's rebuke and advice can help us reflect theologically about

203

what we are doing when we come together as a church around the table. Three matters stand out as important themes of the passage.

1. The Lord's table must first of all express *the community's unity as the new covenant people of God.* Divisions and conflicts in the church are incongruous with the meaning of this common meal; indeed, disunity turns the celebration into a hollow parody of the Lord's Supper. This point pertains not only to doctrinal conflict but also and especially to divisions caused by social and economic disparity in the community. The major emphasis of Paul's pastoral response to the Corinthians is to be found in verses 21–22 and 33: those with more resources must stop shaming the poor and begin sharing their food with "those who have nothing."

Paul is thinking about this problem at the level of the local congregation, but the same logic applies to the church on a larger scale: as long as some Christians go hungry, the Lord's Supper should call the prosperous to share their bread with those in need. This is a challenging word indeed for Christians who live in the affluent societies of North America and Europe. We have tended to separate into different churches distinguished by social class, and we have made the Lord's Supper into a tidy rite disconnected from real eating and drinking. Consequently, it is hard for many economically comfortable Christians to envision the connection between the Lord's table and the needs of the poor. Pastors and teachers should work patiently to enable their congregations to understand the Eucharist not just as a private act of piety focused on receiving individual forgiveness but as a coming together of the Lord's people at a common meal. An important aspect of that common meal is "discerning the body": perceiving the connection between ourselves and our brothers and sisters in Christ. If we discern the body rightly, we will symbolize our oneness in Christ by sharing what God has given us to eat and drink.

2. The Lord's Supper also *focuses the church's memory on the death of Jesus.* We remember him rightly by telling again and again the story of his death. The specific form of the story that Paul received and handed on highlights his self-offering: "This is my body that is for you." Jesus' death was not an accident, nor is it to be understood as a tragic mistake of the judicial system; Jesus freely gave himself up to death for us, and the sharing of the bread and the cup signifies our acceptance of that incalculably great gift. To know Jesus rightly is to know him through the eucharistic story. Further, to know ourselves rightly is to know ourselves as the recipients of his self-giving. That means first of all that we acknowledge our desperate need: we were strangers alienated from God who could be brought into the new covenant only

204

through this costly act of God's radical grace. It means also, in the second place, that we are a people called to live in a way that answers fitly to such divine generosity: we too are to live sacrificially, not pursuing our own interests and pleasures but giving ourselves for others in remembrance of the one who gave himself for us. Because the Corinthians failed to grasp this connection, Paul told them the story yet again: the task of all Christian preaching is nothing more—and nothing less—than that.

3. Finally, the Lord's Supper is an occasion for us to ponder *God's judgment*. Some Christians are so acutely conscious of their own guilt and unworthiness that they shy away from the Lord's Supper, because they intuitively recognize that here their lives are laid bare before God. Such persons need to be taught that the Eucharist is first of all an offer of grace, not condemnation, and that in any case we cannot ultimately avoid accountability to God by staying away from the table. Paul's point in verses 27–32 is that the Lord's Supper provides an occasion for us to exercise discernment about our own lives in preliminary anticipation of God's eschatological judgment. This does not mean, however, that sinless perfection is a prerequisite for eating of the bread and drinking of the cup: if so, none of us could ever come to the table. It does mean that this supper calls us again and again to confess our sin and to open ourselves to leading a new life. In particular, this meal summons us to live—as the invitation to the table in the older Methodist communion service proclaimed—"in love and charity with [our] neighbors." The preacher or teacher should emphasize that when Paul speaks of eating the bread and drinking the cup "in an unworthy manner" (v. 27), he is referring to those who ignore their poorer brothers and sisters in the church. In that respect, the function of judgment language in this passage is very much like the parable of the sheep and the goats in Matthew 25:31–46: it summons the community to care for "the least of these" in their midst.

But what are we to make of Paul's idea that God has punished the church by causing illness and death among those who have failed to discern the body (v. 30)? Insofar as we find this conception disturbing, we reveal our more fundamental discomfort with the very notion of God's judgment. Paul's assertion stands in continuity with Israel's prophetic tradition from Amos onward, and particularly with the theology of Deuteronomy, which proclaims that curses and misfortunes will fall upon Israel if they disregard the covenant that God has made with them. (We might also recall Jesus' description of the fate of the disobedient in Matt. 25:46: "eternal punishment.") Paul certainly does not have a simpleminded theology that posits a one-to-one correspondence

205

between disobedience and suffering; that would hardly be coherent with his emphasis on the cross as the center of the gospel. He does, however, believe that God takes human sin seriously and sometimes acts to discipline those who defy his will. It was a message that the Corinthians needed to hear; as we read their mail, we might ask ourselves whether the church in our own day needs to hear it also.

Spiritual Manifestations in Worship (12:1—14:40)

The final section of Paul's treatment of community worship deals with the issue of spiritual gifts in the Corinthian worship assembly. Some of the Corinthians have placed inordinate emphasis on showy displays of spirituality, especially the gift of speaking in tongues; it seems that some of them are disrupting or dominating the church's meetings by disorderly spirit-inspired utterance that is unintelligible to other members of the community. The length of Paul's response, extending from the beginning of chapter 12 to the end of chapter 14, suggests that he considers this matter highly important and perhaps rather sensitive; as we shall see, he exercises considerable pastoral tact in dealing with this topic.

The three-part structure of the discussion is reminiscent of his treatment of the idol-meat problem in chapters 8—10. An opening section frames the issue in general terms by describing the complementary role of spiritual gifts within the one body of Christ (12:1–31a); a middle section extolling the preeminence of love appears to be a digression but actually provides the norm governing all spiritual manifestations (12:31b—13:13); and the closing section gives specific directions for regulating the gifts, especially the gift of tongues, in worship (14:1–40). Only in chapter 14 does the "presenting problem," the role of tongues and prophecy in worship, come to the surface of the discussion. Nevertheless, the theological reflections in chapters 12 and 13 provide the essential presuppositions for the specific advice that is finally given in chapter 14; therefore, our reading of these two preliminary chapters should always keep in mind the particular pastoral goal toward which Paul is working: He is seeking to bring the disorderly and self-centered worship practices of the Corinthians under control so that the church as a whole may be built up (14:5, 12, 26, 40).

Varieties of gifts, but the same Spirit (12:1–31a)

206   Chapter 12 of 1 Corinthians establishes Paul's theological categories for evaluating spiritual gifts in the church. Its structure may be broadly outlined as follows:

1. Introduction: the Spirit empowers all Christian confession (vv. 1–3)
2. Manifestations of the Spirit: common source, common aim (vv. 4–11)
3. The body analogy: diversity and interdependence (vv. 12–26)
4. Application: gifts and offices in the church (vv. 27–31a)

The broad contours and implications of Paul's discussion are crystal clear, but some points along the way require explication and further comment.

Introduction: The Spirit empowers all Christian confession (vv. 1–3). Paul introduces the new subject by employing the *peri de* formula ("now concerning"), which we have encountered before in 7:1; 7:25; and 8:1. It is possible, though not certain, that this formula signals that he is once again taking up a topic raised by the Corinthians in their letter to him. This inference is made more likely by the fact that there is no indication in chapters 12—14 that Paul is responding to reports about the Corinthians (in contrast, e.g., to 5:1 or 11:18). It seems probable, therefore, that the Corinthians had in some way introduced the issue of public manifestations of the Spirit in worship, though it is very difficult to reconstruct exactly what they might have said. We may infer that they expressed joy and pride about their ability to enter the heavenly sphere and speak with "tongues of angels" (13:1). Paul's response is cautionary and corrective, but he never disputes the authenticity of their experience or of the gifts that they have received from God.

The translation "spiritual gifts," which appears in almost all English renderings of 12:1, is an interpretive paraphrase. The Greek reads simply, "Now concerning spiritual things" (or, alternatively, if the word *pneumatikōn* is read as masculine rather than neuter, "spiritual persons"; on the basis of 14:1, where the neuter form *pneumatika* appears, the neuter is to be preferred in 12:1 as well). The idea of "gifts" (*charismata*) is first introduced by Paul in verse 4. This change of terminology is significant for Paul's argument. Probably the Corinthians used the term *pneumatika* to describe spiritual manifestations such as tongues and prophecy. They may well have been following Paul's own example in this usage, for Paul employs the same language elsewhere to characterize aspects of his own ministry: "We speak . . . in words not taught by human wisdom but taught by the Spirit, interpreting spiritual things [*pneumatika*] to those who are spiritual [*pneumatikois*]" (2:13). Or again, in 9:11, he observes that he has "sown spiritual things

207

[*pneumatika*]" among the Corinthians. In any case, it is evident that the Corinthians are well acquainted with manifestations of the Spirit in their worship; thus, when Paul writes that he does not want them to be "ignorant" (NIV, NEB) about *pneumatika* (12:1), there may be more than a trace of irony in his tone. The Corinthians consider themselves authorities on such matters already. The trouble is that they are treating these manifestations of the Spirit as signs of their own spiritual sophistication and power. Therefore, when Paul shifts to the term *charismata* in verse 4 (and thereafter in vv. 9, 28, 30, and 31), the semantic difference is significant: verbal displays of spiritual inspiration must be interpreted as God's gifts of grace (*charis*), not as the personal achievement or property of the speaker. For that reason, verses 4–11 particularly stress the sovereign initiative of God in allocating and empowering all spiritual gifts in the community.

Before Paul can move into that discussion, however, he must establish the qualitative difference between the activity of the Holy Spirit and other forms of spiritual "inspiration" that surrounded the church in Corinth. The realm of the "spiritual" is hardly unambiguous, Paul reminds his readers, recalling their recent pagan past. The NEB translation accurately captures the force of Paul's expression: "You know how, in the days when you were still pagan, you were swept off to those dumb heathen gods, however you happened to be led" (12:2; cf. the emphatic disavowal of idolatry in 10:14–22). In contrast to that experience of being blown about willy-nilly by various spiritual powers (cf. Eph. 4:14), the Corinthians are now rooted in their relation to Jesus Christ. The one certain criterion of the Holy Spirit's inspiration is that it empowers the simple confession "Jesus is Lord" (12:3). This has two important implications.

First, anyone who utters that confession (not just mouthing the words but making a self-involving confession of the lordship of Jesus) is ipso facto living in the sphere of the Holy Spirit's power. Those who exalt themselves in the possession of spiritual gifts such as tongues or words of wisdom and knowledge (v. 8) should not suppose that others in the church who lack such endowments are thereby strangers to the Spirit. Thus, verse 3 anticipates the theme of verses 12–13: All who are in Christ have entered the realm of the Spirit, and no one should be despised.

Second, and more closely related to Paul's immediate concerns, discernment is necessary to discriminate between spiritual experiences of various kinds. Only where the lordship of Jesus is authentically confessed can we know that the Holy Spirit is at work. To illustrate the point, Paul formulates a hypothetical counterexample: "No one speaking by the Spirit of God ever says, 'Let Jesus be cursed.' " This formulation has given rise to many fanciful hypotheses of commentators seeking to explain how persons in the Christian assembly might actually say such a thing: for example, Gnostic Christians cursing the fleshly Jesus or Christians cursing Jesus in order to escape imperial persecution. (Such explanations are at best anachronistic: in Paul's time there was no organized persecution of Christians by Roman authorities, nor is there any evidence at this early date of Gnostic groups that repudiated the earthly Jesus.) In fact, we can be sure that if Paul believed some of the Corinthians were actually saying such things he would have responded in a considerably more vehement manner to put a stop to it! Worthy of consideration is Jouette Bassler's suggestion that Paul may be recalling his own former life in Judaism when he, as a persecutor of the church, might well have cursed Jesus as a "servant of sin" who stood under the Torah's curse (cf. Gal. 1:13; 2:17; 3:13). In the present context, however, Paul is simply using this dramatic fiction of cursing Jesus to emphasize that those who are inspired by the Holy Spirit will speak and act in ways that glorify the lordship of Jesus. This provides him with a fundamental criterion that allows him to critique the behavior of those at Corinth who are in effect denying the lordship of Jesus even while engaging in inspired spiritual speech—even though the actual critique is deferred until chapter 14.

One other point in Paul's brief introduction should not be allowed to slip by without comment. Paul's statement in 12:2 implies that the Gentile Corinthian Christians have now been made part of Israel. This implication is not clear in English translations that use the word "pagans," because we tend to assume to assume that the opposite of "pagans" is "Christians"—a word that Paul himself never uses. In fact, the Greek word that Paul uses here is *ethnē* ("Gentiles"), whose opposite is "Jews." We would see the force of Paul's claim more clearly if we translated as follows: "*When you were Gentiles* you were carried away to mute idols. . . ." This is the standard language of Jewish polemic against Gentile idolatry. When he indicates that the Corinthian believers are no longer Gentiles, Paul is unmistakably suggesting that they have turned away from idols to serve the living God of Israel (cf. 1 Thess. 1:9) and thereby become grafted into Israel (cf. Rom. 11:17–24). That is why he can speak of Israel in the wilderness as "our fathers" (1 Cor. 10:1): He includes the Corinthian Gentiles among those who can rightly claim ancestry from the Israel of the Old Testament stories. Paul does not develop this point here in 12:1–3, but his offhanded turn of phrase reveals much about his ecclesiology and his understanding of the place of his converts in relation to the people of Israel.

209

Manifestations of the Spirit: Common source, common aim (vv. 4–11). The next section (vv. 4–11) lays the foundation of Paul's understanding of spiritual gifts in the church. They are, first of all, gifts (*charismata*), signs of God's free grace. Furthermore, they are distributed in the community in diverse ways. This means that the church can never be homogeneous; it is to be made up of various individuals exercising different gifts and ministries "for the common good" (v. 7). Paul explains this point by means of a trinitarian formula in verses 4–6.

varieties of gifts (*charismata*)	but the same Spirit
varieties of services (*diakoniai*)	but the same Lord
varieties of activities (*energēmata*)	but the same God who activates all of them in everyone.

Paul of course had no explicit doctrine of the Trinity; this doctrine was not articulated formally by theologians until hundreds of years later. This passage shows, however, that he *experienced* God as Trinity: he can describe the activity of God in the community in three synonymous parallel clauses as the working of the Spirit and of the Lord Jesus and of God. The point of the three-pronged formulation is not to parcel out different spheres of activity to different persons within the Godhead but rather to insist that the many different divinely inspired manifestations in the church have finally one single source. (We should recall the confessional statement of 8:6, which declares that all things are "from" the one God, the Father, and "through" the one Lord, Jesus Christ.)

Similarly, the three terms that describe God's working in the church (gifts, services, activities) should not be sharply distinguished from one another. The use of "services," however, may be intended to broaden the Corinthians' field of vision: They were concentrating on "charismatic" spiritual manifestations, but Paul points also to humbler forms of service (linked with the Lord Jesus, who for Paul exemplifies servanthood) as manifestations of God's presence. The threefold repetition of the term "varieties" is surely significant; Paul is emphasizing the importance of diversity in the church. The creative imagination of God is so many-faceted that God's unitary power necessarily finds expression in an explosion of variegated forms.

The sense of the threefold formula is summed up in verse 7. "To each is given the manifestation [*phanerōsis*] of the Spirit for the common good [*to sympheron*]." Here "Spirit" stands in for all three persons of the Trinity, and the word "manifestation" is employed as the generic category that includes "spiritual gifts" in the narrower sense as well as other activities inspired by God in the church. The emphasis of this sentence falls at the beginning and end: the manifestations are given *to each*, and these manifestations are *for the common good*. All members of the community receive gifts of the Spirit, not just a few leaders or spiritually super-endowed prodigies; furthermore, the whole purpose of God's distribution of these gifts is for the benefit of the community as a whole, not merely the private edification of the individuals who receive the gifts (cf. 6:12; 10:23). This sentence contains in a nutshell the burden of Paul's teaching in chapters 12—14.

In verses 8–10, Paul gives a list of examples of the "manifestations of the Spirit" that he has in mind. This is by no means an exhaustive list of spiritual gifts, as we can see the differing lists found in Romans 12:6–8; Ephesians 4:11–13; and even later in this same unit in 1 Corinthians 12:28–30. The gifts enumerated here simply serve to represent the diversity of the workings of the Spirit. Consequently, it is futile to speculate at length about the precise meaning of each gift, because Paul does not give us enough information to construct a clear picture. It may be possible, however, to see some significance in the grouping of the nine gifts listed here. The key, as Gordon Fee (591) has suggested, is to note the divisions in the list marked by Paul's use of a different word meaning "another":

> To one is given through the Spirit the utterance of wisdom,
> and to another (*allō*) the utterance of knowledge according to the same Spirit.
>
> To **another** (*heterō*) faith by the same Spirit,
> to another (*allō*) gifts of healing by the one Spirit,
> to another (*allō*) the working of miracles,
> to another (*allō*) prophecy,
> to another (*allō*) the discernment of spirits,
>
> to **another** (*heterō*) various kinds of tongues,
> to another (*allō*) the interpretation of tongues.

Classically, *allos* means "another of the same kind" while *heteros* means "another of a different kind." This distinction is not strictly observed in Koine Greek, but it appears that Paul may have used *heteros* here to mark, as it were, pauses for breath, thus dividing the list of gifts into three groups. The two gifts in the first group are the word of wisdom (*sophia*) and the word of knowledge (*gnōsis*)—precisely the characteristics in which the leading Corinthians especially pride themselves (see the discussions of chapters 1—4 and 8, above). The two gifts in the final group are tongues and interpretation of tongues—the spiritual manifestations that are the particular target of Paul's discourse in chapters 12—14. The remaining five gifts in the middle group, then, appear to be a random list

211

of supernatural workings of the Spirit; presumably "faith" here refers not to ordinary Christian faith in God but to the sort of special faith that can "move mountains" (13:2), that is, perform miracles. Thus, Paul brackets a general list of gifts with more pointed references to the spiritual gifts that particularly shape the self-conception of the superspiritual Corinthian Christians whom Paul seeks to correct. By ordering the list in this way, Paul implies that the gifts on which the Corinthians are fixated are by no means the only gifts operative in the church.

Readers today may be surprised to learn that the very same Corinthian Christians who prized philosophically informed wisdom and knowledge might also have displayed enthusiasm for speaking in unknown tongues; the former seems soberly intellectual, while the latter seems irrationally emotional. This is, however, to superimpose modern stereotypes on the ancient situation. Dale Martin has assembled a considerable body of ancient evidence to demonstrate that esoteric "angelic" speech was sometimes seen as a mark of refined spirituality and high status in Jewish and Christian circles (Martin, *Corinthian Body*, 87–92). In such a context, to speak under the inspiration of the Spirit in unintelligible "tongues of angels" might be seen as an activity entirely appropriate for the person gifted with spiritual illumination and wisdom. Thus, the tongue-speakers in the Corinthian community may have been precisely the same "strong," affluent persons who were claiming special knowledge that set them apart from the community in various other ways as well.

In any case, the overall picture of the church that is implied in these verses is, to put it mildly, remarkable: "each one" (v. 7) is empowered by the Spirit with one of these extraordinary gifts. The church as a whole is envisioned as a charismatic community in which the power of the Holy Spirit is palpably present, operating through the complementary gifts of its various members. Healings, miracles, and revelatory speech are portrayed as everyday occurrences within this Spirit-endowed community. Paul seems to take all this for granted and to expect his readers to do the same. Any responsible interpreter of 1 Corinthians 12 must hold this image of the Christian community up against his or her own church community and reflect seriously about the differences. (See "Reflections for Teachers and Preachers," below.)

The conclusion of this section (v. 11) repeats Paul's central point so that no one can possibly miss it: the diverse gifts—of which those listed in verses 8–10 are only a sample—are all "the work of one and the same Spirit" (NIV), and they are allocated within the church just as the Spirits wills to distribute them. The possession of any gift is therefore not a matter of individual merit or worthiness but of the sheer free grace of God. The implication for the spiritually ambitious Corinthians should be clear: There is no ground for boasting about being "spiritual," no matter what gifts one may possess. All the manifestations of the Spirit are to serve God's purpose for the common benefit of the community.

The body analogy: Diversity and interdependence (vv. 12–26). In support of this interpretation of spiritual gifts, Paul sets forth an analogy between the church and the human body (vv. 12–26). The comparison between the body and human societies was a rhetorical commonplace (*topos*) in the ancient world, particularly in speeches calling for social concord. (For detailed references, see M. Mitchell, 157–64). As well shall see, Paul develops this well-worked rhetorical *topos* in an unexpected direction. This figure was ordinarily used to urge members of the subordinate classes to stay in their places in the social order and not to upset the natural equilibrium of the body by rebelling against their superiors (the classic example is the oration of Menenius Agrippa to the plebeians of Rome, recounted in Livy, *Urb. cond.* 2.32 and in Dionysius of Halicarnassus, *Ant. Rom.* 6.86). Paul uses the body image in a somewhat more complicated way to argue for the need of *diversity* in the body (vv. 14–20) and, at the same time, *interdependence* among the members (vv. 21–26). Thus, he employs the analogy not to keep subordinates in their places but to urge more privileged members of the community to respect and value the contributions of those members who appear to be their inferiors, both in social status and in spiritual potency.

The opening sentences of the section (vv. 12–13) introduce the body analogy and explain the basis for thinking of the church as one body. The conclusion of verse 12, however, offers a surprising twist: "For just as the body is one and has many members, . . . so it is with Christ." We expect Paul to say, "so it is with *the church*." Instead, by identifying the many members of the church directly with Christ, Paul seems to press beyond mere analogy to make an ontological equation of the church with Christ (cf. v. 27). Exegetes have long debated whether the designation of the church as "the body of Christ" is for Paul a mere metaphor or a mystical reality. The truth is that this is a false dichotomy; Paul would probably not understand the terms in which the problem is posed. Certainly "body of Christ" is a metaphor; just as certainly, Paul believes that this metaphor illumines the truth about the church's union with and participation with Christ. The church is not merely a human organization; rather, it is brought into

213

being by the activity of the Holy Spirit, which binds believers into a living union with the crucified and risen Lord. We should not be afraid to speak of such truths in metaphorical language, for there is no other way to speak of them adequately.

In verse 13 Paul recalls for the Corinthians the basis of their unity in the one body: all of them, at the time of their conversion and initiation into the community of Christ's people, were "in the Spirit . . . baptized into one body" and "made to drink of one Spirit." The Spirit is not the agent who does the baptizing, but the figurative element into which the new converts were immersed, being plunged into a new world of Spirit-experience. The two clauses of verse 13 are equally metaphorical, and both refer to this same experience. "Drinking the Spirit," contrary to the suggestion of Luther and Calvin, has nothing to do with the Eucharist: it is simply a vivid expression for Paul's conviction that the one Spirit has been given in overflowing abundance to everyone in the community (cf. John 7:37–39). Similarly, the use of the metaphor of being "baptized in the Holy Spirit" elsewhere in early Christian tradition (Matt. 3:11; Mark 1:8; Luke 3:16; John 1:33; Acts 1:5) suggests that it should be distinguished from water baptism rather than simply identified with it. Immersion in water provides the literal reference point for Paul's metaphorical description; his point is that the community as a whole has been immersed in the Spirit's power.

The result of that immersion in the Spirit is that all have been made one. They have come from very different ethnic and social backgrounds—Jews and Greeks, slaves and free—but they have been bonded together by the Spirit into one body. Consequently, the old markers of identity should no longer divide the community. This is a fundamental aspect of Paul's teaching about the church (cf. Gal. 3:27–28; Col. 3:9–11). The closely parallel formula in Galatians 3:28, also associated with baptism, includes a third polarity that has been overcome in Christ: "There is no longer Jew or Greek, there is no longer slave or free, there is no longer *male and female.*" This sentence may well have been a traditional baptismal formula in the Pauline churches. If so, Paul alludes to it here in 1 Corinthians 12:13 but omits the reference to "male and female." Probably the omission is intentional, for the Corinthians' attempts to transcend sex and gender distinctions were, in Paul's view, causing significant problems in the church (see the commentary on chapter 7 and on 11:2–16 above). Paul does not want to revisit those issues here, because it would distract attention from his major point: that all in the church have been joined together in one body.

Paul's immediate concern is to show that the different gifts given

to different members of the church should not provide grounds for in-
vidious distinctions (cf. v. 25). He pursues this theme by developing the
body analogy at considerable length, imagining scenarios in which various body parts ridiculously seek to secede from the body (vv. 14–26).
No detailed commentary on this material is necessary, because its basic lesson is evident to every reader. It should be noted, however, that
two related but different themes are emphasized in Paul's elaboration
of the body metaphor. In verses 14–20, the major theme is *the necessity of diversity*. The body is internally differentiated in accordance
with the design of God (v. 18); without such differentiation, the body
would be grotesque and helpless (v. 17), all eye or all ear. For that reason, no member of the body (church) should ever think that he or she
is worthless or unimportant (vv. 15–16); each constituent part has its
own distinctive purpose in the functioning of the whole. This also
suggests—though Paul does not develop this point—that members
should neither envy nor mimic one another, "desiring this man's gift
and that man's scope" (T. S. Eliot, "Ash-Wednesday," *Complete Poems
and Plays*, p. 60). Rather, each person should accept gracefully and
gratefully whatever gifts God has given and use them for the benefit of
the community.

The focus shifts slightly in verses 21–26 to the *interdependence* of
the members of the body. The apparently "higher" members (eyes and
head) cannot scorn the hands and feet, without whom they would have
no power to act (vv. 21–22); likewise, the different members of the
church need one another. This observation allows Paul to draw a subtly pointed conclusion: "the members of the body that seem to be
weaker are indispensable" (v. 22). Since this comment does not follow
strictly from verse 21 (the hands and feet are hardly "weaker" than the
eyes and head), we must assume that Paul's word choice here is determined by the pastoral situation in Corinth; those who fancy themselves
strong and knowledgeable are exalting themselves above those whom
they regard as "the weak" (see the commentary on 8:7–13, above). Paul
has already played ironic inversions of this theme earlier in the letter
(1:27; 4:10; 9:22), associating weakness with the cross and with his own
apostleship. Here he straightforwardly asserts that the (apparently)
weak have an "indispensable" role in the life of the community and that
the strong ignore them at their own peril.

The social class dimension of this tension between strong and
weak is suggested by Paul's further elaboration of the body metaphor
in verses 24–25: those members that are considered "dishonorable" or
even "shameful" (in the metaphor, the sexual organs) must be treated
with all the greater respect. Here Paul is making a joke and scoring an

215

effective point at the same time. The high-status Corinthians may look down their noses at their uncouth lower-class brothers and sisters in the faith, regarding them as something of an embarrassment, but Paul insists that they must be "clothed" with dignity and honor. This echoes his earlier insistence that the strong must accommodate their behavior to the needs of the weak (8:7–13; 10:28–29a), as Paul himself has done (9:19–23; 10:31—11:1). In the body metaphor, however, Paul goes farther than before to validate the legitimacy and importance of these weaker and less honorable members within the community: not only are they indispensable to the healthy functioning of the whole body, but God has arranged the body in such a way that greater honor is to be given to those who in the natural order of things might be despised (v. 24).

Because God has arranged the body as an interdependent organism in which diversity is essential, the differences between the members should not lead to division (*schisma*—cf. 1:10; 11:18), but to the members' caring for one another (v. 25). Here Paul explicitly relates the "body" discourse back to the theme which has dominated the letter from the first: the appeal for unity. His reference here to "dissension" (NRSV) suggests that indeed the Corinthians are dealing with conflict over the manifestation of spiritual gifts—which is, we must remember, the overarching topic of these chapters. Paul, however, places these conflicts within the larger framework of his vision for a unified church. He envisions not just the tolerance of differences within the community but a gracious and compassionate synergy in which all the members share one another's sorrows and joys (v. 26). Here again the body metaphor serves his hortatory purpose well; everyone knows how a pain in the ankle or finger can absorb the entire body's energy and attention. That, Paul contends, is how things are in the church. He does not speak of what should be, but of what is: the body really is diminished and pained by the suffering of any of its members. The same principle applies also to the honor shown any one member: the body really does celebrate it together. In view of the way Paul has spoken of giving honor to "the inferior member" in verses 23–24, the last sentence of this unit should also be read as an implicit exhortation: The more obviously honorable members of the church should rejoice in showing honor to the less honorable.

Application: Gifts and offices in the church (vv. 27–31a). In the final section of chapter 12, Paul makes explicit the figurative meaning that has been only thinly veiled throughout verses 14–26. "Now you are the body of Christ and individually members of it." The various bodily organs and functions of the foregoing analogy are not linked with the spiritual gifts and offices "in the church" enumerated in verse 28. Again, we should take this list as representative rather than comprehensive. The numbering of the first three items (apostles, prophets, and teachers) may indicate a certain hierarchy of authority (cf. Eph. 4:11), but it may also indicate something about the temporal order in which these gifts come into play in the construction of the Christian community: the itinerant apostle comes first and founds the church, while prophets and teachers follow to continue the work of constructing and instructing the community. Just this sort of sequence has been described already in 3:5–14. (Further teaching on prophets and prophecy will follow in chapter 14.) Certainly the other items in the rest of the list (miracles, gifts of healing, assistance, direction, tongues) are not arranged in any hierarchical order. Indeed, the inclusion in the list of "ability to help others or power to guide them" (v. 28, NEB) shows that Paul is seeking to broaden the range of the Spirit's activity beyond the range of ostentatiously supernatural manifestations that the Corinthians prized. Paul's main concern, however, is to show that the gift of tongues—pointedly left for last in the list—is only one among many gifts appointed by God in the church. The rhetorical questions of verses 29–30 are formulated in the Greek in such a way that each expects a self-evidently negative answer: "Not all are apostles, are they?" and so forth. No one person has all these different gifts, and—more importantly—no one of these gifts is exercised by everyone in the community. This is one more way of putting the point that diversity in the church is both healthy and necessary.

In light of this message, the counsel of verse 31a comes as a surprise: "But eagerly desire the greater gifts" (NIV). After the careful argument throughout the chapter that all members of the community should prize a diversity of complementary gifts and be content with the particular gifts allotted them by the Spirit, why does Paul suddenly rank some gifts above others and tell the Corinthians to strive for them? This advice is so unexpected that some interpreters have proposed reading the sentence not as an imperative but as an accusatory indicative, closely linked with verse 31b: "You Corinthians [wrongly] desire the [so-called] 'greater' gifts, but I will show you a better way." This interpretation, however, disregards the clear directive of 14:1, which is a continuation of the same theme: "Eagerly desire [*zēloute*, precisely the same verb used in 12:31a] spiritual gifts, especially the gift of prophecy" (NIV; cf. also 14:39a). Furthermore, in 14:5 Paul explicitly describes the one who prophesies as "greater" than the one who speaks in tongues. These verses are the explicit elaboration of the meaning of 12:31a. Paul really does regard prophecy as better than tongues, and he does think that all members of the community may rightly aspire to exercise this gift (14:31). His reasons for these opinions will be more fully explained in chapter 14, after an excursus characterizing the spirit in which all the gifts are to be exercised.

REFLECTIONS FOR TEACHERS AND PREACHERS

First Corinthians 12 presents a challenge for preaching, because its message is already so familiar and so obvious that it is hard to know what is left for the preacher to say after the text is read in worship. Still, several important issues rise to the surface as we read the text closely and reflect on how it speaks to the church in our time.

1. *The confession of Jesus as criterion of spirituality.* Not everything that presents itself as "spiritual" is consonant with the gospel. As "spirituality" becomes a buzzword in shopping-mall bookstores, Christians would do well to question which voices are really inspired by the Spirit of God and which seek to lead us astray to idols (v. 2). The simple criterion set forth by Paul in verse 3 is a good place to begin the discernment process. Those who confess that Jesus is Lord are speaking under the influence of the Holy Spirit; those who deny his lordship are not speaking by the Spirit of God. Of course, this simple criterion will not resolve all questions, but it may at least awaken our congregations to the need for critical discernment. The Corinthians had left a pagan past to follow a new Lord. The confession "Jesus is Lord" meant for them that Caesar was *not* Lord, that other gods and lords were nothing (8:4–6), and that they were giving themselves over to a new fundamental allegiance. The danger in the church today, on the other hand, is that we will slide imperceptibly into a generic, self-indulgent religiosity in which anything that comes to us under the guise of "religion" will be uncritically embraced. The simple confession "Jesus is Lord" remains the Spirit-inspired watchword that separates the work of the Holy Spirit from the work of deceiving spirits. At the same time, this confession unites the church at the most basic level. In the midst of serious disagreements within the church, we must recognize that all those who share the confession of Jesus' lordship are our brothers and sisters to whom we are bound by the one Spirit.

2. *Spiritual manifestations as gifts.* Paul repeatedly emphasizes that the workings of the Holy Spirit in the church are *gifts* distributed by God. There is always a danger that we will fall into the error of regarding these gifts as if they were simple natural capacities or talents, for which we might claim credit or in which we might take pride. Against this tendency, Paul's whole discussion in 1 Corinthians 12

218

reminds us of the questions posed in 4:7: "What do you have that you did not receive? And if you received it, why do you boast as if it were not a gift?" Every gift of the Spirit is given "for the common good" (12:7) and must be exercised in the church for the sake of ministry to the whole community. As soon as gifts start to be treated as possessions for the private thrills or personal aggrandizement of individuals, they become corrupted and may begin to cause dissension. I have participated in well-meaning church discussion groups that ask each person to answer the question "What are your spiritual gifts?" While such conversations can be helpful in some ways, they run the risk of turning Paul's lists of gifts (vv. 8–10, 28) into a sort of spiritualized Myers-Briggs inventory of personality types. Paul would not want us to spend our time gazing into the mirror and asking what profile of gifts each of us has; he would prefer that we simply be about the business of using our gifts in service to the community.

3. *The church is a* **charismatic** *community.* As we have noted, Paul pictures the church as a community in which the Holy Spirit operates in powerful and palpable ways through gifts of healing, miracles, and revelatory speech, including tongues and prophecy. Churches in the Pentecostal tradition and communities that have experienced charismatic renewal have recovered such gifts as an integral part of Christian worship and ministry; these manifestations of the Spirit have particularly characterized the rapidly expanding churches of the Third World. In many churches, however—perhaps most churches in the historic Protestant traditions—such phenomena are unknown and may be perceived as threatening. For such churches, 1 Corinthians 12 will indeed look like somebody else's mail. While Paul is aware that the workings of the Holy Spirit are not limited to the more spectacular manifestations that we now characterize as "charismatic," we should not domesticate his conception of the Spirit's power by excluding such gifts from our field of vision—as though he had been talking only about serving on the finance committee or planning the Sunday school curriculum. Teachers working through this text with a class unfamiliar with the manifestations of the Spirit that Paul describes in verses 8–10 might plan to take the group to visit a contemporary community where tongues and prophecy are manifested in the worship service. Such communities should not be hard to find, for in our time the Spirit has chosen to distribute these gifts in churches all around the world. Any community committed to taking Paul's vision for the church as a model for its life will have to ask seriously whether 1 Corinthians 12 does not summon us to open ourselves more radically to the possibility of such manifestations of the Spirit in our midst.

4. *The church is a charismatic* **community**. Paul is also insistent that the gifts of the Spirit must be exercised within the body of Christ for the benefit of the community as a whole. As we have seen, this leads him to highlight the twin themes of *diversity* and *interdependence*: it is good that different individuals have different gifts, and all these different gifts must be orchestrated together for the common good of the community. An important part of the preacher's task will be to discern how these motifs should be balanced to address the needs of the particular local congregation. Some churches, more susceptible to the error of "Lone Ranger" Christianity, may need to hear the appeal for interdependence emphasized, while others, more inclined to press for conformity of Christian experience, may need to hear Paul's affirmation of diverse gifts within the body of Christ. In any case, the image of the body of Christ, as Paul has developed it, provides a vision for authentic community in which there is both great individual freedom (vv. 14–20) and powerful interpersonal sharing and support (vv. 21–26). The goal of our ministry should be nothing less than the formation of such communities.

5. *The privileged are bound in one body with the weak.* This last point is likely to be overlooked in our reflection about 1 Corinthians 12, because it requires a bit of reading between the lines, but it is actually the underlying concern of the whole chapter. Paul is writing to correct the behavior of some haughty Corinthians whose undisciplined flaunting of spiritual gifts has caused the weaker and less honorable members of the community (vv. 22–23) to feel despised and even ostracized from the body because they do not have the same exalted spiritual experiences (vv. 15–16). It is likely, though not certain, that this split with the community reflects the same social and economic differences that we have seen with regard to other problems in the letter, such as the use of law courts (6:1–8) and the abuse of the Lord's Supper (11:17–34). Seeking to overcome this sad division (*schisma*, 12:25) in the church, Paul calls upon all the Corinthians to see themselves joined together as members of one body with a stake in one another's peace and wellbeing. This message makes particular demands on those who hold the upper roles in the social structure and upon those who receive the most impressive spiritual gifts. "From everyone to whom much has been given, much will be required" (Luke 11:48). Minimally, the holders of power are enjoined to receive and honor the weaker members as their peers in the body of Christ, to "have the same care" for them that they have for themselves, and to share in their joys and sufferings (vv. 25–26). A conversion of the imagination will be necessary for those in a position of privilege truly to see themselves as bound together with

220

the weaker members of the body. Such a conversion is the aim of Paul's letter, and it should be the aim of our teaching and preaching as well.

Here the lectionary provides the preacher with some help: on the Third Sunday after the Epiphany in Year C, 1 Corinthians 12:12–31a is linked with Luke 4:12–21. A sermon on these texts might draw connections between the workings of the Spirit in both texts: the Spirit not only empowers Jesus' ministry of good news to the poor but also shapes the body of Christ in which the distinction between slave and free, the barrier between privileged and poor, is broken down.

The preeminence of love (12:31b—13:13)

The purpose of chapter 13 is to portray love as the sine qua non of the Christian life and to insist that love must govern the exercise of all the gifts of the Spirit. Paul's lyrical prose in this unit has encouraged many readers to take it out of context as a lovely meditation on the nature of love; nevertheless, the many verbal and conceptual links between 1 Corinthians 13 and the rest of the letter show that this chapter is not a hymn or an independently composed oration on love. Within 1 Corinthians it serves a clear argumentative purpose: Paul is trying to reform the Corinthians' understanding and practice of spiritual manifestations in worship.

After an introductory sentence (12:31b) that announces the beginning of an epideictic interlude (in ancient rhetoric, *epideictic* referred to a type of demonstrative speech in praise or blame of some person, thing, or quality), the unit breaks clearly into three parts:

13:1–3	The futility of all religious practices without love
13:4–7	Encomium to love
13:8–13	Contrast: The provisional character of all the spiritual gifts, juxtaposed to the abiding character of love

While we may be sure that Paul's understanding of love is fundamentally formed by the love of God shown in the death of Jesus Christ (cf. Rom. 5:8; Gal. 2:20b; 1 Cor. 13:13), there is no explicit reference in this chapter to Jesus or to christology. *Agapē* is presented here as a quality or character attribute that is to be shown forth in the actions of members of the church, as in 16:14: "Let all that you do be done in love." In other words, the purpose of this chapter is straightforwardly ethical. By describing the qualities of love, Paul is seeking to promote the *character*

221

formation of the members of the Corinthian community. As John Calvin observed, "I have no doubt that Paul intended it [1 Corinthians 13] to reprimand the Corinthians in an indirect way, by confronting them with a situation quite the reverse of their own, so that they might recognize their own faults by contrast with what they saw." Of course, the description of love, particularly in 13:4–7, offers not only a reprimand but also a positive model for the construction of character. At the same time, we must not overlook the important role that this chapter plays in Paul's overall appeal for the healing of divisions in the church. Love, as Margaret Mitchell has persuasively argued, is the Pauline antidote to factionalism in the Corinthian church: "Love is the principle of Christian social unity which Paul urges on the Corinthians" (M. Mitchell, 274). As we shall see, this concern decisively shapes Paul's descriptions, both negative and positive, of love. The argument for unity builds cumulatively throughout the letter and reaches a rhetorical climax in chapter 13.

Two common misunderstandings of the chapter must be set aside in the beginning. First, Paul does not write about love in order to debunk tongues and other spiritual gifts. His point is not that love should supersede spiritual gifts but that it should govern their use in the church—as chapter 14 will clearly demonstrate. Love is not a higher and better gift; rather, it is a "way" (12:31b), a manner of life within which all the gifts are to find their proper place. Second, love is not merely a feeling or an attitude; rather, "love" is the generic name for specific actions of patient and costly service to others. If we attend closely to what Paul actually says in this chapter, all sweetly sentimental notions of love will be dispelled and replaced by a rigorous vision of love that rejoices in the truth and bears all suffering in the name of Jesus Christ.

Spiritual actions without love are meaningless (13:1–3).

Spiritual actions without love are meaningless (13:1–3). The first unit of the chapter (vv. 1–3) consists of three sentences that describe various religious practices, all of which are declared futile where love is not present: speaking in tongues (v. 1), prophesying, receiving revealed knowledge, working miracles by faith (v. 2), and ascetic self-deprivation (v. 3) are all worthless if not accompanied by love. The items listed in verses 1 and 2 include gifts of which the Corinthians are particularly fond (tongues and knowledge), but Paul also lists here prophecy, which he himself prizes highly (14:1–25). This demonstrates that his intention is not to polemicize against tongues and revelatory gifts of the Spirit; instead, he merely wants to place them within the proper evaluative framework. By themselves they are of no account. This same judgment applies even to morally praiseworthy acts such as giving away one's possessions, presumably to the poor (v. 3). Paul's broad formulation in these verses can be understood in two ways. On the one hand, he could be condemning "doing the right thing for the wrong reason" and calling for love as the proper motivation for religious practices. On the other hand, he could be condemning moral inconsistency (doing some of the right things but lacking love in other areas of one's life) and calling for love to be lived out in all aspects of existence. Both readings make good sense, and there is no need to exclude either.

The expression "speak with the tongues of men and of angels" (v. 1) does not simply mean to speak with great eloquence. It refers to speaking not only human language but also, by the special inspiration of the Holy Spirit, the language spoken by heavenly beings. One of the most illuminating ancient parallels is found in the *Testament of Job*, an Egyptian Jewish text of the first century B.C.E. or first century C.E. This text contains the legend of the three daughters of Job, each of whom is given a multicolored cord as an inheritance; the cord confers upon them the power of angelic speech and song. "Thus, when the one called Hemera arose, she wrapped around her own string just as her father said. And she took on another heart—no longer minded toward earthly things—but she spoke ecstatically in the angelic dialect, sending up a hymn to God in accord with the hymnic style of the angels" (*T. Job* 48:1–3a). Presumably, this is how "speaking in tongues" was understood by the Corinthians and by Paul also; as Paul says in 14:2, "those who speak in a tongue do not speak to other people but to God; for nobody understands them, since they are speaking mysteries in the Spirit." Tongue-speaking, then, was revered as a mode of communication with the superior heavenly world. But even something as glorious as speaking with the tongues of angels is of no value without love.

The one who speaks in this way but lacks love has become, in Paul's telling metaphor, "an echoing bronze or a clanging cymbal" (v. 1, au. trans.). Corinth was particularly famous for its production of bronze vessels. Since the term *chalkos* ("bronze") is never used elsewhere to refer to a musical instrument, some scholars have proposed that Paul's phrase refers to bronze acoustic vases that were used in the theater to echo and amplify the voices of the actors (see Murphy O'Connor, *St. Paul's Corinth*, 75–77). The "clanging cymbal" was particularly associated with the cult of Cybele, noted for its wild ecstatic worship practices. Thus, Paul's point in verse 1 might be paraphrased as follows: "Even if you can speak with the heavenly language of angels, but have no love, your high-toned speech has become like the empty echo of an actor's speech or the noise of frenzied pagan worship." This is forceful imagery; Paul is pulling no punches with his readers.

Prophecy (v. 2), already mentioned in 12:10 and to be discussed at greater length in chapter 14, means speaking a word from God to the gathered congregation; no doubt Paul understood this gift against the background of the activity of the Old Testament prophets. Understanding "all mysteries and all knowledge [*gnōsis*]" means having access to inside information about the plans of God; for example, Paul uses the term "mystery" in 15:51 to refer to revealed knowledge about the final resurrection of the dead. As this example shows, the background of this language for Paul is the world of Jewish apocalyptic thought, in which the seer receives revelation of the heavenly mysteries from God. The prototype of the apocalyptic seer is Daniel, to whom "the mystery was revealed" of how to interpret Nebuchadnezzar's dream concerning "what will happen at the end of days" (Dan. 2:19, 28), and who therefore praises God, saying:

> Blessed be the name of God from age to age,
> for wisdom and power are his. . . .
> He gives wisdom to the wise
> and knowledge to those who have understanding.
> He reveals deep and hidden things;
> he knows what is in the darkness,
> and light dwells with him.
>
> (Dan. 2:20–22)

The Corinthians, as we have seen, may have adopted from Paul the apocalyptic emphasis on wisdom and knowledge but fused it with interpretations of these terms derived from Greek philosophical traditions. (For other references to the Corinthians' "knowledge," see 1:5; 8:1; 8:7–13; 12:8; 14:6). In any case, no matter whether one gains an understanding of mysterious truths through revelatory experience or through philosophical reflection, such knowledge counts for nothing without love. Paul rhetorically holds himself up as an example: though he has described himself as one who speaks "God's wisdom, secret and hidden, which God decreed before the ages for our glory" (2:7), without love he would be "nothing" (13:2).

Similarly, the person who can perform mountain-moving miracles by faith is nothing without love. ("Faith," we should recall, was also one of the manifestations of the Spirit listed in 1 Cor. 12:9.) Paul may be alluding here to a tradition about the teaching of Jesus, as attested by Mark 11:22–24 and Matthew 17:20 (cf. also Isa. 40:4). In substance, however, Paul's point is closer to the teaching of Matthew 7:21–23: those who are excluded from the kingdom may have prophesied and done mighty works, but such works count for nothing if they have not done the will of the Father in heaven—which, in the Gospel of Matthew,

224

is closely linked with love and mercy. In sum, the revelations and miracles mentioned in verse 2 must be placed within the framework of love if they are to have any significance at all.

In verse 3, the religious practices held up against the standard of love are two different forms of self-denial: giving away one's possessions (cf. Luke 14:33) and giving up one's own body. The meaning of the second example is complicated by a notoriously difficult textual problem: some ancient Greek manuscripts read *hina kauthēsomai* ("to be burned"), while others read *hina kauchēsōmai* ("so that I may boast"). One of the usual objections against "be burned" is that Christian martyrdom by fire was not yet known in Paul's time; however, this objection carries little weight, for traditions of martyrdom by fire were thoroughly familiar in Judaism, as demonstrated by the narratives of the deaths of the Maccabean martyrs (e.g., 2 Macc. 7:1–6; 4 Macc. 6:24–30). Nevertheless, it is hard to imagine why later scribes would have changed "be burned" to the rather perplexing "boast," whereas the reverse change is entirely understandable. Thus, on balance, the reading *kauchēsōmai* ("so that I may boast") is to be preferred.

Still, if Paul wrote "in order that I may boast," what could he have meant? Paul has used "boast" several times in the letter, and not always in a pejorative sense. The evidence of 1 Corinthians 9:15–16 is particularly pertinent; there Paul declares that his ground for boasting is that he has surrendered his legitimate rights for the sake of the gospel. In that passage, the idea of boasting seems to be linked with the motif of eschatological reward for apostolic labors (cf. also Rom. 5:3; 2 Cor. 1:14). If this sense of eschatological boasting can be carried forward from 9:15 into 13:3, the meaning then would be, "if I hand over my body so that I might boast/glory in the eschatological reward for my self-sacrifice."

A possible further sense for "giving up the body" is provided by *1 Clement*, a late-first-century text that refers explicitly to Paul's correspondence with Corinth. Offering examples of what it means to be "filled with love" (54:1), *1 Clement* says, "We know that many among ourselves have given themselves to bondage that they might ransom others. Many have delivered themselves to slavery, and provided food for others with the price they received for themselves" (55:2). This passage is particularly interesting because the two verbs translated as "delivered" and "provided food" are precisely the same two verbs that appear in 1 Corinthians 13:3, there rendered by the NRSV as "hand over" and "give away." It seems likely that *1 Clement* is explicitly echoing 1 Corinthians 13:3 and interpreting the giving over of the body as a reference to voluntary slavery rather than martyrdom by fire (Fee, 634, n.46).

225

Whatever the precise nuance of the phrase, Paul insists that there is nothing to be gained by self-sacrifice where love is absent. With this declaration, his impressive opening paragraph comes to an end, having asserted forcefully that all religious action is meaningless unless encompassed by *agapē*.

Love as the antithesis of the Corinthians' behavior (13:4–7). In the next unit (vv. 4–7) Paul speaks descriptively in praise of love by detailing what love (now poetically personified) does and does not do. The first two positive items in the catalogue ("Love is patient; love is kind") attribute to love qualities that Paul elsewhere ascribes to God (Rom. 2:4). It is evident, however, that the weight of Paul's interest falls upon the eight negative items in the list, most of which correspond closely to the behavior of the Corinthians as described elsewhere in the letter.

The first clue is found in the first negative description of love: "love is not envious [*zēloi*]." This is the same language that Paul had applied to the contentious Corinthians in 3:3: "For as long as there is jealousy [*zēlos*] and quarreling among you, are you not of the flesh?" Paul thus tips off the alert reader immediately that love is the opposite of the divisive rivalry that he has deplored in Corinth. Likewise, the second item ("boastful") echoes Paul's repeated reprimands of the Corinthians for boasting (1:29–31; 3:21; 4:7; 5:6), though he uses a different Greek word here, perhaps because he has just used the verb "boast" in a positive sense in 13:3.

With the third item in the list, even the dullest of Paul's Corinthian readers would have to recognize that he is explicitly contrasting *agapē* to their own behavior: love "is not puffed up [*physioutai*]. (Most English translations opt for a less colorful synonym, such as "arrogant" or "proud.") This is precisely the word that Paul has used to castigate the Corinthians in 4:6; 4:18–19; and 5:2. Furthermore, in 8:1, Paul deflates the Corinthians' pretensions of knowledge by declaring that "Knowledge puffs up [*physioi*], but love builds up." Thus, the appearance of this item in Paul's catalogue of what love does *not* do functions as a virtual cross-reference back to these earlier passages, especially 8:1.

The fourth item—weakly translated by NRSV, NIV, NEB, and JB alike as "rude"—is actually a stronger term referring to shameful behavior. For example, Paul uses the cognate noun in Romans 1:27 to characterize the "shameful act" of male homosexual intercourse. In the context of 1 Corinthians, the only previous explicit use of this word has been in the hypothetical reference to an unmarried man who is "behaving shamefully" in relation to his betrothed virgin (7:36), but Paul's

226

use of the term here probably also reflects the sexual misconduct that he has condemned in 5:1–2 (note the link with "puffed up" in 5:2) and 6:12–20, as well as the "shameful" behavior of women prophesying with heads uncovered (11:2–16) and the humiliation of the poor at the Lord's Supper (11:20–22). All of these Corinthian offenses would constitute the sort of "acting shamefully" that Paul sees as contrary to love.

The fifth item in Paul's negative catalogue again provides an explicit link back to an earlier part of the letter: love "is not self-seeking" (NIV). This repeats precisely the language that Paul had used in 10:24 in his response to the idol-meat controversy: "Do not seek your own advantage but that of the other." Furthermore, the behavior attributed to love in this phrase in 13:5 is identical to Paul's self-description in 10:33: "not seeking my own advantage but that of many." We might also remember that Paul links his own self-renunciation for the sake of others to the example of Christ (11:1; cf. Phil. 2:4).

By this time the Corinthians will surely have gotten the picture: Paul is implying that everything about their behavior contradicts the character of love. The next two negative items are harder to relate to specific passages in the letter, but they are probably to be seen in contrast to the rivalry and dissensions in the Corinthian church: love "is not easily angered" and "keeps no record of wrongs" (NIV; these forceful formulations are much closer to the Greek than the NRSV's pallid adjectives, "not irritable or resentful").

With verse 6, Paul closes the list of negative attributes and offers a positive contrast: love "does not rejoice in wrongdoing [*adikia*], but rejoices in the truth." The term *adikia*—which might better be translated as "injustice"—was featured prominently in 6:1–11, where Paul deplored the Corinthians' practice of taking one another to court unjustly. Given the juxtaposition with "wrongdoing," the term "truth" here surely has a moral sense, as it does in the Johannine tradition (e.g., John 3:21; 1 John 3:18). Thus, to rejoice in the truth would mean, among other things, to embrace God's way of righteous living—a pointed contrast to the Corinthians' present conduct as Paul sees it.

In light of the way that Paul has used the figure of "love" in counterpoint to the Corinthians' divisive and self-centered behavior, we may conclude that *1 Clement* well understood the import of 1 Corinthians 13 in its reprise of the passage: "Love beareth all things, is long-suffering in all things. There is nothing base, nothing haughty in love; love admits no schism, love makes no sedition, love does all things in concord" (*1 Clement* 49:5; note the explicit references to 1 Corinthians in *1 Clement* 47). As this very early interpretation recognizes, Paul's poetic

227

depiction of love's character is aimed at calling the members of the Corinthian community out of schism and into unity with each other (see M. Mitchell, 168 n.624).

After telling us what love is not, Paul ends this unit with four strong verbs that characterize positively the action of *agapē*). "Love bears all things, believes all things, hopes all things, endures all things" (v. 7). Paul has already used the first of these verbs to characterize his own conduct as an apostle: he will "bear anything rather than put an obstacle in the way of the gospel of Christ" (9:12, au. trans.). This observation strengthens the impression that grows on the reader throughout this section: if the Corinthians embody the antithesis of *agapē*, Paul himself models authentic *agapē* in his long-suffering apostolic role. Paul shows them "a more excellent way" not only through his word-picture of love but also through his example, which he wants them to imitate (11:1).

The two verbs "believes" and "hopes" of course foreshadow the conclusion of the chapter, in which faith and hope join love as the abiding marks of Christian character. And the final verb ("endures") creates an *inclusio* with the first item in verse 4 ("Love is patient") and suggests the eschatological location of love in the present time: love persists in a hostile world, awaiting the coming of the Lord. The hyperbole of the repeated "all things" in verse 7 should not lead us to think that love is infinitely credulous and utterly indiscriminate in its believing and hoping. Love does not make its adherents into foolish Pollyannas. Paul's point is accurately conveyed by the NEB's translation: "there is no limit to its faith, its hope, and its endurance."

Spiritual gifts and love (13:8–13). The final section of chapter 13 (vv. 8–13) moves the discussion in a different direction, as Paul now contrasts the permanence of love to the transitory character of the spiritual gifts. This is the part of the chapter that most clearly shows that it was composed to deal with the specific problem of the evaluation of spiritual gifts in the Corinthian community. Love is mentioned only in the beginning and end of the unit (vv. 8a, 13); all the intervening material (vv. 8b–12) highlights the temporary status of spiritual gifts, especially tongues, prophecy, and knowledge (vv. 8b–9). Had Paul been writing a general "hymn to love," he would hardly have emphasized this contrast so strongly.

The treatment of the gifts is set up by an opening affirmation that establishes the point of contrast: "Love never falls." (The NRSV's "Love never ends" is an interpretative paraphrase.) On the other hand, prophecy, tongues, and knowledge will all be brought to nothing eschatologically. The verb that Paul uses in verse 8 of prophecy and knowledge (*katargein*) is a favorite word of his; it consistently refers to God's nullification and abolition of everything that is ephemeral or— in some cases—opposed to him. For example, in 1:28 Paul declares that God has chosen lowly and despised nonentities "to reduce to nothing [*katargēsē*] things that are" (cf. 2:6; 6:13; 15:24–26; Rom. 6:6). In verse 8, to be sure, the gifts listed are not allied with powers hostile to God; rather, they will be abolished simply because they will no longer be necessary when the Lord returns and the fullness of his kingdom is present. These gifts of revelation are suited to the time between the times, when the church must walk by faith; prophecy and *gnōsis* are only "partial" (v. 9), giving believers a real but imperfect glimpse of God's future truth. When that which is complete comes, however, these partial instruments of knowledge will no longer have any purpose, and so they will be discarded by God (v. 10).

(In dispensationalist Christian groups, it is sometimes claimed that "the complete" [*to teleion*] in v. 10 refers to the completion and closure of the New Testament canon, so that the charismatic gifts were only for the apostolic age and have now ceased to function in the church. This interpretation is simply nonsense. There is nothing in the passage about "the New Testament" or about a future revocation of revelatory gifts in the church. Paul had no inkling that Israel's Scripture would be supplemented by a new collection of canonical writings. Verse 10 is simply a general maxim stating that the perfect supplants the partial. Paul's references to the abolition of the gifts [v. 8] are to be understood in light of the patently eschatological language of v. 12: the contrast between "now" and "then" is the contrast between the present age and the age to come.)

The logic of Paul's argument is impeccable within the eschatologically determined symbolic world of his gospel. The Corinthians, however, seem to have lost hold of the future temporal orientation of Paul's preaching. They have moved into a frame of reference that thinks only in spatial categories of "above" and "below." They believe that their spiritual gifts give them immediate access to the divine world, and they are not thinking at all about the future event of God's judgment and transformation of the world (cf. 15:20–28). In their frame of reference, therefore, revelatory spiritual gifts have assumed ultimate significance, because they provide the open, "hot line" links to heavenly reality. Paul wants to relativize these gifts by situating them within the unfolding epic narrative of God's redemption of the world: they have a role to play for now, but the time of their usefulness will pass.

The analogy of verse 11 reinforces this point; just as the perceptions and communicative strategies of childhood are put aside when one arrives at maturity, so also the church's present spiritual gifts will be put aside in the eschaton. The analogy is calculated to ruffle the feathers of those Corinthian readers who consider themselves far advanced in their spirituality and who think of the gift of tongues as the pinnacle of spiritual maturity. Just as in 3:1–4, when Paul addressed them as *nēpioi* (little children not able yet to eat solid food), so here too Paul confronts them with a different assessment of their place in the unfolding plot of God's story.

One last analogy drives home Paul's point. The knowledge provided by the spiritual gifts is like the picture of the world reflected indirectly in a mirror (v. 12), not false but indistinct. (Again Paul is using a metaphor well suited to his audience, for one of the noted industries of Corinth was the manufacturing of mirrors.) The time will come, Paul affirms audaciously, when God will speak to us face to face—as he did to Moses:

> When there are prophets among you,
>   I the LORD make myself known to them in visions;
> I speak to them in dreams,
>   Not so with my servant Moses;
>   he is entrusted with all my house.
> With him I speak *face to face*—
>   clearly, not *in riddles* [LXX: *di' ainigmatōn*; cf. 1 Cor. 13:12];
> and he beholds the form of the LORD.

> (Num. 12:6–8, emphasis added)

This direct encounter with God, Paul insists, belongs to the eschatological "not yet" of salvation. The contrast between "now" and "then" is critical to understanding verse 12. Only "then," in the consummation of God's kingdom, will we know fully—as God knows us already in the present. This last turn of phrase deftly sets the Corinthians who claim "knowledge" in their proper place. God alone is the one who really "knows" (cf. Gal. 4:9).

Now, however, in the time between the times, even with our partial knowledge, "faith, hope, and love remain." In light of the eschatological imagery of verses 8–12, the "now" of verse 13 must surely be read as a temporal adverb, not merely a logical connective. Paul is *not* saying, contrary to the opinion of some exegetes, that faith, hope, and love will all abide eternally. (This statement would be nearly nonsensical in relation to hope; after "the complete" has come [v. 10], after we have seen God face to face [v. 12], what will remain to hope for [cf. Rom. 8:22–25]?) No, faith, hope, and love are the enduring character marks of the Christian life in the present time, in this anomalous interval between the cross and the *parousia*. Faith is the trust that we direct toward the God of Israel, who has kept faith with his covenant promises by putting forward Jesus for our sake and raising him to new life; hope focuses our fervent desire to see a broken world restored by God to its rightful wholeness (Rom. 8:18–39); and love is the foretaste of our ultimate union with God, graciously given to us now and shared with our brothers and sisters. Paul returns repeatedly in his letters to this triad of terms, grouped in various ways, to portray Christian existence (Rom. 5:1–5; Gal. 5:5–6; Col. 1:4–5; 1 Thess. 1:3; 5:8; cf. also Eph. 4:2–5; Titus 2:2; Heb. 6:10–12; 10:22–24; 1 Peter 1:3–8). Love is the greatest of the three because—unlike the revelatory gifts and even unlike faith and hope—it will endure eternally when the love of God is all in all (1 Cor. 15:28). It is also the greatest because, even in the present time, it undergirds everything else and gives meaning to an otherwise unintelligible world (cf. 13:1–3). Only when love presides over our common life in the church will the spiritual gifts find their rightful place and achieve the purposes for which God has given them to us.

REFLECTIONS FOR TEACHERS AND PREACHERS

The first task for the interpreter of 1 Corinthians 13 is to rescue the text from the quagmire of romantic sentimentality in which popular piety has embedded it. The common use of this text in weddings has linked it in the minds of many with flowers and kisses and frilly wedding dresses. Such images are far removed from Paul's original concerns. He did not write about *agapē* in order to rhapsodize about marriage; he was writing about the need for mutual concern and consideration *within the community of the church,* with special reference to the use of spiritual gifts in worship. It may be legitimate to appropriate his words in another context to speak of the love that binds man and woman in marriage, but only if we are clear about the hermeneutical transfer that we are performing when we do that. Most members of our congregations will find their thoughts about love challenged and sharpened if they are invited to reflect in a sustained way about the connection between 1 Corinthians 13 and its original historical context. The passage is originally an impassioned vision of the "more excellent way" in which members of the Corinthian church should treat one another.

Once that point is clearly in focus, we can ask how Paul's word to the Corinthians on this matter might speak also to us. The question that should surface immediately is this: How do our own actions and relationships within our congregation express—or fail to express—love for one another? This would apply not only to the use of charismatic gifts

231

in worship but also to the whole network of actions and interactions that make up the life of a community. Love is the criterion by which we should assess all that we do. Having said that, we must hasten to add that love does not mean uncritical acceptance; Paul's own example of vigorous confrontation of the Corinthians on various issues should demonstrate that point beyond all question! The love that "rejoices in the truth" may also require us to speak hard truth at times to those whom we love.

As we reflect about the theological implications of 1 Corinthians 13, three major observations stand out, one based on each subsection of the passage.

1. *Love is the ground of meaning.* As verses 1–3 emphasize, even the most apparently spiritual and meritorious activities become, without love, literally meaningless. First Corinthians 13 ought to encourage us to step back from even our most cherished projects and ask, "Why am I doing this?" If we cannot honestly say, "I am doing this *for* love and *in* love," then the legitimacy of the whole enterprise must come under serious doubt. This test applies, of course, not just to explicitly religious practices but to everything that we do: business, academics, politics. All of us know of sad cases where laudable causes are promoted by people who have lost this frame of reference and turned into loveless zealots. Indeed, this is not far from what was happening at Corinth: precisely those Corinthians who were most singlemindedly focused on spirituality had become guilty of dividing the community and despising their brothers and sisters. We are so susceptible to self-deception in such matters that we need others around us who can keep us honest and remind us, as Paul does, that love is what really counts ultimately.

2. *Love requires the formation of character.* Love is not just a matter of feelings; feelings come and go, while love abides. Paul's description of the attributes of love in verses 4–7 offers a picture of habitual actions and dispositions. One cannot merely decide in a day's time to start doing these things. They are learned patterns of behavior that must be cultivated over time in the context of a community that models and supports such behavior. We must learn patience; we must be taught how not to keep score of wrongs done against us. As Paul's correspondence with Corinth suggests, the church should be a school for the cultivation of these habits and practices. Regrettably, as the church has tended to adopt the political habits and strategies of secular democracies, far too little attention has been given in our communities to this character-forming task of the church. We must deliberate carefully about how to reform the church so that we can more fully devote our

energies to learning how to love. This is the context in which 1 Corinthians might fruitfully be brought to bear upon our understanding of marriage—and of celibacy and friendship.

3. *All our knowledge is partial.* The eschatological reservation looms heavily over all that we say and do: We know only in part and act constantly on the basis of incomplete information. We have no choice about that in this time between the times. The force of verses 8–13, however, is to encourage us to have a sense of humility and a sense of humor about even our gravest convictions and activities. When the perfect comes, when God judges the secrets of human hearts, when we can see this life from the other side of the resurrection, we will discover that even the things that have seemed most glorious and exalted to us (whether tongues or technology) have been like child's play. Paul tries to teach us to sit loose to the cares and conflicts of present existence and particularly to what we think we know. Only love will not be rendered obsolete in the end.

A final word for preachers: one thing we can learn from this passage is the power of vivid language. Why is this passage so memorable? Its power comes from its metaphorical richness: sounding bronze and clanging cymbal, mountains moving, memories of childhood play and speech, dim reflections in the mirror. The images carry the message with a minimum of didactic commentary. We should learn from Paul the concision and power of metaphorical preaching. At the same time, the diction of the passage is clear and simple, with short phrases, repeated syntactical patterns, and forceful verbs. Love "bears all things, believes all things, hopes all things, endures all things." Long before Lincoln's Gettysburg Address or Strunk and White's *The Elements of Style*, Paul knew that less could say more.

Regulating spiritual gifts in worship (14:1–40)

Having laid the groundwork in chapters 12 and 13, Paul now addresses the problem of the Corinthians' worship in more specific terms. Some of the Corinthians—presumably those who consider themselves gifted with wisdom and knowledge—are placing inordinate emphasis on the gift of tongues. They believe that their ability to speak in a heavenly language that surpasses human understanding is the ultimate sign of their spiritual power and maturity. The community's worship assembly, however, has fallen into disorderly confusion, as various members speak simultaneously and unintelligibly under the inspiration of the Spirit, perhaps even competitively seeking to outdo one another in the display of glossolalia. In this matter, as in the case of their abuse of the Lord's Supper, Paul cannot commend them, for their behavior fractures the community.

233

Nonetheless, this situation poses a difficult pastoral problem for Paul, because he firmly believes that these spiritual manifestations (*pneumatika*)—including tongues—are gifts (*charismata*) of the Holy Spirit given by God to the church (12:10, 28). Paul shares with the Corinthians a vision for community worship as the setting in which God will speak and act powerfully through spontaneous supernatural revelations. How, then, can he seek to create order in the community's worship without squelching the Spirit? His solution, set forth at some length in chapter 14, is to insist that love (chapter 13) requires the gifts to be used for building up the community (14:12, 26). Consequently, *intelligible* speech is necessary in the assembly for the common good; unintelligible tongues must be either interpreted or reserved for private prayer. In preference to tongues, Paul advocates *prophecy* as the highest gift, because the prophet speaks inspired intelligible messages from God directly to the congregation, thereby building up the church.

There is a long tradition of interpreting this text as though Paul only grudgingly allowed the practice of tongues-speaking—as though he were damning this gift with faint praise and implicitly trying to root it out. Such a reading, characteristically advocated by interpreters whose own ecclesiastical traditions have no experience of the gifts about which Paul writes, fails to do justice to the specific language of the passage. What Paul actually says is that the person who speaks in tongues is praying, under the inspiration of the Spirit, to God (v. 2). In some mysterious way, this sort of prayer does spiritually build up the individual (v. 4). Paul himself prays and sings in tongues more than all of the Corinthians (v. 18) and wants all of them to enjoy this gift as well (v. 5). He gives constructive directions for how tongues might play a role in community worship (vv. 26–28) and explicitly directs that speaking in tongues should not be prohibited (v. 39). His major concern is simply to counteract the excessive valuation and undisciplined practice of tongues-speaking in the community.

At the same time, he urges his readers to desire earnestly the gift of prophecy (v. 1). It must be emphasized that for Paul "prophecy" is not the same thing as composing and preaching a sermon; prophecy is also a spiritual gift (12:10, 28), exercised spontaneously under the inspiration of the Spirit and tested by the discernment of the community (14:29–32; cf. 1 Thess. 5:19–21). We must not rationalize away Paul's vision of Christian worship as the spontaneous Spirit-led encounter of the community with God.

Over the entire chapter, however, looms the theme of building up the church. The verb *oikodomein* ("to build up") and the noun *oikodomē* ("upbuilding, edification") occur seven times in this chapter, including in the summarizing formulations of verses 5, 12, and 26. The watchword and guiding principle for Christian worship is "Let all things be done for building up" (v. 26). In light of that framing exhortation, let us examine Paul's specific advice a bit more closely.

Chapter 14 falls into two major parts. In verses 1–25, Paul argues for prophecy as the preferable mode of manifestation of the Spirit in the community's gatherings, putting forward several different arguments and concluding with a fascinating (but difficult) reflection on the divergent impact of tongues and prophecy on those who are outsiders to the community (vv. 20–25). The second part (vv. 26–40) gives specific guidelines for orderly worship (vv. 26–33), asserts Paul's authority to promulgate such guidelines (vv. 36–38), and briefly recapitulates the message of the chapter as a whole (vv. 39–40). In the midst of this last section appears an abrupt and thematically incongruous demand for women to be silent and subordinate (vv. 34–35); this is almost certainly an early gloss interpolated into the text of the letter, and it will be treated separately in an excursus below.

Prophecy builds up the community (14:1–25). After the interlude of chapter 13, Paul resumes his discussion from chapter 12 of the various roles of spiritual gifts in the body of Christ. The first clause in 14:1a sums up the message of chapter 13: pursue the way of love (cf. 12:31b). The second clause ("eagerly desire spiritual gifts") picks up the same verb (*zēloute*) used in 12:31a, now specifying more closely the proper aim of such desire: the gift of prophecy should be especially sought. The reason for the high value of this particular gift is explained in verses 2–4, by way of contrast to tongues: tongues are unintelligible and therefore benefit the speaker alone, while prophecy builds up (*oikodomei*) the church. These verses give us Paul's most informative account of these two gifts. The speaker in tongues is addressing *God* in prayer and speaking "mysteries in the Spirit." According to verses 15–17, this sort of prayer "in the Spirit" is a means of expressing praise and thanksgiving. This is a discourse not intended for human hearers, who cannot understand it (v. 2). Prophecy, on the other hand, is addressed not to God but to human beings "for their upbuilding [*oikodomēn*] and encouragement and consolation" (v. 3). This description shows that Paul does not think of prophecy as predicting future events; instead, its purpose is to address the hearts of the hearers and to encourage them in the faith. That is why it builds up the church.

In verse 5, Paul explicitly indicates that prophecy is among the "greater gifts" mentioned earlier in 12:31a, because it is of greater benefit to the community. The one who prophesies is "greater" than the

235

one who speaks in tongues, unless the latter also interprets the utterance in tongues. Contrary to the NRSV, Paul's statement in verse 5 does not envision a second interpreter ("someone"); the tongue-speaker himself or herself is the subject of the verb "interpret" in this sentence, as in the NIV. Accordingly, in verse 13 Paul indicates that the one who speaks in tongues should pray for the gift of interpretation—again, so that the utterance might benefit the church (v. 12). All of this shows that Paul is not averse to ranking the relative importance of the spiritual gifts; the major difference between him and the Corinthians is that they are using different evaluative criteria for their rankings. Paul, for his part, continually presses for the primacy of community building.

Paul restates his argument in verses 6–12 by using analogies, the first two musical in character. He compares inspired speech in the church to the sounds produced by harp and flute (v. 7), to the call of a military horn (v. 8), and to the varieties of natural human language (vv. 10–11). In the first analogy, he observes that the flutist or harpist cannot merely play random notes; in order for the melody to make sense to the hearer, there must be an order or pattern to the notes sounded. (Furthermore—a point that Paul does not make—different musicians trying to play together cannot simply play whatever occurs to them; their parts must be orchestrated in a complementary fashion.)

The second analogy—the trumpet sounding a call to battle—is even more telling. Paul sometimes uses military metaphors to describe the calling of Christians (e.g., Rom. 6:12–14; Cor. 10:3–6; Phil. 1:27–30; 1 Thess. 5:8; cf. Eph. 6:10–20; 2 Tim. 4:7); his metaphor in 1 Corinthians 14:8 suggests that public speech in the Christian assembly should awaken members of the church to action in the cosmic conflict in which the church is engaged. The "indistinct" sound of incoherent speech in tongues will do nothing to marshal the troops for battle. The speaker in tongues will merely be talking "into the air" (v. 9).

In the third analogy, Paul shifts the metaphorical field and points to the great variety of languages in the world (rightly NIV, JB, not just "sounds" as in NRSV). Estrangement occurs when we encounter someone who does not share a common language with us, because meaningful communication is impossible. Similar estrangement will divide us from one another in the church, he suggests, if incomprehensible tongue-speaking dominates the church's discourse.

Paul's conclusion to this unit gives a revealing characterization of the Corinthians: they are "eager for spiritual gifts" (literally "eager for spirits"; cf. v. 1). Paul seeks to direct their zeal into a constructive path by urging them to "excel" in using their gifts *to build up the church*. By now this exhortation is becoming a familiar refrain. Interestingly,

236

however, he does not single out prophecy in this section in the same way he had done in verses 1–5. Prophecy is mentioned as one of four operations of the Spirit, along with revelation, knowledge, and teaching, that benefit the church through intelligible instruction (v. 6). This suggests that the term "prophecy" should be read throughout chapter 14 as synecdoche for all forms of intelligible speech gifts that edify the church. If Paul had any specific understanding of the distinctions between these four terms, he does not explain it, and it is therefore useless for us to speculate.

The phrasing of verse 6 ("Now, brothers and sisters, if I come to you speaking in tongues") echoes the wording of 2:1, in which Paul wrote, "When I came to you, brothers and sisters, I did not come proclaiming the mystery of God to you in lofty words or wisdom." The echo may be deliberate. Gordon Fee (661–62) has suggested plausibly that there is "an undercurrent of apologetic" in 14:6. The Corinthians had perhaps reproached Paul for failing to come to them with a fireworks display of glossolalia. If so, Paul replies that this was strictly for *their* benefit, for his speaking in tongues would have done them no good. He chose instead, as he has already explained, to come to them with simple understandable words proclaiming Jesus Christ crucified (2:1–2).

We gain a little further insight about the phenomenon of praying in tongues in verses 14–17. When praying in a tongue, Paul indicates, the worshiper's mind is in neutral and "fruitless." Consequently, Paul suggests, it is best to pray and sing not only with the spirit but also with the mind. Whether these two forms of prayer are meant to be simultaneous or sequential is difficult to say from Paul's brief remarks. If verses 14–15 are read as elaborations of verse 13, the latter is perhaps more likely: the worshiper prays in tongues ("with the spirit") and then, still under the guidance of the Spirit, offers an interpretation ("with the mind also"). Otherwise, everyone else in the congregation remains an uninitiated "outsider" (*idiōtēs*) to the mysterious communication between the tongues-speaker and God. When the utterance of praise is interpreted, however, the other person can say "Amen," joining in the expression of thanksgiving and thereby being built up (v. 17).

Paul has held back one important bit of information. Now he drops it in for rhetorical impact: He claims to speak in tongues more than any of the Corinthians, including those who pride themselves on this gift! He explains, however, that he has not employed this gift "in church" (*en ekklēsia:* NEB's "in the congregation" is a better translation) because he would rather speak "five words with my mind" to instruct the congregation than to pour forth a torrent of incomprehensible words

(vv. 18–19). Paul has now played his ace, seeking to trump the Corinthians' claims. He could beat them at their own game of superspirituality, he says, but he has chosen not to play that game because he has another goal in mind. Here again Paul holds himself up as an example to be imitated—an example of renouncing spiritual glory and status for the sake of others. Thus, his ethical example concerning the use of spiritual gifts matches the pattern already outlined in chapters 8–10: Paul renounces rights and privileges for the benefit of others in the church. The *instruction* of the community is a higher value than any amount of exalted religious experience.

This part of the argument could easily be concluded with verse 19, but Paul raises one more issue for consideration: the effect of tongues and prophecy on unbelievers. Throughout the argument so far, he has focused on the effects of these gifts within the community of believers, but in verses 20–25 he shifts attention to people on the periphery of the church community. He begins by suggesting that the Corinthians' absorption with spiritual gifts as an end in themselves is childish (v. 20; cf. the similar accusation concerning their divisiveness in 3:1–4). A more mature perspective would consider the impact of these gifts on others, not only those immediately within the church but also others in Corinth who might be confronted by the gospel.

It is often suggested that Paul might be thinking particularly of the unbelieving spouses of Christians, mentioned in 7:12–16. There is no reason, however, to restrict his concern to this group alone. Evidently, he thinks of the house church meetings as open to nonbelievers; his argument assumes that their presence in worship might be a normal event in the community's life. It is difficult to know whether the *idiōtai* NRSV: "outsiders") constitute a separate group or whether—as is perhaps more likely—this is simply a synonym for unbelievers. Whoever they are, the present context requires that they be people who are not yet committed worshipers of the one God of Israel.

In any case, Paul compellingly works out the implications of his concern for unbelievers in verses 23–25: Outsiders who enter and find the whole community speaking in tongues will think that this Christian group is simply one more mystery cult that whips its partisans into a frenzy of frothy enthusiasm. In the Greek cultural context the verb *mainesthe*, translated by both NRSV and NIV as "you are out of your mind" (v. 23), does not necessarily have the pejorative sense that this translation suggests for readers today. It does not mean that the persons in question are crazy, just that they have temporarily been caught up in a fit of religious ecstasy, a common phenomenon in that culture. The typical pagan Corinthian observing such a scene would say, "Oh, this is just another group like the devotees of Dionysius or Cybele"—one more consumer option in a pluralistic religious market. On the other hand, if outsiders come and find the members of the community prophesying in clear, sober language, they will encounter the word of the Lord, which will disclose "the secrets of the heart," that is, their real moral condition before God (cf. 4:5). This does not mean that Paul thought of Christian prophecy as a fortune-telling trick that disclosed personal secrets about individuals; rather, we should think of something more like the argument of Romans 1—3, a discourse in which all human pretensions to righteousness are stripped away by the proclaimed message of the severity and kindness of God. Paul envisions that unbelievers who encounter this sort of unparalleled truth-telling in the form of Spirit-inspired utterance will be cut to the heart (cf. Acts 2:37) and brought to "bow down before God and worship him" (1 Cor. 14:25).

When Paul imagines that outsiders who are converted by the word of prophecy will declare, "God is really among you," he is recalling a scenario long envisioned by Israel's prophets: the Gentiles will come to acknowledge that the God of Israel is the one God of the whole world. First Corinthians 14:25 echoes the language of Isaiah 45:14, which says Gentiles from Egypt and Ethiopia will come and bow down before Israel, saying, "God is with you alone, and there is no other; there is no god besides him" (cf. also Zech. 8:22–23; Isa. 49:23; 60:10–16). Thus, when the church prophesies authentically, it becomes the instrument through which God accomplishes the eschatological conversion of the nations—or at least a foretaste of that final event. In short, Paul sees prophecy as a powerful tool of evangelism, but he sees tongues (in public worship) as a hindrance to making the gospel understood.

All this seems clear and logical. Unfortunately, great confusion is caused by the way Paul introduces the issue of the unbelievers in verses 21–22. He quotes an approximation of Isaiah 28:11–12 and then offers an exegetical comment on it: "Tongues, then, are a sign not for believers but for unbelievers, while prophecy is not for unbelievers but for believers" (v. 22). This comment seems to stand in direct contradiction to the explanation that follows in verses 23–25, in which unbelievers are turned away by tongues and converted by prophecy. It is impossible here to undertake a full discussion of the exegetical problems surrounding this passage. Some of the difficulties can be cleared up by attending closely to the context of the passage that Paul quotes from Isaiah 28, but other problems remain unresolved. It seems best to acknowledge that Paul's argument here is somewhat garbled—or at least that it rests upon a complex (and insufficiently explained) interpretation of a notoriously obscure Old Testament passage.

Isaiah 28 is a judgment oracle directed particularly against the "scoffers who rule this people in Jerusalem." They have refused to listen to the word of the prophet, mocking it as unintelligible baby-talk (Isa. 28:9–10). The phrase translated in Isaiah 28:10 and 28:13 as "Precept upon precept . . . line upon line . . . here a little, there a little" is actually completely obscure in the Hebrew text (see NRSV footnote); it may be nothing more than a string of nonsense syllables. The point of Isaiah 28:11–13 is that because the scoffing rulers have refused to listen to the prophetic promise of rest, but have instead tried to create security for themselves by making an alliance with Egypt, the word of God will henceforth be to them gibberish spoken in an alien tongue. Thus, the "sign" of unintelligible speech is a prophetic sign of judgment.

This is what Paul means when he says that tongues are "a sign for unbelievers": they are a sign of *condemnation*, symbolizing the inaccessibility of divine revelation. We know that Paul must have meditated on this passage from Isaiah at some length, because he cites Isaiah 28:16 at a crucial point in the argument of Romans where he is pondering the mystery of Israel's unbelief (Rom. 9:33). In 1 Corinthians 14, however, he cites just an excerpt on the run without explaining its context. Perhaps he expects some of his Corinthian readers to understand the allusion. The text works for him here because it links "strange tongues" with unbelief and disobedience. (That this is not Paul's primary way of understanding the phenomenon of speaking in tongues is made clear by everything else he has said in 1 Cor. 14:1–19). In light of this, we can make sense of his comment in verse 22a that tongues are a sign for unbelievers. More difficult, however, is the statement in verse 22b that prophecy is "not for unbelievers but for believers." Clearly, prophecy is for believers in the sense that Paul has already explained: it encourages and builds up the church (vv. 3–6, 12, 19). The problem is with the negative formulation; in light of verses 24–25 it certainly appears that prophecy can be powerfully effective for unbelievers. Paul seems to have gotten carried away by the rhetorical antitheses of verse 22 to say something that he does not strictly mean; perhaps we should interpret him to mean "prophecy is not [primarily] for unbelievers but for believers." In any case, the force of his argument is more clearly stated in verses 23–25, as already explained above; therefore, the preacher or teacher working with this passage should keep the focus there.

240

Order in the assembly (14:26–40). Paul has finished explaining why prophecy (along with other modes of comprehensible revelation and teaching) is preferable to tongues in the gathered Christian community. He now turns to offer some general guidelines about how the Corinthians' worship meetings should be conducted.

In verses 26–33, Paul sketches a picture of a free-flowing community gathering under the guidance of the Holy Spirit in which "each one" contributes something to the mix. Clearly there was no fixed order of service, no printed bulletin for the worshipers! Nor—more remarkably—is anything said of a leader to preside over the meeting. Apparently Paul expects all the members to follow the promptings of the Spirit, taking turns in offering their gifts for the benefit of the assembly, deferring to one another (vv. 29–30) and learning from one another. The meeting will include singing, teaching (probably exposition of Scripture), revelatory utterances (prophecy and its cognates, cf. v. 6), and praise to God in tongues with interpretation.

Nothing is said in this passage of the celebration of the Lord's Supper; it is impossible to be sure whether Paul is thinking here of a prayer and praise meeting separate from the meeting for the common meal, or whether the gathering described here is of the same sort as the one discussed in 11:17–34. In favor of the latter interpretation is Paul's use of the phrase "when you come together" in verse 26, the same language that he had used in 11:17–18, 20, and 33. In all probability the celebration of the Lord's Supper would have included the same features sketched in verse 26.

Paul's concern here, as elsewhere throughout chapter 14, is that all things in this Spirit-led assembly should be done for building up the community (v. 26). The danger, of course, in such a spontaneous assembly is that the worship will become chaotic or that some members will dominate the time for speaking. In order to facilitate good order, therefore, Paul lays down some ground rules.

Only one person at a time should speak in tongues; thereby the scene imagined in verse 23—a room full of babbling believers—is excluded. There are to be no more than two or three utterances in tongues at any one meeting, and each prayer in tongues is to be interpreted for the benefit of the whole congregation. Presumably, Paul does not mean that the prayer in tongues is spoken in a natural language (such as Aramaic) that someone else in the assembly can translate; these tongues are, after all, "the tongues of angels" (13:1). Rather, the "interpretation" is also a supernatural gift of the Spirit. If there is no one present who has this gift, the tongues-speakers are to be silent (v. 28). All these directives presume that the gift is in some sense under the speaker's control. One can *choose*

241

whether to speak out in tongues or to remain silent. This shows that Paul does not think of the gift of tongues as an overpowering emotional experience in which the speaker is possessed by the Spirit in some sort of ecstatic trance. English translations that use the word "ecstacy" to describe the phenomenon of tongues (as the NEB does throughout this chapter) are supplying an interpretive category that is absent from the Greek text and at variance with the picture that Paul draws in verses 26–28. Clarity would be served if preachers and teachers would avoid using such terminology to discuss this material.

Similarly, prophets are also able to control their exercise of the prophetic gift; that is the meaning of verse 32. They also should speak in turn; verse 30 prohibits two or more prophets from competing for the community's attention. If new revelation is given to someone, the first speaker should be silent and listen. This instruction also shows clearly that Paul understands prophecy as a revelatory charismatic gift which may be given in the congregation as the wind of the Spirit blows freely. As with the tongues-speakers, however, only two or three should prophesy at any one meeting.

One of the most intriguing aspects of Paul's directives is that the other members of the church (*not* just the other "prophets") are told to judge (*diakrinein*; cf. 11:31) the prophetic words that are spoken in the assembly, exercising spiritual discernment about whether these words really are authentic words from God. Paul gives similar instructions to the Thessalonians: "Do not quench the Spirit. Do not despise prophecies, but test everything" (1 Thess. 5:19–21a). (This passage shows, incidentally, that the *charismata* were not a uniquely Corinthian phenomenon. We hear less about them in Paul's other letters, in part no doubt because they did not create the sort of difficulties that seem to have developed at Corinth; cf. 1 Cor. 14:32–33). This discipline of submitting the prophetic word to the community's discernment is an outward and visible sign of the message that Paul is trying to impress upon them: The gifts are for the service of the community, not the community for the gifts. The one who prophesies does not thereby become exalted to a spiritual plane beyond the other members; because all have the Spirit (12:3, 13) all are able to participate in the spiritual reception and assessment of the proferred prophetic word. In a community that consistently exercised such discipline, no one prophet should ever be able to seize undue authority or influence.

Paul's attitude on this point may be instructively contrasted to the only slightly later counsel offered in the *Didache*: "Do not test or examine [*diakrineite*] any prophet who is speaking in the spirit, 'for every sin shall be forgiven, but this sin shall not be forgiven'" (*Didache* 11:7; cf. Matt.

12:31–32). In the *Didache*, prophets are to be judged on the basis of their moral conduct, but their prophetic utterances are treated as sacrosanct. For Paul, on the other hand, the role of prophets was neither so sharply defined nor so authoritative as in some other early Christian groups.

The other extraordinary feature of Paul's worship guidelines is his encouragement to *all members* of the church to try their hands at prophesying: "For you can all prophesy one by one, so that all may learn and be encouraged" (1 Cor. 14:31; cf. 14:1, 5). When Paul writes "you can [*dynasthe*] all prophesy," he is not giving permission but acknowledging a *power* given to all by the one Spirit. As always, he stresses that this power is given for the benefit of others in the community. Hardly anywhere do we see a clearer expression of Paul's desire to see all the members of the community grow up into spiritual maturity and full participation in the church's ministry.

The overall picture that emerges from these instructions is of a church in which the Spirit is palpably present, flowing freely in the communal worship through the complementary gifts of different members. In Paul's vision for Christian worship there is neither stiff formality nor undisciplined frenzy: the community's worship is more like a complex but graceful dance, or a beautiful anthem sung in counterpoint. If some at Corinth were claiming that spiritual inspiration moved them to uncontrollable displays of pneumatic enthusiasm, Paul flatly contests the claim, for "the spirits of prophets are subject to the prophets" (v. 32). This basic truth is not the result of some purely human desire for orderliness; it is grounded in the character of God, for "God is a God not of disorder [*akatastasis*] but of peace" (v. 33). As Fee (697) remarks, "the character of one's deity is reflected in the character of one's worship." If the Corinthian worship meetings are chaotic and conflictual, the question must be raised: What God are they really worshiping? The term *akatastasis* has connotations of civil strife and rebellion (M. Mitchell, 173). This is one more hint that the problems in Corinthian worship are not merely the result of overheated spirituality; they are also linked to the factionalism and defiance of Paul's authority that have been the consistent concern of this letter. If, however, God is a God of *peace*, the Corinthians should learn to be at peace with one another and to express that peace in a style of worship that emphasizes concord and complementarity.

Paul rhetorically anticipates that the Corinthians might protest the directives of verses 26–33. "But Paul," they might say, "these guidelines will cramp our style and squelch the freedom of our worship; indeed, important revelations from God may be silenced if we follow your rules." Paul defuses this objection by pointing to the practice of other Christian communities whose worship conforms to more orderly norms. The paragraphing in the NRSV obscures the structure of the discourse. In order to see how the logic of the argument runs, we must read the text with the interpolation of verses 34–35 deleted (see the excursus, below, on that passage).

> And the spirits of the prophets are subject to the prophets, for God is a God not of disorder but of peace, as in all the churches of the saints. . . . Or did the word of God originate with you? Or are you the only ones it has reached? Anyone who claims to be a prophet, or to have spiritual powers, must acknowledge that what I am writing to you is a command of the Lord. Anyone who does not recognize this is not to be recognized.
>
> (1 Cor. 14:32–33, 36–38)

The prideful Corinthian enthusiasts are acting as though they alone have received revelations so powerful as to override standards of community discipline in worship. With withering sarcasm, Paul replies in effect, "Oh really? That's funny: in all the other churches of the saints, it seems that God is a God of order and peace. Or perhaps you are the only ones who really have heard the word of God?"

Having painstakingly explained the theological reasons for his directives for the past three chapters (12:1—14:33), Paul now seems to be running out of patience. He points to the example of the other churches and then bluntly asserts his own apostolic authority in verses 37–38. In contrast to some of his advice on earlier topics (e.g., 7:10–11, 25–38), Paul explicitly claims that his teachings on orderly worship are "a command of the Lord." Furthermore, anyone who defies these teachings by refusing to recognize Paul's authority in this matter will suffer the consequences. Thus, once again, as in 4:18–21, Paul concludes a long section of the letter by challenging the "puffed-up" Corinthians to yield to his authority, an authority backed by sanctions of divine power. The NRSV rendering of verse 38, quoted above, suggests that Paul is telling other members of the Corinthian community not to recognize the person who rejects his teaching. In fact, however, the verse should be understood as a "sentence of holy law," announcing God's eschatological punishment on those who reject the word of God. (For example, cf. Mark 8:38: "Those who are ashamed of me and of my words in this adulterous and sinful generation, of them the Son of Man will also be ashamed when he comes in the glory of his Father with the holy angels." For a classic Old Testament example of this form, see 1 Sam. 15:26: "For you have rejected the word of the LORD, and the LORD has rejected you from being king over Israel.") Accordingly, the NEB translation of 1 Corinthians 14:38 captures the sense of Paul's compact saying: "If he does not acknowledge this, God does not acknowledge him."

Such strong sanctions are invoked against a circle of people in the Corinthian church who have persistently set themselves up as too high and mighty to listen to Paul or to concern themselves with the problems and weaknesses of other Christians at Corinth. The formulation of verse 37 (literally, "If anyone thinks himself to be a prophet or a spiritual person . . .") repeats a rhetorical pattern that we have seen twice before in the letter (Fee, 711). The parallels are revealing:

"If anyone among you thinks himself to be *wise* in this age . . ."
(3:18)
"If anyone   thinks himself to *know* something . . ."
(8:2)
"If anyone   thinks himself to be a *prophet* or *spiritual* . . ."   (14:37)

It is hardly a coincidence that these three formulations target precisely the terms that characterize the self-understanding of the "strong" Corinthians: wisdom, knowledge, and spirituality. Paul's consistent response to them has been to insist that the word of the cross brings all boasting in such qualities to nothing; consequently, they should acknowledge Paul's apostolic authority over them and conform their lives to his example. The minimal expression of such obedience would be for them to constrain their overwrought spiritual impulses and to abide by Paul's directives for orderly worship.

These directives are concisely summarized in the final words of chapter 14: "So, my friends, be eager to prophesy [cf. vv. 1, 5, 31], and do not forbid speaking in tongues [vv. 5, 26–27]; but all things should be done decently and in order" (vv. 39–40). With that Paul has brought his treatment of spiritual manifestations in worship to a close. It must be emphasized, though, that Paul does not seek order for order's sake. The order that he desires to see in the Corinthian assembly allows for great flexibility and for the diverse and unpredictable spiritual contribution of all the members of the body of Christ. Order is necessary only to constrain self-indulgent abuses and to create an atmosphere in which the gifts of all can work together to build up the community in love.

EXCURSUS:
"Women should be silent in the churches" (14:35–35)

In the midst of Paul's directions about tongues and prophecy in the worshiping assembly, there appears an abrupt interjection commanding women not to speak in meetings of the congregation (vv. 34–35). Several

245

ancient manuscripts place these verses not in this location but as an addendum at the end of the chapter, and at least one ancient manuscript includes markings suggesting that the scribe considered these words to be a gloss inserted into the text. If these sentences are an addition to Paul's letter, however, the addition must have occurred at an early stage, since all extant manuscripts contain these words either between verses 33 and 36 or following verse 40. (For a full discussion of the textual problem, see Fee [699–708], who makes a strong argument that these verses are an early interpolation.)

Some critics (e.g., Conzelmann, 246) have treated verses 33b–36 as a unit interpolated into the text, and this theory has influenced the paragraphing found in many English translations: for example, in the NRSV the verses are treated as a separate paragraph and set in parentheses. There is, however, no justification for this arbitrary division of the text. The ancient manuscript evidence suggests that it is only verses 34–35 whose authenticity is suspect, and—as the foregoing discussion in this commentary has shown—the passage makes excellent sense when these two verses are deleted. The debate about the authenticity of these words should be focused on verses 34–35 alone.

One of the strongest reasons for regarding these verses as an interpolation is that their demand for women to remain silent in the assembly stands in glaring contradiction to 11:2–16, in which Paul teaches that women may in fact pray and prophesy in church as long as they keep their heads appropriately covered. It is hard to imagine how Paul could have written those instructions and then, just a few paragraphs later, have written that "it is shameful for a woman to speak in church" (14:35b). Furthermore, all the other available evidence indicates that women played an active role in preaching, teaching, and prophesying in the early Pauline communities: for example, Phoebe (Rom. 16:1–2), Prisca (Rom. 16:3–4; cf. Acts 18:18–28), Junia (Rom. 16:7), and Euodia and Syntyche (Phil. 4:2–3). (For extended discussion of the evidence, see Schüssler Fiorenza, 160–84).

Two other factors cast doubt upon the Pauline authorship of verses 34–35. First, the command in verse 34 is suddenly addressed not to the specific Corinthian situation but to "the churches." Nowhere else in 1 Corinthians does Paul shift in this way to generalized instruction for the churches at large; indeed, this makes no sense at all from a rhetorical point of view in a letter written to a specific congregation, but it does make sense rhetorically if the passage was added at a later time when the letter was being circulated for the guidance of a wider circle of communities.

Second, the unqualified appeal to "the Law" as requiring women's subordination (v. 34b) is—to say the least—uncharacteristic of Paul's way of appealing to Scripture as a source of behavioral norms.

All things considered, this passage is best explained as a gloss introduced into the text by the second- or third-generation Pauline interpreters who compiled the pastoral epistles. The similarity of 1 Corinthians 14:34–35 to 1 Timothy 2:11–12 is striking: Both command women to "learn" in silence and submission. Such directives assume a later historical situation in which there was a conscious effort to restrict the roles played by women in the first-generation Pauline churches.

Those interpreters who do regard 1 Corinthians 14:34–35 as belonging originally to Paul's letter have to explain how these verses fit together with 11:2–16 and how they work within Paul's argument. Four different explanations have been proposed. I list them here, beginning with the most plausible and moving to the least plausible.

First, some interpreters have proposed that Paul is not really prohibiting women from praying and prophesying in the assembly. Rather, he is addressing a specific local problem at Corinth and restricting certain *kinds* of disruptive speech, such as chattering and asking questions (v. 35a). (A variant on this explanation is Ben Witherington's suggestion that the women thought of Christian prophets on the analogy of the Delphic Oracle, which prophesied in response to particular questions about the personal life of the seeker [Witherington, 287].) The difficulty with this explanation is that it fails to reckon with the categorical declaration that it is "shameful" for women to speak in church at all (v. 35b) and with the clear statement that this rule is for "the churches" at large, not just for a particular problem at Corinth.

Second, Elisabeth Schüssler Fiorenza has argued that the women who are allowed to pray and prophesy in the assembly (11:2–16) must be unmarried and that the speech restriction of 14:34–35 applies only to married women, who have husbands to instruct them at home. This explanation introduces a distinction that is not explicit in the text, and it overlooks the evidence that married women such as Prisca did in fact exercise leadership roles in the Pauline churches.

Third, Antoinette Wire has suggested that 11:2–16 should be read as a tactical concession by Paul, allowing women to speak with certain restrictions, but that his real aim is to silence the female prophets altogether. On this reading, 14:34–35 is the rhetorical goal and climax of the letter. Wire's proposal depends upon an elaborate speculative reconstruction of the role of the women prophets at Corinth, and it also ignores the evidence that Paul elsewhere heartily supports the leader-

247

ship role of women in ministry. If Paul's aim was to suppress women, why did he send Phoebe as his emissary to the Roman churches?

Finally, some interpreters have tried to avoid the contradiction between chapters 11 and 14 by reading verses 33b–36 as Paul's quotation of the Corinthians' position. According to this theory, it is the *Corinthians* who want to silence women, and Paul quotes their opinion in order to reject it. (Notice that this is the polar opposite of Wire's interpretation.) This explanation is farfetched in the extreme. There is no indication in the text that Paul is quoting anything (unlike 7:1) or that the Corinthians held such views about women; furthermore, the other Corinthian views cited by Paul are always short slogans, not extended didactic arguments.

In short, none of these attempted explanations succeeds in making sense out of the text as we have it and placing this passage within what we otherwise know about women in the Pauline churches. The best explanation is that the passage is a gloss, inserted in the text at this point because of the catchword connection to Paul's instruction to prophets to "be silent" under certain circumstances (v. 30) and because of Paul's appeal to the general practice of "all the churches of the saints" in verse 32. The whole passage is much more coherent without these extraneous verses. Paul never told women to be silent in churches: this order is the work of a subsequent Christian generation.

Nonetheless, the passage remains in our Bibles, even if we think it is an interpolation. Furthermore, passages such as 1 Timothy 2:11–15 reinforce the same teaching. How, then, is the interpreter to deal with such passages? It is not sufficient to say "Paul didn't write it" and let the question drop. Recognizing that the teaching of 1 Corinthians 14:34–35 is the work of a later hand that sought to squelch women's public role in the church is only the first step toward getting the issues clearly into focus. The task of the teacher or preacher is to encourage the congregation to develop a more nuanced view of the authority and diversity of the canon. The Bible is not a homogeneous or systematic body of teachings; there are many points of internal tension. (For example, Romans 13 and Revelation 13 take radically different views of the power of the state.) One such point of tension is the unresolved discussion in the early church about the appropriate role of women as public witnesses to the gospel; this discussion has left its marks in the divided teaching of our canonical New Testament.

Our hermeneutical responsibility is to recognize these tensions where they exist and to make *theologically informed* judgments about how the different texts speak to our situation. We must try to discern the fundamental themes of the New Testament's teaching and make decisions about contested matters in light of that discernment. (For a full-

248

scale discussion of such problems, see Hays, *The Moral Vision of the New Testament*.) For example, the church ultimately came to decide that the institution of slavery—though widespread in the ancient world—was incompatible with the New Testament's fundamental vision of the freedom and dignity of human beings; consequently, those New Testament texts that support slavery (such as Eph. 6:5–9; Col. 3:22—4:1; 1 Tim. 6:1–2; Titus 2:9–10; 1 Peter 2:18) must be rejected, or understood as provisional adaptations of the gospel message to a particular cultural setting. Such texts should not be used normatively to perpetuate slavery in the church.

Similarly, with respect to the issue of women's public leadership, there are good theological reasons to insist that we should be guided by Paul's vision of Christian worship in which the gifts of the Spirit are given to *all members of the church, men and women alike*, for the building up of the community. The few New Testament texts that seek to silence women (such as 1 Cor. 14:34–35, and 1 Tim. 2:11–15) should not be allowed to override this vision. As our congregations wrestle with the ongoing task of discerning God's will for our life together—a task to which 1 Corinthians repeatedly calls us—we must be faithfully attentive to Paul's wider vision of men and women as full partners in the work of ministry.

REFLECTIONS FOR TEACHERS AND PREACHERS

If Paul came to visit most of our churches today, he would have little cause to chastise us for disorderly and excessive displays of the spiritual gifts. Consequently, most of us, reading chapter 14 of his letter to the Corinthians, may be inclined to shrug and say, "Well, at least we don't have *those* problems." (Presumably the framers of the Revised Common Lectionary thought something like this, for when 1 Corinthians 12—15 is being read sequentially during the Sundays after the Epiphany in Year C, 1 Corinthians 14 is omitted entirely.) Such a response, however, would betray a shallow and unimaginative reading of the text. Upon reflection, we can see that Paul raises a number of issues here that remain of crucial importance for the church today.

1. *Building community.* The overriding concern of this chapter is that the members of the church worship collaboratively in a way that builds up the community through the participation of each member. Worship, Paul emphatically insists, is not just a time for private spiritual blessings; it is a time for the members of the community to share with each other God's gifts so that all may learn and be encouraged. For many congregations, this understanding of the purpose of worship would constitute a revolution of consciousness—or, as we have been saying, a conversion of the imagination. We must ask ourselves how our present styles of meeting and worship actually serve the end of building community.

249

Few churches can read 1 Corinthians 14 seriously without finding themselves invited to discover more broadly participatory styles of worship.

2. *Focusing on the message rather than the medium.* Paul seeks to discipline the use of spiritual gifts not just by focusing on the attitude of the speaker but also by insisting on the substantive content of the message conveyed through the gifts. Intelligible speech is valued for its capacity to instruct others, as well as to encourage and console them. One of the major effects of prophecy is "that all may learn" (v. 31). Even the outsider who is confronted by prophecy will be moved by the disclosive power of what the prophets say, not by their friendly smiles or winsome delivery. This point is worth pondering. Even in churches today that do not practice glossolalia, there is often a huge imbalance on the side of purely affective religious experience, coupled with inattention to substantive teaching of the Christian message and tradition. Against such sheer affectivity, Paul insists that the right use of the gifts is to build up the church through proclaiming and interpreting the gospel. When such substantive proclamation and teaching are not being given in the church, the church's talk becomes "an indistinct sound" that will rightly be ignored.

3. *Order without hierarchy.* One of the most remarkable features of 1 Corinthians 14 is that Paul nowhere seeks to solve the problem of order in the Corinthian worship service by telling his readers to stick to the liturgy or to follow the leadership of the priest or preacher. Indeed, the evidence of the letter as a whole suggests that there was no established authority structure at all within the Corinthian church: no bishops, presbyters, and deacons; no mediating structure between the apostle and his unruly flock. The absence of such recognized structures may have contributed to the problems of order that Paul was forced to address in his letter; yet we should not too hastily conclude that the Corinthian situation was simply an unqualified debacle that forced the Pauline movement to evolve in the direction of the more institutionalized church depicted in the pastoral epistles. Paul does, after all, give thanks for the very real gifts and graces that were manifested in this community (1:4–7). We might at least consider whether Paul's vision for worship, as expounded in chapter 14, deserves more of a try than the church has historically given it. Paul pictures a church in which all the members wait together on the moving of the Spirit, and all take responsibility for discerning what God is saying to them. Could our churches learn to listen to the Spirit in this way? If we did, would we stand to gain something that has been lost? Might many members of our churches discover a new openness to the power of the Spirit working through them? Could we on some occasions experience worship as a graceful extemporaneous dance of the whole body?

4. *Welcoming the Spirit.* The emergence of the charismatic renewal

movement in the twentieth century has made Paul's specific teaching about tongues and prophecy newly relevant in very specific ways. There are some churches in which Paul's cautionary words and disciplinary restrictions on the use of these gifts still need to be heard. Few members of such churches, however, are likely to read this commentary. For the greater number of readers of this book, 1 Corinthians 14 might serve quite a different function. Rather than warning of the dangers of excess, this chapter might beckon us to a window through which we glimpse a strange new world of spiritual power. As the wave of "modernity" recedes and its confident rationalism looks more and more illusory, the reductive strategy of "demythologizing" that dominated much Protestant theology and preaching during the middle of the twentieth century looks increasingly like a museum curio. Other ways forward must be found. Upon reading Paul's account of tongues and prophecy, we may echo Horatio's line, "O day and night, but this is wondrous strange!" If so, Paul whispers back Hamlet's reply:

> And therefore as a stranger give it welcome.
> There are more things in heaven and earth, Horatio,
> Than are dreamt of in your philosophy.
> (*Hamlet*, I.v.)

The church that ponders 1 Corinthians 14 seriously will be led to pray for the gift of prophecy and welcome it when it is given.

5. *Evangelism: Telling the truth to outsiders.* Finally, Paul's sketch of the outsider's encounter with Christian worship (vv. 23–25) is of more than passing interest. As the church ponders the challenge of evangelism in a post-Christian culture, there have been many proposals for packaging the gospel in smooth, unthreatening ways that will appeal to consumers conditioned by the slick come-ons of advertising and mass entertainment. Paul's account offers a stark contrast: the outsider who wanders in to the Christian meeting "is reproved and called to account by all," and hears the secrets of the heart disclosed through Christian prophecy. One of two things will happen. Either the outsider will turn and run, or she will fall down and declare, "God is really among you." If our preaching and prophecy have integrity, they will force such stark choices and radical responses. Preaching that presents the Christian message as a reassuring word of self-affirmation does not elicit from unbelievers the response that "God is really among you." Such preaching is analogous to the tongue-speaking assembly of verse 23, offering a form of Christian experience that looks little different from lots of other feel-good experiences in the pagan world. Only when our proclamation plumbs the depth of the human predicament and narrates the extraordinary story of God's

251

costly redemptive act in Jesus Christ will outsiders and unbelievers recognize that something different is here, that the truth is being told and God is really present.

15:1–58
The Resurrection of the Body

Paul now turns to address the fourth and last of the major contested issues in Corinth: the resurrection of the body. Paul's comments in chapter 15 are not aimed at correcting any particular aberrant behavior among the Corinthians; in this respect, the chapter differs from his discussions of the previous issues (sex in marriage, idol meat, and community worship). Still, Paul is deeply concerned to correct their *beliefs* about the resurrection, and he suggests that these beliefs do have definite behavioral consequences (15:32–34, 58). The many moral failings of the Corinthians may in fact all be surface symptoms of their underlying misapprehension of the very heart of the gospel: the death and resurrection of Jesus. Paul fears that the Corinthians who deny the resurrection of the dead have abandoned the most fundamental conviction of the Christian faith and that their believing is therefore "in vain" (v. 2).

Because it deals with this life-and-death issue, 1 Corinthians 15 is a profound witness to the content of the gospel. Clearly, Paul has saved the weightiest matter for last—as any good preacher would do. This eloquent chapter, coming at the end of the body of Paul's long letter, anchors the whole discussion.

Some of the Corinthians were saying that there is no resurrection of the dead (v. 12). That is the problem that triggers Paul's response. This seems like a puzzling situation: How could a group of people only recently converted from paganism by Paul's preaching of the crucified and risen Lord have turned so quickly to denying the resurrection?

Many scholars, attempting to account for the Corinthian denial of the resurrection, have hypothesized that their error was a manifestation of "overrealized eschatology." On this theory, the Corinthians were not really denying the resurrection; rather, they were claiming to have attained it already, like Hymenaeus and Philetus in 2 Timothy 2:17–18, who "swerved from the truth by claiming that the resurrection has already taken place." Despite the popularity of this explanation among commentators, it requires us to suppose arbitrarily that Paul had misunderstood the situation, for there is no indication in

252

chapter 15 that the Corinthians held such a premature belief in the resurrection. As Dale Martin (*Corinthian Body*, 106) observes, "what they found objectionable about Paul's teaching was not the *future* aspect of the resurrection but that it was to be a *bodily* resurrection." This is especially clear in verses 35–37, whose entire purpose is to counter objections to the notion of an embodied resurrection.

We should not suppose that these Corinthians understood themselves as debunkers of the gospel. On the contrary, as we have seen throughout the letter, they thought of themselves as hyperspiritual Christians (*pneumatikoi*), rich in every spiritual gift. That, however, was just the problem: they were so spiritual that they found the notion of a resurrection *of the body* crass and embarrassing. The phrase translated "resurrection of the dead" (*anastasis nekrōn*) means literally "rising of the corpses." For the spiritually refined Corinthians, this was not the stuff of Christian hope; it was a scenario for a horror story. This would have been particularly true for those members of the community with greater education and philosophical sophistication—precisely the higher-status members of the church whose infatuation with wisdom, knowledge, and tongues was creating the problems with which Paul wrestles throughout the letter. His talk of a future "resurrection of the dead bodies" would have sounded to them like the superstitious foolishness of popular legends.

These Corinthians who claim the possession of a higher *gnōsis*, a more sophisticated theological understanding of the world, identify salvation with escape from the brute physical world and hold the body in contempt. These are the same people who try to transcend their sexuality by renouncing sexual relations within their marriages. Some of them say, "Food is meant for the stomach and the stomach for food, and God will destroy both one and the other" (6:13a). Paul has already replied briefly to this error by declaring that, on the contrary, "The body is meant . . . for the Lord and the Lord for the body; and God raised the Lord and will raise us by his power" (6:13b–14). Now, at the end of the epistle, he addresses the issue of resurrection head on.

Paul insists that the fundamental logic of Christian proclamation demands belief in the resurrection of the dead; therefore, Christian hope necessarily affirms rather than rejects the body. To proclaim the resurrection of Christ is to declare God's triumph over death and therefore the meaningfulness of embodied life. That is why, according to Paul, our future hope must be for a transformed body in the resurrection, not an escape from the embodied state.

To see the argument of chapter 15 in these terms helps us to understand more clearly why both major subdivisions of the argument

253

conclude with appeals for righteous behavior and faithfulness in doing the Lord's work (vv. 32b–34, 58). What we do with our bodies in the present time matters. The gospel's proclamation of resurrection of the body serves both as a warning that we will be held accountable for what we do with our bodies and, at the same time, as a promise that our bodily labor is significant rather than meaningless.

The structure of Paul's discussion may be outlined broadly as follows:

The resurrection of the dead is constitutive of the gospel. (vv. 1–34)
  The *kērygma* proclaims the resurrection of Christ. (vv. 1–11)
  Denial of resurrection of the dead negates the gospel. (vv. 12–19)
  Because Christ has been raised, all who belong to him will be raised. (vv. 20–28)
  Otherwise, hope, suffering, and faithfulness are pointless. (vv. 29–34)
Resurrection means transformation of the body. (vv. 35–58)
  What kind of body is the resurrection body? (vv. 35–49)
  Both the dead and the living will be transformed. (vv. 50–57)
  Therefore, our labor is not in vain. (v. 58)

It is not clear how Paul learned that "some" of the Corinthians (v. 12) were denying the resurrection of the dead. The indirect manner in which he approaches the topic suggests that it was not one of the matters about which they had written him; therefore, it is presumably one of the matters reported to him by other informants (cf. 1:11; 5:1; 11:18). Only some of them are taking this revisionist position, while others are not; therefore, the question of the resurrection is one more cause of division in the community. Seeking to overcome this division, Paul crafts his treatment of the issue with great rhetorical skill: he begins by reminding the Corinthians of common tradition, expecting to gain their assent to his recapitulation of the basic *kērygma*. This is the foundation on which he then constructs his argument.

The Resurrection of the Dead Is Constitutive of the Gospel (15:1–34)

The kērygma proclaims the resurrection of Christ (15:1–11)

Paul begins by reminding the Corinthians of the form in which he had originally proclaimed the gospel to them. The language of "handing on" and "receiving" that he uses in verses 1 and 3 is the same terminology employed earlier in describing the transmission of the Lord's Supper tradition (11:23). This fact, along with the carefully balanced structure of the kerygmatic material that follows, indicates that Paul is quoting an early confessional formula (vv. 3b–5). The fact that he "received" this tradition from others (presumably from the witnesses mentioned in vv. 5–7) shows that this confession is very ancient indeed, probably datable to the time surrounding Paul's own call to apostleship—in other words, back to within about three years after Jesus was crucified in Jerusalem. Thus, the opening paragraph of 1 Corinthians 15 is a testimony of inestimable value concerning the form in which the gospel was preached in the very first generation of Christianity.

Paul goes back to this bedrock confession in order to make the point that "the resurrection of the dead" is not merely some idiosyncratic speculation that can be set aside by those who claim more sophisticated knowledge; rather, it is a matter "of first importance" (v. 3). It is an integral part of the *euaggelion* ("good news") on which those who believe take their stand (v. 1; cf. Gal. 1:11). The resurrection of Jesus and his subsequent appearance to a long list of witnesses is at the heart of the gospel proclaimed in the church; without this foundational truth, there would be no church because there would be no gospel. Those who hold fast to this truth are saved by it—unless, Paul remarks in a deft foreshadowing of verses 12–19, the whole thing is a sham and their faith is "in vain" (v. 2; cf. vv. 10, 14, 17, 58).

The confession itself consists of four clauses. The first and third are the fundamental faith affirmations, while the second and fourth fill out the story of Christ's death and resurrection and provide supporting warrants for the fundamental claims in the other two clauses. The structure, then, is as follows. Paul handed on the tradition:

> that *Christ died for our sins* in accordance with the Scriptures
> and that he was buried,
> and that *he was raised* on the third day in accordance with the Scriptures
> and that he appeared to Cephas, then to the twelve.
>
> (1 Cor. 3b–5)

The two central events of Christ's death and resurrection are said to have occurred "in accordance with the Scriptures." It is highly significant that this early creed specifies that the story of Jesus' passion and resurrection must be interpreted in light of Scripture: the earliest church understood the gospel as the continuation and fulfillment of God's dealings with Israel. The meaning of these world-transforming

255

events must be found in their relation to the Law and the prophets (cf. Rom. 1:2; 3:21; Luke 24:44–47).

Unfortunately, the confessional statement does not stipulate *which* Scriptures are in view. The description of Christ's death as having been "for our sins" calls to mind the portrayal of the suffering servant in Isaiah 53, but this allusion is not very explicit (cf. Isa. 53:5–6, 11–12). Nor does the confessional formula explain *how* the death of Christ was vicariously effective to deal with sins. Even more difficult is the assertion that the resurrection of Jesus was somehow "according to the Scriptures." The reference to "the third day" has led some to suggest Hosea 6:2 or Jonah 1:17 as possible sources for this idea. More likely, however, the phrase "according to the Scriptures" modifies the verb "was raised" rather than the temporal reference to the third day (cf. the similar syntax in 1 Macc. 7:16). Consequently, we could translate the clause as follows: "and that he was raised in accordance with the Scriptures, on the third day." In that case, the Scriptures that point to the resurrection are probably those Psalms that praise God for deliverance of the righteous sufferer; for a clear example of this sort of exegesis in the early tradition, see the reading of Psalm 16 in Acts 2:24–32. The psalm is understood here as prefiguring "the resurrection of the Christ" (Acts 2:31):

> . . . my flesh will live in hope.
> For you will not abandon my soul to Hades,
> Or let your Holy One experience corruption.
> (Ps. 16:9b–10, as quoted in Acts 2:26b–27)

There are several indications in Paul's letters that the Psalms were understood at a very early date as spoken by or referring to the Messiah (=Christ). (See, for example, the use made of Ps. 69:9 in Rom. 15:1–3 and the interpretation of Psalms 110 and 8 in 1 Cor. 15:24–28). This is the primary context in which the references to the Scriptures in 1 Corinthians 15:3–4 should be understood.

The stark reference to Christ's burial in verse 4 confirms the reality and human finality of his death. Similarly, the narration of resurrection appearances in verse 5 serves to confirm that he really was raised from the dead. (The absence of any mention of the empty tomb tradition here shows nothing except that such stories were not a part of the traditional *kērygma*. It certainly does not mean that Paul or any other early Christian could have conceived of a "resurrection from the dead" in which the body remained in the tomb.) Of some importance is the perfect passive verb form "he was raised" (*egēgertai*) in verse 4. The passive voice indicates that God is the one who raised him up, and

256

the perfect tense (in contrast to the aorist forms "died" and "was buried") indicates that he remains risen. Thus, the confessional formula does not just narrate past events: It proclaims Christ as risen Lord.

The traditional confessional formula ends with verse 5. In verse 6, Paul adds additional witnesses in support of the claim that Christ was raised from the dead, which is the major point that he wants to emphasize in the confessional formula. Not only did Cephas (Peter) and the Twelve see the risen Lord, but so did more than five hundred others. Paul's note that most of them are still alive (v. 6) is clearly calculated to provide further evidential support for the resurrection of Jesus; anyone who is disposed to be skeptical will find a formidable gallery of witnesses waiting to testify that they have seen him alive. This shows that Paul did not think of the resurrection of Jesus as some sort of ineffable truth beyond history; rather, it was an event that had occurred in the immediate past, an event for which historical eyewitness testimony was readily available. The inclusion of James (the brother of Jesus, who became a major leader of the Jerusalem church [Gal. 1:19; 2:9, 12; Acts 15:13–21; 21:18]) and of "all the apostles" (indicating a circle wider than the Twelve [see, e.g., Rom. 16:7; Acts 14:14]) extends the range of witnesses still further. There is no point in trying to match Paul's list here with the various resurrection appearance stories in Matthew, Luke-Acts, and John, because the accounts do not correspond precisely. Paul, who of course did not have the gospel narratives known to us, says nothing of the women who were elsewhere remembered as the first witnesses to the resurrection (Matt. 28:9–10; John 20:11–18). He only wants to emphasize the well-attested reality of Jesus' resurrection from the dead; therefore he supplements the traditional kerygmatic formula (vv. 3b–5) by mentioning a string of other traditions known to him (vv. 6–7), culminating in his own testimony that he had seen the risen Lord (v. 8).

By describing this appearance as "last of all," he links it with the resurrection appearances to Jesus' original circle of followers and distinguishes it from all subsequent visions and from the personal experience of Christ that all believers possess through the Holy Spirit; he is claiming to have come face to face with Jesus the Messiah whom God had raised up. Paul says strikingly little here about this encounter with the resurrected Christ (in contrast with the extended accounts in Acts 9:1–9; 22:1–11; 26:12–23); the only point that matters for his present purpose is that he can add his own name to the list of those who attest the truth of the news that Christ was raised from the dead.

When Paul brings himself into the story, however, he digresses

257

somewhat from his immediate purpose of reminding the Corinthians about the substance of the gospel proclamation. We may fairly suspect that his digression is purposeful. As we have seen earlier in the letter (e.g., 4:3–5; 9:3), Paul's apostolic authority is being questioned by some at Corinth; therefore, he takes the opportunity here to include himself in the list of those to whom the risen Christ appeared and to mention discreetly that God's grace has enabled him to work harder than any of the other apostles. God's grace was not "in vain"—an expression that becomes an important refrain in this chapter—rather, God's grace was effectual to and through Paul in bringing communities of believers into existence, including the Corinthians themselves. Even the odd description of the resurrection appearance to him "as to one abnormally born" (v. 8, NIV) may have an apologetic purpose. The term *ektrōma* ordinarily refers to an aborted fetus. It has been suggested that this term was applied to Paul by detractors who considered his bodily presence "weak" and contemptible (2 Cor. 10:10), making fun of his physical ugliness or handicaps (cf. Gal. 4:13–14; 2 Cor. 12:7b–10). If so, Paul here takes up the derisive epithet ironically and turns it into a clever way to talk about the untimeliness of Christ's appearance to him, even while affirming that God's grace has worked through his apostleship in spite of his unworthiness. He makes it clear, however, that his unworthiness is not a function of his physical appearance but of his past role as persecutor of the church (v. 9).

After this digression, the concluding sentence of this section brings the discussion back to the central point. The identity of the witnesses does not matter; whoever the preachers were, all of them preached the same gospel delineated in the formula of verses 3b–5, a gospel focused on the death of Jesus and on his resurrection from the grave. Furthermore, the Corinthians themselves believed this proclaimed word when Paul preached it to them. This was the message that drew them out of the pagan world and into the sphere of God's power and grace. Thus, for them now to question or deny the resurrection of the dead is—as Paul will argue in the next section—an absurd repudiation of their own experience and of the gospel itself.

Denial of resurrection of the dead negates the gospel (vv. 12–19)

The problem that has evoked Paul's recitation of the kerygma is at last disclosed specifically in verse 12: "Now if Christ is proclaimed as raised from the dead, how can some of you say there is no resurrection of the dead?" The verb "proclaimed" is the same word used in verse 11 to sum up the content of the gospel that had been preached to the

Corinthians: "so we proclaim and so you have come to believe." Thus, verse 12 first sums up the content of the preached gospel, with specific focus on Christ's resurrection, and then indignantly confronts the Corinthians with the illogic of their disbelief.

Paul indicates that only some among them were saying that "there is no resurrection of the dead." Who were they, and why were they denying the resurrection? Paul does not give us very much information about the deniers, but we can make some reasonable inferences. It bears repeating that nowhere in this chapter does Paul suggest that any of the Corinthians think the resurrection has already occurred. Instead, Paul's arguments are aimed at affirming a resurrection of the *body* against persons who find this notion intellectually unpalatable. That this was a point of ongoing controversy in the early church is confirmed by a fiercely polemical passage in the writings of Justin Martyr, the great second-century apologist. In his debate with Trypho the Jew, Justin acknowledges that there are "some who are called Christians . . . who say that there is no resurrection of the dead [*anastasis nekrōn*], and that their souls, when they die, are taken to heaven." Against such "godless, impious heretics," Justin takes an uncompromising stand: "Do not imagine that they are Christians" (*Dialogue with Trypho*, 80). These second-century Christians against whom Justin railed were no doubt repeating much the same views that Paul had combated at Corinth a century earlier. (In "Reflections for Teachers and Preachers," below, we must ponder the fact that the position rejected by Paul and Justin as heretical has now become the popular understanding of the Christian faith among most churchgoers.) In any case, Justin continues, "I and others, who are right-minded Christians on all points, are assured that there will be a resurrection of the dead [*sarkos anastasin*, literally, resurrection of the flesh]" (ibid.).

As we have noted, the people in Paul's church at Corinth most likely to be skeptical about *anastasis nekrōn* ("the rising of corpses") would have been those members of the community with greater cultural pretensions, those who knew enough philosophy to distance themselves from the apocalyptic worldview of Paul, whom they may have viewed as an unsophisticated, literalist Jewish preacher. Like many thinkers in the ancient Mediterranean world, they may have desired the escape of the rational soul from the body, viewing the body as a dark and corrupt tomb from which the enlightened person ought to seek release. Plutarch, for example, insisted that only the soul could attain to the realm of the gods, through freeing itself of attachment to the senses and becoming "pure, fleshless, and undefiled" (*Romulus* 28.6). Having been schooled in such refined philosophical thought, perhaps the "wise" Corinthians said something like this:

> The resurrection of Jesus is a wonderful metaphor for the spiritual change that God works in the lives of those who possess knowledge of the truth. "Resurrection" symbolizes the power of the Spirit that we experience in our wisdom and our spiritual gifts. But the image of resuscitated corpses (*anastasis nekrōn*) is only for childish fundamentalists. Those of us who are spiritual find it repugnant.

Paul reacts to their refined skepticism with astonishment and outrage, because he sees it as denying in principle the claim made at the heart of the gospel story: "If there is no resurrection of the dead, then Christ has not been raised" (v. 13). The story of Jesus' resurrection is not just an illustrative fable; Paul insists that it is the story of a real event, a bodily resurrection. "Christ" is not just a symbol for some set of abstract theological truths. Those who deny that God really has the power to raise the dead have placed themselves in contradiction to the gospel story, and it is illogical for them to continue speaking in the name of Christ.

Furthermore, "if Christ has not been raised," the whole foundation of Christian faith has been removed, and a series of disastrous consequences follow. Paul enumerates some of these in verses 14–18, building a rhetorically devastating cumulative picture of the logical entailments of denying the resurrection. The major points are these:

> If Christ has not been raised:
> Our proclamation (*kērygma*) is in vain (v. 14)
>> Result: We are false witnesses about God (v. 15)
> Your faith is in vain (v. 14) and futile (v. 17)
>> Result: You are still in your sins (v. 17)
> Those who have died in Christ are lost (v. 18)

The repeated emphasis in this paragraph on the vanity and futility of Christian talk apart from the reality of the resurrection is striking (see also vv. 2, 10, 32b, 58). For Paul, the whole web of Christian discourse is airy nonsense if it is not anchored in the truth of the resurrection of Jesus. Christian preaching becomes a system of delusions, offering nothing but lies and empty gestures. The gospel has no power to save us if Christ is not raised, and therefore the Corinthians are still lost in their sins, their hope of reconciliation with God based on futile human fantasy.

260

Interestingly, this formulation of the problem leaves intact Paul's basically Jewish picture of reality: God is still real and still judges human sin. The Corinthians—precisely as Gentiles alienated from

Israel's God—are left with no hope, standing under the threat of God's final verdict. Only the resurrection of Jesus offers a real possibility of their transformation into a new life with God in which their sin is forgiven and overcome. Thus, Paul offers us in this paragraph a glimpse into the plight of Gentiles apart from the death and resurrection of Jesus: they are, in the apt summary of Ephesians 2:12, "aliens from the commonwealth of Israel, and strangers to the covenants of promise, having no hope and without God in the world." If we run the film backward and edit out the resurrection of Jesus, that hopeless situation still prevails.

Paul points also to the plight of those believers who have already died (literally "fallen asleep"): If Christ has not been raised, then they are "utterly lost" (NEB). They have simply been destroyed by death and consigned to eternal oblivion. Paul addresses this pastoral problem in 1 Thessalonians 4:13–18 by assuring the Thessalonians that those who are left alive until the coming of the Lord will not be separated from those who have "fallen asleep," for the dead will be raised first and the dead and living *together* will meet the Lord at his return. Here in 1 Corinthians, however, Paul's pastoral objective is very different: he is not trying to reassure believers who have anxiety over the ultimate fate of their loved ones. Instead, he is trying to *induce* some anxiety among the Corinthians about this point! He wants them to consider the full consequences of denying the resurrection of the dead: those who have gone to their graves hoping in Christ have simply gone into limbo.

These horrifying inferences lead up to a chilling conclusion: "If for this life only we have hoped in Christ, we are of all people most to be pitied" (v. 19). The translation of this sentence is difficult because of the position of the word "only" in the Greek text. A very literal translations would read, "If in this life in Christ we have only hoped. . . ." Most interpreters agree, however, that "only" should be understood to modify "this life" (as in NRSV, NIV, NEB, JB) rather than the verb "hoped." Alternatively, the meaning could be, "If, during this life in Christ, we have only hoped [but hoped in vain, since there is no resurrection], we are of all people most to be pitied." Either way, the sense is much the same.

On the surface, the thought expressed here is similar to a prayer found in the Syriac *Apocalypse of Baruch* (a Jewish text from the late first or early second century (C.E.), which laments the necessity of decay and death: "For if only this life exists, which everyone possesses here, nothing could be more bitter than this" (2 *Apoc. Bar.* 21:13). The point in Baruch's prayer, however, is slightly different from Paul's. Baruch is saying that death casts a pall over everything in life, because of the transience of all

261

human strength and beauty. (His prayer is answered by a subsequent divine revelation showing that death is a necessary part of God's plan for the world and promising an ultimate divine salvation for the righteous [2 *Apoc. Bar* 22—30].) Paul, on the other hand, is not speaking generally about human mortality; rather, he says that Christians in particular should be most pitied if there is no resurrection. Why should that be so? If Christ is not raised, does that not simply put us back in the same condition with everyone else in the world? Paul does not elaborate, but at least two good answers can be given to this question. First, if Christ has not been raised, we Christians mock ourselves with falsehood. We preach a message that turns out to be an illusion. We offer for the world's ills a pious lie that veils from ourselves the terrifying truth that we are powerless and alone. Second, as Barrett (350) observes, Christians—in Paul's view—are called to a life of "embracing death," suffering through selfless service of others (cf. 10:33—11:1), not seeking their own advantage or pleasure. If there is no resurrection, this self-denying style of life makes no sense; those who follow the example of Jesus and Paul are chumps missing out on their fair share of life's rewards.

Does this mean that the Christian faith is only a promise of "pie in the sky" with no value for the present life? Of course that is not the case: Paul, along with all the rest of the New Testament writers, believes that life in Christ is a source of great joy and peace and consolation in the present (see, e.g., Rom 5:1–5; 8:1–11; Gal. 5:22–23; Phil 4:4–7)—though he has said remarkably little about these themes in this particular letter to the Corinthians! His point here, however, is that the complex and fulfilling life of the Christian community has integrity only if it is premised on the truth and ordered towards the ultimate fulfillment of God's promises. If the *telos* (goal) of our life together in Christ is merely a mirage on an ever-receding horizon of time, then we are living an unhealthy self-deception—as Christianity's critics, ancient and modern, have charged. There is no authentic Christian faith without fervent eschatological hope, and there is no authentic eschatological hope without the resurrection of the dead.

Because Christ has been raised, all who belong to him will be raised (vv. 20–28)

In fact, however, all the "if" clauses of verses 12–19 are counterfactual conditions. With the ringing affirmation of verse 20, Paul moves from illusion to reality: "But in fact Christ has been raised from the dead." This triumphant declaration resumes the glad story told in verses 3–8 and sweeps away all the gloomy hypothetical consequences that follow from denying the resurrection.

There is also a new element in the story here, an aspect of Christ's resurrection not made explicit in the traditional kerygmatic formula of verses 3b–5: the risen Christ is "the *first fruits* of those who have fallen asleep." His resurrection is not merely a wondrous event that confirms his special status before God; rather, it is the beginning of a much greater harvest. This is the crucial point that some of the Corinthians had failed to understand: they did not see that there was a direct connection between Christ's resurrection and their own future fate. It may seem remarkable to us that anyone could have become an adherent of the early Christian movement without understanding this point, but, as both 1 Corinthians 15 and 1 Thessalonians 4:13–18 demonstrate, Paul had to explain it repeatedly to his Gentile congregations. (Paul's correspondence in general suggests that a fundamental task of ministry is to teach the basics of the faith again and again.) Perhaps he had not articulated this connection fully enough while he was with them, precisely because it was so obvious to him.

Here again we see that Paul interprets the death and resurrection of Jesus in Jewish apocalyptic categories. For one man alone to be raised is a great surprise in the Jewish apocalyptic framework. (Indeed, nowhere in the Judaism of Paul's day was there any expectation that the Messiah would be killed and rise from the dead.) Instead, it was expected that a great general resurrection would accompany God's judgment of the world; the resurrection of the dead cannot be something that happens to one person only. Consequently, the early Christians, Paul among them, took the resurrection of Jesus as a sign that the end of the age was breaking in. If Christ had been raised, then the resurrection of others must follow in due course. The metaphor of "first fruits" serves to express the idea that the great harvest of the general resurrection is at hand.

In verses 21–22, Paul turns from metaphor to typology to make the same point. Christ's rising is not an isolated event: its consequences correspond (antithetically) to the consequences of Adam's sin, which brought death upon all humanity. The impact of Jesus' death and resurrection is therefore equally sweeping: "for as all die in Adam, so all will be made alive in Christ" (see also vv. 45–49; Rom. 5:12–21). A powerful chorus in Handel's *Messiah* is based on this passage, because it so compactly narrates the great reversal of the gospel, the promise that our ultimate destiny is transformed from death to life through Christ's resurrection. This is the first reference to Adam in 1 Corinthians, and the manner of Paul's allusion shows that he expects his readers to know the story of Genesis 1—3 already. Presumably he had taught it to them during his time in Corinth. This is another illustration of the way in

263

which Israel's Scripture defines the symbolic world within which Paul thinks (cf. the discussions of 1 Cor. 5:6–8 and 10:1–22, above). In any case, Paul's point is that the resurrection of Christ has broken the power of death, which had prevailed over all human beings since Adam (Rom. 5:12).

Does the logic of this claim lead to a belief in universal salvation of all human beings through Christ's resurrection, as verse 22b ("all will be made alive") might suggest? Many of Paul's other statements make it difficult to suppose that he held such a view: within 1 Corinthians alone, see 1:18; 2:6; 3:17; 4:5; and 6:9–10. Indeed, the unqualified "all" of verse 22 is given further specification in the sentence immediately following: it is "those who belong to Christ" who will be raised at the time of his coming (v. 23). Paul believes firmly in election—another characteristic doctrine of Jewish apocalyptic—and he is concerned in the present passage only about the way in which Christ's resurrection prefigures the fate of *hoi tou Christou*, "those who are Christ's people." He says nothing one way or the other in this passage about the resurrection and judgment of unbelievers.

Having asserted so strongly that "the resurrection of the dead *has come*" through Christ (v. 21, NRSV) and that we also have a share in the benefits of his resurrection, Paul now thinks it necessary to qualify what he has said so that there can be no misunderstanding: the resurrection of our bodies remains an eschatological hope. "But each in his own order: Christ the first fruits, then at his coming [*parousia*] those who belong to Christ" (v. 23). Since Paul so carefully delineates the sequence of these events in time, this is the one sentence in the chapter that might offer some support for the view that some of the Corinthians were prematurely claiming to be enjoying the life of the resurrection. Paul carefully situates the church's present life in the interval between Christ's resurrection and *parousia* and insists that our resurrection must await his coming. This does not necessarily mean, however, that the Corinthians had an "overrealized eschatology." It simply means that Paul is concerned to tell the story rightly and to correct a possible misreading of what he himself had just said in verses 20–22. The resurrection of the dead will occur at the time of Christ's *parousia*, not sooner.

God has planned the assault on death that way: Christ comes first, then, in the second line of attack, those who belong to him. Paul's use of the term *tagma* ("order, rank"—usually used of a unit of soldiers) in verse 23 signals the beginning of a military metaphor that dominates verses 23–28. Death is an "enemy" to be subdued by Christ as he destroys all the enemies of God and takes control of everything in creation. The final defeat of Death at the general resurrection will constitute the collapse of all resistance to Christ's power and bring us to "the end [*to telos*], when he hands over the kingdom of God the Father, after he has destroyed every ruler and every authority and power" (v. 24). We have seen hints of Christ's triumph over the powers of this world earlier in the letter (the same verb *katargein* that is translated "destroyed" in 15:24, 26 appeared in a similar eschatological sense in 1:28 and 2:6), but here for the first time Paul spells out the story in full.

The terms "rule" (*archē*), "authority" (*exousia*), and "power" (*dynamis*) refer in the first instance to cosmic spheres or forces arrayed in opposition to God (cf. Rom. 8:38; Col. 1:16, 2:10–15; Eph. 1:21; 3:10; 6:12), but they also have concrete political implications. The idea that Christ is Lord and that the kingdom ultimately belongs to God the Father stands as a frontal challenge to the ideology of imperial Rome (Witherington, 295–98). For the inhabitants of the Roman colony Corinth—who walk about a city replete with statues and temples dedicated to the glory of the Roman rulers—Paul's words serve as one more summons to a conversion of the imagination, seeing the world as standing ultimately under the authority of another who will overturn the arrangements of power that now exist. Resurrection of the dead is a subversive belief, because it declares that God alone is sovereign over the created world.

The ultimate victory of Christ over death is also confirmed by Scripture. Paul alludes in verses 25 and 27 to Psalms 110:1 and 8:7, both of which, on Paul's reading, confirm that all things are to be put under the feet of Christ. Paul's use of these Old Testament texts in this allusive manner—with no explanation or justification given for relating them to Christ—shows how early and how fundamental was the Christian conviction that these psalms were to be read christologically. (See also Mark 12:35–37 and parallels; Heb. 1:13; 2:5–9.) As we have already noted, these passages are probably among the scriptural witnesses that Paul has in mind when he says that the resurrection of Jesus was "in accordance with the Scriptures" (1 Cor. 15:4). For some reason, most English translations treat the reference to Psalm 8 in verse 27 as a quotation, but not the reference to Psalm 110 in verse 25. (The exception is the JB, which correctly treats both as quotations.)

Paul works these passages into his argument to confirm the resurrection of the dead in the following way. There is a divinely decreed necessity (*dei*, v. 25) for Christ to reign until he has subdued every adversary, and Scripture bears witness to this truth. Verse 26 ("The last enemy to be destroyed is death") is Paul's interpretive comment on Psalm 110:1, explaining that death must be included among the enemies.

The personification of Death (see also 15:54–55) is characteristic of Paul's understanding of salvation as a great narrative drama in which the protagonist Jesus Christ delivers God's people from bondage to Sin and Death through his obedience in going to death on a cross (cf. Rom. 5:12–21; Phil. 2:5–11). This interpretation of Death as one of the defeated eschatological enemies is in turn justified by appeal to Psalm 8:7, which shows that God has put *all* things (including death) under Christ's feet. Thus, according to Paul's reading, these Psalm texts prove that Christ will finally overcome death.

Here Paul offers the fascinating tangential remark that "all things" of course does not include God himself, for Christ will at the end also "be subjected to the one who put all things in subjection under him, so that God may be all in all" (vv. 27–28). It is impossible to avoid the impression that Paul is operating with what would later come to be called a subordinationist christology. The doctrine of the Trinity was not yet formulated in Paul's day, and his reasoning is based solely on the scriptural texts themselves, read in light of his Jewish monotheistic convictions and his simultaneous conviction that Jesus is proclaimed as "Lord" by virtue of his resurrection.

In any case, the passage as a whole (1 Cor. 15:20–28) places death and resurrection in eschatological perspective, declaring that *Christ's victory over death is assured* and that *this necessarily entails the future resurrection of all who belong to him.* These affirmations stand as a powerful reply to those at Corinth who say there is no resurrection of the dead.

If the dead are not raised, hope, suffering, and faithfulness are pointless (vv. 29–34)

Having asserted his fundamental position, Paul returns to the argumentative strategy of verses 12–19, attempting to show that the denial of the resurrection of the dead undermines the meaningfulness and integrity of the community's life. In verses 12–19 the dire consequences of denying the resurrection were formulated in very general terms. In verses 29–34, however, Paul gives some specific examples of practices that would make no sense in a resurrectionless world (vv. 29–32a) and concludes with a word of warning suggesting that the Corinthians' abandonment of belief in the resurrection has led the community into sin (vv. 32b–34).

The specific examples are given in the form of rhetorical questions that allude briefly to matters well known to his original readers but almost completely opaque to us. Rather than getting bogged down in speculative attempts to explain the details of these obscure references, the preacher working with this text should supply some analogous contemporary examples of activities in the life of our congregations that make no sense if the dead are not to be raised; for example, "If the dead are not raised, why do we sacrifice our time and resources in running a soup kitchen for the homeless?" The examples that Paul gives are of two sorts: baptism on behalf of the dead (v. 29) and the danger and suffering of his own apostolic labors (vv. 30–32a).

The first example is notoriously puzzling, because vicarious baptism for the dead is not otherwise attested in first-century Christianity and because the practice seems so superstitious and objectionable (particularly to Protestant interpreters) that it is hard to believe that Paul would countenance it. Nonetheless, there it stands in the text. Some among the Corinthians are performing baptisms on behalf of others who have died (family members? catechumens?); this sort of activity would be consistent with their high view of baptism, perhaps implied by Paul's cautionary words about the limitations of baptism in 1:14–17 and 10:1–13. Although Paul certainly does not hold a "magical" view of baptism, he apparently gives sanction to this activity by pointing out—quite reasonably—that it is unintelligible unless there is to be a resurrection. All of the numerous attempts to explain away the obvious sense of this verse are strained and unpersuasive. (Those who are interested can consult more detailed critical commentaries.) However unsettling we may find it, this passage serves as one more piece of evidence that Pauline soteriology is far less individualistic than Christians since the Reformation have usually supposed and that Paul is at least open to believing that the community can act meaningfully on behalf of those who are not able to act in their own behalf. It is useful to compare the account of actions taken by Judas Maccabeus to atone for the sin of some of his slain soldiers:

> He also took up a collection, man by man, to the amount of two thousand drachmas of silver, and sent it to Jerusalem to provide for a sin offering. In doing this he acted very well and honorably, *taking account of the resurrection. For if he were not expecting that those who had fallen would rise again, it would have been superfluous and foolish to pray for the dead.* But if he was looking to the splendid reward that is laid up for those who fall asleep in godliness, it was a holy and pious thought. Therefore he made atonement for the dead, so that they might be delivered from their sin.
>
> (2 Macc. 12:43–45, emphasis added)

This text shows that at least some Jews of Paul's era held beliefs that might have made baptism for the dead an intelligible practice. Still, it is fair enough to note that Paul neither cites this passage nor *commends*

267

vicarious baptism in 1 Corinthians 15:29; he merely points out that it is contradictory for the community to practice it while at the same time doubting the resurrection.

The second example is a bit clearer: Paul has repeatedly put his own life and health at risk in order to proclaim the gospel (see, e.g., 4:11–13; 2 Cor. 4:8–12; 6:3–10; 11:23–33). If there is to be no resurrection, why should he bother? These remarks may be taken as an expansion of the ideas already expressed in 1 Corinthians 15:14–15, 19. The reference to fighting with wild animals at Ephesus (v. 32) is a metaphor for contending with opposition of some sort. Paul's subsequent reference to encountering "many adversaries" to his missionary work in Ephesus (16:8–9) should almost surely be taken as a more literal statement about the same events (cf. 2 Cor. 1:8–11; Acts 19:23–41). The metaphor of fighting wild beasts is found also in Ignatius of Antioch, almost certainly echoing Paul: "From Syria to Rome I am fighting with wild beasts, by land and sea, by night and day, bound to ten 'leopards'—that is, a company of soldiers" (Ignatius, *To the Romans* 5:1). (Parenthetically, we may also note that the word here translated "company" of soldiers is *tagma*, the same term used by Paul in 1 Cor. 15:23; this nicely illustrates its normal use in a military context.)

If Paul's own apostolic labors provide a positive example of how one should live in light of the promise of resurrection, the behavior of some of the Corinthians illustrates the opposite possibility (v. 32b). Paul suggests that their skepticism has led them to act like the frenzied inhabitants of Jerusalem who faced siege and annihilation at the hands of the Assyrians (Isa. 22:12–14): instead of facing their fate with repentance and weeping, they decided to "party like there was no tomorrow," as the colloquial English expression has it. The slogan "Let us eat and drink, for tomorrow we die" (quoted from Isa. 22:13) is a devastatingly apt characterization of these resurrection-denying Corinthians, whose own misbehavior has much to do with eating and drinking (1 Cor. 10:21–22; 11:20–22). Of course, they themselves did not explicitly justify eating idol meat and gorging themselves at the Lord's Supper by connecting these behaviors with their denial of resurrection, but Paul suggests that there is a hidden inner connection.

The logical link between this thought and verses 33–34 is at first sight obscure. Why does Paul suddenly quote a Greek proverbial saying taken from a lost play of Menander: "Bad company ruins good morals"? Dale Martin has suggested an answer that is fully consistent with the picture of the troublemaking Corinthian wisdom-enthusiasts that has emerged gradually from the letter as a whole: "The abrupt interjection of the saying in Paul's argument may indicate that he believes the Corinthians' skepticism to be due to influences from other sources—in fact to persons who have only 'ignorance of God'—a designation often used by Jews to refer to Gentiles. . . . All this suggests that Paul attributes the Corinthians' doubts to Greek philosophy, especially, perhaps, the skepticism of Epicureanism" (Martin, *Corinthian Body*, 275 n.79). Note that the concluding reproach, "I say this to your shame" repeats almost verbatim the scolding that Paul administered in 6:5 for their practice of taking legal disputes before pagan judges. Rather than correcting the "ignorance of God" of their pagan neighbors, the "knowing" Corinthian Christians are trying to tailor their faith to the intellectual standards of pagan philosophy, with the result that they are surrendering the heart of the gospel and being drawn into idolatrous and immoral behavior. This is the usual fate of those who undertake to "demythologize" the gospel, from Paul's day to ours. To those Corinthians who want to demythologize the resurrection, Paul has only a stern word of admonition: "Come to a sober and right mind, and sin no more." To proclaim the resurrection of Christ is to enter a world made new by God and therefore to lead a transformed life as well, even in the present age.

Resurrection Means Transformation of the Body (vv. 35–58)

What kind of body is the resurrection body? (vv. 35–49)

Paul now addresses the root causes of the Corinthians' skepticism about resurrection. Although they scoffed, it seems, at *anastasis nekrōn* as the stuff of popular superstition, their incredulity was not based primarily on scientific doubts about the possibility of supernatural events. After all, these same Corinthian Christians believed themselves to be infused with divine power to speak in tongues of angels and to work miracles (see chapters 12—14). Rather, their denial of the resurrection was based on an aversion to the idea that the *body* could be reanimated after death. Such a turn of events would seem positively undesirable to ancient Hellenistic thinkers devoted to an ideal of spirituality that sought to transcend corporeality.

Paul frames the introduction to this next major section in a way that confronts their disdain for the notion of a resurrected *body*. He uses the standard rhetorical device—particularly characteristic of the genre of teaching discourses called diatribe—of putting a hypothetical objection in the mouth of his readers so that he can launch into an explanation: "But someone will ask, 'How are the dead raised? With what

269

kind of body do they come?' " (v. 35). The second rhetorical question is a more precise specification of the first. Thus, "How are the dead raised?" does not mean "How is it possible?" or "By what agency?" (for it is clear that Paul and other advocates of the resurrection of the dead claim that they are to be raised by God's power). Rather, the pressing question here is, "In what form?"

In answer to this question, Paul spits out a scornful response: "Fool!" (cf. Ps. 14:1; certainly this psalm was well known to Paul, for he quotes vv. 2–3 of it in Rom. 3:11–12). This word of stern rebuke introduces a section in which Paul turns the tables on the Corinthians, suggesting that they, not he, are the ones guilty of crude literalism. Paul insists that the concept of "resurrection of the dead" should not be naively understood to refer to the resuscitation of corpses; rather, the concept of resurrection necessarily entails transformation into a new and glorious state. Any fool should realize that, Paul implies. In verses 36–41, he argues his case by using a number of analogies from nature. Verses 42–44 then state the central thesis of the unit—that the resurrection body is a *spiritual body*, free from the decay and weakness that we know in the present life. Finally, this claim is supported in verses 45–49 by an appeal to Scripture and the Adam-Christ typology. The passage as a whole constitutes a sweeping redefinition of the meaning of "resurrection of the dead." Paul in effect argues that his understanding of the term is not subject to the reductive critique posed by those who seek to debunk it.

Another way of putting the point would be to say that he characterizes the skeptical queries of verse 35 as silly, small-minded questions. In effect, the answer is already given by what he says about the transformation of a seed into a plant: "God gives it a body *just as he has chosen [kathōs ethelēsen]*" (v. 38a). We do not understand how this transformation occurs (cf. Mark 4:26–28), and no one could predict the final shape and texture of the mature plant from the appearance of the seed. God is the one who chooses what sort of body to give, and we would be presumptuous to suppose that we should know in advance the answer to the question, "With what kind of body do they come?" We must wait for the harvest to find out. The answer to such a question will necessarily confound the categories of our finite understanding—as the paradoxical expression "spiritual body" demonstrates.

The analogy of the seed enables Paul to walk a fine line, asserting both the radical *transformation* of the body in its resurrected state and yet its organic *continuity* with the mortal body that preceded it. This delicate balance between continuity and discontinuity characterizes the discussion as a whole. Paul shares with the Corinthian deniers of

270

the resurrection the conviction that "flesh and blood cannot inherit the kingdom of God" (v. 50), yet he insists that our future life must nonetheless be *embodied*. That is why he is at some pains to argue that the concept of "body" is not univocal; there are many different kinds of bodies, including not only the endless diversity of animal life but also the diverse "heavenly bodies" of sun, moon, and stars (vv. 39–41). Once this notion of "different bodies" is established, we can more easily make the imaginative inference to a different kind of human body, a body raised up by God with a glory like that of the heavenly bodies—in short, a "spiritual body" (vv. 42–44). This sort of body is entirely outside our present experience (except insofar as we know something about it through the body of the risen Christ), but it is nonetheless a *body*. So Paul argues.

The reference to heavenly bodies might also have helped the philosophically inclined Corinthians make better sense of the concept of a resurrection body. It was a common belief in the ancient world that the human soul and/or mind was made of the same ethereal stuff as the celestial bodies and that the soul would return to the stars after death (for references, see Martin, *Corinthian Body*, 117–20). Paul, of course, did not share this view, but his description of heavenly "bodies" that possess varying degrees of glory could help his readers conceptualize a future glorified body unlike the bodies we now know. Paul found such analogies congenial because they are also found in the Jewish apocalyptic tradition, from which his own understanding of resurrection came. Particularly pertinent in relation to 1 Corinthians 15 is Daniel 12:2–3, one of the very few passages in the Old Testament that prefigure belief in the resurrection of the dead:

> Many of those who sleep in the dust of the earth shall awake, some to everlasting life, and some to shame and everlasting contempt. Those who are wise shall shine like the brightness of the sky, and those who lead many to righteousness, like the stars for ever and ever.

In Daniel, as in Paul's teaching, there is no thought that the risen righteous ones actually *become* stars; rather, the metaphor is used to suggest something about the glorious state they will enjoy when they rise from the dead.

All of the analogies of verses 36–41 lead up to the pivot point of the argument in verse 42: "So it is with the resurrection of the dead." The binary contrasts that follow, affirming that the resurrected body transcends the limitations of earthly bodies known to us, are structured by the seed/plant metaphor ("sown . . . raised"). Whereas our present bodies are "sown" (in this life) perishable, dishonorable, and weak, the

271

resurrection body will be raised (in the next life) imperishable, glorious, and powerful (vv. 42–43). Paul thus produces an impressive piece of visionary preaching, extolling the glories that await us. He is seeking to make the resurrection of the dead seem appealing rather than appalling to the Corinthians.

Yet the last item in this sequence is the one that he is driving toward: "It is sown a natural body [*psychikon sōma*], it is raised a spiritual body [*pneumatikon sōma*]" (v. 44, NIV). This is the nub of his argument. This last contrast, however, presents a vexing problem for translators (cf. 2:14, where the same contrast occurs). The phrase *psychikon sōma* is notoriously difficult to translate into English. The NRSV's translation ("physical body") is especially unfortunate, for it reinstates precisely the dualistic dichotomy between physical and spiritual that Paul is struggling to overcome. In any case, *psychikon* certainly does not mean "physical." Furthermore, although *pneumatikon sōma* is easier to translate, "spiritual body" sounds like an oxymoron. What sense are we to make of this?

By far the most graceful translation of verse 44, and the one that best conveys the meaning of Paul's sentence, is found in the *Jerusalem Bible*: "When it is sown it embodies the soul, when it is raised it embodies the spirit. If the soul has its own embodiment, so does the spirit have its own embodiment." That is Paul's point: our mortal bodies embody the *psychē* ("soul"), the animating force of our present existence, but the resurrection body will embody the divinely given *pneuma* ("spirit"). It is to be a "spiritual body" not in the sense that it is somehow made out of spirit and vapors, but in the sense that it is determined by the spirit and gives the spirit form and local habitation.

All of this is a bit hard to follow in translation, but the drift of Paul's argument is clear in the Greek, where his use of *psychikon* in verse 44 is explained by the key reference to *psychē* in the story of the creation of Adam (v. 45). Paul's use of the difficult term *psychikon sōma* is determined by the fact that he wants to cite Genesis 2:7 (LXX) in support of his position: "The first *man*, Adam, as scripture says, *became a living soul* [*psychē*]; but the last Adam has become a life-giving Spirit" (v. 45, JB). The *psychē* is linked with Adam, the initiator of decay and death, but Christ, by his resurrection, becomes "life-giving Spirit" (cf. v. 22), the initiator of a new order of humanity. The body associated with Adam (which Paul therefore calls *psychikon*) is mortal and bound to the earth from which it came; on the other hand, the body associated with the risen Christ (which Paul therefore calls *pneumatikon*) will be immortal and stamped by the image of "the man of heaven" (vv. 48–49). Once again, as in verses 21–22, we see that our salvation entails

272

participating in Christ and being transformed into his image (cf. Rom. 8:29). A similar point is made somewhat more clearly in Philippians 3:20–21:

> But our citizenship is in heaven. And we eagerly await a Savior from there, the Lord Jesus Christ, who, by the power that enables him to bring everything under his control [cf. 1 Cor. 15:23–28], *will transform our lowly bodies so that they will be like his glorious body.*
> (Phil. 3:20–21, au. trans.)

As in the Philippians passage, so also in 1 Corinthians 15:42–49, the transformation of our bodies is an eschatological event, a future resurrection associated with the *parousia* of Jesus Christ. This future eschatological orientation sharply distinguishes Paul's use of Genesis 2:7 from the reading of the creation story given by Philo, who finds both the archetypal heavenly man (Gen. 1:27) and the earthly man (Gen. 2:7) within the text of Genesis (*Allegorical Interpretation* 1.31–32). For Paul, the heavenly man is Christ, manifested in his resurrected body, who will come from heaven (cf. Dan. 7:13–14; 1 Thess. 4:16–17) *at the end* to raise his people and transform them into his likeness. That is why Paul remarks in 15:46 that "It is not the spiritual that is first [i.e., not in Gen. 1:27], but the natural/soulish [i.e., Gen. 2:7]; *then* the spiritual [i.e., in the resurrection]." It is possible that all of this is a subtle rebuttal to an interpretation of Genesis that was influencing those Corinthians who thought of themselves as *pneumatikoi*. Perhaps their reading was more like Philo's, connecting "the heavenly man" with their own exalted knowledge and wisdom; if so, Paul's opposition between Adam and Christ seeks to reshape their understanding and to beckon them to look to the future transformation of their bodies.

This might also help to explain a notorious textual difficulty in the final verse of this unit. By far the better attested reading in the ancient manuscripts is, "Just as we have borne the image of the man of dust, *let us* also bear [*phoresōmen*] the image of the man of heaven" (v. 49). Almost all modern translations, however, have opted for the more weakly attested reading, ". . . *we will* also bear [*phoresomen*] the image of the man of heaven." Translators have chosen to follow this text because it seems to fit much better with Paul's future eschatological emphasis. The other reading, "let us bear," seems to suggest that this is some sort of ethical choice, as though we could by our own efforts conform ourselves to the image of Christ. In fact, such an ethical twist would not be incongruous with other conclusions of paragraphs within 1 Corinthians 15 (see, e.g., vv. 33–34, 58). Another possibility, however, is that Paul wrote "let us bear the image of the man of

273

heaven" as an exhortation to his readers to look to the coming one, Jesus Christ, as source and hope of transformation, rather than looking to their own wisdom or to some alleged primal divine image within.

Both the dead and the living will be transformed (vv. 50–57)

Paul recognizes that the going has gotten a bit thick in verses 45–49, so he breaks off and starts again by summarizing his argument so far: "What I am saying, brothers and sisters, is this: flesh and blood cannot inherit the kingdom of God, nor does the perishable inherit the imperishable" (v. 50). This sounds, of course, a good deal like what those Corinthians who *denied* the resurrection of the dead must have said; however, by this time in the argument, we recognize that Paul is simply reiterating his argument that the resurrection body must be imperishable (the same word has already been used in v. 42; cf. vv. 52–54) and therefore different in kind from our present bodies. If that is right, however, a new problem arises: What about those who are left alive in their present bodies at the time of Christ's *parousia*? Are they to be stranded, as it were, in deficient mortal bodies? This is for Paul not merely a scholastic problem: He expects Christ to come very soon and he expects to be among those left alive to see this event come to pass (v. 52; cf. 1 Thess. 4:17).

Paul's solution to this problem is presented as a "mystery"—a piece of hidden knowledge about God's preordained purposes now disclosed through revelation (see Rom. 11:25 and 1 Cor. 2:7 for especially good parallels; cf. also Rom. 16:25–26; 1 Cor. 4:1; 13:2; Eph. 3:3–4, 9; Col. 1:26–27). The mystery is that *even the living will undergo transformation into a new form*, receiving their resurrection bodies without having to pass through death. Paul puts it more poetically: "Listen, I will tell you a mystery! We will not all sleep, but we will all be changed, in a moment, in the twinkling of an eye, at the last trumpet. For the trumpet will sound, and the dead will be raised imperishable, and we will be changed" (vv. 51–52). The trumpet as a sign of "the day of the Lord" is a standard symbol of Jewish prophetic-apocalyptic literature (see, e.g., Isa. 27:13; Joel 2:1; Zeph. 1:14–16; 2 Esdras 6:23; Matt. 24:31; Rev. 9:14). On the final day when God's power is manifested, there will be a general transformation: "we will all be changed," dead and living alike. No one should underestimate the power of God to bring salvation by transfiguring everything in a flash. If Paul's earlier argument has stressed *continuity* between the present life and the resurrected body, he now stresses the other side of the dialectic: *transformation*. This constitutes one final way of replying to the "what kind of body?" question: the resurrection body will be radically transformed in a way that remains utterly mysterious.

274

Yet our present existence will not be simply annihilated. The metaphor of putting on new and glorious clothes suggests that our mortal bodies will not be abolished but encompassed, somehow taken up into the eschatological life of the resurrection: "For the perishable body must *put on* imperishability, and this mortal body must *put on* immortality" (v. 53; cf. 2 Cor. 5:2–5 for a more extended development of this metaphor). This is part of God's mysterious plan to *redeem* creation, not to reject it.

When the transformation occurs and our flawed bodies are clothed in immortality at the resurrection, that will be the fulfillment of God's long-promised triumph over the powers of sin and death. Paul brings his lengthy discussion of resurrection to a resonant climax by citing a pair of scriptural texts (vv. 54–55) that portend God's ultimate victory.

The first citation, from Isaiah 25:8 ("Death has been swallowed up in victory"), shows clearly that Paul is reading the prophetic text with careful attention to its original context. (It also shows, by the way, that he is following the Hebrew textual tradition here rather than the LXX, which reads, "Death, being strong, has swallowed people up.") The salvation oracle of Isaiah 25:6–10a does envision God's ultimate destruction of the power of death, and the reader who follows the allusion to its source will find a richly evocative portrayal of God's universal salvation for "all peoples," a picture that Paul, as apostle to the Gentiles, surely must have cherished:

> On this mountain [Mount Zion] the Lord of hosts will make for all
> peoples
> a feast of rich food, a feast of well-aged wines. . . .
> And he will destroy on this mountain
> the shroud that is cast over all peoples,
> the sheet that is spread over all nations;
> he will swallow up death for ever.
> Then the Lord God will wipe away the tears from all faces,
> and the disgrace of his people he will take away from all the earth,
> for the Lord has spoken.
>
> (Isa. 25:6–8)

It is no accident that the culminating vision of "a new heaven and a new earth" in the book of Revelation also alludes to this same passage in Isaiah:

> He will wipe every tear from their eyes.
> Death will be no more;
> mourning and crying and pain will be no more,
> for the first things have passed away.
>
> (Rev. 21:4)

275

INTERPRETATION

By citing Isaiah's eschatological vision at the conclusion of his argument in 1 Corinthians 15, Paul ties God's triumph over death to the resurrection of the body and shows that resurrection is the necessary outcome of God's intent to redeem his people.

Paul's use of the second passage (Hos. 13:14, quoted in v. 55), however, seems at first glance to pull the scriptural material out of its context. In the Hebrew text of Hosea, these words are part of a judgment oracle, actually summoning Death and Sheol to work their punishments on an unfaithful Israel. Yet Paul transforms the words into a taunt of Death personified, now rendered powerless by Christ's resurrection. The key to understanding Paul's use of the text is to recognize that this time he is following the Septuagint loosely. Hosea 13:14 in the Septuagint reads as follows:

> I will deliver them from the hand of Hades,
> and I will redeem them from Death.
> Death, where is your penalty [dikē]?
> Hades, where is your sting?

Paul changes *dikē* (penalty) to *nikos* (victory), thus creating a word-link with the Isaiah quotation, and he addresses both of the mocking questions to Death itself. It is not clear whether Paul intends to allude explicitly to Hosea or whether he is merely "writing freely, in scriptural language, of the ultimate victory over death" (Barrett, 383). If he does intend an allusion to Hosea, he may be thinking not just of the immediate context of Hosea 13:14 but of that prophetic book's larger message of God's ultimate mercy (see, e.g., Hos. 11:8–9; 14:4–8). In any case, Paul's reworking of the text in 1 Corinthians 15:55 creates a provocative declaration of challenge to the "last enemy," Death. The subjugation of Death, which will not be complete until the end of all things (vv. 23–26) is already assured by the resurrection of Christ; therefore, as Paul contemplates the vision of the resurrection at the last day (vv. 51–54), he already sings a triumph song over the fallen enemy. Death's victory will be snatched away when God raises those who belong to Christ, now imperishable, and Death's sting—its power to evoke fear and inflict suffering (cf. Heb. 2:14–15)—is therefore already plucked out, like the stinger of a malevolent insect, by Christ's resurrection from the grave. The unit ends on a note of joyous celebration: "But thanks be to God, who gives us the victory through our Lord Jesus Christ" (v. 57; cf. Rom. 7:25). The phrase "gives *us* the victory" contains the message of chapter 15 in a nutshell: When God raised Jesus the benefit was not for him alone; rather, all of us in the church, the body of Christ, share in the victory in such a way that we too can expect to be raised from the dead.

276

The parenthetical interjection of verse 56 looks like a non sequitur, but in fact it shows how closely linked the powers of death,
sin, and law are in Paul's thought (cf. Rom. 5:12–14; 7:7–13). He
cannot recount the story of Christ's victory over one of these powers
without also mentioning the others, for the full story includes the
good news that all three have been subdued by Jesus Christ. The
nexus between sin and death goes all the way back to the story of
Adam's fall (Gen. 2:17; Rom. 5:12), but Christ will make alive those
who died in Adam. Therefore, those who bear the image of the man
from heaven in their resurrected bodies (v. 49) will be set free not
only from death, but from sin as well. We should remember also that
sin is not far from Paul's mind throughout this argument about the
resurrection, for he is convinced that there is a connection between
the Corinthians' misbehavior and their confusion about resurrection
of the dead (vv. 32b–34).

Therefore, our labor is not in vain (v. 58)

This brief epilogue might seem anticlimactic after the rhetorically
exalted conclusion of verses 50–57, but it actually ties together the concerns of chapter 15 in an illuminating way (Fee, 808). Throughout this
chapter, Paul has repeatedly asserted that if there is no resurrection,
all the faith and labor of Christians is futile (vv. 3, 10, 12–19, 29–32a).
Now that he has confidently declared the victory over death through
Christ, Paul can affirm with equal confidence that "in the Lord your labor is *not in vain.*" The resurrection of the dead serves as a warrant val-
idating not only Christian preaching but also "the work of the Lord"
more generally; everything that we do stands under the sign of Christ's
resurrection, and all our actions are thereby given worth and meaning.
*The resurrection is the necessary foundation for faithful action in the
world.* Therefore, the Corinthians are urged to remain "steadfast, im-
movable" in holding the faith and putting it into action. Though the
words used are different here, Paul has come full circle back to the
theme of verses 1–2: he wants his readers to stand fast and hold firmly
to the gospel. Those who affirm the truth of Christ's resurrection will
be given the moral confidence to live in a way that shows that their
hope is not in vain.

REFLECTIONS FOR TEACHERS AND PREACHERS

Paul saw that underneath all the dismaying problems of the Corinthians lay one massive theological fallacy: they denied the resurrection
of the dead. And by doing that, they denied the importance of the
world that God created. They denied—whether they meant to or not—

that these flawed bodies of ours are loved by God and will be re-deemed. And therefore—whether they meant to or not—they denied that what we do with these bodies is of ultimate significance in God's eyes. So they lapsed into confusion, both moral and theological.

These are sobering observations for a Christian church that all too often denies the resurrection in one way or another. On the one hand, we are confronted by individually self-designed versions of Christianity in which Jesus is seen not as the crucified and risen one but only as a great moral teacher; in such pallid facsimiles of Chris-tianity, the resurrection, if it is preached at all, is understood only as a symbol for human potential or enlightened self-understanding. On the other hand, we find forms of otherworldly pietism that dream warmly of "going to heaven" but ignore the resurrection of the body—and thereby ignore the challenge of the gospel to the world we inhabit: such pietism falls unwittingly into the heresy that Justin Martyr decried as a "godless, impious" betrayal of the faith. It would not be difficult to document the various moral failings that follow from each of these errors.

In such a situation, Paul's treatment of the resurrection of the dead presents the church with a compelling word that needs to be heard again and again. It is no accident that his teachings on the cross (1:18—2:16) and resurrection (15:1–58) stand like bookends—or sentinels—at beginning and end of the body of his letter to the Corinthians. These are the fundamental themes of the gospel story. All our theology and practice must find its place within the world framed by these truths. How then shall we respond to Paul's exposition of the resurrection of the dead? As we reflect on 1 Corinthians 15, a number of key issues stand out.

1. *The resurrection of the dead is necessary in order to hold cre-ation and redemption together.* If there is no resurrection of the dead, God has capriciously abandoned the bodies he has given us. The promise of resurrection of the body, however, makes Christian hope concrete and confirms God's love for the created order. God, the cre-ator of the world, has not abandoned the creation. Furthermore, this teaching is consistent with what we have come to understand about the psychosomatic unity of the human person. Contrary to the ideas that held sway in much of Hellenistic antiquity, we are not ethereal souls imprisoned in bodies. Rather, our identity is bound up inextricably with our bodily existence. If we are to be saved, we must be saved as embodied persons, whatever that may mean. That is why, as Karl Barth observes in a ponderous but theologically exact phrase, the Christian doctrine of resurrection entails "the repredication of our corporeality."

278

Paul writes in Romans 8:23 that we who have the first fruits of the Spirit nonetheless groan along with an unredeemed creation while we await "the redemption of our bodies"—not redemption *from* them, but *of* them. To affirm the resurrection of the dead is to confess that the God who made us will finally make us whole—spirit, soul, and body (1 Thess. 5:23).

2. *In a culture that evades telling the truth about death, the teaching of the resurrection comes as a blast of fresh air.* If asked, "What do we hope for after death?" many devout Christians would answer with sentimental notions of their souls going to heaven and smiling back down on the earth. Such ideas have virtually no basis in the Bible, and those who exercise the teaching office in the church should seek to impress upon their congregations that the predominant future hope of the New Testament writers is precisely the same as the hope presented here in 1 Corinthians 15: resurrection of the body at the time of Christ's *parousia* and final judgment.

I have never forgotten a conversation I had with a young woman in my church years ago. I will call her "Stephanie." Her eighteen-year-old sister (whom I will call "Lisa") had been killed in a car accident. All the members of her family were saying things like "Lisa is so much happier now in heaven; she was always such an unhappy child here" or "God must have wanted her to be with him" or "I just know that Lisa is watching us now and telling us not to be sad." Stephanie was infuriated by such sweet, pious talk, for it seemed to deny both the reality of Lisa's death and its tragedy. Yet Stephanie felt guilty, because as a Christian she thought she ought to believe the pious things her family was saying. Thus, it came as a liberating word to her to learn that Paul speaks of death as a destructive "enemy" that will be conquered only at the end of this age. First Corinthians 15 enabled her to acknowledge soberly that Lisa was now really dead and buried in the ground, while at the same time realizing that she could hope to hold Lisa in her arms again, in the resurrection. Obviously, such matters must be handled with the greatest pastoral sensitivity, but we need to find ways to communicate these matters more clearly in the church. The resurrection of the dead is, after all, the classical teaching of the New Testament and the Christian tradition; we might find that such teaching would go a long way to promote healthier attitudes towards death and life in our congregations.

3. *The doctrine of resurrection of the dead affirms the moral significance of life in the body.* This point has been noted repeatedly in the commentary. The Corinthians deprecated the body and thereby

279

cut the nerve of moral action. When we live within the story told by Paul, however, a story whose climactic conclusion is the triumphant fulfillment/transformation of our mortal bodies, we will use these bodies in ways appropriate to their *telos* (goal/end), which is to be conformed to Christ. That is what Paul means when he writes "The body is not meant for fornication but for the Lord, and the Lord for the body. And God raised the Lord and will raise us by his power" (6:13b–14). Knowing that gives us both confidence and courage to devote ourselves wholeheartedly to God's work, even in the face of danger and opposition, for we know that what we do is finally valid and valued by God.

4. *The moral action to which the resurrection calls us may put us at odds with the established powers in our society*, just as Jesus and Paul found themselves in trouble with the authorities of their day. Why? Because Christ has not yet destroyed every rule and every authority and power (v. 24), and the logic of resurrection—like the logic of the cross—is profoundly subversive of the status quo. This is true in America today no less than in first-century Corinth.

5. *The resurrection binds us to Israel*. This binding occurs because the resurrection of Jesus happened "in accordance with the Scriptures" (v. 4). Thus, it is a matter of "first importance" that our telling of the resurrection story must always situate the *kērygma* (proclamation) in relation to God's promises to Israel and the history of God's dealing with this people, as disclosed to us in Scripture. The one whom God raised from the dead was not chosen at random in a worldwide lottery: rather, his mission was in obedience to Israel's God, and his resurrection confirms God's faithfulness to his covenant promises. Precisely because Paul does not explain *how* the resurrection accords with the Scriptures, we are compelled to delve into those Scriptures to ponder its meaning. One of the most important clues in 1 Corinthians 15 is found near the end of the chapter (v. 54) in Paul's allusion to Isaiah 25: the resurrection of Jesus us a sign of God's intention to gather the nations to a great feast on Mount Zion and to destroy "the shroud that is cast over all peoples" by embracing Gentiles as well as Jews at the time when death is swallowed up in victory.

6. *All Christian proclamation must be grounded in the resurrection*. The faith stands or falls with this, as Paul insists throughout the chapter. This has several crucial implications.

First, it means above all else that the gospel is a word of radical grace, for resurrection is one thing that we can neither produce nor control nor manipulate: our hope is exclusively in God's hands.

Second, it means that the faith is based on a particular event in human history, to which a definite circle of people gave testimony; the resurrection is not simply a symbol for the flowers coming up every spring or for the hope that springs eternal in the human heart. The Christian faith is grounded in the rising from the grave of Jesus Christ, who suffered under Pontius Pilate, was crucified, dead, and buried.

Third, the foundational character of the resurrection means that eschatology is at the heart of the gospel. Because Christ is the first fruits, his resurrection points to the resurrection of all those who belong to him. That remains inescapably a future event. Thus, the effect of the resurrection of Christ is to turn our eyes to God's coming future.

Fourth, if we deny the resurrection, we will find ourselves turning inward and focusing on our own religious experience as the matter of central interest. That is what some of the Corinthians were doing, and it has also been the besetting temptation of Protestant theology since Schleiermacher. This inward turn can take the form of pietistic religion interested only in soul-saving, or it can take the form of "New Age" religion interested only in cultivating personal "spirituality." Either way it comes to much the same thing. The gospel of the resurrection of the dead, by contrast, forces us to take seriously that God is committed to the creation and that God has acted and will act in ways beyond our experience and external to our subjectivity.

7. The resurrection calls for conversion of the imagination. This is particularly clear in 1 Corinthians 15:35–57, in which Paul calls us to expand our categories and to conceive "bodies" unlike anything we now know. The promise of God's final justice and transformative power is beyond the power of ordinary comprehension. This means that our preaching should not seek to defend propositions so much as to evoke the imaginative leaps that will enable us to grasp the gospel through metaphor and song.

Conclusion. Finally, let us consider briefly the place of 1 Corinthians 15 in the Revised Common Lectionary. Readings from 15:1–11 and 15:19–26 are appointed for Easter Sunday in years B and C, respectively. These texts, with their fundamental narration of the earliest kerygmatic tradition and of Christ's eschatological triumph over the last enemy, Death, give the preacher meaty material for exploring the substance of the gospel on this most joyous of feast days.

A continuous reading of the chapter as a whole is prescribed for four Sundays of Epiphany in Year C, omitting only verses 27–34 and 39–41. Some of the thematic linkages with other readings for these Sundays are suggestive.

281

On the fifth Sunday, the resurrection appearances of 15:1–11 are connected with Isaiah's vision of God in the Temple (Isa. 6:1–8) and with the call of Simon, James, and John in Luke 5:1–11. A sermon here could develop the themes of encountering God/Christ and the subsequent call to mission.

On the sixth Sunday, 15:12–20 is linked with Luke 6:17–26, containing Jesus' pronouncement of beatitudes and woes. Thematic connections here are not obvious, but the preacher could explore the relationship between the resurrection and the great reversal proclaimed by Jesus. Both texts have to do with God's unexpected raising of the lowly. Interpreters who are persuaded that the deniers of the resurrection at Corinth were probably among the affluent members of the community will find some provocative grounds for reflection here. Do the wealthy resist the idea of resurrection of the dead because they have already received their consolation (cf. Luke 6:24)? For whom is the promise of resurrection and judgment good news, and for whom should it be a terrifying prospect?

On the seventh Sunday, 15:35–38, 42–50 is paired with the Old Testament reading of Genesis 45:3–11, 15. This is the story of Joseph's meeting with his brothers in Egypt, which has historically been read as a typological prefiguration of the resurrection story.

On the eighth Sunday, 15:51–58 is linked with Isaiah 55:10–13. The sermon could pursue the connection between resurrection and Isaiah's prophecy about the sovereign fruitfulness of God's word. Just as the word that goes forth from God's mouth shall not return empty, so also God's "sowing" of the body is not in vain, and the labors of the faithful are not in vain. All will bear fruit—even miraculous fruit—as God has willed. Isaiah's celebratory vision of "an everlasting sign that shall not be cut off" (Isa. 55:12–13) could be interwoven with Paul's thanksgiving to God that the perishable body will put on imperishability (1 Cor. 15:53–54). The interaction of these two visionary poetic texts could be powerfully generative.

The preacher should beware, however, of getting caught up in complicated demonstrations of relationships between the various lectionary readings. The first responsibility of the preacher working with 1 Corinthians 15 is to make sure that Paul's message about the resurrection of the dead is heard distinctly, for this is the matter "of first importance."

Concluding Matters: A Community Called to Love

1 CORINTHIANS 16:1–24

With the grand conclusion of chapter 15, Paul has finished responding to the various contested issues at Corinth. The final chapter deals with some practical loose ends, gives the Corinthians information about Paul's travel plans, and closes, like all Paul's letters, with a few admonitions and greetings. That is not to say that the content of this final chapter is unimportant; Paul is a savvy pastor who makes every sentence serve a purpose in shaping the life of the church. These brief comments and directives seek to cement Paul's relationship with the Corinthian community and to shape the members' attitudes about Paul's associates Timothy and Apollos. Furthermore, Paul's directions about the collection (16:1–4) and about the role of Stephanas in the community (16:15–17) touch upon matters that would have been of vital concern to the original readers of the letter. It is not surprising that these specific issues are not of direct concern to us; this concluding chapter reminds us once again that 1 Corinthians really is a *letter,* not a theological treatise, and that we are after all reading someone else's mail. Still, here as elsewhere in the letter, we stand to learn something by observing closely how Paul brings the gospel to bear upon practical issues.

At the same time, chapter 16 gives us a glimpse of Paul's larger missionary work. One of the most important functions of this closing chapter is to remind the Corinthians that their church belongs to a wider network of communities (note the references to Galatia, Jerusalem, Macedonia, Ephesus, and "the churches of Asia") and that their life in Christ necessarily involves them in a mission that links them with the wider world. The "work of the Lord" (v. 10) is an urgent matter, and the church at Corinth must learn to see themselves as participants in the larger missionary enterprise.

The content of chapter 16 may be broken neatly in half. In the first part (vv. 1–12), Paul gives directions about the collection and discusses his future itinerary. It is likely that in some of these remarks he is responding, albeit briefly, to questions posed by the Corinthians in their letter. In the second part (vv. 13–24), Paul brings the letter to a close with words of farewell, while underlining some of his major concerns

283

one last time. It is no accident that this final section places particular emphasis on love (vv. 14, 22, 24).

16:1–12
The Collection and Travel Plans

Paul's directions about "the collection for the saints" (16:1–4) presuppose that the Corinthians already know about this project. No explanation is given here of the reasons for this offering, nor are the recipients explicitly designated, though it is clear that the offering is to go to Jerusalem (v. 3). Perhaps Paul had explained things more fully in a previous letter (cf. 5:9); here he addresses only the mechanism for gathering and delivering the collection. From the information in Paul's other letters, we know that the collection was for "the poor among the saints in Jerusalem" (Rom. 15:26) and that Paul had made it a major undertaking among his Gentile congregations, involving at least the churches in Galatia, Macedonia, and Achaia. He interpreted this financial offering as a way for the Gentile churches to be of service for the spiritual blessings that had come to them through the witness of the Jerusalem community (Rom. 15:27), and it is likely that he also saw the collection as an eschatological sign, symbolizing the Gentiles' recognition of Israel's God as the one God of all the earth (Isa. 2:2–3; 60:10–16). Precisely because the collection was symbolically freighted as a sign of unity between Gentiles and Jews in Christ, however, Paul later had cause to worry about whether the Christians in Jerusalem would accept it (Rom. 15:30–31)—despite the fact that the original impetus for the project may have been the Jerusalem leaders' request that Paul should "remember the poor" (Gal. 2:10). In his lengthiest discussion of the collection, however, Paul does not stress these symbolic factors as a motive for the Corinthians to participate in it; rather, he speaks of the sharing of resources as a matter of economic fairness and generosity (2 Corinthians 8—9).

In any case, none of these reasons and motivations is elucidated in 1 Corinthians 16:1–4. Paul merely instructs the Corinthian Christians to put aside "on the first day of the week" any surplus that they have and to save it up for the time of his arrival. Interestingly, this seems to show that there was no established administrative structure in the church for collecting and saving money; each person is to store up his or her contribution privately. (It is also significant that Paul does not

target his appeal to the wealthy members of the community, who might
be expected to provide the necessary patronage for this sort of enterprise; instead, he calls upon all to participate in accordance with their
ability.) Paul is seeking to avoid the unpleasant necessity of launching
a fund drive when he arrives in Corinth; he would prefer that all the
money be stored up before he appears on the scene. Further, he wants
it to be clear to everyone that the money is not for *him*, but for the poor.
Thus, rather than taking the money himself, he plans to send emissaries of the Corinthians' own choice to deliver it to Jerusalem; this
procedure will eliminate any possible suspicion that Paul might be
planning to misappropriate the money. Not incidentally, it will also en-
hance the symbolic value of the gift: the offering of the Gentiles to
Jerusalem is to be brought *by the Gentiles themselves.*

Paul has not yet, at the time of the writing of 1 Corinthians, decided whether he will go to Jerusalem himself. He may be waiting to
see, among other things, how large the gift is before he decides; that is
one possible reading of verse 4, which says literally, "If it be *worthy* for
me to go also, they will go with me." In any case, he is giving them fair
warning to get their money saved up before he comes to Corinth. As
we see from his further cajoling in 2 Corinthians, their response was
not immediately as generous as he had hoped. In the end, however, it
appears that the Corinthians must have participated in a satisfactory
manner, for Paul did decide to go to Jerusalem, and his letter to the
Romans indicates that the churches of Achaia were supporting the
project (Rom. 15:26).

In the meantime, before returning to Corinth, Paul has other
plans. He intends to stay in Ephesus—from where he is writing the
letter—"until Pentecost"—because he is facing both opportunities and
opposition there (vv. 8–9). The reference to Pentecost is another
indication, among many in his letter, that Paul is still thinking in a Jewish frame of reference and expecting his Corinthian converts to do
likewise. Pentecost was, of course, not yet a Christian liturgical celebration in Paul's day; its later emergence as a Christian holy day is a
consequence of the narrative artistry of Luke (see Acts 2). For Paul,
Pentecost was the Jewish festival of the offering of new grain, fifty days
after Passover (Lev. 23:15–21). By this reference to the Jewish calen-
dar, Paul indicates that he intends to stay in Ephesus until early summer before traveling through Macedonia (the region including Paul's
less problematical churches in Thessalonica and Philippi) and then on
to Corinth, where he may spend the winter (vv. 5–6). After his stay
among them, he hopes that the Corinthians will "send him on" to his
next, as yet undetermined, destination with financial and logistical

285

support (v. 7; the verb *propempein* seems to be a technical term for the support of missionaries). If he does accept their financial assistance for his mission, that will represent a change of his previous policy toward them (cf. 9:12; 15–18), but he does not elaborate on his reasons for this shift. Fee (819) suggests that this is an implicit "peace offering": he is now giving the Corinthians the opportunity to "have a share in his ministry" by supporting his work.

Paul gives no details of the events in Ephesus. The "wide door for effective work" refers to favorable circumstances for preaching the gospel, despite the presence of adversaries. This reference to opposition recalls his earlier cryptic allusion to fighting with wild animals at Ephesus (15:32; cf. Acts 19:23–41) and prefigures his later—and equally vague—comments about a terrible affliction that he suffered in Asia (2 Cor. 1:8–11). Despite the present danger, however, Paul sees the opportunity to spread the Word, and so he intends to stay where he is for the time being. We who live in a time and place where the church is comfortably established should not underestimate the uncertainty and risk that attended Paul's missionary work. His description of his plans here shows that Christians may sometimes be called upon to stand and testify in dangerous circumstances, and that the place of greatest risk may also be the place of greatest opportunity for proclaiming the gospel.

In any case, Paul is planning his travel with careful deliberation. Since traveling—especially by sea—was impossible during the wintertime, he aims to time his arrival in Corinth so that he can settle in to stay with them for an extended period of months. His comment that he does not want to see them "just in passing" (v. 7) is not merely a polite convention; given all that he has said in the letter, this is a measure of his serious concern about the spiritual health of the Corinthian community. He anticipates having to do a good deal of corrective counseling and teaching work when he gets there (cf. the pointed reference in 11:34 to further instructions that will be necessary when he arrives). Indeed, it is possible that his appearance in Corinth will provoke a showdown that might require him to stay for some time in order to undo the damage that has been done by the "puffed up" ones in their midst (4:18–21).

In the meantime, Paul has sent Timothy to try to straighten things out by reminding the Corinthians of Paul's "ways in Christ Jesus" (4:17; 16:10–11). This is, to say the least, a tough pastoral assignment for Paul's junior colleague. Paul is plainly worried about the reception that Timothy will find among the Corinthians, for he advises them to provide an atmosphere in which Timothy can work "without fear," and pointedly warns them not to "despise" him. A comparison with 1 Timothy 4:12 might suggest that the concern arises from Timothy's relative youth and inexperience, but another explanation lies close at hand within 1 Corinthians itself. Timothy has been sent as Paul's surrogate into a situation where influential factions in the community have become disenchanted with Paul. Furthermore, Paul, *by the very act of writing this letter*, has heightened the tension. He has sternly castigated powerful members of the church and called for basic changes in their behavior, including their sex lives, social contacts, forms of worship, and legal dealings. If the Corinthians heed Paul's letter, then Timothy's job will not be too hard, but if—as is likely—they reject Paul's appeals, it is Timothy who will be there to take the flak. The most direct way for any Corinthians who are offended by Paul's letter to demonstrate their displeasure will be to attack Timothy. Paul anticipates this difficult situation and calls on the Corinthian church to "send him on his way in peace," with support rather than hostility.

The Corinthians may also be disappointed that it is Timothy rather than Apollos who is coming to visit them. Paul's remarks in verse 12 suggest that the Corinthians had asked Paul to prevail on Apollos to return. The political crosscurrents here are treacherous, for some members of the community seem to be acclaiming Apollos as a leader in opposition to Paul (1:12). Thus, for Apollos to go to Corinth now in Paul's absence could be construed as a power play to undermine Paul's authority. Paul, however, sees himself and Apollos as teammates rather than rivals (3:5–9); thus, he has "strongly urged" Apollos to go to Corinth (16:12), since Apollos might be able to defuse some of the internal conflict in the church. We do not know why Apollos was unable to go to Corinth; Paul's sentence here is ambiguous: literally, "it was not at all *the will* for him to come now." This could mean either that Apollos was unwilling (as in most English translations) or that it was not *God's* will for him to go to Corinth (Barrett, 391–92; see the footnotes in NRSV and NEB). The former interpretation is likelier, though we know nothing of Apollos's reasons for declining to go.

It has sometimes been suggested that Paul's account here of his and Timothy's plans is in conflict with 4:17–21. In chapter 4, Paul definitely says that he has sent Timothy and declares his own intention to come to Corinth "soon"; in chapter 16, on the other hand, there seems to be some doubt about Timothy's arrival in Corinth, and Paul indicates that his own appearance there is to be some months in the future. Consequently, some critics have argued that these paragraphs must originally have belonged to different letters. As most recent commentators have noted, however, this is to read Paul's language much too

287

woodenly. In chapter 4, he is warning the Corinthians not to be arrogant and is making the rhetorical point that he will soon enough be there in person to confront them, whereas in chapter 16 he is giving a more precise account of his actual travel plans. As for Timothy, it is not clear what we should make of the conditional clause "if Timothy comes" (16:10). Perhaps Paul is reckoning realistically with the possibility that Timothy could be delayed or diverted. (We might suggest half-facetiously that—in view of the fears expressed by Paul—Timothy might well remember that he has a pressing engagement in some other town.) In any event, these small discrepancies are insufficient cause to split chapter 16 off from the rest of the letter. The overall account of Paul's travel plans, and of his relation to Timothy and Apollos, is coherent with what he has said in the body of the letter.

16:13–24
Farewell

Paul now shifts into his characteristic letter-closing form. The five brief general exhortations in verses 13–14 signal the transition into the conclusion of the epistle. At first glance, this looks like boilerplate material, for all of these admonitions could be addressed to any church anywhere. On closer inspection, however, we can see that Paul may have chosen at least some of the words in verses 13–14 with an eye towards the particular needs of the Corinthian community.

The first imperative, "Keep alert" (*grēgoreite*) is a verb with strong eschatological overtones. Paul uses it elsewhere to admonish his readers to watch intently so that they will not be caught by surprise by the coming of the day of the Lord: "[L]et us not fall asleep as others do, but let us *keep awake* (*grēgorōmen*) and be sober" (1 Thess. 5:6; for a similar call to eschatological watchfulness, see Rom. 13:11–14; cf. also Mark 13:33, 35, 37). In view of his many reminders throughout the letter for the Corinthians to see their lives in light of the coming eschatological judgment, Paul's call to watchfulness here in 16:13 should certainly be understood as a call for them to look intently for the coming of the Lord and to conduct themselves in a way appropriate to that hope.

288

"Stand firm in the faith" (rightly so translated by the NIV) echoes the words with which Paul opened and closed his chapter on the resurrection (15:1–2, 58). The Corinthians are reminded here to ground their identity in the gospel by holding fast to the message that he proclaimed to them. The NRSV's "stand firm in *your* faith"—supplying a possessive pronoun that is not present in the Greek text—unfortunately shifts the emphasis from the content of the faith proclaimed in the *kērygma* to the believer's subjective attitude or experience of faith. The difference is subtle but important: we stand in the proclaimed word, not in our own subjectivity.

The next two imperatives, "be courageous, be strong" (*not*, by the way, the same Greek word that Paul elsewhere uses to describe the "strong" Christians who think that all things are permitted for them), have no obvious connection to the themes of the letter. They do, however, echo the language of Psalm 31:24, where precisely the same two verbs are used. Paul may have had the Psalm in mind, for its concluding verses resonate richly with his message to the Corinthians:

> Love the LORD, all you his saints [cf. 1 Cor. 16:22].
> The LORD preserves the faithful,
> but abundantly repays the one who acts haughtily [cf. 1 Cor. 4:18–19;
>   5:2–6; 8:1; 10:12; 11:21–22; 14:36; etc.]
> *Be strong, and let your heart take courage* [1 Cor. 16:13],
>   all you who wait for the LORD [cf. 1 Cor. 1:7].
> (Ps. 31:23–24, emphasis added)

Of course, Paul's simple and straightforward exhortations make perfect sense to a reader who does not hear the Psalm echo, but those who do hear will understand that strength and courage are rooted in love for God and set in opposition to boasting and arrogance. Authentic strength is grounded in trustful *waiting* for the Lord; it is the opposite of the spiritual machismo that says "I am free to do anything" (6:12; 10:23).

Finally, the last of this string of pithy exhortations powerfully reinforces one of the central themes of 1 Corinthians: "Let all that you do be done in love" (16:14). This distills the message of the letter into a single sentence. Hearing these words, the Corinthians should certainly remember 8:1–3 and the entirety of chapter 13. Paul hopes they will be moved to action.

Next Paul gives an example of what love in action looks like in the Corinthian setting. The members of the household of Stephanas are praised, for they have "devoted themselves to the service of the saints" (16:15). Stephanas and his household were the first converts (literally *first fruits*—the same word used of Christ in 15:20) in Achaia, and they had been among the few Corinthians baptized by Paul (1:16). Furthermore, it is Stephanas, along with two companions (Fortunatus and Achaicus, possibly members of his household), who had come to Paul in

289

Ephesus, delivering the letter from the Corinthian church and providing further information about what was going on back in Corinth. No doubt they are to be the bearers of Paul's return letter—that is; the present 1 Corinthians. Paul now finds himself in a politically delicate situation, for he wants to commend Stephanas and urge the other Corinthians to acknowledge his ministry and leadership. At the same time, however, he must do so in a way that will not simply exacerbate the partisan splits that have already divided the community. Stephanas and his household are clearly among those identified as supporters of Paul; therefore, if Paul merely endorses Stephanas, the endorsement may carry little weight with those who are already resisting Paul's authority.

Paul's solution to this problem is to point to the work that Stephanas and his household have already done in service to the community. Their authority is legitimated through their service. Paul singles them out as examples of a principle that can be applied more generally: it is those who "work and toil" (v. 16, cf. 15:58) in *service* to the gospel and to the saints (that is, the community of the faithful) who earn authority in the church. It is to "such people" that Christians should be subject. This shows that Paul is not trying to appoint Stephanas and his entourage to some formal office in the church. In fact, Paul's turn of phrase in the Greek says literally, "*they have appointed themselves* for service (*diakonia*) to the saints" (v. 15). That is how authority works in a community where believers are subject to one another in love (cf. Eph. 5:21): people volunteer to serve and thereby gain the esteem of others in the community. Thus, Stephanas and his household exemplify the "way" (12:31b) that Paul is seeking to inculcate among his churches. For that reason, the Corinthians are encouraged to "give recognition" to them (v. 18).

Whether Paul's commendation of Stephanas and his household had the desired effect is impossible to say. Certainly, however, the attention he gives to this matter—a paragraph of several sentences embedded in the midst of otherwise terse parting words—suggests that he saw this as a matter of signal importance for the community. Stephanas and his companions returned to Corinth commended by Paul as faithful representatives of the gospel.

In verses 19–20, Paul continues "networking," passing along greetings from "the churches in Asia," and especially from his missionary associates Aquila and Prisca, who had formerly resided in Corinth at the time of Paul's first arrival there (Acts 18:2–3). These words of greeting remind the Corinthians again that they are not an autonomous club for the promotion of knowledge and spirituality, but that they belong to a larger fellowship of communities under the authority of Jesus Christ.

290

More precisely, they belong to a new *family* in Christ; by addressing them as "brothers and sisters" (*adelphoi*) throughout his letter, he seeks to reinforce this sense of familial intimacy, and he now urges them to symbolize this deep relatedness through the practice of the "holy kiss" (v. 20; cf. Rom 16:16; 2 Cor. 13:12; 1 Thess. 5:26; 1 Peter 5:14). This later became formalized as part of the eucharistic liturgy (cf. Justin Martyr, *Apology* 65), but there is no indication here that Paul thinks of it as anything more than a sign of greeting among people who love one another. In the context of the community's divisions at Corinth, however, the holy kiss would necessarily serve as a powerful sign of *reconciliation* among people who had previously been estranged. It is easy to interpret this brief imperative ("Greet one another with a holy kiss") as a perfunctory gesture, until we try to visualize the Corinthians actually putting it into practice in a community where conflict has prevailed. Within our divided denominations can we envision the members of opposed factions and caucuses coming together and embracing in a holy kiss? As usual, Paul's call to love is simple, radical, and embodied.

In the final three verses of the letter, Paul himself takes up the pen to sign his name and add a postscript. (For similar postscripts, see Gal. 6:11–18; Col. 4:18; 2 Thess. 3:17; and Philemon 19.) Paul characteristically dictated his letters to a scribe (see Rom. 16:22), but he sometimes authenticated and personalized the letter by adding a few words at the end in his own hand. So he does at the end of 1 Corinthians. After his signature, he appends four short sentences:

Let anyone be accursed who has no love for the Lord.
Our Lord, come!
The grace of the Lord Jesus be with you.
My love be with all of you in Christ Jesus.

The sentences are not linked by any conjunctions; each seems to be a self-contained parting thought that Paul wants to leave with his readers.

The first of these sentences will strike many present-day readers as needlessly abrasive. Why, at the conclusion of a letter appealing for love in the community, does Paul feel the need to pronounce a curse on those who do not share his passion for the Lord Jesus? The question is an important one, because it reminds us of the substantial attention that Paul gives in this letter to the call for community discipline (see especially chapters 5 and 6). The Christian community as a community of love is not infinitely inclusive: those who reject Jesus are not and cannot be a part of it. There is great danger to the church, in

291

Paul's view, when some people represent themselves as Christians while rejecting the apostolically proclaimed gospel. In Galatians 1:8–9, for example, Paul pronounces a solemn curse on those who proclaim "another gospel." Even in 1 Corinthians 12:3, where Paul is introducing a plea for acceptance of difference within the community, he prefaces his remarks with an exclusionary warning: "No one speaking by the Spirit of God ever says 'Let Jesus be cursed!' " Those who do say such things are not speaking by the Spirit, are not part of the community of faith, and in turn are subject to a curse. Similarly, those who "do not love the Lord" (16:22a) are those who willfully reject the proclamation of Christ's lordship and place themselves outside the community of faith. It should also be noted, however, that in 1 Corinthians love for the Lord is closely tied to love for all the members of the body of Christ. Those who love the Lord will necessarily seek to build up the community. Those who destroy the community are, virtually by definition, not loving the Lord. Thus, the curse of 16:22 is a thinly veiled threat against those Corinthians who have turned spirituality into a competitive sport, a way of aggrandizing themselves rather than adoring their Lord and maker.

The second sentence is actually a fervent prayer, written in Aramaic rather than Greek: *Marana tha* ("Our Lord, come). The prayer addresses the risen Lord and implores him to return—thus bringing about the consummation that Paul sketched in 15:20–28: the resurrection of the dead, the subjugation of all hostile powers, and the final triumph of God. While it is technically possible to understand the phrase as an indicative statement, a transcription of the Aramaic *Maran atha* ("Our Lord has come"), the use of this same prayer in the *Didache* at the end of a string of eschatological intercessions strongly suggests that it was understood in the early church as a prayer calling upon the Lord Jesus to come. The point may be seen clearly if the *Didache* reference is read in context:

> Remember, Lord, thy Church, to deliver it from all evil and to make it perfect in thy love, and gather it together in its holiness from the four winds to thy kingdom which thou hast prepared for it. For thine is the power and the glory for ever. Let grace come and let this world pass away. Hosannah to the God of David. If any man be holy, let him come! if any man be not, let him repent: "Maranatha, Amen."
> (*Didache* 10.5–6)

In such a context, the phrase can scarcely mean anything other than "Our Lord, come." (This interpretation is confirmed by Rev. 22:20, which brings the book to a close with the equivalent prayer in Greek: *erchou kyrie Iēsou* ["Come, Lord Jesus"].) Paul's uncharacteristic use

292

of an *Aramaic* expression, in a letter written in Greek to a Greek-speaking congregation, shows that the cry *Marana tha* must have been an established element of the worship of the earliest Aramaic-speaking Christian community. This shows two important things. First, the acclamation of Jesus as *Lord* (a title reserved in the Old Testament and Jewish usage for God alone) goes back to the earliest known layer of Christian tradition. Second, this early tradition is eschatological at its very roots. Thus, those modern scholars who have imagined a hypothetical non-eschatological Jesus movement at the beginnings of Christianity can do so only by utterly ignoring the evidence of the Pauline letters.

For anyone who is acquainted with Paul's normal letter-closing format, 1 Corinthians 16:23 sounds like the end of the letter, a benediction pronouncing the *grace* of the Lord Jesus upon the readers. Paul nearly always ends on this note of grace; even the letters usually considered deutero-Pauline have preserved this stylistic feature (cf. 2 Cor. 13:13; Gal. 6:18; Eph. 6:24; Phil. 4:23; Col. 4:18; 1 Thess. 5:28; 2 Thess. 3:18; 1 Tim. 6:21; 2 Tim. 4:22; Titus 3:15; Philemon 25). Furthermore, 1 Corinthians opened with thanks for "the *grace* of God that has been given you in Christ Jesus" (1:4); here the letter seems to have come full circle to the end with a wish for that grace to be continually bestowed on the community. God's grace seemingly has encompassed everything—a fitting conclusion for Paul's message.

Yet there is more. Distinctively in 1 Corinthians, Paul adds a final note *after* the grace benediction: "My love be with all of you in Christ Jesus." In the midst of a stormy and still unresolved relationship with the Corinthian community, in the midst of stern rebukes and incredulous protests against their behavior, Paul nonetheless reaches out to them with this final word. He affirms not only that God still loves them through the grace of the Lord Jesus (v. 23), but that he, Paul, does too. The grace and love of God has created between Paul and these aggravating Gentiles an unlikely but unbreakable bond of love in Christ Jesus. In that love, which reaches out to overcome conflict, lies a sign of hope for the ultimate healing of their divisions.

REFLECTIONS FOR TEACHERS AND PREACHERS

Since Paul does not develop any themes at length in the final chapter of the letter, our observations about the significance of this material for teaching and preaching can be relatively concise. First Corinthians 16 does not appear in the lectionary; doubtless, this text will be more often studied than preached. Those who want to use the letter as a historical window into the social world of the earliest Christian

293

communities will find much interesting material here. As we read closely through this chapter several matters call for our attention.

1. *Money and trust.* Paul's remarks about the collection suggest that there may have been some distrust within the Corinthian church about the administration of this offering for the poor among the saints in Jerusalem. Paul's instructions seek to defuse potential problems by assuring the Corinthians that their representatives will retain oversight of the funds until they are delivered to Jerusalem (v. 3). It is not surprising that if some of the Corinthians doubted Paul's authority they would have been unwilling to entrust him with their money. The passage reminds us that money is one of the most reliable indicators of our commitments and relationships. Even though Paul does not explain the purpose of the collection here, his other discussions of it (Rom. 15:25–29; 2 Corinthians 8–9) make it clear that the collection was for the poor and that Paul saw it as a way of sharing resources within the community of faith. By giving generously, the Corinthians could follow the example of Jesus Christ and demonstrate the genuineness of their love (2 Cor. 8:8–9). Consequently, Paul's directives about the collection invite us also to consider how we are using our money. What do our financial practices say about our relationship to God and our relationships with one another?

2. *Political dynamics and leadership in the church.* Chapter 16 as a whole shows Paul hard at work to repair and cultivate relationships and to solicit support for certain people (Timothy and Stephanas) as leaders in the community. We should not make the mistake of supposing that such "political" concerns are unworthy of the church and the gospel. As long as the present age endures, there must always be leadership within the church, and the exercise of authority is unavoidable. The crucial question is *how* authority is to be recognized and used within the community of faith. The model that Paul commends to the Corinthians, exemplified by Stephanas, is leadership through service (*diakonia*, vv. 15–18). This recalls Paul's earlier descriptions of his own example (3:5–9; 4:1–2; 9:1–27; 10:31—11:1). This model is perhaps at odds with the understanding of some of the Corinthians, who see authority (*exousia*) in terms of exercising rights and standing free from attachments to others. Chapter 16, therefore, may provide the occasion for us to ask once again how we recognize authority within our communities. Is it conferred by institutional mechanisms or earned through service to the saints?

294

3. *The church as network for mission.* As we have noted, one effect of Paul's discussion of his travel plans is to draw the Corinthians into a vision of the church as a fellowship that transcends human

borders. To be in Christ is to be affiliated with other Christians in far-away communities, who are brothers and sisters committed to the same task of proclaiming the gospel to the world—whether in Corinth, Ephesus, Macedonia, or Jerusalem. That is the "work of the Lord," and all communities of Christians are a part of that far-flung work. The mission entails risks and sacrifices; therefore, to be a member of the community of faith necessarily requires participation in these risks and sacrifices in one way or another, even if only through sharing resources with those in need. Despite the focused attention given to the local community at Corinth throughout the letter, Paul does not want his readers to lose this larger ecumenical perspective. As we come to the end of Paul's letter, we would do well to ask ourselves how our churches participate in the international network of the people of God and what we are doing to sustain those servants who undertake the risk of carrying the gospel to a sometimes hostile world.

4. *Watching for the coming of the Lord.* Throughout the letter we have seen the strong and consistent eschatological bent of Paul's thought. The most obvious expressions of this motif in chapter 16 are the call to eschatological watchfulness in verse 13 and the prayer for the coming of the Lord in verse 22. At the same time, there are more subtle signs as well: Paul's metaphorical description of the household of Stephanas as the "first fruits of Asia" (v. 15) suggests the image of the eschatological harvest in which the entire Gentile world will come to offer obedience to the Lord. The collection itself (vv. 1–4) may be intended to symbolize this eschatological fulfillment of the purposes of God. As the letter concludes, we are reminded again that Paul's gospel interprets the world comprehensively within an apocalyptic narrative that moves from the cross (1:18—2:16) to the coming of the Lord and the resurrection of the dead (15:1–58). We should ask ourselves first whether we too return again and again to this story to interpret our vocation; if not, why not? Second, we should ask how the particular forms of our obedience might be affected by living with the lively expectation of the coming of the Lord.

5. *Love as the final word.* The last sentence of the letter, written in Paul's own hand, reaffirms his love for all the Corinthians—despite their failings, despite their arrogance. What would it mean for us in our tragically divided churches to come in the end to a similar affirmation of love for one another? Clearly, in the case of 1 Corinthians, this parting word does not mean that all the problems in Paul's relationship with the Corinthians had been solved by his act of writing this letter. Indeed, as we learn in 2 Corinthians, the relationship was to deteriorate still further before it began to improve. Nonetheless, Paul's parting

word in 1 Corinthians 16:24 is neither perfunctory nor gratuitous, for he has been called along with his Corinthian readers into the *koinōnia* of Jesus Christ (1:9). They are members of the same body, and they all suffer when there is division. Paul's love for them in Jesus Christ means that he is willing to suffer for them and with them as he seeks to call them back to faithfulness and reconciliation. Love under the sign of Jesus Christ crucified can mean nothing less. We desperately need to learn in our communities the discipline of continuing to love one another in the midst of adversity and arguments. For such love, Paul offers us a model. Thus, 1 Corinthians 16:14 remains the test and watchword for all our labors: "Let all that you do be done in love."

BIBLIOGRAPHY

1. For further study

Beardslee, William A. *First Corinthians: A Commentary for Today.* St. Louis: Chalice Press, 1994.

Betz, Hans Dieter and Margaret M. Mitchell. "Corinthians, First Epistle to the." In *Anchor Bible Dictionary,* edited by D. N. Freedman. New York: Doubleday & Co., 1992. Volume 1, pp. 1139–48.

Bruce, F. F., ed. *1 and 2 Corinthians.* New Century Bible Commentary. Grand Rapids: Wm. B. Eerdmans Publishing Co., 1971.

Furnish, Victor P. *The Moral Teaching of Paul: Selected Issues.* Rev. ed. Nashville: Abingdon Press, 1985.

————. *The Theology of the First Letter to the Corinthians.* New Testament Theology. Cambridge: Cambridge University Press, forthcoming 1997.

Hay, David M., ed. *Pauline Theology,* Volume II: *1 & 2 Corinthians.* Minneapolis: Fortress Press, 1993.

Malherbe, Abraham J. *Social Aspects of Early Christianity,* 2d ed. Philadelphia: Fortress Press, 1983.

Murphy-O'Connor, Jerome. *1 Corinthians.* New Testament Message. Wilmington, Del.: Michael Glazier, 1979.

Snyder, Graydon F. *First Corinthians: A Faith Community Commentary.* Macon, Ga.: Mercer University Press, 1992.

Thrall, Margaret E. *The First and Second Letters of Paul to the Corinthians.* The Cambridge Bible Commentary. Cambridge: Cambridge University Press, 1965.

Winter, Bruce W. *Seek the Welfare of the City: Christians as Benefactors and Citizens.* Grand Rapids: Wm. B. Eerdmans Publishing Co.; and Carlisle: Paternoster, 1994.

2. Literature cited

Barrett, C.K. *A Commentary on The First Epistle to the Corinthians.* Harper's New Testament Commentaries. New York: Harper & Row, 1968.

Barth, Karl. *The Resurrection of the Dead,* translated by H. J. Stenning. London: Hodder & Stoughton, 1933.

Bassler, Jouette M. "1 Cor 12:3—Curse and Confession in Context," *Journal of Biblical Literature* 101 (1982): 415–18.

Bonhoeffer, Dietrich. *Life Together*, translated by John W. Dober-
stein. New York: Harper & Row, 1954.

Conzelmann, Hans. *I Corinthians*, translated by James. W. Leitch.
Hermeneia. Philadelphia: Fortress Press, 1975.

Eliot, T. S. *The Complete Poems and Plays, 1909–1950* (New York:
Harcourt Brace & World, 1952).

Fee, Gordon D. *The First Epistle to the Corinthians*. New International Commentary on the New Testament. Grand Rapids: Wm.
B. Eerdmans Publishing Co., 1987.

Hays, Richard B. *Echoes of Scripture in the Letters of Paul*. New
Haven, Conn.: Yale University Press, 1989.

———. *The Moral Vision of the New Testament: Community, Cross,
New Creation*. San Francisco: HarperSanFrancisco, 1996.

Hock, Ronald F. *The Social Context of Paul's Ministry: Tentmaking
and Apostleship*. Philadelphia: Fortress Press, 1980.

Martin, Dale B. *The Corinthian Body*. New Haven, Conn.: Yale University Press, 1995.

———. *Slavery as Salvation: The Metaphor of Slavery in Pauline
Christianity*. New Haven, Conn.: Yale University Press, 1990.

Meeks, Wayne A. *The First Urban Christians: The Social World of the
Apostle Paul*. New Haven, Conn.: Yale University Press, 1983.

Mitchell, Alan C. "Rich and Poor in the Courts of Corinth." *New Testament Studies* 39 (1993): 562–86.

Mitchell, Margaret M. *Paul and the Rhetoric of Reconciliation: An Exegetical Investigation of the Language and Composition of 1
Corinthians*. Louisville, Ky.: Westminster/John Knox Press, 1992.

Murphy-O'Connor, Jerome. "Corinthian Slogans in 1 Cor 6:12–20."
Catholic Biblical Quarterly 40 (1978): 391–96.

———. *St. Paul's Corinth: Texts and Archaeology*. Good News Studies 6. Wilmington, Del.: Michael Glazier, 1983.

Robertson, A., and Alfred Plummer. *A Critical and Exegetical Commentary on the First Epistle of St. Paul to the Corinthians*. 2d ed.
International Critical Commentary. Edinburgh: T. & T. Clark,
1914.

Rosner, Brian S. *Paul, Scripture, and Ethics: A Study of 1 Corinthians
5–7*. Arbeiten zur Geschichte des Antiken Judentums und des
Urchristentums 22. Leiden: E.J. Brill, 1994.

Schrage, Wolfgang. *Der erste Brief an die Korinther*, volumes 1 and 2.
Evangelisch-Katholischer Kommentar zum Neuen Testament.
Zurich and Braunschweig: Benziger Verlag, and Neukirchen-
Vluyn: Neukirchener Verlag, 1991–95 (volume 3 forthcoming
1997).

Schüssler Fiorenza, Elisabeth. *In Memory of Her: A Feminist Theological Reconstruction of Christian Origins.* New York: Crossroad, 1983.

Scroggs, Robin. "Paul and the Eschatological Woman: Revisited." *Journal of the American Academy of Religion* 42 (1974): 532–37.

Talbert, Charles H. *Reading Corinthians: A Literary and Theological Commentary on 1 and 2 Corinthians.* New York: Crossroad, 1987.

Theissen, Gerd. *The Social Setting of Pauline Christianity: Essays on Corinth,* translated by John H. Schütz. Philadelphia: Fortress Press, 1982.

Weiss, Johannes. *Der erste Korintherbrief.* Meyer Kritisch-exegetischer Kommentar über das Neue Testament. Göttingen: Vandenhoeck & Ruprecht, 1910.

Willis, Wendell Lee. *Idol Meat in Corinth: The Pauline Argument in 1 Corinthians 8 and 10.* Society of Biblical Literature Dissertation Series 68. Chico, Calif.: Scholars Press, 1985.

Wire, Antoinette Clark. *The Corinthian Women Prophets: A Reconstruction through Paul's Rhetoric.* Minneapolis: Fortress Press, 1990.

Witherington, Ben, III. *Conflict and Community in Corinth: A Socio-Rhetorical Commentary on 1 and 2 Corinthians.* Grand Rapids: Wm. B. Eerdmans Publishing Co., 1995.

CPSIA information can be obtained at www.ICGtesting.com
Printed in the USA
BVOW012019020212

282059BV00001B/72/P